TO ADVANCE THE GOSPEL

TO
ADVANCE
THE
GOSPEL

New Testament Studies

JOSEPH A. FITZMYER, S.J.

Crossroad • New York

1981
The Crossroad Publishing Company
18 East 41st Street, New York, NY 10017

Printed in the United States of America

Library of Congress Cataloging in Publication Data

Fitzmyer, Joseph A
    To advance the Gospel.

    Includes indexes.
    1. Bible.   N.T.—Addresses, essays, lectures.
I. Title.
BS2395.F58   225.6   80-39627
ISBN 0-8245-0008-3

CONTENTS

PREFACE

> ". . . what has happened to me has really served
> to advance the gospel . . ."   (Phil 1:12)

THE ELEVEN essays which are gathered together in this book were
written over a period of thirteen years and present reflections on a
number of important New Testament problems. They fall into two
main categories, which have been the object of my research and
investigation over the years, the Synoptic Gospels and the Pauline
corpus. Some of the essays in part I, devoted to "Gospel Topics," make
use of new Palestinian evidence that has recently come to light to aid in
the interpretation of old Gospel problems; others (chaps. 1 and 2) are
attempts to reformulate older problems in the light of modern Gospel
research. Topics such as the Marcan priority and the Lucan use of "Q,"
the virginal conception of Jesus, the Matthean form of the divorce
prohibitions, the play on Peter's name in Matt 16:18, and the question
of crucifixion in ancient Palestine are of continual interest to modern
readers. Among "Pauline Topics" those dealing with the meaning of
the gospel, the law, reconciliation, the power of Jesus' resurrection, the
meaning and origin of *kyrios,* and the use of Hab 2:3–4 are of perennial
concern. These two bodies of essays may not be a closely-knit unit, but
they seem to be of sufficient interest to present them together between
the covers of one volume.

None of these essays repeats those in either of the two previous
volumes of my collected essays, either *Essays on the Semitic Background of
the New Testament* (London: Chapman, 1971; reprinted, Missoula, MT:
Scholars Press, 1974) or *A Wandering Aramean: Collected Aramaic Essays*
(SBLMS 25; Missoula, MT: Scholars Press, 1979). One essay, however,
"New Testament *Kyrios* and *Maranatha* and Their Aramaic Background," gives a résumé of the discussion of the *Kyrios*-title in *A*

Wandering Aramean, but presses further in the contextual discussion of *Maranatha.* Hence its inclusion here.

In gathering these essays for republication in this volume, I have made some slight alterations. References have been made uniform, and some calling attention to new material bearing on the topics have been added; a number of minor changes in wording and occasionally a paragraph or two have been introduced in the interest of clarity. On one or other occasion, I have added a postscript to discuss views of those who might have commented on earlier forms of the essays. Apart from such changes the essays remain substantially as they originally appeared; the basic thesis in none of them has changed.

Grateful acknowledgement is hereby expressed to the editors of the following periodicals who have granted permission for the reprinting of the essays which originally appeared as articles in their publications: *Catholic Biblical Quarterly, Interpretation, The Jurist, Perspective,* and *Theological Studies.* My gratitude is also hereby expressed to Cambridge University Press for permission to reprint "Aramaic *Kephāʾ* and Peter's Name in the New Testament" from the Festschrift for Matthew Black; to the Institute for Antiquity and Christianity, Claremont for permission to reprint "Reconciliation in Pauline Theology" from the Festschrift for John L. McKenzie; to Editions J. Duculot of Gembloux, Belgium for permission to reprint " 'To Know Him and the Power of His Resurrection' (Phil 3:10)" from the Festschrift for Béda Rigaux; to the editor for permission to reprint "New Testament *Kyrios* and *Maranatha* and Their Aramaic Background" from the Festschrift destined for Bo Reicke; and to Editions Desclée of Paris for permission to reprint "Habakkuk 2:3–4 and the New Testament" from *De la Loi au Messie, Mélanges* for Henri Cazelles. Full details about the credits will be given in the asterisked footnote at the beginning of each chapter.

Finally, I must express sincere thanks to my colleague, Juan B. Cortés, S. J., who has helped me in many ways in the production of this book; and to Richard Ressa and Joseph Wysocki for furnishing me with the Hebrew text of the passages quoted.

JOSEPH A. FITZMYER, S. J.
The Catholic University of America
Washington, DC 20064

ABBREVIATIONS

A   Alexandrinus (New Testament Greek MS)

AAS   *Acta apostolicae sedis*

AB   Anchor Bible (Garden City, NY: Doubleday)

ALBO   Analecta lovaniensia biblica et orientalia

ALUOS   *Annual of the Leeds University Oriental Society*

AnBib   Analecta biblica

ANTF   Arbeiten zur neutestamentlichen Textforschung

AOS   American Oriental Series

AP   A. E. Cowley, *Aramaic Papyri* (Oxford, 1923)

ASAE   *Annales du service des antiquités de l'Egypte*

ASNU   Acta seminarii neotestamentici upsaliensis

ATR   *Anglican Theological Review*

B   Vaticanus (New Testament Greek MS)

b.   Babylonian Talmud (prefixed to name of tractate)

BA   *Biblical Archaeologist*

BAC   Biblioteca de autores cristianos

BAG   W. Bauer, W. F. Arndt, and F. W. Gingrich, *A Greek-English Lexicon of the New Testament* (Chicago: University of Chicago, 1957)

BDF   F. Blass, A. Debrunner, and R. W. Funk, *A Greek Grammar of the New Testament* (Chicago: University of Chicago, 1961)

BDR   F. Blass, A. Debrunner, and F. Rehkopf, *Grammatik des neutestamentlichen Griechisch* (14th ed.; Göttingen: Vandenhoeck & Ruprecht, 1976)

BETL   Bibliotheca ephemeridum theologicarum lovaniensium

BEvT   Beiträge zur evangelischen Theologie

BGU   *Ägyptische Urkunden aus den königlichen Museen zu Berlin: Griechische Urkunden* (11 vols.; ed. W. Schubart et al.; Berlin: Weidmann, 1895–1976)

BHT   Beiträge zur historischen Theologie

Bib   *Biblica*

BibLeb   *Bibel und Leben*

BibOr   Biblica et orientalia

BJRL   *Bulletin of the John Rylands (University) Library (of Manchester)*

BLE   *Bulletin de littérature ecclésiastique*

BMAP   E. G. Kraeling, *Brooklyn Museum Aramaic Papyri* (see p. 122 n. 31)

BNTC   Black's New Testament Commentaries

BR   *Biblical Research*

BSac   *Bibliotheca sacra*

BSOAS   *Bulletin of the School of Oriental (and African) Studies*

BTB   *Biblical Theology Bulletin*

BVC   *Bible et vie chrétienne*

BZ   *Biblische Zeitschrift*

BZNW   Beihefte zur *ZNW*

CBQ   *Catholic Biblical Quarterly*

CBQMS   Catholic Biblical Quarterly—Monograph series

CC   Corpus christianorum

CD   Damascus Document (from Cairo Genizah)

ChrC   *Christian Century*

ChrT   *Christianity Today*

CIG   *Corpus inscriptionum graecarum*

CNT   Commentaire du Nouveau Testament

col(s).   column(s)

CRAIBL   *Comptes rendus de l'Académie des inscriptions et belles-lettres*

CSCO   Corpus scriptorum christianorum orientalium

CSEL   Corpus scriptorum ecclesiasticorum latinorum

CTM   *Concordia Theological Monthly*

CurTM   *Currents in Theology and Mission*

D   Codex Bezae (New Testament Greek MS)

DACL   *Dictionnaire d'archéologie chrétienne et de liturgie*

DBS   *Dictionnaire de la Bible, Supplément*

Did.   *Didache*

DJD   Discoveries in the Judaean Desert

DS   Denzinger-Schönmetzer, *Enchiridion symbolorum*

EBib   Etudes bibliques

EMar   *Ephemerides mariologicae*

ESBNT   J. A. Fitzmyer, *Essays on the Semitic Background of the New Testament* (London: Chapman, 1971; reprinted, Missoula, MT: Scholars, 1974)

EstBib   *Estudios bíblicos*

EstEcl   *Estudios eclesiásticos*

ETL   *Ephemerides theologicae lovanienses*

ETR   *Etudes théologiques et religieuses*

EvQ   *Evangelical Quarterly*

EvT   *Evangelische Theologie*

ExpTim   *Expository Times*

frg.   fragment

FRLANT   Forschungen zur Religion und Literatur des Alten und Neuen Testaments

G   Boernerianus (New Testament Greek MS)

GCS   Griechische christliche Schriftsteller

GGA   *Göttingische gelehrte Anzeigen*

Greg   *Gregorianum*

Hennecke-Schnee-melcher, NTA   E. Hennecke and W. Schneemelcher, *New Testament Apocrypha* (2 vols.; London: Lutterworth, 1963, 1965)

HNT	Handbuch zum Neuen Testament	"L"	Lucan private source
HTKNT	Herders theologischer Kommentar zum Neuen Testament	LCL	Loeb Classical Library
		Leš	*Lěšonénu*
		LQ	*Lutheran Quarterly*
		LTK	*Lexikon für Theologie und Kirche* (2d ed.; 11 vols.; ed. J. Höfer and K. Rahner; Freiburg im B.: Herder, 1957–67)
ICC	International Critical Commentary		
IDB	*Interpreter's Dictionary of the Bible* (4 vols.; Nashville: Abingdon, 1962)	LXX	Septuagint
IDBSup	Supplementary volume to IDB (1976)	"M"	Matthean private source
		m.	*Mishnah* (prefixed to name of tractate)
IEJ	*Israel Exploration Journal*	MeyerK	H. A. W. Meyer (ed.), Kritisch-exegetischer Kommentar über das Neue Testament
Int	*Interpretation*		
ITQ	*Irish Theological Quarterly*		
j.	Jerusalem Talmud (prefixed to name of tractate)	MGWJ	*Monatsschrift für Geschichte und Wissenschaft des Judentums*
JB	A. Jones (ed.), *Jerusalem Bible* (Garden City, NY: Doubleday, 1966)	Midr.	*Midrash*
		MM	J. H. Moulton and G. Milligan, *The Vocabulary of the Greek Testament* (London: Hodder and Stoughton, 1930)
JBC	R. E. Brown et al. (eds.), *The Jerome Biblical Commentary* (Englewood Cliffs, NJ: Prentice-Hall, 1968)		
JBL	*Journal of Biblical Literature*	MNT	R. E. Brown et al. (eds.), *Mary in the New Testament* (New York: Paulist; Philadelphia: Fortress, 1978)
JES	*Journal of Ecumenical Studies*		
JJS	*Journal of Jewish Studies*	MS(s)	manuscript(s)
JPS	Jewish Publication Society	MT	Masoretic Text
JQR	*Jewish Quarterly Review*	MTZ	*Münchener theologische Zeitschrift*
JR	*Journal of Religion*		
JSS	*Journal of Semitic Studies*	Mur	Murabba'at (see p. 181. n. 18)
JTS	*Journal of Theological Studies*		
		NAB	*New American Bible*
		NEB	*New English Bible*
KAI	H. Donner and W. Röllig (eds.), *Kanaanäische und aramäische Inschriften* (3 vols.; Wiesbaden: Harrassowitz, 1962)	NIV	*New International Version*
		NovT	*Novum Testamentum*
		NovTSup	Supplements to *NovT*
		NRT	*La nouvelle revue théologique*
KD	*Kerygma und Dogma*	NTAbh	Neutestamentliche Abhandlungen

NTD	Das Neue Testament deutsch		bingen: Mohr [Siebeck], 1957–65)
NTS	*New Testament Studies*	RNT	Regensburger Neues Testament
NTT	*Norsk teologisk tidsskrift*		
NTTS	New Testament Tools and Studies	*RSR*	*Recherches de science religieuse*
		RSV	*Revised Standard Version*
P	Papyrus	*RTAM*	*Recherches de théologie ancienne et médiévale*
PCTSA	*Proceedings of the Catholic Theological Society of America*		
		RTL	*Revue théologique de Louvain*
PG	J. Migne (ed.), Patrologia graeca	*RTP*	*Revue de theólogie et de philosophie*
PL	J. Migne (ed.), Patrologia latina	*SBFLA*	*Studii biblici franciscani liber annuus*
PNT	R. E. Brown et al. (eds.), *Peter in the New Testament* (New York: Paulist; Minneapolis: Augsburg, 1973)	SBLMS	Society of Biblical Literature Monograph Series
		SBLSBS	Society of Biblical Literature Sources of Biblical Study
P.Oxy.	*Papyrus Oxyrhynchus*		
PSI	*Pubblicazioni della società italiana per la ricerca dei Papiri greci e latini in Egitto* (15 vols.; ed. G. Vitelli et al.; Firenze: E. Ariani, 1912–57)	SBM	Stuttgarter biblische Monographien
		SBS	Stuttgarter Bibelstudien
		SBT	Studies in Biblical Theology
		SE I, II, etc.	*Studia evangelica I, II, III, IV, V, VI* (= TU 73 [1959], 87 [1964], 88 [1964], etc.)
PVTG	Pseudepigrapha Veteris Testamenti graece		
PW	Pauly-Wissowa, *Real-Encyclopädie der classischen Altertumswissenschaft*	*SEA*	*Svensk exegetisk årsbok*
		Sem	*Semitica* (Paris)
		SJLA	Studies in Judaism in Late Antiquity
"Q"	The Q-Source in the Synoptic tradition (see p. 35)	*SJT*	*Scottish Journal of Theology*
		SNTSMS	Society for New Testament Studies Monograph Series
RB	*Revue biblique*		
RechBib	Recherches bibliques	*ST*	*Studia theologica*
RES	*Revue des études sémitiques*	Str-B	[H. Strack and] P. Billerbeck, *Kommentar zum Neuen Testament* (6 vols.; 4th ed.; Munich: Beck, 1963–65)
RevExp	*Review and Expositor*		
RevistB	*Revista bíblica*		
RevQ	*Revue de Qumran*		
RGG	*Religion in Geschichte und Gegenwart* (3d ed.; 7 vols.; ed. K. Galling et. al.; Tü-	*SUNT*	*Studien zur Umwelt des Neuen Testaments*

TBT	*The Bible Today*	*VT*	*Vetus Testamentum*
TD	*Theology Digest*	VTSup	Supplements to *VT*
TDNT	G. Kittel and G. Friedrich (eds.), *Theological Dictionary of the New Testament* (Grand Rapids, MI: Eerdmans, 1964–76)	*WA*	J. A. Fitzmyer, *A Wandering Aramean: Collected Aramaic Essays* (SBLMS 25; Missoula, MT: Scholars, 1979)
Tg.	*Targum* (prefixed to a proper name)	WMANT	Wissenschaftliche Monographien zum Alten und Neuen Testament
TLZ	*Theologische Literaturzeitung*		
TP	*Theologie und Philosophie*	*WTJ*	*Westminster Theological Journal*
TQ	*Theologische Quartalschrift*		
TS	*Theological Studies*	*ZAW*	*Zeitschrift für die alttestamentliche Wissenschaft*
TTZ	*Trierer theologische Zeitschrift*		
TU	*Texte und Untersuchungen*	*ZKG*	*Zeitschrift für Kirchengeschichte*
TZ	*Theologische Zeitschrift*	*ZKT*	*Zeitschrift für katholische Theologie*
UBSGNT	United Bible Societies *Greek New Testament*	*ZNW*	*Zeitschrift für die neutestamentliche Wissenschaft*
		ZRGG	*Zeitschrift für Religions- und Geistesgeschichte*
VD	*Verbum Domini*		
VS	Verbum salutis	*ZTK*	*Zeitschrift für Theologie und Kirche*
VSpir	*Vie spirituelle*		

Part I

GOSPEL TOPICS

One

THE PRIORITY OF MARK
AND THE "Q" SOURCE IN LUKE*

THE STEERING COMMITTEE for the Pittsburgh Festival on the Gospels, held in April 1969 to celebrate the 175th anniversary of the Pittsburgh Theological Seminary, asked me to prepare a survey of the state of the question of Luke's dependence on Mark and "Q." This question is part of the so-called Synoptic Problem, a vast area of New Testament study. I had been asked to do this because I once espoused the priority of Mark.[1] To admit the priority of Mark over Luke and the use of "Q" would be to adopt a form of the Two-Source Theory as a solution to the Synoptic Problem.[2] This solution has been called in question from time to time; indeed, recently there has been a call for the reopening of the entire Synoptic question.[3] My task is, obviously, not to re-examine the problem itself *ab ovo*, even with respect to the limited part with which I have been asked to deal. It is rather a survey of the current scene, as this is known to me.

Before I begin the survey proper, several preliminary remarks seem to be called for. First of all, the Synoptic Problem has been debated for over 150 years, during which time the corporate effort of scholars has come a long way, and yet no wholly satisfying solution has been found. Indeed, the literary source analysis of the Synoptic Gospels has long since yielded to other phases of gospel study: to form criticism and to *Redaktionsgeschichte*, to mention only the two most important phases. These advances have all been the result of *critical study* of the Gospels, carried on with the developing philological tools of literary and historical research. Sometimes the advances were made in one phase or another because of previous misdirected or even false steps, as we can recognize today when we view the process with hindsight. To admit this, however, does not mean that one who accepts elements of past solutions necessarily agrees with all the presuppositions that were in vogue at the time. The subsequent recognition of false steps does not necessarily imply that the whole process has been somehow vitiated, unless, of course, one subscribes to some sort of determinism in history. Thus, few will support today the priority of Mark because this Gospel is judged to serve as a better bridge to the historical Jesus than the Gospels of Matthew or Luke, which are considered to be more artificial. On the other hand, if arguments used in the past seem to have been inadequate or weak, it does not necessarily mean that they are such today; presuppositions affecting them may have changed, or the arguments may have received further analysis, confirmation, or support.

Second, the history of Synoptic research reveals that the problem is *practically insoluble.*[4] As I see the matter, we cannot hope for a definitive and certain solution to it, since the data for its solution are scarcely adequate or available to us. Such a solution would imply a judgment about the historical genesis and literary relationship of the first three Gospels, whereas the data for a historical and literary judgment of this nature are so meagre and of such a character as to preclude certitude. It is in this *general* context that I believe B. H. Streeter's oft-quoted statement ought to be repeated (and not apropos of some specific difficulty). Streeter wrote, ". . . we cannot possibly know, either all the circumstances of churches, or all the personal idiosyncrasies of writers so far removed from our own time."[5] I stress this point at the outset, because one finds often enough in recent discussions a straining after what is called "the truth" of the matter.[6] I submit, however, that "the truth" of the matter is largely inaccessible to us, and that we are forced to live with a hypothesis or a theory. This means too that there are loopholes in the theory, and that the value of the hypothesis may have to be judged by criteria other than its sheer truth.

Third, because the corporate critical study of the Synoptic Problem has resulted only in a theory or theories about its solution, there are at least two other criteria that have been operative in this work, and I am speaking of criteria that involve critical judgment, not "non-scientific" or "extra-scientific" factors. One of these is appeal; the other is usefulness. The Two-Source Theory has certainly appealed to the majority of twentieth-century scholars.[7] In saying this, I do not intend "an appeal to authority," as if the sentiment of the majority closed the issue. It is a simple statement of fact. Opponents complain of "the consensus" or the "collective bias," and subtly contrast the majority to "all careful students of the Synoptic Problem" and to the "perceptive critic," as if these appellations were proper only to those who criticize the theory. Little is obviously gained by this sort of approach; and it certainly does not do away with the fact itself of the appeal of the Two-Source Theory to the critical judgment of many scholars. As for its usefulness—its *Brauchbarkeit* (to repeat a word used by G. Strecker and W. Marxsen that has become a sort of tag, even in English discussions)—who can deny that the Two-Source Theory has served as the springboard for both the form criticism of the Gospels and later on for *Redaktionsgeschichte*? In the latter case it is almost a fundamental prop. I am, however, aware that neither of these methods of critical gospel study is organically or necessarily tied to the Two-Source Theory. In the former case, the method was derived from Old Testament *Gattungsgeschichte*. Yet, historically, it was applied to the Gospels on the basis of the Two-Source Theory, as the works of M. Dibelius and R. Bultmann manifest on almost every page. I know of no comparable form-critical studies that operate on the basis of another theory and have commanded the attention of scholars which can claim to rival the Dibelius-Bultmann approach.[8] As for *Redaktionsgeschichte*, this method of gospel study could theoretically be carried out on the basis of another theory of Synoptic relationships. But it has not really been done.[9] Until it is, the *Brauchbarkeit* argument is a valuable, but extrinsic, criterion for judging the worth of the hypothesis.

These preliminary remarks do not touch the real issue. But they have been made to clear the air on certain aspects of the problem before we confront the major task.

I. *The Priority of Mark*

This survey of the study of the relationship of the Lucan Gospel to the Synoptic Problem may be begun with the priority of Mark. I propose to set forth briefly the main arguments that have normally been proposed for it and comment on them from the standpoint of some recent developments.

First of all, the priority of Mark over Luke (and Matthew) has been espoused in recent times because the bulk of Mark is found in Luke (55 percent of it, according to Streeter) and in Matthew (90 percent of it).[10] This common agreement in subject-matter is often referred to as the Triple Tradition. In itself, the mere common possession of the same matter does not argue for the priority of Mark. The situation could be due to Mark's dependence on Luke (and/or Matthew), as Augustine once held with reference to Matthew (*De consensu evangelistarum*, 1.2,4), and as J. J. Griesbach,[11] and more recently W. R. Farmer,[12] have held with reference to both Matthew and Luke. In other words, "Mark is necessarily the connecting-link between Matthew and Luke in these passages, but not necessarily the source of more than one of them."[13] Thus stated theoretically and abstractly as a propositional argument (often with the aid of diagrams and arrows), the intermediary position of Mark is certain, but the priority of Mark over the other two is still to be shown.

When the argument is thus left on the theoretic level, as it often is, the priority of Mark appears to be more of an assumption than a conclusion. But the retort is made that the priority of Mark over Matthew and Luke depends as well on the concrete comparison of individual texts and on the complex of subsidiary questions related to it that must be answered. For instance, in the case of the latter one may ask a series of questions: (1) Why would anyone want to abbreviate or conflate Matthew and Luke to produce from them a Gospel such as Mark actually is? (2) Why is so much of Matthew and Luke omitted in the end-product? Why is so much important gospel material that would be of interest to the growing and developing church(es) eliminated by Mark? Why, for example, has he omitted the Sermon on the Mount and often encumbered narratives in the retelling with trivial and unessential details (e.g., the cushion in the boat, Mark 4:38; the "four men" in Mark 2:3; etc.). In other words, given Mark, it is easy to see why Matthew and Luke were written; but given Matthew and Luke, it is hard to see why Mark was needed in the early Church. (3) How could Mark have so consistently eliminated all trace of Lucanisms? If he were a modern practitioner of *Redaktionsgeschichte,* the elimination might be conceivable. But was he so inclined? (4) What would have motivated Mark to omit even those elements in the infancy narratives of Matthew and Luke that are common? His alleged interest in narratives, rather than teaching, would have led him instead to present a conflated and harmonized infancy narrative. (5) Mark's resurrection narrative, even if it be limited to 16:1–8, is puzzling. Can it really be regarded as an abbreviation or conflation of the Matthean and/or Lucan accounts? (6) What sort of early theologian does Mark turn out to be if his account is based on Matthew and Luke? Having behind him the certainly more developed christologies and ecclesiologies of Matthew and Luke, what would be his purpose in constructing such a composition? There is an unmistakable Marcan theology, with which one has to cope, as is now evident from the study of the *Redaktionsgeschichte* of the second Gospel. But that this was produced by an abbreviation or conflation of Matthean and/or Lucan theologies is incomprehensible to most students of the Synoptics.

These considerations are admittedly subsidiary; but they do affect the argument that is based on the bulk of the material that is common to the Triple Tradition. It might even be admitted that no one of these reasons is in itself cogent or sufficient to prove the priority of Mark.

This does not mean that there have been no attempts to answer such questions from other points of view.[14] But does the conviction that these other attempts have carried outweigh the more common interpretation?

A second reason usually given for asserting that Luke depends on Mark is the order or sequence of episodes in the Third Gospel that is so similar to that of Mark, even when other material is interspersed in Luke. This sequence is, moreover, even more strikingly compared to Mark's, when Matthew's order is taken into account, for Matthew and Luke agree in sequence only to the extent that they agree with Mark. When one departs from the Marcan sequence and pursues an independent course, the other still agrees with the Marcan order. Or, to put it another way, within the Triple Tradition, Matthew and Luke never agree with one another against Mark in regard to the order of episodes. As far as the common sequence of material in Luke and Mark is concerned, one sees it best in the five blocks of material set forth below:

(1) Mark 1:1–15   = Luke 3:1–4:15 (five episodes)[15]
(2) Mark 1:21–3:19   = Luke 4:31–6:19 (eleven episodes)
    (Luke's Little Interpolation, 6:20–8:3)
(3) Mark 4:1–9:40   = Luke 8:4–9:50 (twenty episodes)
    (At 9:17, Luke's Big Omission, Mark 6:45–8:26)
    (At 9:50, Luke's Little Omission, Mark 9:41–10:12)
    (Luke's Big Interpolation, 9:51–18:14)
(4) Mark 10:13–13:32   = Luke 18:15–21:33 (twenty-two episodes)
(5) Mark 14:1–16:8   = Luke 22:1–24:12 (sixteen episodes)

Within these major blocks of material common in sequence to Mark and Luke, there are occasional insertions from the Double Tradition or from Luke's special source that fill out an episode. Yet they do not affect the common order, for despite them the blocks of material in Mark are still seen as units in Luke. Such insertions can be found at Luke 3:7–14 (John's preaching); 3:23–38 (the genealogy of Jesus); 4:2b–13 (the temptation); 19:1–27 (Zacchaeus and the parable of the pounds); 19:41–44 (lament over Jerusalem); 22:27–32, 35–38 (the discourse at the Last Supper); 23:27–32 (the road to Calvary); 23:39b–43 (two criminals on crosses); 23:47b–49 (Calvary).

Moreover, within these large blocks smaller units are confirmed by the same order or sequence in Matthean episodes:

Matt 9:1–8, 9–13, 14–17	Mark 2:1–12, 13–17, 18–22	Luke 5:17–26, 27–32, 33–39
Matt 12:1–8, 9–14, 15–21	Mark 2:23–28, 3:1–6, 7–12	Luke 6:1–5, 6–11, 17–19
Matt 13:1–9, 10–17, 18–23	Mark 4:1–9, 10–12, 13–20	Luke 8:4–8, 9–10, 11–15
Matt 16:13–23, 24–28, 17:1–9	Mark 8:27–33, 8:34–9:1, 9:2–10	Luke 9:18–22, 23–27, 28–36
Matt 22:15–22, 23–33, 34–40, 41–46	Mark 12:13–17, 18–27, 28–34, 35–37	Luke 20:20–26, 27–40, 41–44

Once again the query is in order, whether the sequence of sections and incidents in Matthew and Luke over against Mark argues for anything more than the intermediary position of Mark, or for anything more than Mark as a connecting-link between Matthew and Luke.[16] To assert that it actually proves the priority of Mark would be to fall into the so-called Lachmann Fallacy.[17] Yet again, one has to make a distinction between the theoretic and abstract presentation of this argument, and the concrete application of it in the Triple Tradition. For many students the telling factor is not simply the comparison of Luke with Mark, but also with Matthew, and the more plausible reasons that can be assigned for the Lucan omission and addition of material within the Marcan order.

It is undoubtedly this argument more than any other that has been assailed as "inconclusive or fallacious." The "fallacious" character of it has been stressed by E. W. Lummis, H. G. Jameson, B. C. Butler, and W. R. Farmer, to cite only the main names.[18] It was especially Butler who insisted on the intermediary position of Mark and maintained that Mark "was not necessarily the source of more than one of them." But H. G. Wood put his finger on a difficulty in Butler's own solution, which argues from this intermediary position, viz., "that Mark is a source only for Luke, and the knowledge of Matthew's order comes to Luke through Mark. This is very strange because Dom Butler claims to have proved that Luke is also dependent on Matthew. Why, having Matthew in his hands, Luke should follow Matthew's order only when it reappears in Mark is difficult to understand and explain. If Dom Butler's thesis were true, there should be numerous agreements in order between Matthew and Luke against Mark, and admittedly there are none or next to none."[19] Wood also criticizes Butler for not having examined the question of order "in detail;" he devotes a large part of his short article precisely to the refutation of Butler in the matter of sequence or order. Unfortunately, it cannot be reproduced here, but many of his points are quite telling; his article should not be overlooked.

One last remark in this matter of order pertains to the so-called Lucan transpositions. In at least five places Mark and Luke do not have the same order of episodes, where they might have: (1) The imprisonment of John the Baptist (Mark 6:17–18) is found in Luke 3:19–20. (2) Jesus' visit to Nazareth (Mark 6:1–6) is found at the beginning of the Galilean ministry in Luke 4:16–30. (3) The call of the four disciples (Mark 1:16–20) appears later in Luke 5:1–11. (4) The choosing of the Twelve (Mark 3:13–19) and the report of the crowds that followed Jesus (Mark 3:7–12) are presented in an inverted sequence in Luke 6:12–16, 17–19. (5) The episode about Jesus' real relatives (Mark 3:31–35) is found after the parables in Luke 8:19–20. Of less significance are two other episodes that appear in a different order: the parable of the mustard seed (Mark 4:30–32), which is found in Luke 13:18–19 (in this instance an independent Lucan source may be involved); and the betrayal of Jesus (Mark 14:20–21 and Luke 23:21–23, an episode of the passion narrative). In any case, a more plausible reason can be assigned for the transposition of the five episodes by Luke than for their transposition by Mark.[20] This would again argue for the priority of Mark over Luke.

Third, the priority of Mark has been espoused because of the actual wording of the passages within the Triple Tradition, which is frequently the same. This affects even the collocation of words and the structure of sentences. Yet from this observation, baldly stated, one might wonder how one can conclude to the priority of Mark. What makes the difference, however, for many scholars is the concrete comparison. Streeter suggested using different colors to distinguish the words that agree in all three, and those that agree in Matthew and Mark, or in Luke and Mark. Such a comparison is facilitated by the use of W. G. Rushbrooke's *Synopticon* or by the more recent book of W. R. Farmer with the same title.[21] Rushbrooke's work openly espoused the Two-Source Theory and presented the matter in colored columns accordingly; Farmer's *Synopticon* presents the text of each of the first three Gospels in its entirety, and not in parallel columns, and highlights the agreements between the various compositions in different colors. It is thus better designed to assist the student to determine the nature and extent of the verbatim agreements without reference to any particular source-theory. Yet even the use of Farmer's book pushes one in the direction of the Two-Source Theory. I cannot help but still be impressed by that part of the argument that singles out the agreement of

Matthew or Luke with Mark, when the other disagrees. This aspect must be taken into account in conjunction with the agreement of all three. When it is so considered, I find it hard to see Mark as a mere connecting-link. And even less can I find a plausible reason for saying that Mark borrowed from Matthew or Luke.

A fourth reason for espousing the priority of Mark over Luke (and Matthew) has been found in the more primitive character of the narrative of the second Gospel, or what has been called its "freshness and circumstantial character." This refers to the greater quantity in Mark of vivid, concrete details, phrases likely to cause offense, roughness of style and grammar, and the preservation of Aramaic words. These traits abound in Mark and are present in Matthew and Luke to a less degree. One cannot regard them as evidence for Mark's "greater historical candour,"[22] since they do not really support such a judgment. Again, they are not found solely in the so-called Petrine passages in Mark, but in others as well.[23]

Streeter's analysis of the details of this Synoptic feature is well known; he regards the differences in Matthew and Luke as improvements and refinements of Mark's version. For instance, he maintains that "the difference between the style of Mark and of the other two is not merely that they both write better Greek. It is the difference which always exists between the spoken and the written language. Mark reads like a shorthand account of a story by an impromptu speaker—with all the repetitions, redundancies and digressions which are characteristic of living speech."[24] He cites as further evidence the "context-supplements" of J. C. Hawkins, those enlargements of the narrative which add nothing to the information conveyed by it,[25] the majority of which are omitted by Matthew, and a large number of which are omitted by Luke as well.

Butler also treated this material, and he admitted that this point was the only one of Streeter's five arguments that tended "to support the theory of Marcan priority to the exclusion of all other solutions . . . , an argument deserving serious attention."[26] Faced, however, with a mass of data on this point, Butler sought a solution in Mark's dependence on Matthew, by insisting that the references in Mark to Peter's remembering (11:21) reveal him to have been a preacher who "was using Matthew as his *aide-mémoire*."[27] "Peter made use of Matthew as the source-book for his own 'instructions', he selected passages which his own memory could confirm and enlarge upon, he omitted incidents that occurred before he met our Lord, and most of Matthew's discourse-material, as not suitable for his purpose and not such as he could reinforce with a personal and independent recollection. He altered his Palestinian-Jewish source in various ways to make it more palatable to his Gentile audience."[28] Thus Butler returned to a form of Augustine's solution, but apparently he has had little following in such an opinion. It is noteworthy that Butler had to interpose between Matthew and Mark a *preacher,* in effect, an oral source. As such, this becomes another stage in his solution of the Synoptic Problem, which he does not formally acknowledge. It is a hypothetical element that is really devoid of any control, and this is its deficiency.

A more frontal attack on this argument, however, was made by Farmer, who pointed out several defects in the argument as it was used by Streeter. Indeed, he turns the usual argument around and maintains that precisely those things that point to the "primitivity" of Mark's language are indications of the Gospel's lateness. It is understandable that Farmer is critical of Streeter's facile distinction between characteristics of spoken and written languages, of his idea that Mark has resulted from dictation, and of his assigning of the second Gospel to John Mark of Acts.[29] But Farmer's attribution of the "interesting and picturesque" details to the "well-attested tendency in the church to make the tradition more specific by the addition of just such details" goes undocumented.

What is really needed in this argument is a set of independent criteria. The more recent book of E. P. Sanders, *The Tendencies of the Synoptic Tradition,*[30] has addressed itself to this question in some detail. But whereas the Synoptic and pre-canonical tradition of what Jesus did and taught was formerly studied in comparison with the tendencies of folk tradition, or of rabbinical tradition, or of the early church as revealed in the epistles, Sanders seeks criteria from the post-canonical tradition. Under three main headings (increasing length, increasing detail, and diminishing Semitism, as possible tendencies of the tradition) he compares the post-canonical tradition and the Synoptic Gospels. From the standpoint of increasing length, Sanders finds that the evidence "weighs against the two-document hypothesis, and especially against Mark's priority, unless it can be offset by the *redaktionsgeschichtlich* consideration that Matthew and Luke were abbreviators."[31] Under the second heading Sanders concludes that "the simple priority of any one Gospel to the others cannot be demonstrated by the evidence of this chapter [i.e., increasing details]. It is clear, rather, that the questions which finally emerge from this section concern redactional method and the relation of Mark to the eyewitness period. The categories which argue for Matthew's priority to Mark are just those which some would explain as containing material which Mark owes to his eyewitness source." "In summary, we must conclude that the principal lesson to be learned from the study of details is that of caution, . . . the criterion of detail should not be used too quickly to establish the relative antiquity of one document or another."[32] Finally, Sanders concludes that "Semitic syntax and grammar do not necessarily prove a tradition to be either relatively or absolutely early," and that Mark is richer in parataxis, asyndeton, and the use of the historic present. "It certainly suited Mark's redactional style to write vernacular Greek more than it did the style of Matthew or Luke, but we cannot thereby prove Mark to be the earliest of the Gospels."[33] The study of Sanders deserves greater attention than this one paragraph I have devoted it, since it bears on a vital aspect of what has been called "an argument deserving serious attention."[34] But the book significantly ends in a *non liquet:* "While certain of the useful criteria support Mark's priority, some do not. Both Matthean priorists and Lukan priorists can find some support in this study."[35] Sander's study may be important, but it is really limited in scope; it has to be considered alongside of other comparative studies of the Synoptic and similar tendencies. Yet even this detailed study has not really undermined the primitive character of the Marcan Gospel.

Undoubtedly the weakest point in the usual line-up of reasons set forth for the Two-Source Theory is Streeter's fifth point. When it is scrutinized today from the vantage-point of hindsight, his presentation is seen to be not so much an argument as a preliminary statement and a preoccupation to answer two objections: (1) Why did Matthew and Luke both omit certain sections of Mark (viz., Mark 1:1; 2:27; 3:20–21; 4:26–29; 7:2–4, 32–37; 8:22–26; 9:29, 48–49; 13:33–37; 14:51–52)? These represent a total of some thirty verses. (2) How can we explain certain minor verbal agreements (omissions or alterations) of Matthew and Luke against Mark in the Triple Tradition?[36]

To explain the omitted sections of Mark, Streeter appealed to a variety of reasons which were not always cogent. To explain the minor verbal agreements of Matthew and Luke against Mark, Streeter classified the passages and offered reasons for the independent changes. In the main, his classification used these headings:[37] (a) *Irrelevant agreements:* Since unnecessary or unimportant Marcan words were often omitted by Matthew or Luke in their compression of details, "coincidence in omission" in these parallel passages proves nothing. Similarly, the common shift in some parallel passages from the historic present to imperfects or aorists, the common substitution of *de* for *kai,* the common insertion of noun-subjects in sentences where Mark merely has "he" or "they," and the common introduction of *idou* in five parallel passages (whereas Mark never uses it in narrating). In all of these details Streeter's point was that changes were otherwise widespread in Matthew or Luke and inevitably led to coincidental, and hence irrelevant, cases of agreement, constituting "considerably more than half the total number of the Minor Agreements."[38] (*b*) *Deceptive agreements:* "When Mark uses a word which is linguistically inadmissible, the right word is so obvious that, if half-a-dozen independent correctors were at work, they would all be likely to light upon it. For instance Mark uses *pherein* of animals or persons as objects, and every time Matthew and Luke concur in altering it to *agein* (or some compound of it).[39] Similarly, common corrections are made for *krabbaton, thygatrion, kentyriōn, basileus* (used of Herod), etc. Streeter applied the same judgment to "coincidences" that extended beyond single word agreements (e.g., the five-word sequence in Matt 9:7; Luke 5:25 over against Mark 2:12—showing that four of the five words are derived from the immediate Marcan context); cf. Mark 16:8; Matt 28:8; Luke 24:9;— Mark 3:1; Matt 12:9–10; Luke 6:6—Mark 4:10; Matt 13:10; Luke 8:9—Mark 4:36; Matt 8:23; Luke 8:22; etc. (*c*) *The Influence of "Q":* Certain phrases were commonly introduced into passages derived from Mark by Matthew and Luke because of the overlapping of "Q" and Mark (i.e., because "Q" also contained versions of John's preaching, the baptism of Jesus, the temptation, the Beelzebul controversy, etc.). Yet Streeter used this influence to explain the agreements in Matthew and Luke in their parallels to only three Marcan passages:

> Mark 4:21 = Matt 5:15 = Luke 8:16 = Luke 11:33
> Mark 4:22 = Matt 10:26 = Luke 8:17 = Luke 12:2
> Mark 8:12 = Matt 12:38 = Matt 16:4 = Luke 11:29

(*d*) *Textual corruption:* ". . . in nearly every case where a minute agreement of Matthew and Luke against Mark is found in B ℵ it is absent in one or more of the other early local texts." From this Streeter concluded, "A careful study of the MS. evidence distinctly favours the view that all those minute agreements of Matthew and Luke against Mark, which cannot be attributed to coincidence, were absent from the original text of the Gospels, but have crept in later as a result of 'assimilation' between the texts of the different Gospels." (*e*) *Some Residual Cases:* Here Streeter treated chiefly Mark 14:65, Matt 26:67–68 and Luke 22:64: the plural participle *legontes* and the phrase *tís estin ho paisas se,* "the most remarkable of the minor agreements." To handle it, Streeter appealed to the addition of the phrase in the Marcan text of MSS W, Θ, 13, etc., 579, 700, and after a rather lengthy discussion concluded that the phrase is really "an interpolation into Matthew from Luke."[40]

The fifth point in Streeter's presentation has often been criticized, and this loophole in the Two-Source Theory has been exploited by its opponents.[41] For instance, in seeking to dispense with "Q," A. M. Farrer drew an argument precisely from Luke's "small alterations in the wording of his Marcan original" which were made in common with Matthew.[42] Though Farrer admits that Luke worked directly "upon the more ancient narrative of St. Mark," yet his alterations of Mark were owing to "Matthean echoes," because Luke was after all acquainted with Matthew. Farrer's premise is that the Two-Source Theory was erected "on the incredibility of St. Luke's having read St. Matthew's book,"—a presupposition that has undergone a change in recent times and that enables Farrer simply to *assert* to the contrary. Farrer criticizes Streeter for classifying the minor agreements and for finding a distinct hypothesis for each class of them (such as scribal error assimilating Luke to Matthew or Matthew to Luke, or scribal error subsequently effacing the text of Mark, or stylistic and doctrinal changes, or dependence on a "Q" parallel). "Thus the forces of evidence are divided by the advocate, and defeated in detail."[43] Farrer's criticism of Streeter on this point was, however, analyzed by R. McL. Wilson, who retorted with the observation that his criticism was written "with the balance tilted against it from the beginning"—an admirable "example of the demolition of one's opponent by means of the gentle art of ridicule."[44] (To another aspect of Farrer's argument I shall return below.)

The one more or less valid point of criticism that Farrer levelled against Streeter—that of classifying the minor agreements and then finding a distinct hypothesis of each—was subsequently developed by W. R. Farmer, who labelled Streeter's procedure as "the atomization of the phenomena."[45] By this he means the separate classification and discussion of the phenomena in one group at a time, which obscured the total concatenation of agreements in a given Synoptic passage. So treated, the reader would scarcely become aware of the "web of minor but closely related agreements" of Matthew and Luke against Mark in any given passage.[46] Farmer analyzes in great detail the arguments of Streeter under four main headings; many of his analyses have detected historical defects in Streeter's presentation, and some of them unveil a rather cavalier procedure.

Yet not all of Farmer's remarks are as telling as they might seem to be. For instance, his claim that the readers of Matthew and Luke "were used to a Greek upon which the influence of Latin had long been felt. At least this is a presumption that would follow naturally from the historic and cultural realities of the times. . . ."[47] One would have expected a little documentation here instead of a presumption. Or again, Farmer's comment on the common Lucan and Matthean shift from the Marcan *legei* (an historic present) to *eipen* in 20 passages: "Possibly all twenty instances of this particular agreement are irrelevant. In each case, however, it is necessary to see this particular agreement in the context of all related phenomena in the concrete passage in which the agreement occurred."[48] In this regard Farmer seems to be uncovering a defect in the process of atomization; indeed, in the abstract it appears to be a point well made. However, if one fishes out the 20 passages (which are undocumented) and compares them, even using Farmer's new colored *Synopticon,* it is difficult to see what the telling "web of minor but closely related agreements" is in most of these passages. True, one will find in these passages other words than *eipen* highlighted in red, i.e., common to Matthew and Luke. Sometimes a few significant words are common, but at times a common *kai* or *de* or *idou* (e.g., Matt 8:1–4; 9:3–4; 12:48) might be the words. In such cases it is hard to discern what the "web" really is. Consequently, until Farmer spells out what is meant by this "web of *closely related* agreements," one may have to live with the atomizing explanation. In most instances, to be sure, Streeter's explanations still command stronger assent than Farmer's alleged web.

Concerning these common minor agreements of Matthew and Luke against Mark in the Triple Tradition, one should recall that they represent only a small fraction of the data to be considered in the Synoptic Problem. They constitute a problem which cannot be denied; they are one of the loopholes in the Two-Source Theory. Whatever explanation (or explanations) may account for this phenomenon, it scarcely weighs as evidence that completely counterbalances the other data pointing to a dependence of Luke (and of Matthew) on Mark. Furthermore, the distinction made long ago between significant and insignificant agreements of Matthew and Luke against Mark is still valid. The longest list of significant agreements, constructed from four earlier attempts to collect them, numbers only 46. And when these are further examined, they can be reduced to six: Matt 26:68, 75; 17:3, 17; 9:7, 20 (and parallels).[49] The last word on this issue has not been said, and unfortunately what has at times been written about it has been laced with more emotion than reason.

These are the main reasons that have been proposed for the priority of Mark over Luke (and Matthew). They are not without their difficulties, but some of them are less cogent than others. But, as I see the situation, the day has not yet come, even in 1980, "when the absolute priority of Mk [is] regarded as an a priori position in an obsolete stage of criticism."[50]

Before leaving the topic of the priority of Mark, a word should be said about the form of Mark that is thought to underlie Matthew and Luke. If the majority consensus seems to favor the priority of Mark over Luke (and Matthew), it can be said to be largely against the idea of *Ur-Markus*, i.e., against a form of Mark that Matthew and Luke would have used which was earlier than and slightly different from canonical Mark. V. Taylor, in his commentary *The Gospel according to St. Mark*, surveyed the various forms in which this hypothesis had been proposed up to that time and felt "compelled to reject all known forms of the Ur-Markus hypothesis"; yet he admitted that "there is something unseemly in an investigation which ends with *Requiescat Ur-marcus*."[51] Unfortunately, the hypothesis has not quite died. Some of the earlier forms in which it had been proposed have, indeed, proved inadequate; but some recent studies have been supporting one or other aspect of it. Aside from the problems of the commonly omitted Marcan passages in Matthew and Luke and the minor verbal agreements, there is also the problematic ending of Mark, the textual evidence for a "Western" (or perhaps "Caesarean") form of Mark, and the textual evidence for a second-century revision of Mark.[52] These are, in the main, the reasons invoked for the Ur-Markus hypothesis. None of this evidence, however, is as cogent as the other factors favoring the Two-Source Theory, and this is basically the reason for the reluctance of many to accept it. Then, too, there is the more recent emphasis on *Redaktionsgeschichte*, which may allow for some of the differences that the hypothesis itself was seeking to handle. To my way of thinking, the possibility of Ur-Markus is still admissible.[53]

II. *Luke's Use of "Q"*

Once again it is almost impossible to discuss the hypothesis of Luke's use of "Q" without bringing in the question of Matthew's use of it too, since by definition "Q" is the postulated Greek written source underlying some 230 verses common to Matthew and Luke and not found in Mark. This non-Marcan material in Matthew and Luke is usually referred to as the Double Tradition. Such common non-Marcan material could be owing to Matthew borrowing from Luke, or to Luke borrowing from Matthew, or to their common use of an earlier source. Today, very few would consider it likely that Matthew has derived such material from Luke.[54] A number of Gospel commentators, however, do maintain that Luke has used Matthew, but the majority rather insist on their common use of a postulated Greek, written source, called "Q."[55]

To establish the independent existence of this source is more difficult than to establish the priority of Mark. Moreover, it is to be noted that some commentators who admit the priority of Mark over Luke[56] deny the existence of the postulated second source (maintaining either the priority of Matthew over both Mark and Luke, or at least that Luke depends on both Mark and Matthew).

Before the survey of the reasons for the postulated "Q" is begun, the more general question of Luke's dependence on Matthew has to be posed.[57] For Luke's dependence on Matthew is an issue that is not restricted only to the Double Tradition. We have already noted Farrer's contention that the Two-Source Theory was erected on "the incredibility" of Luke having used Matthew. Some of the main reasons for denying such use must now be reviewed, before we proceed to the more specific questions of "Q." They can be summed up under the following five headings.

First, the apparent reluctance of Luke to reproduce typically Matthean "additions" within the Triple Tradition. In thus phrasing the matter, I may seem to be prejudging the issue. I am only trying to refer to the fuller Matthean formulation of parallels in Mark, such as the exceptive phrase on divorce (Matt 19:9; cf. Mark 10:11);[58] Jesus' promise to Peter (Matt 16:16b–19; cf. Mark 8:29);[59] Peter's walking on the waters (Matt 14:28–31; cf. Mark 6:50);[60] and the peculiar Matthean episodes in the passion narrative. When Matthew and Mark are considered alone, it may be difficult to decide the dependence or priority in such cases. To my way of thinking, they are more readily intelligible as Matthean "additions" than as Marcan excisions. But the real issue is to explain Luke's failure to adopt the extra Matthean materials in his parallels, or at least some of them, if he has written in dependence on Matthew—or used Mark as his main source and quarried Matthew only for such material as would suit his own edifice.[61] The few examples cited above, having to do with pericopes, do not give a full picture of this phenomenon; it is necessary to compare a whole list of smaller Matthean additions to Mark, which are absent in Luke.[62] For instance,

Luke 3:22	Matt 3:17	(the public proclamation)	Cf. Mark 1:11
5:3	4:18	("who is called Peter")	1:16
5:27	9:9	("Matthew")	2:14
6:4–5	12:5–7	(plucking grain on the Sabbath)	2:26–27
8:18b	13:12a	(being given in excess)	4:25
8:10–11	13:14	(quotation of Isa 6:9–10)	4:12
9:1–5	10:7	(nearness of the kingdom)	6:7–11
9:20b	16:16b	(Peter's confession)	8:29b

Similar instances could still be added. The question is how to account for the Lucan omission of such Matthean material in the hypothesis that Luke used Matthew. It is not convincing merely to state that he preferred the simpler Marcan form.[63]

Second, it is difficult to explain adequately why Luke would want to break up Matthew's sermons, especially the Sermon on the Mount, in order to incorporate a part of it in his Sermon on the Plain and scatter the rest of it in an unconnected and disjointed fashion in the loose context of the travel account. Even though one must admit that this central portion of Luke is redactionally very important in the composition of the Third Gospel and that it constitutes a "mosaic" in its own right, yet the tension between its matter and its form (i.e., between its loosely connected or almost unconnected episodes or sayings and its unifying preoccupation with Jesus' movement toward Jerusalem that appears from time to time [Luke 9:51, 53; 13:22; 17:11; 19:28]) has always been a problem.[64] Whatever explanation is to be given for it and for Luke's redactional purpose in constructing this central section, the explanation that he has quarried the material from Matthew's sermons is the least convincing.

Third, aside from 3:7–9, 17 and 4:2–13 Luke has never inserted the material of the Double Tradition into the same Marcan context as Matthew. If he derives such material from Matthew—and otherwise manifests such respect for a source that he is following, as his dependence on Mark would suggest[65]—it is surprising that at least some of the remaining Double Tradition material does not occur in contexts that parallel Matthew, which are often quite appropriate to this material. The frequent disagreement with the Matthean order in this regard is crucial to any judgment about Luke's dependence on Matthew; in fact it suggests that he does not depend.

Fourth, an analysis of the Double Tradition material in Matthew and Luke shows that sometimes Matthew, sometimes Luke has preserved what can only be described as the more original setting of a given episode.[66] This would seem to be scarcely the case if Luke were always dependent on Matthew within this tradition. It is, however, readily intelligible in the hypothesis that both of them have been following and editing a common source.

Fifth, if Luke depends on Matthew, why has he almost constantly omitted Matthean material in episodes where there are Matthean, but no Marcan parallels, e.g., in the infancy and resurrection narratives?

These are the five main reasons for denying Luke's dependence on Matthew. They have to be coped with in a real way whenever the contrary thesis is maintained. They form, moreover, the background for the more specific discussion of the Lucan and Matthean use of "Q."

That Matthew and Luke both used a common source is a partial hypothesis of the Two-Source Theory. Farrer has maintained that this "is its weakness," and that the Lucan use of Matthew is not "a contrary hypothesis."[67] This view of the situation was exposed by F. G. Downing, who maintained "that Luke used Matthew must in the nature of the case remain as much an hypothesis as the one-time existence of Q."[68] It is but another reason for my own preliminary remark about the "truth of the matter" and the hypothesis with which one must deal in this matter. "Q" is admittedly a hypothetical entity, but it remains to be seen whether it is "an unnecessary and vicious hypothesis," as Butler has labelled it, or "a nebulosity, a capriciousness, an intractability," as S. Petrie has called it.[69]

The following are the main reasons for the postulated Greek written source "Q."[70] First, the number of crucial texts in which Matthew and Luke agree almost with identical wording, at times even word-for-word, is such that common dependence on a source is called for.[71] Thus in passages such as these:

Matt 3:7b–10	Luke 3:7b–9	(The speech of John the Baptist; 60 out of 63 words are identical and two of the differences are clearly Lucan stylistic improvements [*arxēsthe* for *doxēte;* an added adverbial *kai*]).
Matt 6:24	Luke 16:13	(The saying about serving two masters; 27 out of 28 words are identical)
Matt 7:3–5	Luke 6:41–42	(On judging; 50 out of 64 words are identical)
Matt 7:7–11	Luke 11:9–13	(The efficacy of prayer; 59 out of 74 words are identical)
Matt 11:4–6, 7b–11	Luke 7:22–23, 24b–28	(Jesus' answer and testimony about John the Baptist; 100 out of 121 words are identical)
Matt 11:21–23	Luke 10:13–15	(Woes against the towns of Galilee; 43 out of 49 words are identical)
Matt 11:25–27	Luke 10:21–22	(Jesus' praise of the Father; 50 out of 69 words are identical)
Matt 12:43–45	Luke 11:24–25	(Return of the evil spirit; 53 out of 61 words are identical)
Matt 23:37–38	Luke 13:34–35	(Lament over Jerusalem; 46 out of 55 words are identical)
Matt 24:45–51	Luke 12:42–46	(Sayings about vigilance; 87 out of 104 words are identical)

The differences in the above list may seem at times a little high; but one would have to look at the concrete cases, which often enough involve stylistic variants (e.g., Luke eliminating a paratactic *kai* that Matthew has preserved).

Second, it is scarcely coincidental that the material of the Double Tradition inserted into the First and Third Gospels in different contexts manifests a common general underlying sequence or order. This can hardly be due to oral tradition and seems rather to argue for a written source. Most of this material is inserted in Matthew into Marcan contexts and sermon blocks, whereas in Luke it scarcely ever appears in Marcan contexts but is generally grouped in separate, interpolated blocks—or, as Streeter once put it, "Matthew conflates his sources, Luke alternates them."[72] Given this situation, one would scarcely expect a common sequence of any sort in the Double Tradition. And yet, there is a trace of such a sequence.

One way of detecting this common sequence is found in the two-column line-up of parallels of the Double Tradition frequently presented in Introductions to the New Testament (e.g., in that of W. G. Kümmel[73]). This list begins with the order of the Lucan material and compares the Matthean with it; the common order is more apparent at the beginning and the end of the list than in the middle. A better way, however, has been discovered by V. Taylor,[74] who at first set forth the Double Tradition in seven columns: the first of which presented the Lucan order, the next five columns the common material as it appears in each of the five great Matthean sermons, and the seventh as it appears in Matthew outside of the sermons. Taylor's method respects the Matthean scattering of the material, mainly in the sermons, and beyond them. In his first discussion of this matter Taylor had eliminated certain questionable material; but he returned to the issue later and did a more comprehensive study, comparing the Lucan order in detail with each of the sermons in Matthew and the extra-sermon passages. What is striking in this detailed comparison is the amount of agreement in sequence that is revealed, not in the over-all order, but in the individual Matthean sections when they are compared with Luke. When there is lack of agreement, it frequently occurs because Matthew inserts Double Tradition material into blocks of his own special material ("M"), and strives for a topical arrangement. At times this argument from the order of the Double Tradition material has been impugned, but I have so far uncovered no real attempt to cope with or refute the Taylor presentation of it.[75]

A third reason for postulating "Q" is found in the doublets in Luke (and in Matthew). By "doublet" is meant here an account of the same event or a saying occurring twice in either Luke or Matthew and related in such wise that they seem to be part of the Triple Tradition, on the one hand, and of the Double Tradition, on the other—or to put it another way, that one belongs to a tradition parallel to Mark and one to a tradition not parallel to Mark. The conclusion drawn from this phenomenon is that Matthew and Luke have retained in their Gospels the double accounts of the same event or double sayings as they inherited them independently from Mark and from "Q." Thus, in Luke we note the following doublets:

From the Marcan Source		From the "Q" Source	
8:16	(= Mark 4:21)	11:33	(= Matt 5:15)
8:17	(= Mark 4:22)	12:2	(= Matt 10:26)
8:18	(= Mark 4:25; Matt 13:12)	19:26	(= Matt 25:29)
9:3–5	(= Mark 6:8–11)	10:4,5–7,10–11	
			(= Matt 10:1,10–12,14)
9:23–24	(= Mark 8:34–35; Matt 16:24–25)	14:27	(= Matt 10:38–39)
9:26	(= Mark 8:38; Matt 16:27)	12:9	(= Matt 10:33)[76]

These are the three main reasons for postulating "Q." Admittedly, no one has even seen this source isolated; attempts to ferret it out have certainly not been able to command universal agreement.[77] It may never have been the literary unit that Mark is (or that Ur-Markus was). Part of the problem encountered here is the lack of agreement as to how much really belongs to "Q"; this is the loophole in this part of the theory. There is also the difficulty of passages that, considered globally, would seem to belong to the "Q" source and yet display such a disagreement in word order and vocabulary that one hesitates to label them clearly as derived solely from Q. Taylor lists seven such passages:

Luke 10:25–28	Matt 22:34–39	(Saying about the great commandment)
Luke 12:54–56	Matt 16:2–3	(Saying about signs of the times)
Luke 13:23–24	Matt 17:13–14	(Saying about the narrow gate)
Luke 13:25–27	Matt 7:22–23; 25:10–12	(Saying about the shut door)
Luke 14:15–24	Matt 22:1–10	(Parable of the great supper)
Luke 15:4–7	Matt 18:12–14	(Parable of the lost sheep)
Luke 19:22–27	Matt 25:14–30	(Parable of the pounds)[78]

How can one account for the verbal disagreement in such passages? Is it owing to the simultaneous dependence of such passages on another source which had a parallel to "Q" (e.g., on "L" or "M")? Is it owing simply to the redactional work of Matthew or Luke? Is it owing to the fact that "Q" existed in different forms? Was "Q" possibly a composite document? Taylor believes that there is a "wide consent" that Matthew is dependent on a second source other than "Q" and would apparently ascribe such verbal disagreement to the conflation of "M" and "Q."[79] A common understanding of "Q" maintains that Luke presents substantially the original order of "Q," while the more original wording is found in Matthew, since Luke has undoubtedly modified "Q" stylistically, as he has done Mark. Sometimes the verbal disagreement can be ascribed to a known Lucan or Matthean characteristic; yet this does not account for all of it. It is precisely this difficulty of the verbal disagreement in certain Lucan and Matthean passages that one would otherwise be inclined to label as "Q" that hampers scholars from agreeing on the extent of "Q."

It is sometimes argued that "Q" existed in different forms that were used independently by Matthew and Luke. Thus C. K. Barrett would distinguish two written forms of it.[80] This suggestion, however, might be acceptable, if it meant that a passage in the written source was from time to time replaced by a better form of the same story or saying which was derived from oral tradition. So revised, the "Q" source might have been used at different times by Matthew and Luke. Plausible though this suggestion is, it is quite speculative.

Some writers have suggested that "Q" represents only layers of tradition that existed largely in an oral, catechetical, or liturgical form.[81] To admit such a multiple form of "Q," however, fails to account for the almost word-for-word identical phrasing which is met at times and which we have mentioned above. It would mean, in effect, a return to a form of the *Traditionshypothese* with all its consequent difficulties.

An objection to "Q" has often been derived from its content, that it consist almost entirely of sayings of Jesus, contains very few narratives (e.g., the temptation, the cure of the centurion's servant, the disciples of John the Baptist), and lacks a passion narrative. This last defect is claimed to be crucial, for how could the early church have composed an evangelical text that lacked the kerygmatic proclamation of the saving Christ-event itself? This objection, however, stems from a modern, preconceived idea of what *euangelion* was in the early church. No one will deny that *euangelion* was related to *kerygma,* but the two are not necessarily co-extensive terms. Moreover, regardless of the position one takes about the origin of the sayings ascribed to Jesus in the Coptic *Gospel according to Thomas*—whether they are to be regarded as derived from the canonical sources, from Gnostic composition, or from an independent ancient oral tradition—the significant thing is that this collection of 114 sayings was frankly labelled "Gospel" in antiquity. Save for a few small sections (No. 13, No. 22, No. 100, which contain the tiniest bit of narrative), the *logoi* ascribed to Jesus in this text are devoid of contextual settings, and there is no passion narrative. And yet it was entitled *peuaggelion pkata Thōman.*[82] This apocryphal Gospel, then, shows us at least that the argument against "Q" drawn from its content is not necessarily valid. To argue thus, however, does not mean that one ascribes a link between "Q" and the Coptic apocryphal Gospel;

if there be a relation, it must be established on other grounds. Finally, to my way of thinking, the postulated "Q" source may not represent a kerygmatic document of the early church at all. It may rather have been part of the *didachē* of some early community or communities, representing mainly a collection of sayings of Jesus gathered from various oral traditions and formulated anew in view of various *Sitze im Leben* (e.g., preaching, controversy, casuistry, catechetics, liturgy).

Anyone who has made use of the Two-Source Theory in Synoptic Gospel study is aware of the difficulties and the inadequacies of the "Q" hypothesis. Part of the problem is, as Farrer has rightly recognized, that it is a hypothetical entity. That it is unnecessary is another matter; this is still to be established. In my opinion, the "Q" source will continue to command the attention of students, despite its difficulties, until a more useful hypothesis is convincingly proposed—one that is freer of serious objections to it than is "Q."

A subsidiary question involving "Q" must finally be mentioned, before this section is brought to a close. It is the so-called overlapping of "Q" and Mark in the Gospels of Matthew and Luke. This refers to the suggestion that some episodes or sayings were found in both Mark and "Q" and have been combined in passages basically related to the Triple Tradition. For instance, the preaching of John the Baptist (Luke 3:1–18), the baptism of Jesus (Luke 3:21–22), the temptation of Jesus (Luke 4:1–13), the parables of the mustard seed (Luke 13:18–19) and of the leaven (Luke 13:20–21). In these cases there is evidence of conflationary composition. Streeter's view was that Mark and "Q" represent independent traditions in these passages; this seems to be commonly accepted, and only a few would maintain that Mark depends on "Q" or has incorporated part of "Q."[83]

III. *Other Solutions*

Before finishing this survey of the question of Luke's dependence on Mark and "Q," a few words ought to be added concerning other recent theories about the composition of the Third Gospel which differ from the Two-Source Theory. Some remarks have already been made above about such solutions, but there is room for further comment. I restrict myself to the question of Luke's dependence on sources in the theories of L. Vaganay, X. Léon-Dufour, and W. R. Farmer.[84]

The solutions of L. Vaganay and X. Léon-Dufour have in common a desire to give more play to oral tradition in the formation of the Synoptic Gospels.[85] Vaganay also seeks to allow for some of the early church's tradition or extrinsic testimony about the Gospels. He distinguishes seven steps in the formation of the Synoptic Gospels: (1) The stage of oral, Aramaic and Greek, tradition about what Jesus said and did (marked by mnemonic devices of oral style as parallelism, rhythm, catchwords, and inclusion). (2) The stage of early attempts to record the oral tradition in writing, Aramaic and Greek, for different local churches. (3) The Aramaic Gospel of Matthew (M), attested to by Papias, and its Greek translation (Mg), postulated because of long passages in the Triple Tradition having the same systematic sequence, common Old Testament citations, traces of a five-book division, and agreements of Matthew and Luke against Mark. (4) The collection of sayings-material in a secondary, supplementary Synoptic source (S), originally composed in Aramaic, but eventually translated into Greek (Sg), corresponding roughly to the sayings in the Lucan travel account and some 145 verses of Matthew; this is in no way the same as "Q" in content or order. (5) The canonical Mark, composed in ignorance of S, but based on Peter's catechesis, especially at Rome, and also on Mg. (6) The canonical Matthew, a reworking of Mg, Sg, and Mark (changing the order of Mg, displacing the sayings in Sg, and condensing the three sources). (7) The canonical Luke, using Mark as its principal source and both Mg and Sg as secondary and complementary sources (respectively).[86]

Vaganay's solution is thus much more complicated than the Two-Source Theory. With respect to Luke, it differs mainly in postulating a dependence on the Greek translation of Aramaic Matthew and in assigning a different content to Sg than would be in "Q." Significant is Vaganay's conviction that Luke was composed independently of canonical Matthew.[87]

The major difficulty in Vaganay's solution is the assignment of Lucan dependence on both Mark and Mg, when the latter is not really sufficiently distinguished from Mark. Vaganay himself senses the difficulty.[88] Again, the solution is quite conjectural in spots. Vaganay seems to think that his M contained the Sermon on the Mount; but then there is a major problem (already mentioned above) to convince us that Mark, even as an abbreviator, would omit such a section from Mg. Moreover, his view of Sg encounters the same difficulties as "Q," for it admits word-for-word identity in some places, but considerable verbal disagreement in others. This is scarcely an improvement on the "Q" hypothesis. There is, further, a host of small passages about which one wonders, when one reads Vaganay's solution and his assignment of them to one or other source (e.g., the preaching of the Baptist in Matt 3:7–10 and Luke 3:7–9 as a part of Mg). Though I find certain elements in

Vaganay's solution intriguing, I cannot regard it as a more successful rival to the Two-Source Theory.

X. Léon-Dufour emphasizes the tell-tale evidence of *oral style* in the Synoptics (parallelism, rhythm, catchwords, and inclusion), *verbal shifts* which are scarcely due to simple editing, and the *context-supplements* of Mark. He maintains, moreover, that the detailed argumentation usually based on the similarity between Matthew, Mark, and Luke "proves hardly more than the existence of literary contacts between the respective sources."[89] He accordingly abandons "the rigid system of literary interrelationships,"[90] or dependence of one canonical Gospel on another, and insists that his solution is not a return to the facile hypothesis of oral tradition alone. Rather, it is a *via media* that seeks to allow for both oral tradition and literary dependence. Oral tradition has been at work both at the beginning of the gospel tradition and at its end, just before the definitive form of the three Gospels, between the literary contacts and the final redaction. Literary contacts occurred, not between the Gospels as such, but "within a presynoptic documentation already more or less systematized."[91] He would thus postulate five stages of formation: (1) The stage of crystallized oral tradition. (2) The first systematization in Aramaic Matthew. (3) Successive written documents, at least three in number, which enjoyed literary contacts. (4) Oral modifications in the various communities of these documents. (5) The definitive Gospels of Matthew, Mark, and Luke. Thus there is no dependence of Luke on Mark or on Matthew (as we know them), but only an undefined literary contact between them in an early stage, and modifications from subsequent oral tradition.

The difficulties that such a theory encounters are several. First, Léon-Dufour himself admits that it "rests on partial analysis."[92] Second, it cannot wholly escape the charge of being somewhat aprioristic and speculative. Third, the presentation of this solution is built up too much on objections voiced against the Two-Source Theory (as if none of these have an answer) and on opponents to it who do not agree among themselves in their own solutions.[93]

The thesis of W. R. Farmer departs from that of Vaganay and Léon-Dufour in not being concerned with the influence of oral tradition on the formation of the Synoptics. Succinctly put, Farmer's thesis is a renewed appeal for the Griesbach hypothesis: "Matthew is in many respects secondary to the life situation of Jesus, and the primitive Christian community, but . . . this Gospel was nonetheless copied by Luke, and . . . Mark was secondary to both Matthew and Luke, and frequently combined their respective texts."[94] Farmer would date Mark at the beginning of the second century, regarding it as a composition written in Alexandria, or possibly Rome, where a need was felt for a shorter Gospel for some liturgical event in the Church's life in which the whole of Mark was to be read and "in which the worshipper's powers of concentration and his eschatological expectations were sharply focused on the words of the Lord of the cult: 'What I say to you I say to all: Watch!,' followed immediately by a dramatic representation of the final acts in the redemptive drama of universal salvation through the Passion of the Son of God."[95] This shorter Gospel was needed in "mixed" congregations, i.e., in congregations such as at Alexandria or Rome in which Christians lived who had come from different places and were accustomed to different Gospels (e.g., either Matthew or Luke). Mark was fashioned as a text from Matthew and Luke and was to be read on "high liturgical occasions where it would have been particularly important to the adherents of the various Gospels for their favorite Gospel to be read—by creating a new Gospel largely out of existing Gospels concentrating on those materials where their texts bore concurrent testimony to the same Gospel tradition."[96] Thus it is that Farmer has returned to the Griesbach thesis: that Matthew was the first Gospel composed, then Luke in dependence on it, and finally Mark as a conflation or an abridgment of Matthew and Luke.

Farmer's thesis is preceded by a lengthy exposé of Synoptic studies, accompanied by a detailed analysis of certain Gospel parallels, and set forth in a series of sixteen propositions, which unfortunately cannot be reproduced here because of their length. They are, however, essential to his thesis. Finally, he caps his discussion with notes for a history of the redaction of Synoptic Tradition in Mark. Thus it is that Farmer's main preoccupation is with the Marcan Gospel, which for him represents the term of the Synoptic development. Many of the arguments that others have proposed for the primitive character of Mark are cleverly turned by him into reasons for its late date. Farmer's thesis is provocative, even if it has not commanded much assent.

When it is critically viewed, Farmer's thesis raises a number of serious difficulties. Though it sets out to "investigate the history of the Synoptic problem,"[97] the number of American, English, French, and German writers who have dealt with some phase of the Synoptic question and who are passed over in silence is surprising. Farmer proposed to write a "critical review of the history of the Synoptic problem,"[98] but it has turned out to be a sketch interlaced with value judgments and remarks of a "non-scientific" or "extra-scientific" character (to use his own terms).[99] In the course of the above discussion I have already commented on some aspects of his thesis, as they were concerned with the Two-Source Theory (e.g., on Mark as an abridgment or conflation of

Matthew and Luke, or on Luke as dependent on Matthew—admittedly a secondary issue for Farmer).[100] A few more specific remarks, however, may be in order.

First of all, it seems to be an argument from order on which Farmer ultimately depends in his attempt to justify the creation of Mark. The dominant reason for his contention that Mark is an abridgement or a conflation of Matthew and Luke is precisely the agreement, not in subject matter, but in order. If it were true that Mark was composed by a concentration "on those materials where their [i.e., Matthew's and Luke's] texts bore concurrent testimony to the same Gospel tradition," then why has Mark not copied at least some of the so-called Double Tradition? In this case, the order of the material differs greatly in Matthew and Luke. This seems to mean, then, that the mixed congregations of Alexandria or Rome, for which Mark was allegedly composed, were interested on the great liturgical feast-days not only in listening to concurrent parts of the Gospel to which they had been accustomed in the places from which they originally came, but were demanding that the selected episodes from Matthew and Luke be read to them *in the same order*. Only thus can one account for the omission of the Double Tradition in Mark. Accordingly, we must assume that even though these Christians all knew of the stories of Jesus' triple temptation, they were content with the Marcan abridgment. Even though they knew of the Beatitudes, the Lord's Prayer, and a host of other common Gospel episodes, they were apparently so fixed on the order and sequence of episodes as to prefer an abridged form of the Gospel in accustomed sequence to other common and concurrent material in Matthew and Luke.[101]

Second, to cite some difficulties in the details of Farmer's argumentation, no convincing reason has been given why Mark should have omitted the preaching of John the Baptist (Matt 3:7–10; Luke 3:7–9), which not only is an element to which Matthew and Luke bear "concurrent testimony," but even in the same place in the Synoptic tradition. Similarly, the account of the triple temptation of Jesus (Matt 4:1–11; Luke 4:1–13); in this case the inversion of the last two temptation scenes cannot be alleged as a factor for not using them.

Third, Farmer cites a "classic example" of an inconclusive theological or christological argument for the primitive character of Mark: the idea of the virginal conception of Mary, found in the Matthean and Lucan infancy narratives, and the absence of a birth narrative in Mark; from this it would appear that Mark had been written "before this idea had been accepted in the Church."[102] He prefers rather to follow S. Davidson, in thinking that Mark 6:3, which identifies Jesus as "a carpenter, the son of Mary," reflects a later formulation and one stemming from a community in which the idea of Mary's virginal conception was already accepted. Roman Catholics are often said to misinterpret Mark 6:3, and so I hesitate to comment on it. But in this case I find it very difficult to think that the sole meaning of Mark's phrase, "the son of Mary," is a clear and obvious reference to her virginity. I can readily understand how this phrase might have been the seedbed for the belief passed on in the Matthean and Lucan infancy narratives; but to regard that cryptic, and possibly innocuous, Marcan phrase as a factor "weighing in favor of a date for Mark after this development"[103] [i.e., of a belief in the virginal conception] is asking too much.

Unfortunately, this catalogue of disagreements with details in the Farmer presentation of the matter could go on for a long time. Farmer has sought to propose alternate reasons to answer objections often levelled against the Griesbach hypothesis. Some of them are ingenious and challenging; but in the long run they are not convincing.

I have now come to the end of this survey of the question of Luke's dependence on Mark and "Q." As is to be hoped, it represents largely the present state of the question and the chief reactions to it. There are undoubtedly items that should have been included, for one reason or another. Conceivably, the most recent attempts to solve the Synoptic Problem might be on the right track or might be more valid than the Two-Source Theory. However, they are deficient in so many details— some of which I have pointed out above—and raise at least as many problems as the ones they seek to resolve. Until a more convincing way is found to present one or the other of them, the Two-Source Theory is still the most attractive hypothesis.

By the latter I mean chiefly the priority of Mark and the postulated source "Q" as the chief documents underlying the Gospels according to Matthew and Luke. However, I am inclined to allow for the influence of oral tradition, even at the redactional level which is responsible for the canonical form of these Gospels. Indeed, I would be more inclined to admit this for Luke than for Matthew, i.e., for "L" than for "M." My only hesitation is that one has to distinguish between what might be "L" and what migh be Lucan redaction. This distinction is not easily made. Recent studies, however, have made all of us more aware of Lucan characteristics and Lucan compositional devices. Allowance for these must be made in any re-evaluation of the sources "Q" and "L."

This sketch has been intended to spark discussion on the Synoptic Problem which has been something of a moribund issue in gospel studies; there are undoubtedly some who think that it should remain in that state because we have moved on to the more important tasks of studying the Gospels in and for themselves. This has been due in large part to the phases of Form Criticism and *Redaktionsgeschichte* that have succeeded Source Analysis. It remains to be seen whether the reopening of the entire Synoptic question would yield better fruit.[104]

Postscript (1980)

Since the above essay was composed, a few articles have appeared touching on the issue with which it deals. A few comments on one or other of them may be in order here.

First of all, in the volume in which the essay first appeared one finds another by D. L. Dungan, "Mark—the Abridgement of Matthew and Luke."[105] It deals with the same arguments drawn from Streeter which I sought to support anew. Since it appears earlier in the volume than my article, it has seemed to some that I had a copy of Dungan's essay and sought to refute the work of this younger scholar. My article, however, was written in complete independence of his. I did not even know of it until we were sent copies of the page-proofs of the volume prior to the Pittsburgh Festival. I shall leave it to others to judge whether my arguments meet Dungan's objections.

Second, a colloquy was held at Trinity University in San Antonio, Texas, 26–29 May 1977, on the relationships among the Gospels.[106] It was an attempt at an interdisciplinary approach to problems of such interrelationships, discussing them from the viewpoints of oral traditional literature, classical studies (especially of ancient rhetoric), Judaic studies (especially in rabbinic parallels), and literary criticism. Though the colloquy brought the methods of these other disciplines to bear on the study of the Gospels, it scarcely contributed anything to the classic problem of the Synoptic interrelationships. I cannot agree with the conclusion of the last seminar leader, J. B. Tyson, that "most participants in the seminar concluded that the Griesbach Theory had now achieved a position of respectability, that it is at least a possible solution."[107] It has always been a possible solution (otherwise it would not have been proposed), but a respectable one. . . ? As a result of that colloquy, the Two-Source Theory, as a modified form of the Two-Document Hypothesis has suffered no real set-back; "the Colloquy in no way contributed to any alleged 'eroding' of the dominance of the Two-Source Theory"[108]—an allegation heard at times during the colloquy on the lips of convinced Griesbachians.

Third, about the same time W. R. Farmer in a review article entitled "Modern Developments of Griesbach's Hypothesis,"[109] included a section, "Objections to Griesbach's Hypothesis."[110] In it he took up nine objections that I have formulated in the above essay and sought to answer them. They are too long (occupying almost 10 pages) to reproduce here or try to respond to them here. That will have to await another occasion. But even the lapse of seven years did not enable him to come up with more than feeble answers, in almost every paragraph of which there is room for an incredulous expostulation.

NOTES

* Originally published in *Jesus and Man's Hope* (Perspective Books, 1; 2 vols.; Pittsburgh: Pittsburgh Theological Seminary, 1970), 1. 131–70.

[1] "The Aramaic Qorbān Inscription from Jebel Ḥallet et-Ṭûri and Mark 7:11/ Matt 15:5," *JBL* 78 (1959) 60–65; reprinted, *ESBNT,* 93–100. I realize that the admission of having espoused the priority of Mark in the past leaves me open to the charge of beginning with an assumption. I suppose I shall have to live with it; my intention is to survey the current situation, as I see it.

[2] There is a slight difficulty in the topic assigned, which is that of Luke's dependence on Mark and "Q." Formally, it does not include Matthew's dependence. But since what is really at stake in this discussion is the Two-Source Theory, I shall be forced to include the Matthean aspect from time to time for the sake of the argument. In any case, I leave aside the discussion of reasons for modifications of the classic theory (e.g., the special sources, "L" and "M," and their respective natures; possible multiple sources underlying Mark; the relation of "Q" to an Aramaic collection of *logia;* Proto-Luke; etc.). Unfortunately, this means leaving aside some important Synoptic studies such as that of P. Parker, *The Gospel Before Mark* (Chicago: Chicago University, 1953).

[3] See S. Petrie, " 'Q' Is Only What You Make It," *NovT* 3 (1959) 28–33; W. R. Farmer, *The Synoptic Problem: A Critical Analysis* (New York: Macmillan, 1964) vii; J. Bligh, *CBQ* 31 (1969) 390: E. P. Sanders, *The Tendencies of the Synoptic Tradition* (SNTSMS 9; Cambridge: University Press, 1969) 279.

[4] I would qualify this opinion to admit that there may be some as yet undreamed-of application of data-processing by computers to the problem, i.e., some method not tied to the usual sort of literary judgments which have marked the history of Synoptic research so far.

[5] *The Four Gospels: A Study of Origins, Treating of the Manuscript Tradition, Sources, Authorship, Dates* (4th impr.; New York: Macmillan, 1930) 169.

[6] See W. R. Farmer, *Synoptic Problem,* viii, 200. From a different point of view, cf. also W. Marxsen, *Introduction to the New Testament: An Approach to Its Problems* (Philadelphia: Fortress, 1968) 118: "This Two-Source theory has been so widely

accepted by scholars that one feels inclined to abandon the term "theory" (in the sense of 'Hypothesis')."

⁷ This includes at present many Roman Catholic scholars. Perhaps the most significant recent contribution from this quarter to Synoptic study has been the work of B. de Solages, *A Greek Synopsis of the Gospels: A New Way of Solving the Synoptic Problem* (Leiden: Brill, 1959). His application of a mathematical method, involving statistical analysis, combinatory analysis, and the calculus of the probability of causes to word occurrences within pericopes, plus an independent graphic method of demonstration of the common order of pericopes in Matthew, Mark, Luke, again with the aid of combinatory analysis, has resulted in an unexpected confirmation of the Two-Source Theory. De Solages labelled his sources Mk and X; and even though his work is limited in character, it appears as a support for the classic theory.

The significance of the book was not lost on K. Grayston and G. Herdan (*NTS* 7 [1960–61] 97–98), who wrote, "The outcome of this laborious study is that the two-document hypothesis is systematically established; and it is worthy of note that the book has an approving preface by Cardinal Tisserant, President of the Biblical Commission." What is not expressed here, however, is the *volta face* that this work, so prefaced, represents in the history of the Biblical Commission and in the realm of Roman Catholic Synoptic studies in this century. One need only recall the Commission's negative *responsum* of 26 June 1912 to the (quite loaded!) question posed about the Two-Source Theory (see DS 3578; or *Enchiridion biblicum* [7th ed.; Naples: M. D'Auria, 1961], 400; or *Rome and the Study of Scripture* [7th ed.; St. Meinrad, IN: Grail, 1962] 132). I personally find it difficult today to rid myself of the impression that the Commission's earlier opposition to the Two-Source Theory was basically the reason why an older generation of Roman Catholic scholars sought for solutions to the Synoptic Problem that differed considerably from the Two-Source Theory. While there were some who espoused modifications of it that made it possible to live with the *responsum* (e.g., by insisting that Aramaic Matthew was at the basis of "Q," or by adopting other modifications—cf. A. Wikenhauser, *New Testament Introduction* [New York: Herder and Herder, 1958] 252–53; J. Levie, "L'évangile araméen de saint Matthieu est-il la source de l'évangile de saint Marc?" *NRT* 76 (1954) 689–715, 812–43 [reprinted separately, Tournai: Casterman, 1954]; M. Meinertz, *Einleitung in das Neue Testament* [Paderborn: Schöningh, 1950], most of the other attempts at a solution subconsciously at least proceeded from the *responsum* (e.g., J. Chapman, *Matthew, Mark and Luke* [London: Longmans, Green, 1937]; B. C. Butler, *The Originality of St. Matthew: A Critique of the Two-Document Hypothesis* [Cambridge: University Press, 1951]; L. Vaganay, *Le probleme synoptique: Une hypothèse de travail* (Bibliothèque de théologie, 3/1; Paris: Desclée, 1954) 139–310.

The occasion for the *volta face* came with the semi-official clarification provided by the two secretaries of the Biblical Commission in 1955, when they reviewed the new edition of the *Enchiridion biblicum* and admitted that the *responsa* that dealt with literary questions were by and large outdated and that the "interpreter of Sacred Scripture can pursue his scientific investigations with full liberty and accept the results of these investigations. . ." (see A. Miller, *Benediktinische Monatschrift* 31 [1955] 49–50; A. Kleinhaus, *Antonianum* 30 [1955] 63–65; cf. E. F. Siegman, *CBQ* 18 [1956] 23–29).

For a Roman Catholic reaction to de Solages' book, see P. Benoit, *RB* 67

(1960) 93–102; cf. the author's rejoinder, *BLE* 61 (1960) 287–311. See also L. Hartman, "Synoptica," *SEA* 31 (1966) 133–35.

In still more recent times the stauchest defender of the Two-Source Theory has been the Belgian Roman Catholic, F. Neirynck. He has done this in numerous publications, some of which will be cited below at appropriate places.

[8] Perhaps an exception could be made for some of the form-critical work of P. Benoit and L. Cerfaux.

[9] Presumably, chap. VII in W. R. Farmer's book *Synoptic Problem* is an attempt along these lines; but even he admits the incompleteness of the notes in this chapter.

[10] *The Four Gospels,* 151, 159–60. See also G. Bornkamm, "Evangelien, synoptische," *RGG,* 753–66. See further F. Neirynck, "La matière marcienne dans l'évangile de Luc," *L'Evangile de Luc: Problèmes littéraires et théologiques: Mémorial Lucien Cerfaux* (ed. F. Neirynck; BETL 32; Gembloux: Duculot, 1973) 157–201. This is a detailed analysis of T. Schramm, *Der Markus-Stoff bei Lukas: Eine literarkritische und Redaktionsgeschichtliche Untersuchung* (SNTSMS 14; Cambridge: University Press, 1971).

[11] CSEL, 43.4; PL, 34.1043–44. Cf. X. Léon-Dufour, "The Synoptic Problem," *Introduction to the New Testament* (ed. A. Robert and A. Feuillet; New York: Desclée, 1965) 266.

[12] *Synoptic Problem,* 199–232.

[13] B. C. Butler, *Originality,* 65.

[14] See, for instance, W. R. Farmer, *Synoptic Problem,* 278–83, 230–32, 253, 227–28, et passim; X. Léon-Dufour, "The Synoptic Problem," 269–74.

[15] The numbering of the episodes differs with the way various scholars divide up the blocks of material. The exact numbering is immaterial. It is intended merely to give a general indication of incidents involved.

[16] One could also argue that all three evangelists copied an earlier source independently and thus account for the common order. This argument for a sort of *Urevangelium* has been used. But it is of little concern today, and we need not pursue this possibility further.

[17] This title for the error in logic involved was first coined by B. C. Butler (*Originality,* 62–71), even though he was careful not to ascribe directly to Lachmann what he calls a "schoolboyish error of elementary reasoning." This has been made clear in the article of N. H. Palmer, "Lachmann's Argument," *NTS* 13 (1966–67) 368–78, which provides an abridged English translation of Lachmann's article. Farmer (*Synoptic Problem,* 66) traces the fallacy itself to F. H. Woods, "The Origin and Mutual Relation of the Synoptic Gospels," *Studia biblica et ecclesiastica: Essays Chiefly in Biblical and Patristic Criticism* (Oxford: Clarendon, 1890), 2. 59–104. More recently he has pointed out that the first person in the English-speaking world to attribute the error to Lachmann was F. C. Burkitt in his Jowett Lectures for 1906 ("The Lachmann Fallacy," *NTS* 14 [1967–68] 441–43).

[18] See E. W. Lummis, *How Was Luke Written: Considerations Affecting the Two-Document Theory with Special Reference to the Phenomena of Order in the Non-Marcan Matter Common to Matthew and Luke* (Cambridge: University Press, 1915); H. G. Jameson, *The Origin of the Synoptic Gospels: A Revision of the Synoptic Problem* (Oxford: Blackwell, 1922); B. C. Butler, *Originality,* 62–71. W. R. Farmer is content to remark, "Since Streeter's first three reasons for accepting the priority of Mark were exposed as fallacious by Jameson in 1922 and again by Butler in 1951, there is no need to give them further consideration" (*Synoptic Problem,*

169). O. E. Evans, however, still considers the argument from order to be of "decisive importance" (*ExpTim* 72 [1960–61] 296). And in this he is not alone.

[19] "The Priority of Mark," *ExpTim* 65 (1953–54) 17–19; cf. O. E. Evans, *ExpTim* 72 (1960–61) 296.

[20] In each case Matthew has preserved the Marcan order of these five "transpositions," except for a partial transposition of his own in Matt 10:1–4. Luke moves up the report of the Baptist's imprisonment in an effort to finish off the story of the Baptist before the baptism and before the ministry of Jesus is begun, because either John does not belong to the period of Jesus (Conzelmann) or he represents a separate preparatory period within the time of fulfillment (W. Wink). The visit to Nazareth is transferred to the beginning of the ministry for a programmatic purpose, to present in capsule-form the theme of fulfillment and to symbolize the rejection that marks the ministry of Jesus as a whole. The call of the four disciples is given a more plausible, psychological position by Luke in its later appearance, when it is narrated after a certain portion of Jesus' ministry; it makes the response to the call more intelligible than in Mark. The inversion of the choosing of the Twelve and the report of the crowds again produces a more logical setting for the Sermon on the Plain (6:20–49). And the shifting of the episode about Jesus' real relatives provides an illustration of who the real hearers and doers of the word of God are (8:19–20). See further my commentary on *Luke* (AB 28; Garden City, NJ: Doubleday, 1981).

On this whole question of Lucan transpositions, see now F. Neirynck, "The Argument from Order and St. Luke's Transpositions," in *The Minor Agreements* [see n. 49 below], 291–322; cf. *ETL* 49 (1973) 784–815.

[21] See W. G. Rushbrooke, *Synopticon: An Exposition of the Common Matter of the Synoptic Gospels* (London: Macmillan, 1880?); W. R. Farmer, *Synopticon: The Verbal Agreement between the Greek Texts of Matthew, Mark and Luke Contextually Exhibited* (Cambridge: University Press, 1969).

[22] See D. Guthrie, *New Testament Introduction: The Gospels and Acts* (London: Tyndale, 1965) 127.

[23] See V. Taylor, *The Gospel according to St. Mark* (London: Macmillan, 1953) 102, 44–66.

[24] *The Four Gospels*, 162–64. Cf. B. C. Butler, *Originality*, 147–56.

[25] J. C. Hawkins, *Horae synopticae: Contributions to the Study of the Synoptic Problem* (2d ed.; Oxford: Clarendon, 1909), 114–53, esp. pp. 125–26.

[26] *Originality*, 68.

[27] Ibid., 168.

[28] Ibid., 168–69.

[29] *Synoptic Problem*, 170–71.

[30] (SNTSMS 9; Cambridge: University Press, 1969).

[31] Ibid., 87.

[32] Ibid., 188.

[33] Ibid., 255.

[34] The book came into my hands unfortunately only at a date when the original form of this sketch was practically finished.

[35] Ibid., 276.

[36] See the lists in E. A. Abbott, *The Corrections of Mark Adopted by Matthew and Luke* (Diatesserica II; London: Black, 1901) 307–24; or J. C. Hawkins, *Horae synopticae*, 143–53, 208–212; B. de Solages, *A Greek Synopsis*, 1052–66.

[37] *The Four Gospels*, 179–81, 293–331.

[38] Ibid., 298.

[39] This point has been discussed in my article, "The Use of *Agein* and *Pherein* in the Synoptics," *Festschrift to Honor F. Wilbur Gingrich* (ed. E. H. Barth and R. E. Cocroft; Leiden: Brill, 1972) 146–60.

[40] *The Four Gospels*, 325–29. Cf. W. R. Farmer, *Synoptic Problem*, 284–86 (and 148–51).

[41] See A. W. Argyle, "Agreements between Matthew and Luke," *ExpTim* 73 (1961–62) 19–22; N. Turner, "The Minor Verbal Agreements of Mt. and Lk. against Mk.," *SE I*, 233–34; X. Léon Dufour, "The Synoptic Problem," 271–74. Cf. L. Vaganay, *Le problème synoptique*, 69–74, 405–25; J. Schmid, *Matthäus und Lukas: Eine Untersuchung des Verhältnisses ihrer Evangelien* (Freiburg im B.: Herder, 1930).

[42] "On Dispensing with Q," *Studies in the Gospels: Essays in Memory of R. H. Lightfoot* (ed. D. E. Nineham; Oxford: Blackwell, 1957), 55–88, esp. p. 61.

[43] Ibid., 62.

[44] "Farrer and Streeter on the Minor Agreements of Mt and Lk against Mk," *SE I*, 254–57.

[45] *Synoptic Problem*, 118.

[46] Ibid., 125.

[47] Ibid., 124.

[48] Ibid.

[49] See S. McLoughlin, "Les accords mineurs Mt-Lc contre Mc et le problème synoptique: Vers la théorie des Deux Sources," *De Jésus aux Evangiles: Tradition et rédaction dans les évangiles synoptiques* (BETL 25; Donum natalicium I. Coppens, II; Gembloux: Duculot, 1967) 17–40. This article must be used, however, with caution. It is cited here only because it indicates some of the lines along which one may have to proceed in evaluating the thrust of these minor agreements in the Two-Source Theory. See further now F. Neirynck, "Minor Agreements Matthew—Luke in the Transfiguration Story," *Orientierung an Jesus: Zur Theologie der Synoptiker für Josef Schmid* (ed. P. Hoffmann et al.; Freiburg im B.: Herder, 1973) 253–66. cf. F. Neirynck (in collaboration with T. Hansen and F. van Segbroeck), *The Minor Agreements of Matthew and Luke against Mark with a Cumulative List* (BETL 37; Louvain: Leuven University; Gembloux: Duculot, 1974).

[50] X. Léon-Dufour, "The Synoptic Problem," 277.

[51] *Mark* (see n. 23 above), 68–77.

[52] See T. F. Glasson, "Did Matthew and Luke Use a 'Western' Text of Mark?" *ExpTim* 55 (1943–44) 180–84 (and the debate that ensued with C. S. C. Williams, *ExpTim* 55 [1944–45] 41–45; 57 [1945–46] 53–54; 58 [1946–47] 251; 77 [1965–66] 120–21); J. P. Brown, "An Early Revision of the Gospel of Mark," *JBL* 78 (1959) 215–27 (and the note by T. F. Glasson with the same title, *JBL* 85 [1966] 231–33); O. Linton, "Evidences of a Second-Century Revised Edition of St. Mark's Gospel," *NTS* 14 (1967–68) 321–55; A. F. J. Klijn, "A Survey of the Researches into the Western Text of the Gospels and Acts," *NovT* 3 (1959) 162.

[53] R. Bultmann (*Form Criticism: A New Method of New Testament Research* [Chicago: Willett Clark, 1934] 13–14) has made use of this hypothesis; see also G. Bornkamm, *RGG*, 2. 756. The arguments commonly brought against it can be found in W. G. Kümmel, *Introduction to the New Testament* (rev. ed.; Nashville: Abingdon, 1975) 49–50. See further now F. Neirynck, "Urmarcus

redivivus? Examen critique de l'hypothèse des insertions matthéenes dans Marc," in *L'Evangile selon Marc: Tradition et rédaction* (BETL 34; Gembloux: Duculot, 1974) 103–45.

[54] See the discussion in L. Vaganay, *Le problème synoptique*, 294–95. A nuanced position is found in the article of H. P. West, Jr., "A Primitive Version of Luke in the Composition of Matthew," *NTS* 14 (1967–68) 75–95.

[55] For attempts to trace the origin of this siglum, see W. F. Howard, "The Origin of the Symbol 'Q," *ExpTim* 50 (1938–39) 379–80. See further now H. K. McArthur, "The Origin of the 'Q' Symbol," *ExpTim* 87 (1976–77) 119–20; F. Neirynck, "The Symbol Q (= Quelle)," *ETL* 54 (1978) 119–25; "Once More: The Symbol Q," ibid., 55 (1979) 382–83 (writing against L. H. Silberman, "Whence Siglum Q? A Conjecture,' *JBL* 98 [1979] 287–88). The custom of referring to the Double Tradition as "Q" is traced to Johannes Weiss (1891).

For recent studies of "Q," see M. Devisch, *De geschiedenis van de Quellehypothese: I. Inleiding; II. Van J.-G. Eichhorn tot B. H. Streeter; III. De recente Exegese* (2 vols.; Louvain: Katholiek Universiteit te Leuven, 1975); D. Lührmann, *Die Redaktion der Logienquelle* (WMANT 33; Neukirchen-Vluyn: Neukirchener-V., 1969); P. Hoffmann, *Studien zur Theologie der Logienquelle* (NTAbh ns 8; Münster: Aschendorff, 1972); S. Schulz, *Q: Die Spruchquelle der Evangelisten* (Zürich: Zwingli-V., 1972); R. A. Edwards, *A Concordance to Q* (SBLSBS 7; Missoula, MT: Scholars Press, 1975); A. Polag, *Die Christologie der Logienquelle* (WMANT 33; Neukirchen-Vluyn: Neukirchener-V., 1977); P. Vassiliadis, *Hē peri tēs pēgēs tōn logiōn theōria* (Athens: University of Athens Theological School, 1977).

[56] E.g., B. C. Butler, A. M. Farrer.

[57] It has been espoused by J. H. Ropes, *The Synoptic Gospels* (2d ed.; London: Oxford, 1960); H. G. Jameson, *Origin*, 6; B. C. Butler, *Originality*, 22; "St. Luke's Debt to St. Matthew," *HTR* 32 (1939) 237–308; W. R. Farmer, *Synoptic Problem*, 221–25; R. T. Simpson, "The Major Agreements of Matthew and Luke against Mark," *NTS* 12 (1965–66) 273–84; W. Wilkens, "Zur Frage der literarischen Beziehung zwischen Matthäus und Lukas," *NovT* 8 (1966) 48–57; A. W. Argyle, "The Methods of the Evangelists and the Q Hypothesis," *Theology* 67 (1964) 156–57; K. H. Rengstorf, *Das Evangelium nach Lukas* (NTD 3; 9th ed.; Göttingen: Vandenhoeck & Ruprecht, 1962) 8–9; A. Schlatter, *Das Evangelium des Lukas: Aus seinen Quellen erklärt* (2d ed.; Stuttgart: Calwer, 1960) 472–561.

[58] W. R. Farmer treats this passage in the *Synoptic Problem* (pp. 255–57), using it as a prime example for the Griesbach solution. He regards the Lucan text (16:18) as "a conflation" of Matt 19:9 and 5:32 and is mainly concerned with the genuine problems of the assumed remarriage of the divorced woman and of the Roman practice that is reflected in the Marcan version. But he devotes little time to what seems to be a crucial problem: What would have led Luke to excise the exceptive phrase in Matthew? An appeal to Paul's absolute formulation of the prohibition of divorce in 1 Cor 7:10 scarcely solves the problem, because it only raises the larger one whether Luke was acquainted with Paul's letters at all. Again, to picture Mark twice confronted with the exceptive phrase in Matt 5:32 and 19:9 and twice excising it because he was more influenced by Luke's version from which it is absent is not a convincing argument. For another view of this passage, see A. Isaksson, *Marriage and Ministry in the New Temple* (ASNU 34; Lund: Gleerup, 1965) 96–104. See further pp. 82–99 below.

[59] See Farmer's treatment of this passage in "The Two-Document Hypothesis as a Methodological Criterion in Synoptic Research," *ATR* 48 (1966) 380–96. B. C. Butler (*Originality*, 168) sought to defend the Matthean priority of Matthew 16:16ff. But his explanation that Peter, in "telling the Caesarea Philippi incident" and using Matthew as his *aide-mémoire*, tore out "the story of the high praise of himself and the promise of his peculiar status *vis-à-vis* the Church, while leaving the stinging rebuke," because he had learnt "the lesson of Christian humility" is too rhetorical to be convincing. I personally see no difficulty in understanding this passage as a Matthean addition, along with the stories about the coin in the mouth of the fish that Peter is to catch and his walking on the waters. They are three episodes in the First Gospel that were added to the so-called ecclesiastical section to enhance Peter's role. See further R. E. Brown et al. (eds.), *Peter in the New Testament* (New York: Paulist; Minneapolis, MN: Augsburg, 1973) 83–101.

[60] In the hypothesis of Luke's dependence on Matthew, the problem of his apparent reluctance to reproduce Matthean material can also be illustrated in the Double Tradition (e.g., the fuller form of the Beatitudes [Matt 5:3; cf. Luke 6:20; Matt 5:6; cf. Luke 6:21]; the fuller form of the Lord's Prayer [Matt 6:9–13; cf. Luke 11:2–4]). See J. Dupont, *Les béatitudes* (rev. ed.; Bruges: Saint-André, 1958), 43–128. What seems to be at issue here is a Matthean pattern of additions made to dominical sayings, a pattern that accounts readily for his differences from Mark and Luke in the Triple Tradition and from Luke in the Double Tradition.

[61] To paraphrase the words of A. M. Farrer, "On Dispensing with Q," 65.

[62] See F. G. Downing, "Toward the Rehabilitation of Q," *NTS* 11(1964–65) 1969–81 (arguing against Farrer); E. L. Bradby, "In Defence of Q," *ExpTim* 68 (1956–57) 315–18 (despite its title, this article really deals with this issue). *Pace* N. Turner ("The Minor Verbal Agreements of Mt. and Lk. against Mk.," *SE I*, 223–34), this evidence is not all the result of a subjective approach, or the use of the English text alone; nor does it really involve the minor agreements of Matthew and Luke against Mark. Several arguments are confused by him. Cf. J. Schmid, *Matthäus und Lukas*, 25ff.

[63] Perhaps one should also consider the converse phenomenon in Luke, i.e., his apparent failure to follow Matthew in omitting Marcan passages (e.g., Luke 4:34–37 = Mark 1:23–28 [Jesus in the synagogue of Capernaum]; Luke 9:49–50 = Mark 12:41–44 [the widow's mite]). Farrer has sought to offset this and other arguments which bear on Luke's omission of Matthean material by implying that they are based on an antiquated view of Luke as a collector of Jesus' sayings and a failure to realize that he is really "building an edifice" ("On Dispensing with Q," 63). In one form or another he continually comes back to this line of argumentation: Luke as using a Marcan skeleton, clothed with material cut from Matthew; or Luke as the gardener, expressing his preference for his own new arrangement over that which his predecessor has left him (p. 65). To describe Luke's edifice, Farrer indulges in ingenious typological eisegesis. The major part of his article is given over to establishing a pattern between Luke (and Matthew) and the Hexateuch. With the advance of *Redaktionsgeschichte* it is certainly wrong to say that Luke is regarded simply as a collector of Jesus' sayings; most of the modern commentators who espouse the Two-Source Theory would reject this and insist on the theological "edifice" in the Third Gospel as much as Farrer does. That this edifice was constructed,

however, as Farrer sketches it is another matter. In typological interpretation one must always ask the question: Who is seeing the connections and patterns, Farrer or the Evangelist? In this regard one would do well to consult the estimate of Farrer's work on Mark by no less a literary critic than Helen L. Gardner, *The Business of Criticism* (Oxford: Clarendon, 1959) 108–22.

[64] See W. C. Robinson, Jr., "The Theological Context for Interpreting Luke's Travel Narrative (9:51ff.)," *JBL* 79 (1960) 20–31; L. Vaganay, *Le problème synoptique*, 106–8.

[65] For some observations on this problem, see T. R. Rosché, "The Words of Jesus and the Future of the 'Q' Hypothesis," *JBL* 79 (1960) 210–20.

[66] See L. Vaganay, *Le problème synoptique*, 295–99; B. H. Streeter, *The Four Gospels*, 183.

[67] "On Dispensing with Q," 66.

[68] "Towards the Rehabilitation of Q," 180 n. 5. See also W. H. Blyth Martin, "The Indispensability of Q," *Theology* 59 (1956) 182–88, esp. p. 182.

[69] B. C. Butler, *Originality*, 170; S. Petrie, "'Q' Is Only What You Make It," *NovT* 3 (1959) 28–33.

[70] For an attempt to make "Q" out to be a "written Aramaic source," see F. Bussby, "Is Q an Aramaic Document?" *ExpTim* 65 (1953–54) 272–75.

[71] Strictly speaking, one might object that such data argue only for the dependence of Luke on Matthew, or more generically, of one on the other. This would have to be admitted, if this argument stood alone. It must, however, be considered against the background of the general issues already discussed above, which rule out the dependence of Luke on Matthew.

[72] *The Four Gospels*, 187.

[73] *Introduction*, 65–66.

[74] "The Order of Q," *JTS* 4 (1953) 27–31; "The Original Order of Q," *New Testament Essays: Studies in Memory of Thomas William Manson 1893–1958* (ed. A. J. B. Higgins; Manchester: University Press, 1959) 246–69.

[75] Cf. C. K. Barrett, "Q: A Re-examination," *ExpTim* 54 (1942–43) 320–23 (for an earlier denial of the validity of this argument). Taylor quotes some of the results of the investigation of P. Parker (*The Gospel before Mark*, 30) to support his contention: "Since Q has not been assimilated to Matthean types of expression" and "the style of Q does not pervade M, therefore Q and M have different origins" and "Q is really from an autonomous source" (p. 269). O. E. Evans (*ExpTim* 72 [1960–61] 298) is also favorably impressed by Taylor's argument.

[76] See further J. C. Hawkins, *Horae synopticae*, 99–106. Matthew has about 20 doublets (ibid., pp. 82–99). The "doublet" is not a gospel feature derived solely from Mark, since this Gospel has only one of them, or possibly two (see 9:35–37–10:43–44 and possibly 6:31–44–8:1–10). The occurrence of this feature in Mark raises a different issue, which is not related to that of the Matthean and Lucan "doublets."

[77] See the attempts of B. H. Streeter, *The Four Gospels*, 197ff.; A. (von) Harnack, *The Sayings of Jesus: The Second Source of St. Matthew and St. Luke* (New York: Putnam, 1908). Cf. J. Moffatt, *An Introduction to the Literature of the New Testament* (3d ed.; Edinburgh: Clark, 1918), 194–204, for a survey of 16 attempts to reconstruct "Q." Many of these attempts, however, go back to the pioneer days of the investigation; the astronomical figures sometimes found in them for "Q" verses have in large measure been reduced in recent studies. Even though one cannot cite a consensus, recent writers tend to count the common

verses of the Double Tradition in the neighborhood of 230. *Redaktionsgeschichte* in the study of Matthew and Luke has affected this question too; there is the tendency to allow more for the compositional work of the evangelists in this area.

[78] "The Order of Q," 28.

[79] Ibid. Cf. his older article, "Some Outstanding New Testament Problems: I. The Elusive Q," *ExpTim* 46 (1934–35) 68–74. J. P. Brown ("The Form of 'Q' Known to Matthew," *NTS* 8 [1961–62] 27–42) has suggested a combination of "Q" and "M" sayings (without the parables) as the form of "Q" which Matthew used along with Mark, i.e., a "larger sayings-document Q^{mt}." If Taylor's suggestion has any merit, then perhaps Brown's suggestion may prove to be an interesting refinement of it. Léon-Dufour criticizes this blending of "Q" and "M" into Q^{mt}, admitting that "all this solves the difficulty, but at the cost of raising up two logical entities that transform the Two-Source Theory into a Four-Source theory." So what? Such a transformation may be needed as a refinement of the Two-Source theory. Moreover, if "M" or "L" were regarded merely as an oral source, then the modification of "Q" by such material would allow for the influence of later oral tradition on the gospel formation, such as Léon-Dufour himself argues for.

[80] *ExpTim* 54 (1942–43) 320–23; cf. W. Bussmann, *Synoptische Studien* (3 vols.; Halle/S.: Buchhandlung des Waisenhauses, 1931), 2. 110–56. Also R. S. Cherry, "Agreements between Matthew and Luke," *ExpTim* 74 (1962–63) 63.

[81] See J. Jeremias, "Zur Hypothese einer schriftlichen Logienquelle Q," *ZNW* 29 (1930) 147–49; M. Dibelius, *From Tradition to Gospel* (New York: Scribner, 1935), 76.

[82] See H. Koester, "*Gnōmai diaphoroi:* The Origin and Nature of Diversification in the History of Early Christianity," *HTR* 58 (1965) 279–313, esp. pp. 293–299; reprinted in *Trajectories through Early Christianity* (ed. J. M. Robinson and H. Koester; Philadelphia: Fortress, 1971) 114–57. Cf. J. M. Robinson, "*Logoi sophōn:* On the Gattung of Q," *Trajectories,* 71–113, esp. pp. 74–85.

[83] See T. E. Floyd Honey, "Did Mark Use Q?" *JBL* 62 (1943) 319–31; B. H. Throckmorton, Jr., "Did Mark Know Q?" *JBL* 67 (1948) 319–29; J. P. Brown, "Mark as Witness to an Edited Form of Q," *JBL* 80 (1961) 29–44; M. Devisch, "La relation entre l'évangile de Marc et le document Q," *L'évangile selon Marc: Tradition et rédaction* (BETL 34; Louvain: Leuven University, 1974) 59–91; W. Schenk, "Der Einfluss der Logienquelle auf das Markusevangelium," *ZNW* 70 (1979) 141–65.

[84] For another attempt to explain Luke, see L. Cerfaux, "Luc (Evangile selon saint)," *DBS* 5 (1953) 564–72; "A propos des sources du troisième Evangile, proto-Luc ou proto-Mt," *ETL* 12 (1935) 23–26. For still another attempt, mostly by M.-E. Boismard, see P. Benoit and M.-E. Boismard, *Synopse des quatre évangiles en français avec parallèles des apocryphes et de pères* (3 vols.; Paris: Cerf, 1965, 1972, 197). An assessment of this attempt has been written by F. Neirynck (with the collaboration of others), *Jean et les Synoptiques: Examen critique de l'exégèse de M.-E. Boismard* (BETL 49; Louvain: Leuven University, 1979). See also F. Neirynck, "Une nouvelle théorie synoptique (A propos de Mc., I, 2–6 et par): Notes critiques," *ETL* 44 (1968) 141–53 (= ALBO 4/41).

[85] See also J. W. Doeve, "Le rôle de la tradition orale dans la composition des évangiles synoptiques," *La formation des évangiles* (RechBib 2; Bruges: Desclée de Brouwer, 1957), 70–84.

[86] *Le problème synoptique,* 42–313.

[87] Reviews of Vaganay's book can be found in the following places: M.-E. Boismard, *RB* 61 (1954) 453–54; B. Botte, *BVC* 2 (1954) 116–22; *RTAM* 21 (1954) 150; L. Cerfaux, *NRT* 76 (1954) 494–505; A. Gelin, *L'ami du clergé* 64 (1954) 373–75; X. Léon-Dufour, *RSR* 42 (1954) 557–72; J. Levie, *NRT* 6 (1954) 689–715, 812–43 (to which Vaganay replies in *ETL* 31 [1955] 343–56; see Levie's rejoinder, *ETL* 31 [1955] 619–36); J. L. McKenzie, *TS* 15 (1954) 639–44; K. H. Schelkle, *TQ* 134 (1954) 479ff.; C. S. C. Williams, *Theology* 57 (1954) 430–32.

[88] "A notre avis Lc devait avoir pour source principale Mc., pour source secondaire Mg, pour source complémentaire Sg, sans qu'il soit possible de faire le partage entre les deux premières" (p. 313).

[89] "The Synoptic Problem," 276.

[90] Ibid., 282.

[91] Ibid., 286.

[92] Ibid., 285.

[93] In thus criticizing Léon-Dufour's position, I am not espousing what he calls "la sécurité dogmatique du grand nombre de ses partisans" [i.e., of the Two-Source Theory]; nor do I agree that "les chercheurs qui le [the Two-Source Theory] contestent sont l'objet d'une pitié dédaigneuse de la part de la majorité" ("Interpretation des évangiles et problème synoptique," *De Jésus aux évangiles,* 5–16, esp. p. 5) Part of the difficulty which I find with his criticism of various defenders of the Two-Source Theory is his inability to allow them to modify the theory itself. Suppose one does realize that room should be made in it to allow for the influence of some oral tradition (and, in fact, allows for it in the form of "L" or "M," which may be partly oral, partly written); this does, indeed, mean a departure from the *classic* form of the theory. There is no reason why the proponents of the Two-Source theory today have to be tied to the rigid interrelationships of earlier investigators. Compare too his treatment of the so-called "Marcan" sections in which the arrangement of Mark is respected beyond the three usually mentioned, this scarcely undermines the argumentation of the theory. And why *must* all three elements (content, order, expression) concur at once?

[94] *Synoptic Problem,* 277.

[95] Ibid., 279.

[96] Ibid., 280.

[97] Ibid., viii.

[98] Ibid., 121.

[99] See further "A 'Skeleton in the Closet' of Gospel Research," *BibRes* 6 (1961) 18–42; "The Two-Document Hypothesis as a Methodological Criterion in Synoptic Research," *ATR* 48 (1966) 380–96; "The Synoptic Problem and the Contemporary Theological Chaos: The New Testament Parable's Image of Jesus is More Camouflaged than Clarified by the Hypothesis that Mark was the First-Written Gospel," *ChrC* 83 (1966) 1204–6; "Some Thoughts on the Provenance of Matthew," *The Teacher's Yoke: Studies in Memory of H. Trantham* (Waco, TX: Baylor University, 1964) 109–16.

Reviews of Farmer's book, *The Synoptic Problem,* can be found in the following places: F. W. Beare, *JBL* 84 (1965) 295–97; T. A. Burkill, *ChrC* 81 (1964) 1430; S. Cutt, *Theology* 69 (1966) 225–27; F. C. Grant, *Int* 19 (1965) 352–53; W. E. Hull, *RevExp* 65 (1968) 490–92; R. Leivestad, *NTT* 68 (1967) 16–28; W. C.

Linss, *LQ* 18 (1966) 90–91; J. H. Ludlum, *ChrT* 9 (1964–65) 306; H. Meynell, *Theology* 70 (1967) 391–96; C. L. Mitton, *EspTim* 77 (1965–66) 1–3; M. Rese, *Verkündigung und Forschung* 12/2 (1967) 34–38; W. Schmithals, *TLZ* 92 (1967) 424–25; J. Reumann, *Dialog* 4 (1965) 308–11; H. Rhys, *ATR* 48 (1966) 92–94; H. C. Snape, *Modern Churchman* 10 (1966) 184–91.

[100] See pp. 16, 17–18 above.

[102] See further W. E. Hull, *ExpTim* 65 (1968) 490–92.

[102] *Synoptic Problem*, 231.

[103] Ibid., p. 232. Farmer completely passes over the textual problem of Mark 6:3, about which many commentators have been exercised for a long time. I would not defend as more original the reading *ho tou tektonos huios* which is usually relegated to the *apparatus criticus*. But no less a commentator on Mark than V. Taylor has done so: "It is best to conclude that Mark wrote *ho tou tektonos huios* and that an early scribe replaced this reading by *ho tektōn* and added *ho huios tēs Marias*" (*Mark*, 300). This is only an example of the way in which Farmer has sometimes presented the evidence. See further R. E. Brown et al., *Mary in the New Testament* (New York: Paulist; Philadelphia: Fortress, 1978) 59–64; p. 49 below.

[104] See further B. Reicke, "Griesbach und die synoptische Frage," *TZ* 32 (1976) 341–59; M.-E. Boismard, "The Two-Source Theory at an Impasse," *NTS* 26 (1979–80) 1–17; R. H. Fuller, "Die neuere Diskussion über das synoptische Problem," *TZ* 34 (1978) 129–48; F. Lentzen-Deis, "Entwicklungen in der synoptischen Frage?" *TP* 55 (1980) 559–70.

[105] *Jesus and Man's Hope* (see p. 30 above), 1. 51–97.

[106] W. O. Walker, Jr. (ed.), *The Relationships among the Gospels: An Interdisciplinary Dialogue* (Trinity University Monograph Series in Religion, 5; San Antonio, TX: Trinity University, 1978).

[107] Ibid., 340–41.

[108] My comment, ibid., 257; see also p. 11.

[109] *NTS* 23 (1976–77) 275–95.

[110] Ibid., 283–93.

Two

THE VIRGINAL CONCEPTION OF JESUS
IN THE NEW TESTAMENT*

THE VIRGINAL CONCEPTION of Jesus by Mary has recently become the topic of discussion in American Roman Catholic circles. There have been comments in diocesan newspapers and reports of the "dismay" of the Mariological Society in the U.S.A.,[1] and there have been references to the discussion of this topic in many and varied Roman Catholic circles in Europe, in technical theological periodicals, and in not a few specifically devoted to mariology. The discussion ranges far at times, involving systematic theologians as well as exegetes, and in at least one instance a national conference of bishops.

The issue involves the virginal conception of Jesus, i.e., whether he was historically conceived by Mary who was and remained bodily a virgin in the process, or, in other words, whether he was conceived without the intervention of human seed. It is necessary to be precise about this, because in popular writing and sometimes in Protestant theological treatments or in Roman Catholic discussions in other modern languages the question has been referred to as the "virgin birth." This mode of reference may be defensible, for it is based on early credal formulas, such as *natus ex Maria virgine*. But it should be avoided in technical discussions, because it is often ambiguous. The ambiguity comes from a different notion in Catholic tradition which asserts that Mary remained a virgin even at the time of Jesus' birth (i.e., that his birth was miraculous, or caused no rupture of the hymen or other bodily lesions). The notion of the virginal parturition has no basis in Scripture and comes from post New Testament and patristic writings; it even acquired status in mariology.[2] Because of this development it is better to avoid the term "virgin birth" and to insist that the topic under discussion is the virginal conception of Jesus by Mary, or what has often been called her *virginitas ante partum.*

To broach the question, one has to realize that it is multifaceted and has all sorts of ramifications. Since the problem in the modern discussion begins with the biblical data, though it is not restricted to that, I should like to reconsider the New Testament material that bears on the topic. Though I shall be primarily interested in the modern interpretation of that material, other aspects of the problem will have to be touched on. Consequently, I should like to do four things: (1) explain the varied background of the recent discussion among Roman Catholics; (2) survey the discussion briefly in order to highlight the problem; (3) consider the New Testament data on the virginal conception of Jesus; and (4) suggest a mode of interpretation that may prove palatable.

I. *The Varied Background of the Recent Discussion*

Various factors have given rise to the discussion of this topic in recent times. First of all, there is the shift in emphasis in Roman Catholic mariology that has taken place since the Second Vatican Council. It was decided not to issue a separate schema on Mary, after one had actually been prepared by the preparatory theological commission, but rather incorporate the conciliar treatment of her into the dogmatic constitution on the church, as its last chapter—in effect, as an appendage to *Lumen gentium.* [3] Moreover, within the chapter the Council fathers did not hesitate to profess the "subordinate role of Mary," [4] acknowledging that her maternal duty toward human beings in no way obscured or diminished the "unique mediation of Christ." [5] In thus setting forth the role of Mary with reference to her Son and to all Christians, the Council stressed it precisely in relation to the church. [6] This conciliar stance has created a shift in emphasis in Roman Catholic mariological thinking.

True, in chapter 8 of *Lumen gentium* Mary is referred to as the "Blessed Virgin," and one finds there the repetition of traditional titles: "in the mystery of the Church, herself rightly called mother and virgin, the Blessed Virgin stands out in eminent and singular fashion as exemplar of both virginity and motherhood." [7] The passing references to her as virgin are there couched in stock formulas; this is readily intelligible, because the Council was more interested in affirming her maternal role with reference to Jesus and the church. [8]

Second, this shift in emphasis in mariological thinking must also be understood in terms of another affirmation of the Council. In the

Decree on Ecumenism it is admitted that "in Catholic teaching there exists an order or 'hierarchy' of truths, since they vary in their relationship to the foundation of the Christian faith."[9] This admission, though not without some background in the theological past, constituted an official recognition of the centrality or noncentrality of certain ideas in Catholic teachings.[10] Though the Council fathers gave no instance in the decree itself of what truths they had in mind or of their relative position in the hierarchy, it escaped no one's attention that in rejecting the idea of a separate schema on Mary, in making their mariological affirmations in the concluding chapter on the church, and in not hesitating to "profess the subordinate role of Mary," they were supplying a concrete example of a truth that may have to be judged in terms of this hierarchy.

Against such a background since the Council, the modern Roman Catholic discussion of the virginal conception of Jesus has taken place. But there is another factor that has to be considered. Since it is usually thought that this is a matter of Catholic faith, one may wonder how there could be a discussion of it in recent times. No little reason, however, for the discussion comes precisely from the theological status of this notion within Roman Catholic teaching. Standard manuals on mariology have normally assigned a theological note of at least *de fide* to the thesis of Mary's virginity *ante partum*.[11] But systematic theologians have recently been stating that theological status with more precision and great caution. Michael Schmaus, who can scarcely be branded for liberal views, recently summed it up thus:

> . . . Mary conceived Jesus of the Holy Spirit without a male principle of generation. It is the constant teaching of the Church *from the beginning*[12] that she gave birth to Jesus without violation of her integrity and that she remained ever virgin. Though there has been no formal definition on the subject, but only non-infallible declarations of the Church in the course of Christological assertions[13]. . . , the perpetual virginity of Mary is certainly part of the faith and preaching of the Church."[14]

Though Schmaus recognizes the virginal conception as "part of the faith and preaching of the Church," he puts his finger on the problem: there have been only non-infallible declarations of the church, and these in the course of christological assertions. We are thus confronted with a teaching that is said to be of faith because of a long-standing affirmation in the ordinary magisterium. This immediately involves it in the modern theological question about the binding character of the ordinary magisterium.[15] This thorny question has itself been debated ever since *Humani generis* in 1950, and to try to discuss its pros and cons here would distract from the purpose of this paper. But it has to be mentioned since it too forms part of the background of the recent discussion of Mary's virginal conception.

II. *Recent Roman Catholic Biblical and Theological Discussions*

In the Protestant traditions of Christianity the virginal conception of Jesus has not been universally affirmed. One discerns, in fact, a three-fold position: (1) an affirmative position, often expressed as the "Virgin Birth," and clung to as a historical fact as tenaciously as is the virginal conception in most Roman Catholic circles;[16] (2) a negative position, which questions it;[17] and (3) an agnostic position, which sees little relevance in it for Christian faith.[18] While some Roman Catholic mariological tenets have constituted genuine problems in recent ecumenical dialogues (e.g., the Immaculate Conception, the Assumption), Mary's virginal conception has normally not been such an issue. Moreoever, it is hard to say to what extent the understanding of this matter among Protestants has really been operative or influential in the recent Roman Catholic discussion of it. For this reason I shall not try to include Protestant views on the matter in this brief survey.[19]

Though one can trace the beginnings of the Roman Catholic discussion back to about 1970,[20] it gained notoriety in Holland about the time of the publication of the Dutch Catechism in 1966,[21] for which the bishops of the Netherlands had written a foreword, and in which it was stated that Jesus

> was born wholly of grace, wholly of promise—"conceived of the Holy Spirit." He was *the* gift of God to mankind.
> This the evangelists Matthew and Luke express when they proclaim that Jesus' birth was not due to the will of a man. They proclaim that this birth does not depend on what men can do of themselves—infinitely less so than in other human births. That is the deepest meaning of the article of faith, "born of the Virgin Mary". . . . . Mankind has ultimately no one to thank but the Holy Spirit for the coming of this promised one. His origin is not of blood nor of the will of the flesh nor of the will of man, but from God: from the Most High.[22]

What is said here seems to be beyond cavil.[23] But what is *not* said caused a notable reaction, for nothing had been included about Jesus' conception by Mary who was a virgin. A clarifying statement was subsequently issued by the Dutch bishops, and a Roman commission of cardinals suggested various corrections for the Cathechism, among which was a note reaffirming the virginal conception.[24]

But the matter has not rested there. Roman Catholic writers in Germany and elsewhere in Europe have continued to debate the issue. In Germany, in particular, they have referred to the virginal conception of Jesus in the Matthean and Lucan infancy narratives as a theologoumenon,[25] i.e., a theological assertion that does not directly express a matter of faith or an official teaching of the Church, and hence is in itself not normative, but that expresses in language that may prescind from factuality a notion which supports, enhances, or is related to a matter of faith.[26] The German writers who have been using this term to designate the Matthean and/or Lucan affirmation of the virginal conception do not mean by it a mere mythologoumenon. It is not just a way of expressing in mythical language what transcends our limited human notions or judgments. They refer to the virginal conception as theologoumenon because they find it a convenient way of labeling an assertion in the infancy narratives, which they are convinced says nothing about the historical or biological aspects of what they affirm. The German exegetes, in particular, have made use of this term,[27] because they are concerned to stress what is the real christological message in the Matthean and Lucan annunciation scenes and because they are aware of the diversity of the New Testament data in this area.

Discussions of this matter, however, have not been limited to Holland and Germany. The Spanish mariological periodical *Ephemerides Mariologicae* has carried extended surveys of the debate and even recorded a dialogue between its editor, J. M. Alonso, and the Dutch theologian Piet Schoonenberg entitled "The Virginal Conception of Jesus: History or Legend?"[28] No one misses the import of such a dialogue between a Dutchman and a Spaniard, and the entire survey reveals the problems that the topic has raised for Roman Catholic theologians today. The Spanish editor's introductory note speaks of "libertas theologica" in a context fraught with meaning. Issues involved in the problem have been discussed in France and Belgium as well.[29] The first noteworthy discussion of the problem in the English-speaking world was begun by R. E. Brown, in his article "The Problem of the Virginal Conception of Jesus."[30] Careful never to deny it and even to admit that "for some 1600 years of Christian existence (A.D. 200–1800) the virginal conception of Jesus in a biological sense was universally believed by Christians,"[31] he surveyed the problem from many theological angles, both biblical and systematic. From his discussion there emerge two areas in which further study is needed: the extent to which the virginal conception has actually been taught in the Church's tradition and the nature of the New Testament affirmations themselves.

This brief survey of the issues that have been raised in the modern Roman Catholic discussion has highlighted the main problems. I should now like to turn to the biblical data, which constitute the starting point of the discussion.

III. *The Biblical Data Concerning the Virginal Conception*

Mary is not mentioned in the Old Testament. The one text that may seem to bear on this question, because it is used in the Matthean annunciation scene (Matt 1:18–25), is Isa 7:14, "Therefore the Lord himself will give you a sign: Behold, a young woman (is) pregnant and bearing a son, and you/she will call his name Immanuel."[32] Though Old Testament commentators debate about whose son is concerned, there is, in general, no longer any hesitation among them that the original sense of the text had nothing to do with a virginal conception. Neither in Diaspora Judaism prior to Christianity[33] nor in Palestinian Judaism prior to or contemporary with the rise of Christianity was this text understood either of the Messiah or of a virginal *conception*.[34] We find it first so used in the Matthean infancy narrative, and the evangelist's intention is clear. However, the question that has arisen so often today is which came first, a biological fact that was seen as the fulfillment of an Old Testament passage, or a reflection on an Old Testament passage that served as an explanation of the character of the special child to be born and of the gratuitous and divine origin of the messianic era now dawning.[35] It is thus that the modern debate about the use of Isa 7:14 in the Matthean infancy narrative takes shape.

In treating the New Testament data, one notes at the outset that only two passages bear on the topic, the two annunciation scenes in the Matthean and Lucan Gospels: the annunciation to Joseph (Matt 1:18–25) and the annunciation to Mary (Luke 1:26–38). The matter scarcely finds an echo elsewhere in the Matthean and Lucan Gospels, and it is surrounded with silence in the rest of the New Testament. When one further considers the genre of the infancy narratives in which these annunciation scenes occur, one realizes the complicated nature of the question. Moreover, what is generally admitted today as the early Christian kerygma, preserved in various New Testament passages, never includes a formulation such as we find in the latter creeds, "conceived by the Holy Spirit and born of the Virgin Mary."[36] Given this general situation, one can understand how Roman Catholic theologians and exegetes have queried whether this notion was really part of the "constant teaching of the Church from the beginning."[37] In treating the New Testament data that bear on the topic, one has to consider four bodies of material: (1) Pauline passages, (2) the Marcan Gospel, (3) the Johannine data, and (4) the annunciation scenes in Matthew and Luke. I have listed the material here more or less in the accepted chronological order and shall treat it in this way.

(*1*) *Paul.* The first theologian of the Christian church never mentions Mary in any of his writings.[38] This is only part of the general puzzle why Paul manifested so little concern about the origins, life, and ministry of Jesus of Nazareth.[39] Only two texts in his letters bear directly on the topic, and two others are related to it indirectly.[40]

(*a*) In a passage that is often regarded as pre-Pauline and kerygmatic, Rom 1:3,[41] the Apostle refers to Jesus as "born of the seed of David according to the flesh." This assertion is part of a parallelism in which the major theological affirmation bears on Jesus as the "Son of God set up in power according to a spirit of holiness as of the resurrection." But in it Paul does assert Jesus' Davidic descent. The phrase "of the seed of David" (*ek spermatos David*) is obviously meant in the figurative sense of "descent from David"; only a fundamentalist interpretation of it would insist on *sperma* being used to suggest male seed. Actually, it means no more than what Paul means by "the seed of Abraham," used of Jesus in Gal 3:16.[42] At face value, it implies that Jesus had Davidic blood in his veins, and nothing suggests that this was to be taken in a fictive, putative, legal sense alone. On the other hand, it clearly says nothing about his virginal conception.[43]

(*b*) The second Pauline text that bears on the matter is the Apostle's assertion that Jesus was sent forth by God as his Son, "born of woman, born under the law" (Gal 4:4). It is part of Paul's affirmation about the fulness of time and the beginning of a new phase of salvation-history, in which the role of the unnamed woman is clearly motherhood, without the slightest hint of virginity. While it may be idle to insist that Paul did not actually say "born of a virgin," as did Ignatius of Antioch some decades later,[44] the issue for him was really something else: to affirm the redemption and the adoptive sonship of all Christians in v. 5. To do so, he asserts the abasement and the common humanity shared by Jesus and those redeemed, even though he was the Son sent by the Father.[45] Here Paul at least alludes to Jesus' divine pre-existence, as he mentions this mission. But once again there is no awareness of the virginal conception.[46]

(*c*) Indirectly related to these two texts is Phil 2:6–7, part of a pre-Pauline hymn derived from some early Christian liturgy and used by Paul to assert again Jesus' pre-existence, his kenosis and abasement, and finally his exaltation to glory.[47] What is important here is to note that

Paul saw no contradiction in this affirmation of the divine pre-existence of Jesus and his descent from the line of David according to the flesh (Rom 1:3).[48] No reference is made to the virginal conception, and it is not seen as a necessary or indispensable prop for the incarnation. Fully human, with Davidic blood in his veins, he could still be the Son of God, the exalted *Kyrios.*[49]

(*d*) The last Pauline text that bears on the question indirectly has nothing to do with Jesus or Mary but contains a formula that may shed some light on our subsequent discussion. To emphasize the freedom of Christians from the law, Paul introduced into Galatians 4 an allegory of the Old Testament story of Sarah and Hagar.[50] Because of her barrenness, Sarah gave her Egyptian slave-girl, Hagar, to her husband, Abraham, so that he might have a son by her; but God intervened and promised Abraham a son from Sarah, his real wife (Gen 16:1–15; 21:1–14). Paul insists that Christians "like Isaac are children of promise" (Gal 4:28), born to be free, not to be slaves. He continues: "But as at that time he who was born according to the flesh [Ishmael] persecuted him [Isaac] who was born according to the Spirit, so it is now" (Gal 4:29). Here one encounters again Paul's contrast, "according to the flesh . . . according to the Spirit." He considers Ishmael born to Abraham from Hagar as "born according to the flesh," and Isaac born to him from the barren Sarah as a result of God's promise as "born according to the Spirit." This is, indeed, Paul's allegorical *interpretation* of the Genesis story, where there is a promise, but no mention of the Spirit. Thus, Paul invokes the influence of the Spirit in Isaac's birth to explain how Sarah's sterility was overcome; but it is not an influence of the Spirit that substitutes for human intercourse.[51] Though the allegory has nothing to do with the virginal conception of Jesus, it does attest a biblical sense in which the Spirit intervened in the birth of a child without implying virginal conception. It is noteworthy, then, that Paul makes no similar affirmation about the generation of Jesus "according to the Spirit," either in Rom 1:3–4[52] or in Gal 4:4.

In these Pauline passages we note his silence about the virginal conception of Jesus. It raises the question whether he believed in it, cared about it, or just did not know about it. His silence obviously does not exclude it, and by itself or in isolation it would mean perhaps nothing at all. But when it is considered against a larger pattern, it makes its own significant contribution.[53]

(2) *Mark.*[54] In the earliest New Testament writing in which an attempt was made to record who Jesus was and what he did and said, we find the same silence about his origins.[55] In Mark 1:1 "the beginning

of the gospel of Jesus Christ" is related to a starting point in salvation-history and commences with the ministry of John the Baptist. The Marcan Gospel slightly post-dates the composition of the major Pauline letters; it is known to contain all sorts of details about Jesus that later Evangelists, who worked with it as a base, tended to excise or to censor in order to bring their picture of Jesus more into harmony with the developing christology of their day.[56] And in this sort of comparison Mark's Gospel has again and again revealed traces of its more primitive character.

Only in Mark 6:3 do we find a phrase that might seem pertinent to the topic at hand: "Is not this the carpenter, the son of Mary and brother of James and Joses and Judas and Simon, and are not his sisters here with us?" We are not concerned with the latter part of the verse, which speaks of Jesus' "brothers" and "sisters," for that is involved in the discussion of Mary's virginity *post partum.*[57] What is of interest is the identification of Jesus as "the carpenter, the son of Mary." Such an identification of a Palestinian Jew by a matronymic instead of a patronymic is unusual. It might seem to suggest that Mark did have some idea of the virginal conception. But this is to read into a cryptic, and possibly innocuous, Marcan phrase a meaning that is really derived from the Matthean or Lucan infancy narratives. If we did not have the latter compositions, of definitely later vintage, would the idea of virginal conception suggest itself to the reader of Mark 6:3?[58] What is significant in this regard is the way in which the Matthean Gospel changes what it borrows from Mark. Despite its infancy narrative, it rephrases the query of Jesus' townspeople thus: "Is not this the carpenter's son? Is not his mother called Mary? And are not his brothers James and Joseph and Simon and Judas?" (Matt 13:55). Though one can explain the phrase "the carpenter's son" in the putative or legal sense and thus harmonize the data in Matthew, the more significant aspect is that the assertion of the virginal conception in the Matthean annunciation scene finds no echo here in the later chapter.[59]

Even if one were to insist that Mark purposely used the phrase "son of Mary," one would still have the problem of specifying the purpose. Did it refer to Mary as a widow? (Joseph is never mentioned in the Marcan Gospel.) Did it echo an ancient accusation of illegitimacy? Such questions may strain the imagination; but they are answered only by speculation.

The upshot of the investigation of the earliest Gospel is that it too has no clear affirmation of a Christian belief in the virginal conception of Jesus.[60] In this, its data agree with those of Paul.

(3) John. If I introduce the Johannine data next, it is not because the Gospel of John was composed before the Matthean or Lucan Gospels, but because the data are more easily handled next and the Gospel, despite its late final redaction, has apparently preserved material that is often as primitive as that of the Synoptics, but from a parallel Christian setting.[61] In this matter the Johannine tradition may well antedate the annunciations of the Matthean and Lucan infancy narratives.

Unlike the Marcan tradition, the Johannine Gospel identifies Jesus as "the son of Joseph" (1:45; cf. 6:42). It makes no attempt to suggest that this should be understood in a legal, putative, or foster sense. Aside from these passing references, the only passage that has been introduced into the discussion of Mary's virginal conception is a clause in the prologue, 1:13: "But to all who received him, who believed in his name, he gave power to become children of God; who were born, not of blood nor of the will of the flesh nor of the will of man, but of God" (*RSV;* the crucial Greek phrase is *hoi ouk egennēthēsan*). The plural reading, referring to Christian believers, is used in the most recent critical editions of the Greek New Testament, that of the United Bible Societies and of Nestle-Aland (26th edition), but also in older critical editions in general.[62] The *Jerusalem Bible,* however, has preferred to read the singular in 1:13, *hos ouk egennēthē,* which would mean "But to all who did accept him he gave power to become children of God, to all who believe in the name of him *who was born not* out of human stock or urge of the flesh or will of man, but of God himelf."[63] This singular reading would suggest that the tradition of the Johannine Gospel was aware of the virginal conception of Jesus. However, it is really based on wishful criticism. It runs counter to "the overwhelming consensus of all Greek manuscripts"[64] and finds support only in patristic citations and a few isolated Syriac translations (which have a conflated text). The scholarly world has come out strongly against the singular reading, judging it to "have arisen either from a desire to make the Fourth Gospel allude explicitly to the virgin birth or from the influence of the singular number of the immediately preceding *autou.*"[65] Despite the backing of the *Jerusalem Bible,* this sole support for the virginal conception in the Fourth Gospel is alleged and without foundation; it cannot be seriously entertained.

The Johannine Gospel obviously does not deny the virginal conception of Jesus, but it does not affirm it either. This is striking in view of the christological stance that it assumes, presenting Jesus as almost always speaking from glory, even in statements uttered during his earthly ministry.[66] The Johannine christology has pushed the titles and the understanding of Jesus back from the primitive stage already mentioned, where they referred to his future parousiac coming (see Acts 3:20), not only to the ministry itself, but to a stage of pre-existence that even surpasses that of Paul. It is, as it were, a *reflexive* pre-existence that makes the Jesus of the ministry sound as if he were speaking always from "the glory that I had with you before the world was made" (John 17:5). It represents but a logical development of the christological tendencies of other New Testament writings, and it prepares for the Nicene declaration about Jesus as "true God from true God" (DS 125). But even so, the Johannine Gospel can still refer to him as "the son of Joseph" and can remain silent about his virginal conception. In this the Johannine writings join the Pauline and the Marcan testimony, and witness to widespread areas in the early church that did not affirm that which is found in the annunciation scenes of Matthew and Luke. This silence from three distinct local church traditions again raises the modern question about the "constant teaching of the Church *from the beginning.*"[67]

(*3*) *The Annunciation Scenes in Matthew and Luke.* In contrast to the data in Paul, Mark, and John, there are two passages in the Matthean and Lucan Gospels which deal with the virginal conception of Mary. These are the annunciation scenes: in Matt 1:18–25, in which the "angel of the Lord" announces to Joseph, in a dream, that Mary is already pregnant by the Holy Spirit; and in Luke 1:26–38, in which the "angel of the Lord" (1:11), now identified as Gabriel (1:19, 26), promises to Mary a conception through the intervention of the Holy Spirit. Since, however, these annunciation scenes occur in the infancy narratives, some preliminary comments about the nature of these gospel parts are in order for a proper understanding of them.

First of all, it is generally agreed today that the infancy narratives represent the latest part of the gospel-tradition to develop.[68] The earliest Gospel, Mark, has no such introductory section; the Johannine Gospel substitutes a largely hymnic prologue for its introduction.[69] And the tendency manifested here, in this late stage of gospel-formation, became full-fledged when infancy gospels as such emerged in their own right, such as the apocryphal *Protevangelium Iacobi* or the *Infancy Story of Thomas the Israelite Philosopher* (actually an account of the childhood of Jesus ascribed to Thomas).[70]

Second, it is significant that none of the so-called kerygmatic passages of the New Testament ever allude to details of the infancy of Jesus, as we have already noted in part. The most that one finds is the reference to his Davidic descent in the kerygmatic fragment of Rom 1:3–4. Even the most expanded form of such kerygmatic preaching, as claimed by some commentators to be found in Acts 10:37–43, refers only to the "word which was proclaimed throughout all Judea, beginning from Galilee after the baptism which John preached."[71] Whatever one wants to say about these so-called kerygmatic passages in Acts, it is noteworthy that Luke, who is said to have preserved several of them, never so formulates them as to include details from his own infancy narrative, let alone anything specifically connected with the virginal conception in them.

Third, the historicity of details in the infancy narratives has always been a problem, and it has been frankly discussed by Roman Catholic commentators in recent years. In this regard a certain consensus of opinion has arisen: (a) Matthew and Luke *do not depend on each other,* not only in the composition of their Gospels as a whole, but specifically in the writing of their infancy narratives.[72] (b) Both of them make use of *prior early Christian tradition in some details* at least.[73] (c) Despite their mutual independence, the radically different structure of their narratives, and their basically different stories about the infancy of Jesus, they have *certain details in common*—details which both may have inherited from the previous tradition and in which one is disposed to find a historical nucleus (Matthew would seem to be a control for Luke, and vice versa). We shall return to the common details; but for most of the scenes in the infancy narratives there simply is *no* control, biblical or extrabiblical, such as a historian would consider necessary for a judgment about the historical character of long-distant happenings.[74] (d) There is a liberal sprinkling in these narratives of folklore, astrology, christological titles, and interpretation of the Old Testament, which makes the reader realize that he/she is confronted with a literarily embellished account. The extent to which either narrative can be regarded as "midrashic" is debated and need not detain us now.[75] *If* the narratives could ever be accorded the label of historiography, that label would have to be qualified with some adjective like "imitative"— i.e., imitative historiography.[76] For both Matthew and Luke recount their infancy stories in imitation of other traditions, biblical and extrabiblical. In Matthew, the story of Jesus' infancy is modeled in part on the haggadic development of the birth of Moses in contemporary Palestinian Judaism;[77] in Luke, the infancy story about Jesus not only parallels that about John the Baptist (which was probably derived from an independent earlier tradition), but has unmistakable similarities with the story of the childhood of Samuel in the Old Testament (1 Samuel 1–2).[78]

Fourth, the christology of the Matthean and Lucan Gospels differs from that of Mark in that, like the Pauline and Johannine presentation, it represents a form of the three-stage christology of the early church. Mark's christology was two-staged in that it reflects the retrojection of the titles and the understanding of the risen Christ back to the Jesus of Nazareth in the account of the ministry. Both Paul and John pushed the titles and the understanding back to a third stage, viz., that of pre-existence (each in his own way). But Luke and Matthew, who never allude to Jesus' pre-existence, have a three-stage christology of their own, in which the understanding of Jesus as Messiah, Savior, Lord, Son of David, etc. is pushed back to the infancy period.[79] It represents in reality a stage in the developing understanding of him who is the Christian Lord. These evangelists thus seek in the overtures to their Gospels to strike the chords that will orchestrate their presentation; from the beginning of their Gospels they identify this person as if all that is to be said about him were actually patent from the very beginning of his earthly existence. Their major affirmations in these Gospel introductions bear then on his christological identification: He is born of God, son of Abraham, son of David, Messiah, Savior, Lord, and Son of God. To fail to perceive this is to miss the thrust of the infancy narratives.[80]

Against the background of these four generic observations about the infancy narratives we may look at some specific details, and above all at the elements in them that are common to Matthew and Luke despite their great diversity. These have been noted as the following nine points: (1) the principal characters, Jesus, Mary, Joseph; (2) the dating of the stories in the days of Herod the king (Matt 2:1; Luke 1:5); (3) the engagement of Mary a virgin to Joseph (Matt 1:18; Luke 1:27; 2:5); (4) the Davidic descent of Joseph (Matt 1:16, 20; Luke 1:27; 2:4); (5) the involvement of God's Holy Spirit in the conception of Jesus (Matt 1:18, 20; Luke 1:34); (6) the birth of Jesus from Mary in Bethlehem (Matt 1:25; 2:1; Luke 2:7); (7) the heavenly imposition of the name of Jesus prior to the birth (Matt 1:21; Luke 1:31); (8) Jesus' Davidic descent (Matt 1:1; Luke 1:32); (9) the final settlement of the family in Nazareth (Matt 2:23; Luke 2:51).

Some commentators would add to this list two further elements: (*a*) Mary's virginal conception (appealing to Matt 1:18–20; Luke 1:34); (*b*) and this precisely at a time when she was still only engaged to Joseph (Matt 1:18; Luke 1:27; 2:5). These common details I have taken from a Roman Catholic commentator, Josef Schmid, who definitely included the last two elements in his list of 1960.[81] However, a more recent discussion by J. Riedl, who refers to Schmid's list, restricts what it calls the "historical facts" in the two narratives to the following: Mary's engagement to Joseph, the Davidic descent of Jesus via Joseph, the imposition of the name of Jesus, the birth of Jesus from Mary, the birth in Bethlehem, and the final settlement in Nazareth. Though Riedl has telescoped some of the elements that are listed separately above, he has significantly omitted from his list of "historical facts" all mention of the intervention of the Spirit and of the virginal conception.[82] In itself, this may seem merely like a difference of opinion; but it points up the attitude of Roman Catholic commentators today, when they are confronted with the question of the historical character of the Matthean and Lucan infancy narratives.

What lies behind the mode of interpreting the annunciation scenes of the infancy narratives in such a way? Several things are involved. First, the difference in the treatment of the conception of Jesus in the Matthean and Lucan stories. Matthew leaves no doubt that the conception has already taken place, and without the intervention of Joseph. He was on the point of repudiating his fiancée because "she was found to be with child" (Matt 1:18).[83] But he is reassured: "That which is conceived in her is of the Holy Spirit" (1:20). Matthew never indicates how the conception came about; there is no hint of intercourse of any sort, and he uses no language that would suggest a hierogamy or a theogamy after the manner of Greek and Egyptian myths about the births of heroes as the result of the intercourse of a god and a human.[84] Whatever Matthew inherited in this matter from prior Christian tradition he has unmistakably presented as virginal conception, even with defensive, apologetic nuances. Thus, there is no doubt about the Matthean assertion of virginal conception as something that has already taken place.

Does Luke do the same? If he does, it is less clear, and herein lies the difficulty.

The interpretation of the Lucan annunciation is complicated by several things. First of all, it is clearly a parallel to the annunciation made to Zechariah, the father of John the Baptist (1:5–23) and the husband of Elizabeth who was barren, "and both were advanced in years." By contrast, Mary is said to be a "virgin engaged to a man whose name was Joseph" (1:27). Second, she was a *young* Galilean girl, who was still a virgin, and who was not only contemplating marriage but was already engaged. Mary's youth and virginal status stand in contrast to the old age and the barrenness of Elizabeth. Third, the angel's greeting that startles Mary and the subsequent indication to her that she has been favored by God to become the mother of the Davidic Messiah refer to a *future* conception, but it is not immediately understood. Moreover, the question has to be asked whether it really rules out human intercourse. And there may be the further question whether, in reading it as if it did rule it out, one is not importing a Matthean nuance into the story. This may seem surprising, but listen to the Lucan text itself (in the *RSV* rendering):

> [28]And he [Gabriel] came to her and said, "Hail, O favored one, the Lord is with you!" [29]But she was greatly troubled at the saying, and considered in her mind what sort of greeting this might be. [30]And the angel said to her, "Do not be afraid, Mary, for you have found favor with God. [31]And behold, you will conceive in your womb and bear a son, and you shall call his name Jesus. [32]He will be great and will be called the Son of the Most High; and the Lord God will give to him the throne of his father David, [33]and he will reign over the house of Jacob for ever; and of his kingdom there will be no end." [34]And Mary said to the angel, "How can this be, since I have no husband?"[35] And the angel said to her, "The Holy Spirit will come upon you, and the power of the Most High will overshadow you; therefore the child to be born will be called holy, the Son of God."

Eventually Mary says: "I am the Lord's servant; let it happen to me as you say."

When the account in these eight verses is read in and for itself—without the overtones of the Matthean annunciation to Joseph—every detail in it could be understood of a child to be born of Mary in the usual human way, a child endowed with God's special favor, born at the intervention of the Spirit of God, and destined to be acknowledged as the heir to David's throne as God's Messiah and Son. Chap. 2 in the Lucan Gospel supports this understanding even further with its references to Mary and Joseph as Jesus' "parents" (2:41) or as "your father and I" (2:48). And in these references no attempt is made on the part of the evangelist to qualify Joseph's fatherhood as foster or legal.

However, four points may seem to militate against such an understanding of the annunciation scene in Luke. The first is Mary's query, which I shall translate literally from the Greek: "How will this be, since I do not know a man?" (1:34). Or, to paraphrase it with the proper Semitic connotation, "since I have no relations with a man (*or* with a husband)."[85] This query has been subjected to many explanations over the centuries. It has been said to express a vow, a resolve, or an intention not to have marital intercourse;[86] or a protest because she *has* not known a man;[87] or surprise because she is not yet married (which implies that Mary understood the angel's words to mean a conception that was already under way, as in parallel angelic communications in the Old Testament, and one which the further words of the angel clarify and refer to the future);[88] or even some contorted explanations.[89] The one thing that is clear is that there is no unanimous or "Catholic" interpretation of this question.[90] Of the three mentioned, the least forced explanation seems to be the third, surprise at the announcement that is understood in the Old Testament sense that conception is already under way. But the real solution to this problematic verse lies in the realization, as J. M. Creed has expressed it, that "a narrative of this kind ought not to be subjected to the strain of such questions" (i.e., whether Mary's words imply a vow or a resolve of virginity).[91] The purpose of Mary's question to the angel is to give the evangelist an opening for the further angelic communication about the real character of the child to be born: He will not only be the Davidic Messiah to rule over the house of Jacob, but He "will be called holy, the Son of God" (1:35).[92] The main affirmation in the angelic declaration to Mary is thus wholly christological.[93] Mary's query is merely a Lucan stage-prop for the dramatization of the identification of the child; the trouble is that Luke's dramatization has made it sound like a historicization, and the conversation of Mary with the angel has borne the weight of centuries of re-presentation of the scene in Christian art, especially of the sort of Fra Angelico. Unfortunately, such re-presentation does not make history out of what may not have been intended to be such.

A second difficulty for this interpretation comes from the angelic declaration that the "Holy Spirit will come upon you, and the power of the Most High will overshadow you" (1:34). The language used by the angel is highly figurative, but neither verb, *eperchesthai* ("come upon") or *episkiazein* ("overshadow"), has in itself any connotation of conception, let alone of sexual implication. They are otherwise unattested in a context that would suggest either of these nuances.[94] They are, at most, figurative expressions for the mysterious intervention of God's Spirit and power which will be responsible for the divine and messianic character of this child. The figurative use of these verbs here obviously does not exclude the idea of a miraculous conception; but they do not say it either, least of all in an exclusive sense implying no human intervention. In this regard, we may recall here that the birth of Isaac "according to the Spirit" (Gal 4:29), which we discussed earlier,[95] did not imply a virginal conception of him. It was simply Paul's way of accounting for the child so cared for in God's providence and for his role in salvation-history. In the Lucan infancy narrative, then, the real question that has to be asked is whether the Spirit's "coming upon" Mary and its "overshadowing" of her are intended to explain the child's special relation to God (as His Son) or her bodily, virginal integrity. If we had only these eight verses of the Lucan infancy narrative, would this passage be read as it often is—in terms of the virginal conception of Jesus? It may have been so interpreted because of the harmonization of its detail with the Matthean account. But the modern query is raised about this as a "common" element. At most, it is only a possible understanding of the Lucan annunciation scene, not one that is unquestionably such. (See the postscript.)

The third point that may seem to cause a difficulty for this interpretation of the Lucan annunciation scene is Luke 2:5, where we are told that Joseph went to Bethlehem to be enrolled in the census "with Mary, his betrothed, who was with child" (*syn Mariam tē emnēsteumenē autō, ousē enkyō*). This verse has long been a problem and it still remains one, no matter how one interprets 1:26–38, whether of Mary's virginal conception or not. Its description of Mary is dependent on 1:27, "a virgin engaged to a man named Joseph" (*parthenon emnēsteumenēn andri hō onoma Iōsēph*). And the question is still, what is Mary doing in the company of Joseph on a journey if she is still only "engaged"? The participle *emnēsteumenē* would imply that she had not yet cohabited with him. Ancient versions (Vetus Itala, Sinaitic Syriac) easily solved the problem by changing the reading from "his betrothed" to "his wife." And the Koine tradition of Greek MSS (together with some Latin versions) introduced the word *gynaiki* (or *uxori*), which would mean "his engaged wife," but this is clearly a harmonizing gloss that solves nothing. Which was she? His wife or his finacée? The *lectio difficilior preferenda* is that with which we began;[96] it might seem to be a formulation made in the light of the virginal conception, but it is not per se clear, and nothing else in chap. 2 favors it. No hint is given about the cause of Mary's pregnancy,[97] and the original independence of chap. 2 from chap. 1 may suggest that this verse is not even to be thought of in terms of virginal conception.

The last point of difficulty for the interpretation being used here is derived from outside the infancy narrative itself, from Luke 3:23, where we read that "Jesus, when he began his ministry, was about thirty years of age, being the son (as was supposed) of Joseph, the son of Heli," etc., and the genealogy continues backward through some seventy names to "the son of Adam, the son of God." Aside from the details of ancestors in the Lucan genealogy that differ from the Matthean list, Luke significantly traces Jesus' pedigree back not only to Adam but to God himself. Some commentators see in the termination of the genealogy (in God himself) a subtle way in which Luke again affirms the divine sonship of Jesus.[98] Yet, as it begins, the genealogical list says "as was supposed" (*hōs enomizeto*), the son of Joseph. It sounds as if the evangelist is correcting the impression suggested by the (inherited?) genealogy that Jesus was actually the son of Joseph, and correcting it in the light of the infancy narrative's annunciation scene. Leaving aside the strained interpretations of the phrase that have often been proposed in attempts to harmonize the two genealogies of Jesus,[99] we may note that, whatever way the phrase is going to be understood, it will affect not only the paternity of Joseph (in a real sense? in a putative, legal sense?) but also the climax of the genealogy as well. If one opts for the interpretation that Luke suggests here Joseph's "legal" or "putative" paternity, what does that say about the divine filiation at the end? On the other hand, if one were to insist that it refers merely to the beginning of the genealogy, then there is a significant corrective to it in the light of chap. 1. This would then shed some light on the infancy narrative and indicate that the evangelist did want 1:26–38 to be understood of virginal conception. This possibility cannot be excluded. But in the long run, the Lucan Gospel does not assert the virginal conception of Jesus as clearly as does the Matthean annunciation scene.

These, then, are the problems that face one when one tries to read the Matthean and Lucan infancy narratives in terms of the virginal conception of Jesus.

IV. *A Palatable Interpretation of the New Testament Data*

Because of such problems in the Lucan annunciation scene in particular, and because of the isolated testimony to the virginal conception of Jesus in the Matthean and Lucan infancy narratives, Roman Catholic interpreters, both exegetes and theologians, have asked a further question about the virginal conception. Given the silence of the New Testament outside of the two annunciation scenes, is it possible that the real thrust of the infancy narratives is to affirm something other than the historical, biological virginity of Mary? Is the affirmation of these scenes to be found in something else? For instance, in the divine and gratuitous creativity of a new age of salvation-history, inaugurated by the birth of this extraordinary child who will in time be recognized as God's agent of salvation and as the fulfillment of Old Testament promises, the heir to sit on David's throne, the Christian Messiah, the Son of God, the Savior and Lord proclaimed to all men? In other words, is the virginal conception of Jesus, which is clearly asserted in the Matthean infancy narrative, and less so in the Lucan annunciation scene, anything more than a theologoumenon? One has to recognzie that the New Testament data are not unambiguous; they do not necessarily support the claim that this was a matter of faith "from the beginning." When one looks at the complicated assertion in the Lucan annunciation scene, there is a real reason to raise the question whether the evangelist's assertion is anything more than a theological expression in language that may prescind from factuality about a notion which is related to a matter of faith, without being such itself. Roman Catholic exegetes and theologians who so phrase the question are concerned with three things. First, how explain the isolated assertion of the virginal conception in Matthew 1 over against the general thrust of the Matthean infancy narrative, which is more concerned to tell us who Jesus is and whence he comes, "Quis et unde?"[100] Similarly, the less clear Lucan assertion of it is embedded in a twofold angelic announcement, the thrust of which is more concerned with Jesus' messianic or Davidic role and his divine filiation than with Mary's virginal status.

Second, they are concerned to reckon with the "open" character of the two isolated New Testament passages which deal with the question, when they are compared with the striking silence about it in the rest of the Synoptic Gospels and in the remainder of the New Testament itself. Even if one were to say that in this matter Matthew and Luke have inherited traditional material and did not fabricate it themselves out of whole cloth, one has still to ask whether they present it as *Glaubensgut,*[101] as an affirmation of faith, or merely as a theologoumenon. Because this hesitation arises—and not merely because of modern hesitations about the miraculous, but rather because of the difficulties which the texts themselves raise—the assertion, such as it is in the Matthean and Lucan annunciation scenes, is "open," i.e., open to further understanding and/or development.

Third, as in the case of other matters in the New Testament, which are judged today from an exegetical point of view to be open-ended assertions—"open" in the sense that they could develop genuinely within the Christian dogmatic and theological tradition in one direction or another—the New Testament assertion has to be understood for what it really is and not interpreted anachronistically. As less controversial, I may be permitted to cite the example of Paul's assertion of the universal causality of Adam's sin in Rom 5:12–21. That this is somehow related to the dogma of original sin is a commonplace since Trent (DS 1512). What Paul asserts there about it is not exactly the same as the formulation or conception of the matter in the Councils of Orange or Trent. It could actually have developed as it did, or not. In this case the openness of the assertion has been removed; what Trent affirms may be regarded as the *sensus plenior* of Romans 5.[102] So too with the assertions of Matthew and Luke on the matter of the virginal conception. If it eventually were to be judged that the traditional understanding of the virginal conception in a historical, biological sense is a matter of faith, then one would still have the obligation of asking whether that is the clear affirmation of the New Testament data. Here one must learn to distinguish between a New Testament assertion and the legitimate development of it within the Christian tradition. This is complicated. For what I said at the beginning of my discussion about the so-called traditional teaching among Roman Catholics in the reiterations of the ordinary magisterium for centuries obviously colors one's assessment of the normative character of such a development. Should dogmatic theologians agree on the normative character or binding force of the constant and ordinary magisterium—which does not seem to be the case at the moment—the Roman Catholic commentator could live with it. But he would still insist on taking the critical position that his discipline demands about the affirmation of the New Testament text itself. The Matthean annunciation scene asserts indeed the virginal conception of Jesus, and the Lucan may do so less clearly, but whether they make of that assertion an affirmation of faith or a theologoumenon is still a vital question.

In summary, then, the "open" character of the assertion of the virginal conception of Jesus in the New Testament is seen in (a) the isolated declaration of it in the annunciation scenes of Matthew and Luke over against the silence of the rest of the New Testament data, which raises the question whether it was really a matter of Christian faith "from the beginning"; (b) the different treatment of the matter in the Matthean and Lucan annunciation scenes, where it is clearly asserted in the former and only figuratively so in the latter; (c) the hesitation about whether it is affirmed as a historical fact or asserted as a theologoumenon to support some affirmation of faith. These, then, are the issues in the modern debate.

Finally, it must be stressed that the exegetes and theologians who have been involved in this debate have not denied the virginal conception of Jesus; in fact, in many instances, they have not even questioned it. They have indeed raised questions about it and have been honestly seeking to draw the lines between what is of the essence of Catholic faith and what has been uncritically associated with it in unquestioning assumptions. They have been concerned to ascribe critically to the biblical sources only what they affirm, and to dogmatic or systematic development what it has interpreted. Lastly, they have been seeking honestly to assess the entire matter with the sophisticated attitude of their own generation. This may make of them minimalists in the mariological debate. But who says that the maximalists have the corner on the truth?[103]

Postscript (1980)

After the original form of the above article was published, R. E. Brown contributed a note to the same publication in which he took issue with my presentation of an aspect of the virginal conception of Jesus in the Lucan Gospel.[104] He mentioned the four points in the Lucan account in which I found a certain ambiguity,[105] and added a fifth argument, which clinches the matter for him and which I did not take into account. It concerns the step-parallelism between the annunciation of the conception of John the Baptist and that of Jesus.

Brown stresses that one annuciation is clearly patterned on the other and that Luke used this step-parallelism not merely to compare John and Jesus but to underline the superiority of Jesus over John. One element in this parallelism is precisely the "how" questions: "How shall I know this? For I am an old man, and my wife is advanced in years" (1:18); and "How shall this be, since I have no husband?" (1:34). An extraordinary conception is involved in both annunciations; and Mary's faith in the divine intervention in the conception of Jesus is rewarded because it involves an intervention greater than that in the conception of John—a conception which overcomes her lack of sexual relations.[106]

Brown's point is well taken, and I accept the correction that he offers with a slight modification. I do not agree with him that the account of the annunciation of John's conception (and birth) has been fashioned by Luke in dependence on that of Jesus. It is just the other way round. Luke had inherited a Baptist tradition, which recounted the conception (and birth) of John in imitation of Old Testament models; and he fashioned the annunciation of Jesus' conception (and birth) in imitation of it.[107] In any case, the step-parallelism calls for the great intervention of the divine in the conception of Jesus, even though the phrasing of individual verses in the account of Jesus' conception remains ambiguous, as I have already pointed out.

I also accept this correction for another reason. When the twelve of us who were involved in the discussion of the Marian passages of the New Testament as a preparation for *Mary in the New Testament* came to the Lucan scene of the virginal conception of Jesus, my view of the matter as set forth in the above essay surfaced and was discussed. Eventually, the other eleven members of the task force voted against my interpretation of the matter, mainly because of the step-parallelism just mentioned.[108] So I concluded that such a peer-vote in this matter should be given proper attention. Hence this postscript.[109]

NOTES

* This paper was delivered as a lecture at the fifth annual seminar of the Catholic Bishops of the United States, "Theological Developments in Postconciliar Years," at the Catholic University of America, Washington, DC (June 9–12, 1973). Originally published in *TS* 34 (1973) 541–75.

[1] "Virgin Birth Controversy Stirs Convention: Mariological Society Dismayed," *Tablet* (Brooklyn) 65/51 (Jan. 11, 1973) 4; "Mariologists Discuss Virgin Birth Controversy," *Catholic News* (New York) 87/2 (Jan. 11, 1973) 7; "Shadow over Mary," *Catholic Review* (Baltimore) 37/44 (Jan. 12, 1973) 1; "Defend Dogma of Virgin Birth," *New World* (Chicago) (Jan. 12, 1973) 2.

[2] See, among others, K. Rahner, "Virginitas in partu," *Theological Investigations* 4 (Baltimore: Helicon, 1966) 134–62. Even though it is affirmed in various Church documents (see, e.g., Pius IV, *Cum quorundam* [DS 1880]: "B. V. Mariam . . . perstitisse semper in virginitatis integritate, ante partum scilicet, in partu et perpetuo post partum"), M. Schmaus can still state: "From the 3rd century on, the general doctrine of the Fathers of the Church and the theologians was that the birth took place without pangs and without bodily lesions in Mary. But this cannot be regarded as dogma" ("Mariology," *Sacramentum mundi: An Encyclopaedia of Theology* 3 [New York: Herder and Herder, 1969] 379).

[3] *AAS* 57 (1965) 58–67. See W. M. Abbott and J. Gallagher (eds.), *The Documents of Vatican II* (New York: America, 1966) 85–96 (chap. 8: The Role of the Blessed Virgin Mary, Mother of God, in the Mystery of Christ and the Church). See especially the introduction and notes by A. Dulles, pp. 13, 85, 91, 94 (nn. 256, 279, 285). Cf. F. Lakner, "Hat die Mariologie nach dem Vatikanum II wesentliche Fortschritte gezeitigt? Ein Literaturbericht," *ZKT* 90 (1968) 462–75; R. Laurentin et al., *La Vierge Marie dans la constitution sur l'église* (Etudes mariales, 22; Paris: Vrin, 1965); G. Philips, "Le Saint-Esprit et Marie dans l'église: Vatican II et prospective du problème," *Le Saint-Esprit et Marie* (Etudes mariales, 25 [1968] 7–37); *Mariología conciliar* (*L. G. cap. 8*) (Estudios marianos, 30–31; Madrid: Coculsa, 1968); R. Laurentin, *Court traité sur la Vierge Marie: Édition postconciliaire* (Paris: Lethielleux, 1968) 90–100; C. W. Neumann, "The Decline of Interest in Mariology as a Theological Problem," *Marian Studies* 23 (1972) 12–38. For a preconciliar harbinger of this shift in emphasis, see A. Müller, "Contemporary Mariology," in *Theology Today 1: Renewal in Dogma* (Milwaukee: Bruce, 1965 [tr. of *Fragen der Theologie heute,* 1957]) 109–28.

[4] *Lumen gentium,* §64. This was explicitly stated to safeguard the unique mediation of her Son, but the implications of the statement are obvious.

[5] Ibid., §60.

[6] This notion received further stress in the address of Pope Paul VI as he closed the third session of Vatican II, declaring Mary to be the "most holy Mother of the Church" (*AAS* 56 [1964] 1015).

[7] *Lumen gentium,* §63.

⁸ Aside from titles like "the Virgin Mary" (§52, 53, 65), the "most Holy Virgin" (§65), the "Blessed Virgin" (§54, 58, 60, 61, 62, 63, 66, 67), the "Virgin of Nazareth" (§56), the "Immaculate Virgin" (§59), references to the virginal conception are found in §55 (identifying Mary as "the Virgin who is to conceive and bear a son, whose name will be called Emmanuel [cf. Isa 7:14]") and §57 (referring to "Christ's virginal conception" and his not diminishing "his mother's virginal intergrity" at birth [with a note referring to the Lateran Synod of A.D. 649, can. 3]). That these references were made only in passing is readily seen from the intent of the Council Fathers: "The Synod does not . . . have it in mind to give a complete doctrine on Mary, nor does it wish to decide those questions which have not yet been fully illuminated by the work of theologians. Those opinions therefore may be lawfully retained which are freely propounded by schools of Catholic thought concerning her who occupies a place in the Church which is the highest after Christ yet very close to us" (*Lumen gentium*, §54).

⁹ *Unitatis redintegratio*, §11 (*AAS* 57 [1965] 90–112, esp. p. 99; *The Documents of Vatican II*, 354).

¹⁰ Note that the Council here seems to use the word in the sense of "higherarchy." For a discussion of this notion since the Council, see H. Mühlen, "Die Bedeutung der Differenz zwischen Zentraldogmen und Randdogmen für den ökumenischen Dialog: Zur Lehre des zweiten vatikanischen Konzils von der 'hierarchia veritatum,' " in *Freiheit in der Begegnung: Zwischenbilanz des ökumenischen Dialogs* (ed. J.-L. Leuba und H. Stirnimann; Stuttgart: Evangelisches Verlagswerk, 1969) 191–227; "Die Lehre des Vaticanum II über die 'hierarchia veritatum' und ihre Bedeutung für den ökumenischen Dialog," *Theologie und Glaube* 56 (1966) 303–35; L. Jaeger, *A Stand on Ecumenism: The Council's Decree* (New York: Kenedy, 1965) 112–18; G. Thils, *Le décret sur l'oecuménisme du deuxième Concile du Vatican* (Bruges: Desclée de Brouwer, 1966); J. Feiner, "Decree on Ecumenism: Commentary on the Decree," in *Commentary on the Documents of Vatican II* (New York: Herder and Herder, 1968), 2. 57–164, esp. pp. 118–21; U. Valeske, *Hierarchia veritatum: Theologiegeschichtliche Hintergründe und mögliche Konsequenzen eines Hinweises in Ökumenismusdekret des II. Vatikanischen Konzils zum zwischenkirchlichen Gespräch* (Munich: Claudius, 1968) 66; G. H. Tavard, " 'Hierarchia veritatum': A Preliminary Investigation," *TS* 32 (1971) 278–89. Cf. "Report of the Lutheran-Roman Catholic Study Commission on 'The Gospel and the Church,' " *Worship* 46 (1972) 326–51, esp. p. 333 (§24–25).

¹¹ For example, J. M. Hervé, *Manuale theologiae dogmaticae* (Paris: Berche et Pagis, 1935), 2. 648; "de fide divina et catholica" (J. A. de Aldama, "Mariologia," *Sacrae theologiae summa* [*BAC;* Madrid: Editorial católica, 1953], 3. 394); "Es ist Glaubenssatz . . ." (M. Schmaus, *Katholische Dogmatik 5: Mariologie* [Munich: Hueber, 1955] 107); "catholicae fidei dogma" ("commissio cardinalitia de 'Novo Catechismo' ('De nieuwe Katechismus')," *AAS* 60 [1968] 685–91, esp. p. 687. Few, however, would agree today with P. J. Donnelly, ("The Perpetual Virginity of the Mother of God," *Mariology* [ed. J. Carol; Milwaukee: Bruce, 1957], 2. 228–96) that "it is a solemnly defined dogma," appealing to the Lateran Synod of A.D. 649 under Pope Martin I (p. 228); or with L. Lercher, *Institutiones theologiae dogmaticae* (3d ed.; Innsbruck: Rauch, 1942), 3. 288 ("de fide definita").—See K. Rahner, "Dogmatische Bemerkungen zur Jungfrauengeburt," in *Zum Thema Jungfrauengeburt* (ed. K. S. Frank et al.; Stuttgart: Katholisches Bibelwek, 1970) 121–58.

[12] My italics; see further below, pp. 46, 48, 51, 59.

[13] He refers to the Lateran Synod of A.D. 649 (DS 503) and Pius IV's Constitution *Cum quorundam* (DS 1880). Appeal is likewise often made to the *Symbolum apostolicum* in its different forms (DS 11, 30); *Tomus Damasi* (DS 158); First Council of Toledo (DS 189); *Tomus Leonis* (DS 294); Second Council of Constantinople, can. 2 (DC 422); Eleventh Council of Toledo (DS 533); Third Council of Constantinople (DS 555); Fourth Lateran Council (DS 801); Second Council of Lyons, Profession of Faith of Michael Palaeologus (DS 852); Council of Florence (DS 1337). But it has long since been recognized that in most of these texts the major affirmation is christological, not mariological, and that the passing affirmations about Mary bear on the *birth* of Jesus from her as "ever virgin," a stock phrase (*semper virgo, aeiparthenos*).

[14] "Mariology," *Sacramentum mundi*, 3. 379.

[15] See Pius XII, *Humani generis* (*AAS* 42 [1950] 568; DS 3885). What was said there produced considerable immediate discussion; some of the more recent treatments of the topic reveal the real problems involved. See B. Schüller, "Bemerkungen zur authentischen Verkündigung des kirchlichen Lehramtes," *TP* 42 (1967) 534–51 (see *TD* 16 [1968] 328–32). G. Baum, "The Magisterium in a Changing Church," *Concilium* 21 (1967) 67–83; A. B. Vaughan, "The Role of the Ordinary Magisterium of the Universal Episcopate," *PCTSA* 22 (1967) 1–19; J. J. Heaney, "Catholic Hermeneutics, the Magisterium and Infallibility," *Continuum* 7 (1969–70) 106–19; P. Fransen, "The Authority of the Councils," in *Problems of Authority* (ed. J. M. Todd; Baltimore: Helicon, 1962) pp. 43–78, esp. pp. 61–62 ("the ordinary magisterium, which, even in a Council, remains fallible" [p. 61]). What is really at issue here is the role of dogma and of the magisterium in an era of change within the Roman Catholic Church. See A. Dulles, *The Survival of Dogma* (Garden City, NY: Doubleday, 1971) 108–24, 146, 158–62; P. Schoonenberg, *Die Interpretation des Dogmas* (Düsseldorf: Patmos, 1969; = *Tijdschrift voor Theologie* 8 [1968] 243–347); R. A. McCormick, "The Teaching Role of the Magisterium and of Theologians," *PCTSA* 24 (1970) 239–54; K. Rahner, "Theology and the Church's Teaching Authority after the Council," *Theological Investigations* 9 (New York: Seabury, 1972) 83–100. The question is further complicated by the recent discussions about the relationship of "dogma" to the "gospel" or the "word of God." See W. Kasper, *Dogma unter dem Wort Gottes* (Mainz: Matthias Grünewald, 1965); "Evangelium und Dogma," *Catholica* 19 (1965) 199–209. Moreover, it should be recalled that Vatican II clearly stated, in a historic "first," that "the living teaching office [*magisterium*] of the Church . . . is not above the word of God, but serves it" (*Dei verbum*, §10). The expression "word of God" has to be understood in the full sense in which it is used earlier in the Dogmatic Constitution, which, though it is not restricted to or identified with the *written* word of God, does not exclude that form of it. Hence for the first time the Council fathers admitted that the Scriptures stand over the magisterium in some sense (*eidem ministrat; AAS* 58 [1966] 822). Its privileged character as the inspired word of God is also something that the magisterium *serves*, "listening to it devoutly, guarding it scrupulously, and explaining it faithfully by divine commission and with the help of the Holy Spirit" (ibid.).

[16] E.g., H. A. Hanke, *The Validity of the Virgin Birth: The Theological Debate and the Evidence* (Grand Rapids: Zondervan, 1963); J. G. Machen, *The Virgin Birth of Christ* (New York: Harper & Bros., 1930; reprinted 1967); D. Edwards, *The*

Virgin Birth in History and Faith (London: Faber & Faber, 1943). In such Protestant circles it is often feared that the denial of the virginal conception implies the denial of the divinity of Jesus Christ; or it is stoutly asserted as the touchstone of orthodoxy against rationalist criticism. J. Ratzinger (*Introduction to Christianity* [New York: Herder and Herder, 1970] 208) notes apropos of such a position that "according to the faith of the Church the Sonship of Jesus does not rest on the fact that Jesus had no human father; the doctrine of Jesus' divinity would not be affected if Jesus had been the product of a normal human marriage. For the Sonship of which faith speaks is not a biological but an ontological fact, an event not in time but in God's eternity; the conception of Jesus does not mean that a new God-the-Son comes into being, but that God as Son in the man Jesus draws the creature man to himself, so that he himself 'is' man."

[17] With varying nuances, T. Boslooper, *The Virgin Birth* (London: SCM, 1962); R. Bultmann, *The History of the Synoptic Tradition* (Oxford: Blackwell, 1968) 295–96; W. Marxsen, "Jungfrauengeburt (exegetisch)," *RGG*, 3. 1068–69.

[18] See F. V. Filson, *A New Testament History* (Philadelphia: Westminster, 1965) 86.

[19] A. Vögtle ("Offene Fragen zur lukanischen Geburts- und Kindheitsgeschichte," in *Das Evangelium und die Evangelien: Beiträge zur Evangelienforschung* [Düsseldorf: Patmos, 1971] 43–56, esp. p. 43) does make some reference to this aspect of the problem. See further J. M. Alonso, "Cuestiones actuales: La concepción virginal de Jesús: 1. En autores protestantes," *EMar* 21 (1971) 63–109.

[20] See F. J. Schierse, "Weihnachtliche Christusverkündigung: Zum Verständnis der Kindheitsgeschichten," *BibLeb* 1 (1960) 217–22.

[21] *A New Catechism: Catholic Faith for Adults* (New York: Herder and Herder, 1967) 74–75. This is a translation of *De Nieuwe Katechismus: Geloofsverkondiging voor volwassenen* (Hilversum: Brand, 1966), published with the imprimatur of Card. B. Alfrink. The 1970 edition of *A New Catechism* contains "the Supplement to a New Catechism," written by E. Dhanis and J. Visser on behalf of the Commission of Cardinals appointed to examine the Dutch Catechism (pp. 511–74; see especially pp. 538–40).

[22] The Dutch bishops subsequently made it clear that they intended no ambiguity on Mary's bodily virginity; see *De Tijd* (Amsterdam), Aug. 19, 1966; *De nieuwe Gids*, Aug. 20–21, 1966. Cf. "The Dutch Catechism Controversy," *Herder Correspondence* 4 (1967) 156–59; J. M. Alonso, "El catecismo holandés: El tema mariano," *EMar* 19 (1969) 119–43, 457–66. See further W. Bless, *Witboek over de Nieuwe Katechismus* (Utrecht: Ambo, 1969).

[23] It is worth noting that the usual criticism of the Dutch Catechism in this matter passes facilely over a position that it assumed; it blithely ascribes to "the evangelists Matthew and Luke" phrases that sound biblical but were never penned by either of them: "Jesus' birth was not due to the will of a man," or "His origin is not of blood nor of the will of the flesh nor of the will of man, but from God." Such phrases, biblical indeed, are derived from the Johannine prologue (John 1:13), from a passage that has its own problems (see further below, p. 50).

[24] "Commissio cardinalitia de 'Novo Catechismo' ('De nieuwe Katechismus')," *AAS* 60 (1968) 685–91: "3. De profitenda Iesu conceptione ex Maria Virgine.

Petitum est a Commissione Cardinalium ut Catechismus aperte profiteretur Beatam Verbi Incarnati Matrem virginali semper floruisse honore et ut clare doceret factum ipsum virginalis conceptionis Iesu, quod cum mysterio Incarnationis maxime congruit; proindeque ut nullam ansam deinceps daret ad hoc factum—contra Ecclesiae Traditionem in Sacris Litteris fundatam—derelinquendum, servata tantum aliqua eius significatione symbolica, verbi gratia de summa gratuitate doni quod Deus nobis in Filio suo largitus est" (p. 688).

[25] See R. Pesch, "Der Gottessohn im matthäischen Evangelienprolog (Mt 1–2): Beobachtungen zu den Zitationsformeln der Reflexionszitate," *Bib* 48 (1967) 395–420, esp. p. 410; J. Michl, "Die Jungfrauengeburt im Neuen Testament," *Mariologische Studien* 4 (Essen, 1969) 145–84, esp. p. 183 ("The question raised was: Is the conception of Jesus by a virgin to be considered a historical fact or a theologoumenon? A critical investigation can bring forth reasons that suggest the position of a historical fact; but it must also grant that there are circumstantial details that favor the opposite thesis of a mere theologoumenon. The limitations of historico-critical exegesis are manifest here, which stand in the way of a decisive view"); O. Knoch, "Die Botschaft des Matthäusevangeliums über Empfängnis und Geburt Jesu vor dem Hintergrund der Christusverkündigung des Neuen Testaments," *Zum Thema Jungfrauengeburt*, 37–59, esp. pp. 57–58 ("The reticence of the Fourth Gospel [in this matter] suggests the conclusion that the tradition about the virginal conception and birth of Jesus was either not generally known and admitted in the church of the first century or was not regarded as decisive for belief in Christ and for a Christian profession of faith . . . . If this observation is correct, then it lends support to what is today generally admitted in Catholic teaching, that belief in Jesus Christ as true man and true God does not necessarily entail the virginal conception and birth of Jesus"). Cf. A. Vögtle, "Offene Fragen," 43; also his "Die matthäische Kindheitsgeschichte," *L'Evangile selon Matthieu: Rédaction et théologie* (BETL 29; ed. M. Didier; Gembloux: Duculot, 1972) 153–83.

[26] The term "theologoumenon" is not alway used in the same sense; what is given here as the sense is a slightly modified form of that given by K. Rahner ("Theologoumenon," *LTK* 10 [2d ed.; Freiburg: Herder, 1965] 80–82): "A statement which makes a theological assertion that cannot be immediately considered as an official teaching of the Church, or as a dogmatic proposition that is binding in faith, but rather that is first of all the result and expression of a striving for an understanding of faith through the establishment of connections between binding faith-statements and the confronting of (them with) the dogmatic thinking of a person (or a given period)" (col. 80). Further on, Rahner continues: "Revelation that takes place in human awareness must necessarily make use (at least 'between the lines') of theologoumena. But these are not the process of understanding that is affirmed along with the statement itself, in which what is meant is correctly understood but with perspective" (col. 81, with a cross reference to his article on "Perspektivismus").

[27] See n. 25 above; cf. R. E. Brown, *TS* 33 (1972) 5 n. 8; M. Dibelius, *Jungfrauensohn und Krippenkind: Untersuchungen zur Geburtsgeschichte Jesu im Lukas-Evangelium* (Sitzungsberichte der Heidelberger Akademie der Wissenschaften, Phil.-hist. Kl., Abh. 4, 1932; reprinted in *Botschaft und Geschichte: Gesammelte Aufsätze 1* [Tübingen: Mohr (Siebeck), 1953] 1–78, esp. p. 35 n. 46.

[28] "La concepción virginal de Jesús: ¿Historia o leyenda? Un dialogo teológico," *EMar* 21 (1971) 161–206; P. Schoonenberg, "Eine Antwort," ibid., 207–

16. See further P. Schoonenberg, "God concurreert niet," *Theologie en Zielzorg* 61 (1965) 1–10; "Gods oorzakelijkheid en Christus' voortkomst," *Theologie en Pastoraat* 63 (1967) 35–45, esp. p. 42.

[29] See L. Evely, *L'Evangile sans mythes* (Paris: Editions universitaires, 1970); *The Gospels without Myth* (Garden City, NY: Doubleday, 1971) 80–82. From a different standpoint, P. Grelot, "La naissance d'Isaac et celle de Jésus," *NRT* 94 (1972) 462–87, 561–85.

[30] *TS* 33 (1972) 3–34. This article surveys some of the same material from a different viewpoint. It has now appeared in an expanded form in his book *The Virginal Conception and Bodily Resurrection of Jesus* (New York: Paulist, 1973) 21–68. I am indebted to him for a number of leads that he has given to me beyond his original article and for certain sources that he kindly put at my disposal. For other discussions of this matter in the English-speaking world, see Brown's n. 7. For light-weight reactions to Brown's article, see J. S. Brusher, "Waffling Theologians: A Problem for the People of God," *Homiletic and Pastoral Review* 73 (1972) 22–28; T. C. Lawner, "Some Observations on the Brown Article on the Virginal Conception of Jesus," ibid., pp. 61–66. In the same category of reactions belong the remarks of J. B. Carol, *Marian Studies* 24 (1973) 9 and 96.

[31] *TS* 33 (1972) 11.

[32] This is my literal translation of the Hebrew text, *lākēn yittēn ʾădōnāy hûʾ lākem ʾôt hinnēh hāʿalmāh hārāh wĕyōledet ben wĕqārāʾt šĕmô ʿimmānû-ʾEl*. It preserves the participial/adjectival form of *hārāh* and *yōledet;* 1QIsaᵃ 6:29 reads *wqrʾ*, "and he will call." For recent Roman Catholic discussions of this text in the context of the virginal conception, see R. Kilian, "Die Geburt des Immanuel aus der Jungfrau, Jes 7, 14," *Zum Thema Jungfrauengeburt*, 9–35; H. Haag, "Is 7, 14 als alttestamentliche Grundstelle der Lehre von der Virginitas Mariae," *Jungfrauengeburt gestern und heute* (ed. H. J. Brosch and J. Hasenfuss; Mariologische Studien, 4; Essen, 1969) 137–44; M. Rehm, "Das Wort ʿalmāh in Is 7, 14," *BZ* ns 8 (1964) 89–101.—*JB* translates: "The maiden is with child"; *RSV:* "A young woman shall conceive and bear a son"; *NEB:* "A young woman is with child and she will bear a son." The *NAB*, however, has: "The Virgin shall be with child, and bear a son." But cf. the note on this verse in the *NAB*. Similarly, the *NIV:* "The virgin will be with child and will give birth to a son." Cf. A. M. Dubarle, "La conception virginale et la citation d'Is., VII, 14 dans l'évangile de Matthieu," *RB* 85 (1978) 362–80.

[33] It is, of course, well known that the so-called Septuagint rendered the Hebrew *hā-ʿalmāh*, "a young (marriageable) girl," by *hē parthenos*, which is usually taken to mean "a virgin" or "the virgin." In this form Matt 1:23 quoted Isaiah in Greek. Part of the problem here is that the existing mss of the LXX date from Christian times, and no one is sure that the *parthenos* of Isa 7:14 actually belonged to the pre-Christian Greek translation of Isaiah or whether the reading has been influenced by Matthew's text. One LXX ms does use *neanis* instead of *parthenos;* this would mean "young girl" and would be the exact equivalent of Hebrew *ʿalmāh*. Moreover, *neanis* is used in other Greek translations of the Old Testament (Aquila, Symmachus, Theodotion), as well as in one or other patristic citation of Isa 7:14. See J. Ziegler, *Isaias* (Septuaginta Vetus Testamentum graecum, 14; Göttingen: Vandenhoeck & Ruprecht, 1939) 147. Another aspect of the problem is the meaning of *parthenos* in the LXX. In 45 out of 52 instances it translates *bĕtûlāh*, the proper Hebrew word for "virgin," and in these instances

its own natural Greek meaning covers precisely the nuance of the Hebrew. But Greek *parthenos* was apparently not as precise as the Hebrew *bĕtûlāh,* for sometimes in the LXX it renders *ʿalmāh* (Gen 24:43) or *naʿărāh,* "young girl" (Gen 24:14; 34: 3). See further P. Benoit, "La Septante est-elle inspirée?" in *Vom Wort des Lebens: Festschrift für Max Meinertz* (NTAbh 1, Ergänzungsband; Münster: Aschendorff, 1961) 45. Even granting that the Septuagintal reading of *parthenos* does genuinely mean "virgin" and does really go back to Diaspora Jewish circles, it still does not affirm "virginal conception" in the sense in which this is usually understood of Jesus (i.e., excluding a male, human progenitor). One has to reckon with the possibility that the Greek text of Isaiah is not loaded with all the connotations that it has in Matthew. For an attempt to explain the shift from *ʿalmāh* to *parthenos* as the result of influence from Egyptian myths about the god Amon and a virgin, see E. Brunner-Traut, "Die Geburtsgeschichte der Evangelien im Lichte ägyptologischer Forschung," *ZRGG* 12 (1960) 97–111. This has been too facilely adopted as plausible by Kilian, "Die Geburt des Immanuel," 32–34. The Egyptian myth does not refer to parthenogenesis, but rather to a *hieros gamos,* involving intercourse of the god with the woman who was a virgin. See further T. Boslooper, "Jesus' Virgin Birth and Non-Christian 'Parallels,'" *Religion in Life* 26 (1956–57) 87–97; J. Hasenfuss, "Die Jungfrauengeburt in der Religionsgeschichte,' in *Jungfrauengeburt gestern und heute,* 11–23.

[34] To date at least there is no indication in Palestinian Jewish literature of Isa 7:14 being so understood. See StrB, 1. 75. The later Targum of Jonathan on the Prophets does not introduce a messianic nuance here. A Davidic (and hence indirectly messianic) sense of the passage is admitted by some commentators, who relate chap. 7 to Isa 9:1–6 and 11:1–9; but to admit this is still a far cry from the "virginal conception" of the Messiah.

[35] See Vögtle, "Offene Fragen," 46–47.

[36] Not even the maximal approach to the early Christian kerygma that is taken by C. H. Dodd (*The Apostolic Preaching and Its Developments* [London: Hodder & Stoughton, 1950] 7–35) would include this. See further M. Dibelius, *From Tradition to Gospel* (New York: Scribner, n.d.) 17; R. Bultmann, *Theology of the New Testament* (London: SCM, 1956), 1. 33–52; B. van Iersel, "Saint Paul et la prédication de l'église primitive," *Studiorum paulinorum congressus internationalis catholicus, 1961* (AnBib 17–18; Rome: Biblical Institute, 1963) 433–41; C. F. Evans, "The Kerygma," *JTS* 7 (1956) 25–41; W. Baird, "What Is the Kerygma? A Study of I Cor 15:3–8 and Gal 1:11–17," *JBL* 76 (1957) 181–91.

[37] Schmaus, quoted above, p. 43.

[38] Not even in Rom 16:6. For a fuller discussion of the Pauline passages, see now *MNT,* 33–39.

[39] As is well known, his concern was with the interpretation of the Christ-event, the explanation of the significance for mankind in the complex of the final events of Jesus' existence: His passion, death, burial, resurrection, exaltation to glory, and heavenly intercession. See further my *Pauline Theology: A Brief Sketch* (Englewood Cliffs, NJ: Prentice-Hall, 1967) 12–14. Even Paul's rare references to "words" or "commands" (1 Thess 4:15; 1 Cor 7:10; 11:23; 14:37) are ascribed not to the historical Jesus but to the risen "Lord," thus indicating his concern with the present influence of the risen Christ rather than with the historical Jesus. Cf. D. L. Dungan, *The Sayings of Jesus in the Churches of Paul: The*

Use of the Synoptic Tradition in the Regulation of Early Church Life (Philadelphia: Fortress, 1971) xvii–xxix.

[40] Paul's reference to James as "the brother of the Lord" (Gal 1:19) raises another problem, but we cannot treat it here. See J. Blinzler, *Die Brüder und Schwestern Jesu* (SBS 21; Stuttgart: Katholisches Bibelwek, 1967) 17, 23, 92, 96, 107, 119, 121, 132–33, 137–38; *MNT,* 65–67.

[41] On Rom 1:3–4 as "kerygmatic," see my commentary in *JBC,* art. 53, §15–16. Cf. O. Michel, *Der Brief an die Römer* (MeyerK 4; 13th ed.; Göttingen: Vandenhoeck & Ruprecht, 1966) 38–39; O. Kuss, *Der Römerbrief übersetzt und erklärt: Erste Lieferung (Röm 1, 1, bis 6, 11)* (2d ed.; Regensburg: Pustet, 1963) 4–9, 12–15; M.-E. Boismard, "Constitué fils de Dieu (Rom., I, 4)," *RB* 60 (1953) 5–17; H. Schlier, "Zu Röm 1, 3f.," in *Neues Testament und Geschichte* (Festschrift O. Cullmann; Tübingen: Mohr [Siebeck], 1972) 207–18.

[42] The phrase is, of course, derived from the Old Testament in this sense; see Ps 89:3–4; cf. 2 Sam 7:12; John 7:42; 2 Tim 2:8.

[43] Even such a commentator as H. Schürmann, who traces the virginal conception back to a "historisches Faktum," has to admit that "Paul would have formulated things differently here, had he known of the Virgin Birth" (*Das Lukasevangelium: Erster Teil* [HTKNT 3; Freiburg im B: Herder, 1969] 61). The further question is sometimes raised whether Paul may have derived the parallel kerygmatic affirmation from early Christian tradition which already knew of the genealogies of Matt 1:1–16 and Luke 3:23–38. However, the real question is whether the genealogies were part of the early tradition or not. The more frequent understanding of this matter is to regard them as attempts to spell out the Davidic (and divine) relationships attested in the earlier Pauline passages, and not the other way round. See Vögtle, "Offene Fragen," 49.

[44] *Ad Smyrn.* 1, 1 (*alēthōs onta ek genous Dauid kata sarka, huion theou kata thelēma kai dynamin theou, gegennēmenon alēthōs ek parthenou*). The dependence of Ignatius' wording here on Rom 1:3 is unmistakable; his addition of "truly born of a virgin" is significant, but it still has not clearly enunciated virginal conception. Did Paul actually write Gal 4:4–5? J. C. O'Neill (*The Recovery of Paul's Letter to the Galatians* [London: SPCK, 1972] 58) regards these verses as "not originally written by Paul," but introduced later as a gloss from "Jewish Christian liturgy." If they were introduced later, they would almost surely have been formulated otherwise.

[45] Years ago J. B. Lightfoot (*The Epistle of St. Paul to the Galations* [reprinted, Grand Rapids, MI: Zondervan, 1967] 168) perceived the force of these verses expressed in Paul's chiasmus: " 'The Son of God was born a man, that in Him all men might become sons of God; He was born subject to law, that those subject to law might be rescued from bondage.' " The attempts of T. Zahn (*Der Brief des Paulus an die Galater* [2d ed.; Kommentar zum Neuen Testament, 9; Leipzig: Deichert, 1923] 201–2) to interpret this text as evidence for the virginal conception, because no father is named in it, has convinced no one. More recently, W. C. Robinson ("A Re-Study of the Virgin Birth of Christ: God's Son Was Born of a Woman: Mary's Son Prayed 'Abba Father,' " *EvQ* 37 [1965] 1–15) has tried to draw an argument from Paul's use of *genomenon* for Jesus, "born" of a woman in contrast to Ishmael or Isaac, who were "begotten" (*gegennētai*) according to the flesh or the Spirit. The trouble with his view is that *genesthai* can mean either to "be born" or "be begotten" (see BAG, 157) and *gennan* can mean

either to "beget," i.e., become the father of, or to "bear," i.e., become the mother of (ibid., 154). So the distinction proposed by Robinson breaks down.

[46] M. Dibelius (*Jungfrauensohn*, 29 n. 47) remarks appositely: "If the text read *genomenon ek parthenou* [born of a virgin], the words would be stripped of their meaning" in the Pauline context.

[47] The literature on this Pauline passage is vast; for a recent treatment of it, see J. T. Sanders, *The New Testament Christological Hymns: Their Historical Religious Background* (SNTSMS 15; Cambridge: University Press, 1971) 58–74; R. P. Martin, *Carmen Christi: Philippians ii.5–11 in Recent Interpretation and in the Setting of Early Christian Worship* (SNTSMS 4; Cambridge: University Press, 1967).

[48] Some authors have even asked whether, if one were to take Paul at his word about kenosis and humiliation, the idea of virginal conception would not introduce a Docetic notion and thus really weaken his argument. See H. Räisänen, *Die Mutter Jesu im Neuen Testament* (Suomalaisen Tiedeakatemian Toimituksia, Annales academiae scientiarum fennicae, ser. B, nide-Tom 158; Helsinki: Academy of Sciences, 1969) 24; Vögtle, "Offene Fragen," 49. Whether the query is all that important, the more significant thing is that Paul inherits here an early Christian (Hellenistic? Jewish?) hymn that affirms Jesus' pre-existence (and incarnation) and feels no concern to correct it in terms of virginal conception.

[49] See further Rom 8:32. The ideas of pre-existence (or incarnation) that are implied in these texts are notions that Paul seems to have derived from the early Christian community which he joined as a convert. Yet these notions scarcely reflect the earliest levels of that community's christological beliefs. Remnants of still earlier christologies, in which notions and titles were applied to Jesus in terms of his parousiac coming, are found in the New Testament. These were then first retrojected back to his earthly ministry; in Paul's writings we see some of them being pushed back to the stage of pre-existence. See further R. E. Brown, *TS* 33 (1972) 17–19.

[50] See my commentary on Galatians in *JBC*, art. 49, §28.

[51] Cf. Dibelius, *Jungfrauensohn*, 42–52. See E. Schweizer, "Pneuma," *TDNT*, 6. 429.

[52] In Rom 1:3–4 Paul does use the phrase "according to the spirit of holiness," but though this may be equated with the "Holy Spirit" in the Old Testament sense, it is strikingly related by Paul to Jesus' resurrection, not his birth. See further *MNT*, 38–39.

[53] Commenting on the *argumentum ex silentio*, H. von Campenhausen (*The Virgin Birth in the Theology of the Ancient Church* [Naperville, IL: Allenson, 1964] 17–18) admits that it "must not be pressed in relation to an isolated text or document; it may be that in one case or another the silence is a matter of pure chance. But as regards Paul such qualifications are not relevant; his legacy is too big for that, and too rich in Christological assertions and formulae. . . . In any case, a generation 'according to the Spirit' is not thought of in his writings, even remotely, as a physiological miracle. In this he was certainly no exception. There is nothing to indicate that, for example, the letters composed later under his name, or the other writings of the New Testament, knew and put forward anything more than he did in this matter." Von Campenhausen does not include the infancy narratives in these "other writings of the New Testament"; see the context of his discussion.

⁵⁴ Mary appears in the Marcan Gospel only in 6:3. It is highly unlikely that the "Mary the mother of James the younger and of Joses" (15:40; cf. 15:47; 16:1) refers to her. It is inconceivable that the evangelist would have used such a circumlocution to indicate the presence of Jesus' *own mother* near the cross. See further *MNT*, 68–72, also 65–67.

⁵⁵ If one were to prefer the postulated "Q" source as earlier than Mark, the situation would still be the same; nothing in it about the virginal conception. For a fuller discussion of the Marcan material, see now *MNT*, 51–72.

⁵⁶ See, among other discussions, R. E. Brown, *Jesus God and Man* (Milwaukee: Bruce, 1967) 45–46; A. Robert and A. Feuillet, *Introduction to the New Testament* (New York: Desclée, 1965) 179, 212–13.

⁵⁷ On this issue see J. Blinzler, *Die Brüder und Schwestern Jesu* (n. 40 above); J. J. Collins, "The Brethren of the Lord and Two Recently Published Papyri," *TS* 5 (1944) 484–94. It should be noted, however, that a Roman Catholic interpreter of Mark 6:3 has maintained that the four "brothers" and the "sisters" of Jesus mentioned there are actually blood brothers and sisters. See R. Pesch, *Das Markusevangelium, I. Teil* (HTKNT II/1; Freiburg im B.: Herder, 1976) 322–24.

⁵⁸ The text of Mark, as we have given it above, is found in all the chief Greek MSS; see B. M. Metzger, *A Textual Commentary on the Greek New Testament* (New York: United Bible Societies, 1971) 88–89. Some inferior MSS, however, identified Jesus rather as "the carpenter's son," which seems to be a harmonization of the Marcan text with Matt 13:55. Yet such an astute commentator on the Marcan Gospel as Vincent Taylor preferred this reading as the original (*Mark*, 300). But see J. Blinzler, *Die Brüder und Schwestern Jesu*, 28–30; H. J. Vogels, "Die 'Eltern' Jesu," *BZ* 11 (1913) 33–43; E. Stauffer, "Jeschu ben Mirjam: Kontroversgeschichtliche Anmerkungen zu Mk 6:3," in *Neotestamentica et semitica: Studies in Honour of Matthew Black* (ed. E. E. Ellis and M. Wilcox; Edinburgh: Clark, 1969) 119–28; *Jesus and His Story* (New York: Knopf, 1960) 23–25, 165–66; and more recently H. K. McArthur, "Son of Mary," *NovT* 15 (1973) 38–58 ("the phrase had no special connotation," 58).

⁵⁹ A similar situation is found in the Lucan Gospel; see "Joseph's son" (4:22); cf. 2:41, 48; and see further pp. 54–58 above. Luke completely omitted the Marcan episode (6:1–6a).

⁶⁰ It should not be overlooked that this Marcan passage and the phrase "son of Mary" have been taken by W. R. Farmer as a "classic example" of an inconclusive theological or christological argument for the primitive character of the Marcan Gospel. See pp. 27–28 above. Cf. *MNT*, 62–63.

⁶¹ See C. H. Dodd, *Historical Tradition in the Fourth Gospel* (Cambridge: University Press, 1963) 1–18, 423–32; R. E. Brown, *The Gospel according to John (i–xii)* (AB 29; Garden City, NY: Doubleday, 1966) xli–li; A. J. B. Higgins, *The Historicity of the Fourth Gospel* (London: Lutterworth, 1960) 63–82.

⁶² It is the reading adopted in *The Greek New Testament* (ed. K. Aland et al.; 3d ed; New York: United Bible Societies, 1975) 321; Nestle-Aland, *Novum Testamentum graece* (26th ed.; Stuttgart: Deutsche Bibelstiftung, 1979) 247; E. Nestle, *Novum Testamentum graece* (24th ed.; Stuttgart: Württembergische Bibelanstalt, 1960) 230; A. Merk, *Novum Testamentum graece et latine* (9th ed.; Rome: Biblical Institute, 1964) 306; [G. D. Kilpatrick], *Hē kainē Diathēkē* (2d ed.; London: British and Foreign Bible Society, 1958) 276; R. V. G. Tasker, *The Greek New Testament* (London: Oxford University, 1960) 140 [the Greek text presupposed in the *NEB* New Testament]; H. J. Vogels, *Novum Testamentum graece et*

latine 1 (3d ed.; Freiburg: Herder, 1949) 287; J. M. Bover, *Novi Testamenti biblia graeca et latina* (3d ed.; Madrid: Consejo superior de investigaciones científicas, 1953) 271; B. F. Westcott and F. J. A. Hort, *The New Testament in the Original Greek* 1 (London: Macmillan, 1890) 187; C. Tischendorf, *Novum Testamentum graece* 1 (8th ed.; Leipzig: Giesecke & Devrient, 1869) 743–44; H. von Soden, *Griechisches Neues Testament: Text mit kurzem Apparat* (Göttingen: Vandenhoeck & Ruprecht, 1913) 182. I have not been able to find a critical edition of the Greek New Testament that has preferred the singular reading to the plural.

[63] *The Jerusalem Bible* 2 (Garden City, NY: Doubleday, 1966) 146. For the worth of this English translation one should not fail to consult the pointed review of W. J. Harrington, an Irish confrère of the French Dominicans who produced the remarkable French original. His review is published in French, to spare the sensibilities of English-speaking readers enamored of this English version (*RB* 75 [1968] 450–52). In this case, however, the fault lies not with the English version, for it reflects the French original of John 1:13: "lui qui ni sang, ni vouloir de chair, ni vouloir d'homme, mais Dieu a engendré"(*La sainte Bible* [de Jérusalem]: *L'évangile . . . de saint Jean* [2d ed.; Paris: Cerf, 1960] 69). The note reads: "Allusion à la génération éternelle du Verbe, mais sans doute aussi, vu l'insistance sur l'exclusion du sang et de la chair, à la naissance virginale de Jésus. . . ." It seems rather obvious that the Dutch Catechism derived its questionable formulation of what "the evangelists Matthew and Luke" said from this reading of the Johannine Gospel (see n. 23 above). A good instance of how a well-meaning, popular version of the Bible can lead the untutored astray!

[64] Metzger, *A Textual Commentary*, p. 197. The patristic evidence stems mainly from Latin Fathers or versions (e.g. Vetus Itala[b], Irenaeus [Latin], Tertullian, Origen [Latin], Ambrose, Augustine, Pseudo-Athanasius). Metzger lists the following modern scholars who have argued for the originality of the singular: T. Zahn, A. Resch, F. Blass, A. Loisy, R. Seeburg, C. F. Burney, F. Büchsel, M.-E. Boismard, J. Dupont, F.-M. Braun. He could also have listed D. Mollat, the translator of John in *La sainte Bible* [de Jérusalem], and J. Galot (*Etre né de Dieu: Jean 1:13* [AnBib 37; Rome: Biblical Institute, 1969]). But see J. Schmid, "Joh 1, 13," *BZ* ns 1 (1957) 118–25; A. Hossiau, "Le milieu théologique de la leçon *egennēthē* (Jo. I. 13)," in *Sacra pagina* 2 (ed. J. Coppens et al.; BETL 12–13; Gembloux: Duculot, 1959) 170–88; G. D. Fee, "The Text of John in the Jerusalem Bible: A Critique of the Use of Patristic Citations in New Testament Textual Criticism," *JBL* 90 (1971) 163–73, esp. pp. 166–67: "It is quite another [thing] to reconstruct this primitive reading on a purely eclectic basis, so that by a process of picking and choosing one 'creates' an original reading that is supported *in toto* by *no* single piece of evidence. Yet this is precisely the nature of Boismard's resultant text for such passages as John 1:12–13" (Fee refers to Boismard's article, "Critique textuelle et citations patristiques," *RB* 57 [1950] 388–408, esp. pp. 401–8, an article that greatly influenced D. Mollat in his translation of John for *La sainte Bible* [de Jérusalem]).

[65] Metzger, *A Textual Commentary*, 197.

[66] See R. E. Brown, *Jesus God and Man*, 92.

[67] Schmaus, quoted above, p. 43.

[68] See, e.g., V. Taylor, *The Formation of the Gospel Tradition* (London: Macmillan, 1959) 168–89; Bultmann, *The History of the Synoptic Tradition*, 354; O. Cullmann, "Infancy Gospels," in Hennecke-Schneemelcher, *NTA*, 1. 363–69; J. Riedl, *Die Vorgeschichte Jesu* (Stuttgart: Katholisches Bibelwerk, 1968) 11–13. The reader

will find a full exposition of all the problems in the interpretation of the infancy narratives in the excellent work of R. E. Brown, *The Birth of the Messiah: A Commentary on the Infancy Narratives in Matthew and Luke* (Garden City, NY: Doubleday, 1977). See also *MNT,* 74–97, 107–62.

[69] See, e.g., Brown, *John (i–xii),* 18–36; R. Schnackenburg, *The Gospel according to St. John* (New York: Herder and Herder, 1968) 221–81.

[70] See Hennecke-Schneemelcher, *NTA,* 1. 370–417.

[71] See above, p. 47. Cf. G. Friedrich, *"Kēryssō," TDNT,* 3. 710–12. Even if Acts 10:37–43 is basically kerygmatic and pre-Lucan, it also betrays Lucan reworking (e.g., in the formulation of the "beginning" from Galilee, *arxamenos,* 10:37; cf. Luke 3:23; Acts 1:22). Cf. Luke 23:5.

[72] See J. Schmid, *Matthäus und Lukas: Eine Untersuchung des Verhältnisses ihrer Evangelien* (Freiburg: Herder, 1930); W. G. Kümmel, *Introduction to the New Testament* (Nashville: Abingdon, 1966) 64. With reference to the infancy narratives specifically, see J. Riedl, *Die Vorgeschichte Jesu,* 11–13. See also pp. 17–18 above.

[73] R. Pesch, "Eine alttestamentliche Ausführungsformel im Matthäus-Evangelium," *BZ* 10 (1966) 220–45; 11 (1967) 79–95, esp. 88–89. Also A. Vögtle, "Offene Fragen," 44; C. T. Davis, "Tradition and Redaction in Matthew 1:18–2:23," *JBL* 90 (1971) 404–21; A. Paul, *L'Evangile de l'enfance selon saint Matthieu* (Paris: Cerf, 1968) 45–94. There is not time to discuss here the amount which the Matthean or Lucan accounts owe to tradition and to redaction, though this is an important aspect of one's judgment. See C. Burger, *Jesus als Davidssohn: Eine traditionsgeschichtliche Untersuchung* (Göttingen: Vandenhoeck & Ruprecht, 1970) 91–106, 127–37.

[74] It might be good to interject here a consideration from a dogmatic theological point of view, to forestall an obvious difficulty. The events in the infancy narratives are recounted in the past tense and, like the rest of the gospel stories, are inspired. From this one might be tempted to conclude to the guaranteed, inerrant character of the narratives and perhaps even to a guarantee of their *historical* character. But this is to ride roughshod over the literary forms or the types of accounts that one has to deal with in these narratives. To offset such a misunderstanding, one should recall what Pius XII had to say about literary forms in his encyclical *Divino afflante Spiritu* (§314–16 [DS 3829–30]) and the precisions added by Vatican II in *Dei verbum* (chap. 3, §11–12 [*The Documents of Vatican II,* 118–20]). Moreover, neither official ecclesiastical documents treating of biblical inspiration and inerrancy nor the discussions of theologians have ever maintained that the necessary formal effect of inspiration was historicity. Inspiration does not make a historical statement out of what was not intended to be such. It would, however, obviously guarantee the historical character of an intended historical statement, just as it would guarantee the poetic truth of a poem, the rhetorical truth of a sermon or oration, the gospel truth of a Gospel. "Biblical inspiration" is thus an analogous notion; see P. Benoit, "The Analogies of Inspiration," in *Aspects of Biblical Inspiration* (Chicago: Priory, 1965) 13–35; B. Vawter, *Biblical Inspiration* (Philadelphia, 1972) 119–31; Vögtle, "Offene Fragen," 44–45.

[75] See J. Riedl, *Die Vorgeschichte Jesu,* 8–10; A. G. Wright, "The Literary Genre Midrash," *CBQ* 28 (1966) 105–38, 417–57, esp. pp. 454–56.

[76] This term has been used, in a slightly different way, by E. Burrows, *The Gospel of the Infancy and Other Biblical Essays* (London: Burns Oates, 1940) 1–58.

As I am using it, the "imitation" involves the assimilation of details to other literary accounts.

[77] See M. Enslin, "The Christian Stories of the Nativity," *JBL* 59 (1940) 317–38; P. Winter, "Jewish Folklore in the Matthaean Birth Story," *HibJ* 53 (1954) 34–42; H. W. Obbink, "On the Legends of Moses in the Haggadah," *Studia biblica et semitica T. C. Vriezen . . . dedicata* (Wageningen: Veenman & Zonen, 1966) 252–64; P. J. Thompson, "The Infancy Gospels of St. Matthew and St. Luke Compared," *SE I*, 217–22; M. M. Bourke, "The Literary Genus of Matthew 1–2," *CBQ* 22 (1960) 160–75; S. Muñoz Iglesias, "El género literario del evangelio de la infancia en San Mateo," *EstBib* 17 (1958) 243–73 (see *TD* 9 [1961] 15–20). But cf. C. H. Cave, "St Matthew's Infancy Narrative," *NTS* 9 (1962–63) 382–90.

[78] See, e.g., E. Burrows, *The Gospel of the Infancy*, 1–58; S. Muñoz Iglesias, "El evangelio de la infancia en San Lucas y las infancias de los héroes bíblicos," *EstBib* 16 (1957) 329–82; R. McL. Wilson, "Some Recent Studies in the Lucan Infancy Narratives," *SE I*, 235–53. This aspect of the Lucan infancy narrative is strangely neglected by R. Laurentin, *Structure et théologie de Luc I-II* (Paris: Gabalda, 1957).

Cf. M. Miguens, "The Infancy Narratives and Critical Biblical Method," *Communio* 7 (1980) 24–54 [one does not know whether to laugh or to weep over this article].

[79] See, e.g., R. H. Fuller, *The Foundations of New Testament Christology* (New York: Scribner, 1965) 195–97; R. E. Brown, *TS* 33 (1972) 24.

[80] See, e.g., H. H. Oliver, "The Lucan Birth Stories and the Purpose of Luke-Acts," *NTS* 10 (1963–64) 202–26; P. S. Minear, "Luke's Use of the Birth Stories," in *Studies in Luke-Acts: Essays Presented in Honor of Paul Schubert* (Nashville: Abingdon, 1966) 111–30; A. Vögtle, *Messias und Gottessohn: Herkunft und Sinn der matthäischen Geburts- und Kindheitsgeschichte* (Düsseldorf: Patmos, 1971); "Die Genealogie Mt 1, 2–16 und die matthäische Kindheitsgeschichte (I. Teil)," *BZ* 8 (1964) 45–58; "(II. Teil)," ibid., 239–62; "(Schlussteil)," ibid. 9 (1965) 31–49; "Das Schicksal des Messiaskindes: Zur Auslegung und Theologie von Mt 2," *BibLeb* 6 (1965) 246–79.

[81] *Das Evangelium nach Lukas* (4th ed.; RNT 3; Regensburg: Pustet, 1960) 90. See further X. Léon-Dufour, *Les évangiles et l'histoire de Jésus* (Paris: Editions du Seuil, 1963) 90; A. Vögtle, "Offene Fragen," 44.

[82] *Die Vorgeschichte Jesu*, 12–13.

[83] In other words, the conception had already taken place when the angelic announcement was made. What should not be missed here is the loaded form of the statement of the Evangelist (1:18): "She was found to be with child *of the holy Spirit*," and this is given as the basis of Joseph's consideration of divorce (see Deut 22:21 for the Old Testament background to his doubting). See A. Isaksson, *Marriage and Ministry in the New Temple* (Lund: Gleerup, 1965) 135–42. No explanation is given why Joseph, a "just man," wanted to divorce someone who had been found to be with child *of the holy Spirit*. The evangelist's intention is clear, but his mode of formulation raises questions precisely about the thrust of the narrative and its redaction—issues that cannot be pursued here. See C. T. Davis, *JBL* 90 (1971) 413. Contrast the treatment of this episode in J. Daniélou, *The Infancy Narratives* (New York: Herder and Herder, 1968) 40: "The announcement made to Joseph was not intended to inform him that Mary had conceived virginally—that he already knew. . . ." But this goes against the

plain sense and basic thrust of the story, which states that Joseph was about to repudiate Mary and had to be informed by the angel to persuade him to the contrary. However, Daniélou is on the right track when he states that "the object of this account" is not "to defend the virgin birth"; it is rather "to establish how Jesus can be a descendant of David and the Davidic Messiah *despite* the virgin birth which seems so fundamental an objection to his being so" (p. 41). In effect, this is to affirm the virginal conception as a theologoumenon (see below).

[84] For a history-of-religions approach to this question, see W. Marxsen, "Jungfrauengeburt," 1068; G. Gutknecht, *Das Motiv der Jungfrauengeburt in religionsgeschichtlicher Beleuchtung* (Greifswald: Universitätsverlag, 1952). But attempts to find extrabiblical parallels for the virginal conception in Greek and Egyptian literature have not really succeeded, since in almost every instance that is cited the parallels imply at least sexual intercourse. See R. E. Brown, *TS* 33 (1972) 30–32 (and the literature that he cites); A. Vögtle, "Offene Fragen," 45–47; E. Schweizer, "Pneuma," *TDNT*, 6. 397.

[85] Contrast the tendentious translation of this verse in the *Jerusalem Bible*, New Testament, 91: "since I am a virgin." This is not found in the French original, "puisque je ne connais point d'homme."

[86] This understanding of the verse has been traced back to Ambrose (*Expositio evang. Lucae* 2, 14–15 [CSEL, 32. 49–50]) and Augustine (*De sacra virginitate* 4, 4 [CSEL, 41. 237–38]). In one form or another it still has its defenders: R. Laurentin, *Structure et théologie du Luc I-II*, 176–88; G. Grayston, *Virgin of All Virgins: The Interpretation of Luke 1:34* (Rome: No publisher, 1968). Cf. J. F. Craghan, *Mary: The Virginal Wife and the Married Virgin: The Problematic of Mary's Vow of Virginity* (Rome: Gregorian University, 1967) 42–48.

[87] This understanding is found in many ancient versions which rendered the verb *ginōskō* in the past tense and implied that Mary understood the angel to mean that she was already pregnant. See H. Quecke, "Lk 1, 34 in den alten Übersetzungen und im Protevangelium des Jakobus," *Bib* 44 (1962) 499–520; "Lk 1, 34 im Diatessaron," *Bib* 45 (1964) 85–88; "Zur Auslegungsgeschichte von Lk 1, 34," *Bib* 47 (1966) 113–14.

[88] See Gen 16:11; Judg 13:3. This interpretation is widely used today; see, e.g., A. Plummer, *A Critical and Exegetical Commentary on the Gospel according to S. Luke* (5th ed.; Edinburgh: Clark, 1964) 24 ("The words are the avowal of a maiden conscious of her own purity; and they have been drawn from her by the strange declaration that she is to have a son before she is married"). For *ou* in the sense of *oupō* that this interpretation involves, see Mark 8:17–18.

[89] E.g., that of J.-P. Audet, "L'Annonce à Marie," *RB* 63 (1956) 364–74. This interpretation has "not received great support" (J. F. Craghan, "The Gospel Witness to Mary's 'Ante Partum' Virginity," *Marian Studies* 21 [1970] 28–68, esp. p. 56). It is vitiated by an idea that is often repeated, that Luke's annunciation scene is influenced by Isa 7:14. Aside from superficial parallels in the Greek wording of Luke 1:26–38 and the LXX of Isa 7:10–17, there is little evidence that Luke has fashioned his annunciation in dependence on Isaiah. It is necessary to insist on this, because otherwise critical commentators tend at times to gloss over it (see A. Vögtle, "Offene Fragen," 46; H. Schürmann, *Das Lukasevangelium*, 62–63; G. Voss, *Die Christologie der lukanischen Schriften in Grundzügen* [Bruges: Desclée de Brouwer, 1965] 65–81). The possible parallel phrases are seven: *oikou Dauid* (Luke 1:27)—*oikos Dauid* (Isa 7:12); *ho kyrios* (Luke 1:28)—*kyrios* (Isa 7:10); *parthenon* (Luke 1:27)—*hē parthenos* (Isa 7:14);

syllēmpsē en gastri (Luke 1:31)—*en gastri hexei* (Isa 7:14 [cf. *apparatus criticus*]); *texē huion* (Luke 1:31)—*texetai huion* (Isa 7:14); *kai kaleseis to onoma autou* (Luke 1:31)—*kai kaleseis to onoma autou* (Isa 7:14); *epi ton oikon* (Luke 1:33)—*epi ton oikon* (Isa 7:17). But in those Lucan phrases that seem to be similar to Isa 7:14 in this list one should not miss the parallels that are found elsewhere in the Old Testament (e.g., Gen 16:11). The difficulty here is once again the harmonization of the Lucan and Matthean narratives. It is noteworthy that R. Laurentin, for all his discussion of the Old Testament background of Luke 1–2 (*Structure et théologie de Luc I-II*), does not treat Isa 7:14 as part of it.

⁹⁰ J. M. Creed (*The Gospel according to St. Luke: The Greek Text with Introduction, Notes, and Indices* [London: Macmillan, 1953] 19) thinks that Mary's "vow" is the "usual interpretation of Roman Catholic exegetes."

⁹¹ Ibid. This is also acknowledged by H. Schürmann, *Das Lukasevangelium*, 49; he traces the idea back to H. J. Holtzmann and others (n. 68). J. Gewiess ("Die Marienfrage, Lk 1,34," *BZ* 5 [1961] 221–54, esp. pp. 242–43) calls attention to the literary device of the question that Luke often uses (Luke 13:23; 16:5, 7; 17:37; Acts 8:30–31; 10:14; 16:30).

⁹² Or possibly "the holy one to be born will be called the Son of God." This verse (1:35) and v. 32 have recently been found to echo Aramaic phrases that have come to light in pseudo-Danielic apocalyptic fragments from Qumran Cave 4, which J. T. Milik is to publish. "He will be said to be the son of God, and they will call him the son of the Most High" (see *WA*, 90–94). The text is apocalyptic and has nothing to do with an infancy narrative; unfortunately, it is fragmentary and no hint is given about the person who is the subject of the titles used.

⁹³ See G. Voss, *Die Christologie*, 75–76: "The Virgin Birth is regarded in the Lucan presentation not under its biological point of view, but as a theological statement." Also K. H. Rengstorf, "Die Weihnachtserzählung des Evangelisten Lukas," in *Stat crux dum volvitur orbis: Eine Festschrift für Landesbischof D. Hanns Lilje* (ed. G. Hoffmann and K. H. Rengstorf; Berlin: Lutherisches Verlagshaus, 1959) 15–30.

⁹⁴ The verb *eperchesthai* is used in Luke 11:22; 21:26; Acts 1:8; 8:24; 13:40; 14:19; Eph 2:7; Jas 5:1. Only in the programmatic verse of Acts 1:8 is it again used of the Spirit, as the risen Jesus promises the apostles "power" for the ministry of witnessing to him. Luke's use of the verb in 1:35 is often thought to be influenced by the LXX of Isa 32:15, *heōs an epelthē eph' hymas pneuma aph' hypsēlou*, "until the Spirit comes upon you from on high." Here it is used to explain the fertility of the land (in the LXX: of Carmel), but it does not transcend the figurative sense. For other combinations of the verb with *pneuma*, see Num 5:14; Job 1:19; 4:15 (but one must be careful of the sense of *pneuma*). The verb *episkiazein* has a literal sense in Acts 5:15; the use of it in the transfiguration scene (Mark 9:7; Matt 17:5; Luke 9:34) may be literal, but a symbolic connotation cannot be completely ruled out. In the Lucan infancy narrative the use of the verb is wholly figurative, symbolical of God's presence (and power) to Mary and the child to be born of her. It may well reflect the symbolism of Exod 40:35 or Ps 91:4, although this is sometimes contested (see G. Voss, *Die Christologie*, 73–76).

⁹⁵ See p. 48 above.

⁹⁶ In the recently published critical edition of *The Greek New Testament* (UBS, 206) these ancient tamperings with the text are not even noted; and in his

commentary on the text Metzger (*A Textual Commentary*, 132) passes over them in silence. See now Nestle-Aland, 26th ed., 156.

[97] Not only here, but also in connection with the earlier passages discussed above, a distinction has often been proposed between the fact of the virginal conception and its possible literary embellishment in a presentation stemming from a later period of gospel-formation—as if the latter could be admitted to have been freely introduced, whereas the former is really the firm datum. At the end of an excursus, "Jungfrauengeburt—ein Theologoumenon?" E. Nellessen (*Das Kind und seine Mutter* [SBS 39; Stuttgart: Katholisches Bibelwerk, 1969] 109) sought to explain why the data about the conception arose only in the later period of the gospel-tradition: "It should be recalled, however, that an explicit investigation into the peculiar circumstances of the conception and birth of Jesus would only then have recommended itself when the beginnings of Jesus' human life would have become the object of a narrative presentation. Outside of the Matthean and Lucan Gospels that is scarcely the case, and certainly not in Paul, who speaks of the beginnings of Jesus' life only in short confessional formulas (Rom 1:3; Gal 4:4)." To which A. Vögtle ("Offene Fragen," 48) appositely remarked: "But that is to put the cart before the horse! A claim is made for a probative argument out of something that cries out for an explanation. The problem is why the idea of a virginal conception appears only in narrative presentations which make use of Old Testament annunciation forms and in declarations that prepared for these (Matt 1:16) or reflect on them (Luke 3:23), but have no reference to the incarnation of Jesus such as the Pauline passages suggest." The real problem is expressed by Vögtle (ibid., 47): "Without a basic declaration of the original witness, in this case above all of Mary herself, an authentic tradition could not have been established," and it strains the imagination to try to explain it, all pious suggestions about intimate family traditions etc. notwithstanding. See further his "Offene Fragen," 50: A. Weiser, "Überblick über den Verlauf der Diskussion [der Beuroner Tagung]," in *Jungfrauengeburt gestern und heute* (Mariologische Studien, 4) 205–14, esp. pp. 211–12.

[98] See, e.g., H. Schürmann, *Das Lukasevangelium*, 188; E. E. Ellis, *The Gospel of Luke* (London: Oliphants, 1966) 93.

[99] See H. Schürmann, *Das Lukasevangelium*, 198–200.

[100] This is the title of a perceptive article on the Matthean infancy narrative by K. Stendahl, "Quis et Unde? An Analysis of Mt 1–2," in *Judentum—Urchristentum—Kirche: Festschrift für Joachim Jeremias* (BZNW 26; Berlin: Töpelmann, 1960) 94–105. That the Matthean emphasis is on Jesus rather than on Mary is seen in the way the evangelist refers several times over to "the child with Mary his mother" (2:11) or "the child and his mother" (2:13, 14, 20, 21).

[101] This is the term used for what Schürmann calls "das historische Faktum der jungfräulichen Empfängnis," which he traces to an "intimate family tradition" (*Das Lukasevangelium*, 61) and which he claims would have taken time to be transmitted to great church-centers. In using this terminology, *Glaubensgut* and theologoumenon, one should recall the distinction made by K. Rahner, quoted above (n. 26). Protestant writers sometimes use similar terminology with different nuances. Thus, R. H. Fuller (*Foundations*, 202) writes: "For those who are concerned about the historicity of the 'Virgin birth' ('virginal conception' is a more accurate term), let it be stated that to believe in the Virgin birth is

not to accept the historicity of a biological parthenogenesis but to adhere to the Christological intention of the narratives, which is to express the transcendental origin of Jesus' history. See the present writer's essay, The Virgin Birth, Historical Fact or Kerygmatic Truth? *BR* 1 (1956), pp. 1–8. In a letter to me, J. Jeremias proposes to substitute 'Glaubensaussage' ('affirmation of faith') for 'kerygmatic truth', on the ground that the Virgin birth was never actually part of the kerygma as such. Accepting the correction, we may say that to believe in the Virgin birth is to adhere to the *faith* which the story expresses." As proposed above, *Glaubensgut* would not be the same as the *Glaubensaussage* in this comment of Fuller. See further A. Weiser, "Mythos im Neuen Testament unter Berück-sichtigung der Mariologie," in *Mythos und Glaube* (ed. H. J. Brosch and H. J. Köster; Mariologische Studien 5; Essen, 1972) 67–88, esp. pp. 80–84.

[102] See further my commentary on Romans in *JBC*, art. 53, §52–60.

[103] See further E. Carroll, "A Survey of Recent Mariology," *Marian Studies* 25 (1974) 104–42, esp. pp. 125–26; J. A. Saliba, "The Virgin-Birth Debate in Anthropological Literature: A Critical Assessment," *TS* 36 (1975) 428–54.

[104] See "Luke's Description of the Virginal Conception," *TS* 35 (1974) 360–62.

[105] See pp. 55–58 above.

[106] See further Brown's *The Birth of the Messiah*, 299–301.

[107] See further my commentary, *The Gospel according to Luke* (AB 28; New York: Doubleday, 1981).

[108] See *MNT*, 120–21.

[109] See further S. Muñoz Iglesias, "La concepción virginal de Cristo en los evangelios de la infancia," *EstBib* 37 (1978) 5–28, 213–41; A. Vicent Cernuda, "La génesis humana de Jesucristo según San Pablo," *EstBib* 37 (1978) 57–77, 267–89.

Three

THE MATTHEAN DIVORCE TEXTS AND SOME NEW PALESTINIAN EVIDENCE*

THE RECENT publication of a passage from one of the Qumran scrolls that may shed some light on the Matthean divorce texts is the occasion for a fresh consideration of those controverted verses.[1] The Matthean passages are but two among several in the New Testament which record sayings attributed to Jesus about the prohibition of divorce. Four writers, in fact, have recorded the prohibition that is traced to him. The earliest form of it is found in 1 Cor 7:10–11, but each of the Synoptic evangelists has also preserved some form of the prohibition: Mark 10:2–12; Luke 16:18; Matt 5:31–32; 19:3–9. In fact, there are, in all, five passages with seven sayings about the dissolution of marriage.

Despite the tone of a controversy-setting that surrounds the pronouncement preserved in Mark 10 and Matthew 19, which is sometimes thought to reflect more a later church-synagogue debate[2] than a discussion of the historical Jesus with the Pharisees, two features have often been invoked in favor of the authenticity of the prohibition: the independent attribution of the saying to Jesus in First Corinthians and in the Synoptics, and the radical opposition of the prohibition to the well-known Jewish permission of divorce, usually associated with the Mosaic legislation reflected in Deut 24:1–4.[3]

Likewise introduced at times into the discussion of New Testament teaching on divorce are texts that do not deal with it explicitly, but that are instructions sometimes interpreted as implying the prohibition. These are the regulations set down in the Deutero-Pauline letters that Christian *episkopoi, presbyteroi,* and *diakonoi* are to be *mias gynaikos andres,* "husbands of one wife" (1 Tim 3:2, 12; Tit 1:6), and that the widow who was to be enrolled should have been *henos andros gynē*, "the wife of one husband" (1 Tim 5:9).[4] The latter Deutero-Pauline instruction about the widow seems to be merely an extension of what Paul himself writes in 1 Cor 7:39–40, when, insisting that he has "God's Spirit," he recommends, "In my opinion she is happier if she remains as she is" (1 Cor 7:40). To this recommendation some also relate the illustration that Paul uses in Rom 7:2–3, "A married woman is bound by law to her husband as long as he lives; but if her husband dies, she is discharged from the law concerning the husband."[5] However, none of these texts bears directly on the question of divorce; and if they do have any pertinence, it is only indirect. Though they contribute to the complexity of the New Testament data that bear on the question of divorce, they are not of concern to us now.

The problems connected with the prohibition of divorce in the first set of texts mentioned, however, are multiple and notorious. Some of these problems arise from the Synoptic relationships of Matthew, Mark, and Luke; some from form-critical and redaction-critical considerations. Consequently, before discussing the Qumran material that bears on the exceptive phrases in the Matthean passages, I shall have to state briefly how I view these various New Testament texts that treat of divorce. Once the Qumran material has been presented, I shall draw from it the consequences for the Synoptic passages and discuss further theological implications in all of them. My discussion, then, will fall into four parts: (1) preliminary remarks about certain aspects of the New Testament divorce passages; (2) the Qumran material that bears on the Matthean exceptive phrases; (3) consequences to be drawn for the Marcan and Matthean passages; and (4) theological implications of all this for the current debate about divorce.

I. *Preliminary Remarks*

The preliminary remarks about certain aspects of the New Testament divorce-passages are intended to set forth my understanding of the relation between the five main texts and some of the details in them as a background for the Palestinian evidence to be considered in part II. The remarks will be seven in number.

(1) 1 Cor 7:10–11. The earliest attestation of an attitude of Jesus toward divorce is preserved in the Pauline corpus, in the First Letter to the Corinthians (written ca. A.D. 57), where the prohibition is attributed by Paul to "the Lord."[6] What he has almost certainly derived from prior

Christian tradition, he invests with the authority of the risen *Kyrios,* clearly stating that it does not originate with him (in contrast to 7:12, 25):

[10a]*Tois de gegamēkosin parangellō,* [10b]*ouk egō alla ho Kyrios,* [10c]*gynaika apo andros mē chōristhēnai*—[11a]*ean de kai chōristhē,* [11b]*menetō agamos ē tō andri katallagētō*—[11c]*kai andra gynaika mē aphienai.*

[10a]To the married I give charge, [10b]not I but the Lord, [10c]that the wife should not separate from her husband [11a](but if she does, [11b]let her remain single or else be reconciled to her husband)—[11c]and that the husband should not divorce his wife (*RSV*).

Here in indirect discourse Paul formulates the prohibition (which may reflect the pronouncement preserved in Mark 10:4 and Matt 19:7).

The *RSV* has translated the charge *gynaika apo andros mē chōristhēnai* (with an aorist passive) by the intransitive verb "separate": "that the wife should not separate from her husband." It thus takes the passive of *chōrizein* and treats it as a middle or intransitive, thus making it an equivalent of *aphienai* in v. 11b.[7] It casts the prohibition of divorce, which is attributed to "the Lord," into a form suited more to a Hellenistic Christian setting than to a Palestinian Christian setting. It would, moreover, mean that the earliest attested New Testament prohibition of divorce was already set in an elaborated form reflecting the Hellenistic ambiance of Paul's missionary activity. Furthermore, v. 13c would seem to support this interpretation: "she should not divorce him" (*mē aphietō ton andra*). Here it is clear that Paul is envisaging the Hellenistic world, in which it was otherwise possible for the woman to divorce her husband. However, it should be noted that vv. 10c and 11a could just as easily be translated thus: "that the wife should not be separated (*or* divorced) from her husband—but if she is separated (*or* divorced). . . ." With such an understanding of the verses, the charge would reflect the Palestinian Jewish situation in which only the husband was normally permitted to institute divorce.

The *RSV* has also set vv. 11a–b between dashes. This probably reflects the opinion of some commentators, such as H. Baltensweiler,[8] who regard these clauses as a Pauline insert into the charge of the Lord, which is thus only to be identified with vv. 10c and 11c. Paul's insert would be an explication of the charge about divorce itself in terms of subsequent marriage with another person. Since, as we shall see below, other forms of the prohibition do refer to subsequent marriage as well as to divorce, I prefer to regard v. 11a–b as a reflection of what was in the original saying, although the present formulation may indeed be Pauline.

As H. Conzelmann has put it, "the regulation is absolute."[9] Neither husband nor wife is to be divorced from the other; if the woman should be divorced, she should remain *agamos*, "unmarried," or be reconciled. As D. L. Dungan has stated, "It is clear that one of the things this word of the Lord means to Paul is that *it forbids additional marriages after divorce.*"[10] But he also interprets Paul's words in the passage to mean that Paul *"permits the divorce if it has taken place."*[11] He finds that *"Paul's application is in flat contradiction to the command of the Lord, which is a strict prohibition of divorce."*[12] One wonders, however, whether this is really a Pauline "permission" or a mere concession to a factual situation, perhaps reported to him from the Corinthian community. In any case, Paul's attitude in v. 10 is unqualified and envisages no further marriage for the woman after the divorce. It stands in contrast to what he sets forth—he himself, not the Lord[13]—in vv. 12–15 about the believing woman who is "not bound" (*ou dedoulōtai*) if an unbelieving husband separates from her.

(2) Luke 16:18. An equally absolute prohibition of divorce is found in an isolated dominical saying of Jesus in Luke 16:18. A slightly modified form of it stands the best chance of being regarded as the most primitive form of the sayings about divorce in the New Testament. In its present form it runs as follows:

[18a]*Pas ho apolyōn tēn gynaika autou* [18b]*kai gamōn heteran moicheuei,* [18c]*kai ho apolelymenēn apo andros gamōn moicheuei.*

[18a]Everyone who divorces his wife [18b]and marries another commits adultery, [18c]and he who marries a woman divorced from her husband commits adultery (*RSV*).

This form of the dominical saying is a declaratory legal statement which is reminiscent of Old Testament casuistic law.[14] It is related to the saying preserved in Matt 5:32 (minus the exceptive phrase) and is derived from the common source "Q."[15] In its present Lucan form the saying is not only a prohibition of divorce but a judgment about a husband's marriage after the divorce relating both to adultery, proscribed by Old Testament legislation (in the Decalogue, Exod 20:14; Deut 5:18; and elsewhere, Lev 20:10; Deut 22:22; cf. Luke 18:20 and John 7:53–8:11 [the latter implies that Deut 22:22 was still regarded as in force]). The Lucan form of the saying differs from the Pauline in that the subsequent marriage mentioned is that of the man, whereas in 1 Corinthians 7 it is the woman's subsequent marriage.

The phrase in Luke 16:18b, *kai gamōn heteran,* "and marrying another," has been regarded as an addition made by Luke to what is otherwise the original form of the saying.[16] Since, however, that phrase is present in other forms of the prohibition, whether it be the Pauline form or the Synoptic forms (Mark 10:11; Matt 19:9), it is almost certainly part of the original prohibition.[17]

The phrase in Luke 16:18c, *apo andros,* is missing in Codex Bezae; this variant is in itself insignificant, but its omission may represent the more original form of the saying.[18]

Indeed, the whole third part of the saying (18c) may be only an extension of the first part (18a–b). It was probably found in the "Q" source, since it is also present in Matt 5:32b.[19] But whether it actually formed part of the original prohibition may be debated, since it is not hinted at in Paul or Mark.

When all is said and done, the chances are that the most primitive form of the logion is preserved here in Luke 16:18a–b, possibly with 18c (but without *apo andros*): "Everyone who divorces his wife and marries another commits adultery (and he who marries a divorced woman commits adultery)."

What should be noted here is that the prohibition is cast completely from the Old Testament or Jewish point of view, commenting on the action of the husband who would divorce his wife and marry again (or who would marry a divorced woman). Underlying it are the notions of the wife as the chattel of the husband, implied in such passages as Exod 20:17; 21:3, 22; Jer 6:12; Num 30:10–14; Esth 1:20–22; and above all in Sir 23:22–27; and of the Old Testament allowance of divorce to the husband (Deut 24:1–4). What is new is the branding of the man's action as adulterous. Though Paul's form of the prohibition is the earliest preserved, it represents a certain development beyond what seems to be the more primitive form of the prohibition preserved here in Luke.

(3) Matt 5:31–32. The isolated dominical saying about divorce in "Q" has become part of the Sermon on the Mount in the Matthean Gospel, functioning as one of the six antitheses in 5:21–48, where Jesus is depicted reacting to the righteousness of the scribes.[20] Though some commentators have at times tried to relate Matt 5:31–32 to Mark 10:11,[21] it is almost certainly a separate tradition that is reflected here and in Luke 16:18. Both Matt 5:32 and Luke 16:18 have the *pas ho apolyōn* form, whereas Mark 10:11 has *hos an apolysē* (as does Matt 19:9). The text of Matt 5:31–32 reads:

[31a]*Errethē de* [31b]*hos an apolysē tēn gynaika autou, dotō autē apostasion.* [32a]*egō de legō hymin hoti* [32b]*pas ho apolyōn tēn gynaika autou parektos logou porneias poiei autēn moicheuthēnai,* [32c]*kai hos ean apolelymenēn gamēsē, moichatai.*

[31a]It was also said, [31b]"Whoever divorces his wife, let him give her a certificate of divorce." [32a]But I say to you that [32b]every one who divorces his wife, except on the ground of unchastity, makes her an adulteress; [32c]and whoever marries a divorced woman commits adultery (*RSV*).

Whereas v. 31a forms Matthew's stereotyped introduction to the saying, marked with his characteristic *errethē de*, a shortened form of similar earlier formulas (vv. 21a, 27a) or of those that follow (vv. 33a, 38a, 43a), v. 31b (*hos an apolysē tēn gynaika autou, dotō autē apostasion*, "whoever divorces his wife, let him give her a certificate of divorce") purports to quote Deut 24:1 in part, but it is not a verbatim quotation of the so-called LXX.[22] The sense of the quotation, however, is clear and provides the basis of the antithesis. The Matthean form of the prohibition of divorce recorded here differs from Luke 16:18, not only because of the added exceptive phrase *parektos logou porneias*, but in two other ways: (*a*) it lacks the second phrase, Luke 16:18b, *kai gamōn heteran;* and (*b*) it relates divorce itself, and not divorce and subsequent marriage, to adultery. Whereas the Lucan form of the saying also expresses a judgment about the husband's subsequent marriage, the Matthean form regards divorce itself as the cause of adultery (*poiei autēn moicheuthēnai*, lit., "makes her to be adultered"). This is, I suspect, a Matthean reformulation of the original "Q" saying, which is found in a more primitive form in Luke 16:18a–b. One reason for regarding the Matthean form as a reformulation is the immediate context in the Sermon on the Mount, where in v. 27 Jesus' antithesis equates even the lustful look of a man at a woman with adultery, an antithesis that lacks a parallel in either Mark or Luke. Hence it is most likely Matthew who relates divorce itself to adultery.[23] Once again, the prohibition is stated from the viewpoint of the man, as in the Lucan form of the saying.

(4) Mark 10:2–12. This passage dealing with divorce is composite. The first part (vv. 2–9) is a pronouncement-story or *Streitgespräch*, which, having quoted Gen 1:27 and 2:24, ends with the apophthegm "What therefore God has joined together, let not man put asunder." It is addressed to Pharisees who have asked him whether "it is lawful for man to divorce his wife" (v. 2). But joined to this pronouncement-story is a dominical saying, addressed to disciples later on in a house (vv. 10–12), a saying that echoes the judgmental form of "Q." This brings it about that there are here in Mark 10 two sayings of Jesus about divorce. They run as follows:

[9]*ho oun ho Theos synezeuxen, anthrōpos mē chōrizetō.*

[9]What therefore God has joined together, let not man put asunder.

[11a]*kai legei autois.* [11b]*hos an apolysē tēn gynaika autou* [11c]*kai gamēsē allēn* [11d]*moichatai ep' autēn.* [12a]*kai ean autē apolysasa ton andra autēs allon,* [12b]*moichatai.*

[11a]And he said to them, [11b]"Whoever divorces his wife [11c]and marries another, [11d]commits adultery against her; [12a]and if she divorces her husband and marries another, [12b]she commits adultery."

In the pronouncement recorded in v. 9 the third person negative imperative is used and it formulates absolutely Jesus' prohibition of divorce itself. It involves God himself in the matter and has sometimes been said to echo a view of marriage that is otherwise found in Tob 6:18 (LXX[BA]:"she was destined for you from eternity"). It is a pronouncement that is not based on Deut 24:1, about which the Pharisees had inquired, but rather on Gen 1:27 and 2:24.[24]

The dominical saying of vv. 11–12 is again a declaratory legal statement similar to and related to the "Q" saying of Luke 16:18 and Matt 5:32. As in the "Q" statement, it expresses a judgment about divorce and subsequent marriage, which are viewed from the man's standpoint and regarded as adulterous.

Three things, however, are to be noted about the saying. (*a*) The reading of v. 12a given above is that of Sinaiticus and Vaticanus (preferred by Nestle-Aland, 26th ed.). But there are two other forms of the verse that are attested.[25] (*b*) V. 11d as given above includes the words *ep' autēn;* it thus specifies that the divorce and subsequent marriage are an act of adultery "against her." This would seem extraordinary from the Jewish point of view. Indeed, this is probably the reason why it is omitted in some MSS.[26] The phrase *ep' autēn* is almost certainly a Marcan addition made in the light of what is to be said in v. 12. It is an explicative addition, which makes Jesus' words express the fact that adultery against a woman is something now to be considered.[27] (*c*) V. 12 is a further Marcan extension of the first logion, introduced to suit the contingencies of Gentile Christian communities in areas where Roman and Greek law prevailed and where a woman was permitted to divorce her husband.[28] The evangelist Mark has thus extended the logion to a new situation, whereas it was originally formulated in terms of the usual Old Testament understanding of the marriage bond, in which only the man—as *ba'al*—was able to divorce his wife, although we know that divorce was envisaged as a possibility at least for Jewish women living in the military colony at Elephantine in Egypt in the fifth century B.C. A number of Aramaic marriage contracts from that place mention it explicitly.[29] But the evidence for such a practice in Palestine itself is meager indeed, almost nonexistent.[30]

Hence the composite Marcan form of the divorce pericope contains two forms of the prohibition of divorce attributed to Jesus, both of them unqualified. There is one aspect of the pericope—the intelligibility of the Pharisees' question—which will be discussed below.

(5) Matt 19:3–9. Closely related to Mark 10:2–12 is the similar pericope of Matt 19:3–9.[31] In fact, Matthew has derived it from his "Marcan" source, but he has modified it to make it better suit his Jewish-Christian concerns. First of all, he has cast the controversy (*Streitgespräch*) in terms of the Hillel-Shammai dispute, by making the Pharisees ask whether it is lawful to divorce one's wife "for any cause" (*kata pasan aitian*). Second, he has built the dominical saying (of Mark 10:11–12, without the phrase *ep' autēn*, which was unsuited to his concerns) into the controversy itself (19:9), introducing it by the vv. 7–8. Like Mark, he too has thus preserved for us two forms of the saying about divorce:

[6]*ho oun ho Theos synezeuxen, anthrōpos mē chōrizeto.*

[6]What therefore God has joined together, let not man put asunder.

[9a]*legō de hymin hoti* [9b]*hos an apolysē tēn gynaika autou mē epi porneia* [9c]*kai gamēsē allēn,* [9d]*moichatai.*

[9a]And I say to you: [9b]Whoever divorces his wife except for unchastity, [9c]and marries another, [9d]commits adultery (*RSV*).

Aside from the exceptive phrase, to which I shall return, the first saying (v. 6) repeats the absolute prohibition of divorce that is found in Mark, and the second takes over only that which would suit Matthew's Jewish-Christian concerns.

The real problem with this interpretation of Matt 19:3–9 is that it presupposes the Two-Source Theory of Synoptic relationships, at least a modified form of it.[32] Some commentators, who admit such a solution to the Synoptic Problem in general, think at times that the episode preserved here is more primitive than its counterpart in Mark 10 and that the evangelist was here dependent on a tradition independent of Mark and actually more primitive than the Marcan source (e.g., "M").[33] Still others point to this passage in particular as one of the best reasons for abandoning the Two-Source Theory entirely.[34] Part of the reason for such views is the composite character of Mark 10:2–9 and 10:11–12, already mentioned, which is regarded as secondary. Part of it is the double audience or double setting in the Marcan form (an answer to the Pharisees, v. 2, followed by an answer to the disciples, v. 10). Moreover, the question posed in Matthew 19, "Is it lawful to divorce one's wife *for any reason?*" is regarded as more primitive, because it seems to reflect a dispute between the schools of Hillel and Shammai and would thus have a more plausible matrix in a well-known Palestinian Jewish setting.[35] But the question as posed in Mark 10:2 is said to be incomprehensible in such a setting, because divorce was in fact permitted in Palestinian Judaism. The new material that I should like to consider in part II bears directly on this problem; my further comments on the problem will be presented in part III. At the moment I only wish to say that this form of the Matthean prohibition of divorce (minus the exceptive phrase) has to be regarded as derived from Mark 10 and adapted by Matthew for the sake of Christians living in the mixed community for which he was principally writing.[36]

(6) Matthean Exceptive Phrases. The major problem in the Gospel divorce texts is the Matthean exceptive phrases. On the one hand, the judgmental saying in Matt 5:32 relates *divorce* itself to adultery (and not simply divorce with remarriage, as in Mark 10:11, Matt 19:9, Luke 16:18) and levels its accusation against the man.[37] On the other hand, the prohibition of divorce is accompanied by an exceptive phrase in both Matthean passages: *parektos logou porneias,* "except in the matter of *porneia*" (5:32), and *mē epi porneiā,* "except for *porneia*" (19:9).[38] Though the phrases differ in their formulation, they both have to be understood as expressing an exception.[39]

Three aspects of the problem which these exceptive phrases create have to be distinguished. (*a*) Are they possibly part of the authentic logion? Attempts have been made to maintain that the Matthean exceptive phrases go back to Jesus himself, or at least that they are part of the primitive form of the prohibition.[40] However, few critical commentators would go along with such a solution today. There are two main reasons for the reluctance: (i) the greater difficulty in explaining how the more absolute forms of the prohibition in Paul, Mark, and Luke would then have arisen (especially difficult in 1 Cor 7:10: to think that Paul would so record the absolute, unqualified form of the prohibition as a saying of the *Kyrios* in a context in which he himself makes an exception);[41] (ii) the tendency otherwise attested in Matthew of adding things to the sayings of Jesus (e.g., two extra petitions in the Our Father [6:10b, 13b; cf. Luke 11:2–4]; additions to the Beatitudes [5:3a, 6a; cf. Luke 6:20b–21]; Peter's secondary confession [16:16b–19; cf. Mark 8:29]; Matt 13:12b [cf. Mark 4:25, Luke 8:18]; Matt 25:29 [cf. Luke 14:26]).[42] These two considerations make it almost certain that the exceptive phrases stem from the pen of the evangelist, faced with a problem to resolve in the community for which he was writing.[43]

(b) What is meant by *porneia?* Elsewhere in Matthew the word occurs only in 15:19, where it is listed among other evil machinations of the human mind, "murder, adultery, fornication" (*RSV*), lined up side-by-side with *moicheia*, "adultery," and obviously distinct from it. Etymologically, it means "prostitution, harlotry, whoredom," being an abstract noun related to *pornē*, "harlot," and to the verb *porneuein*, "to act as a harlot." Generally speaking, it means "fornication," but, as Bauer-Arndt-Gingrich note, it is actually used "of every kind of unlawful sexual intercourse."[44] Though it is differentiated from *moicheia* in Matt 15:19; Mark 7:21–22; 1 Cor 6:9; Heb 13:4, it is used of a variety of sexual activity: 1 Cor 5:1 (incest), 6:13 (prostitution), 2 Cor 12:21 (parallel to *akatharsia* and *aselgeia*); see further Col 3:5 and Eph 5:3.[45] In Acts 15:20, 29 (cf. 21:25) *porneia* is used, however, in a specific sense, since it is lined up with several dietary tabus,[46] which early Gentile Christians, living in close contact with Jewish Christians (i.e., in predominantly Jewish-Christian communities), were being asked to avoid: "what has been sacrificed to idols, blood, and what is strangled." The letter of James to the local churches of Antioch, Syria, and Cilicia forbids, in fact, four of the things proscribed by the Holiness Code of Leviticus 17–18, not only for "any man of the house of Israel" but also for "the strangers that sojourn among them" (*ûmin haggēr 'ăšer yāgûr bĕtôkām*, 17:8). These were the meat offered to idols (Lev 17:8–9), the eating of blood (Lev 17:10–12), the eating of strangled, i.e., not properly butchered, animals (Lev 17:15; cf. Exod 22:31), and intercourse with close kin (Lev 18:6–18).[47]

Now which of these various meanings of *porneia* can be intended in the Matthean exceptive phrases? For many commentators, *porneia* is simply understood as "adultery."[48] This interpretation is open to the obvious objection that if Matthew had meant that, he would have written *moicheia*, a word that he otherwise knows and uses. It has also been pointed out on several occasions that Matthew keeps *moicheia* and *porneia* distinct (15:19).[49] There is the further difficulty that Matthew is speaking about something that he in effect equates with adultery; so he seems to mean something different from adultery.[50] By another group of commentators the word is understood in the generic sense of prostitution or harlotry, as it seems to be used in most of the Pauline passages quoted above. This meaning, while not impossible, would be imposing on the word a predominantly Pauline and Hellenistic meaning in a passage which may have more Palestinian and Jewish concerns.[51] A third group of interpreters prefers to use the specific meaning of *porneia* that is used in Acts 15:20, 29,[52] understanding it to mean illicit marital unions within the degrees of kinship proscribed by Lev 18:6–18. This is preferred because of the Jewish-Christian problem envisaged in Acts 15 and the concerns of the Matthean Gospel itself. Of these three main positions[53] I think that the last-mentioned is the one to be preferred, since there is now further evidence from Qumran literature to support it. This will be seen in Part II.

(*c*) Why would Matthew add the exceptive phrases? We have already implied the answer to this third aspect of the problem: because he was seeking to resolve a casuistic problem in early Jewish-Christian communities. The *destinataires* of the Matthean Gospel were a mixed community, predominantly Jewish-Christian, and one of its purposes was precisely to explain to them the sense of the Christian message and why it was that the Gentile Christians were taking over the kingdom preached in it.[54] But another aspect of the exceptive phrases was undoubtedly to handle the situation of Gentiles who were coming into it and already found themselves in the marital condition proscribed for Jews by Lev 18:6–18. Just as the letter of James enjoined certain matters on the Gentile Christians of the local churches of Antioch, Syria, and Cilicia, so Matthew's exceptive phrases solve a problem for Gentile Christians living in the same community with Jewish Christians, who were still observing Mosaic regulations.

(7) Greek Words for Divorce in the New Testament. The last preliminary remark has to do with the Greek words for "divorce" which are used in the various New Testament passages dealing with it. The diversity of vocabulary for it is surprising, and attempts to solve some of the foregoing problems have often involved strained explanations of the vocabulary itself. Hence a need to clarify certain matters.

Paul uses the verb *chōrizein* (1 Cor 7:10) of the woman. It is often used of divorce in the strict sense in Greek writers of the classical and Hellenistic periods (e.g., Isaeus 8.36; Euripides, *Frg.* 1063.13; Polybius, *Hist.* 31.26,6), as well as in Greek marriage contracts.[55] But it is unattested in the Greek of the so-called LXX. Yet it does turn up precisely in the apophthegm (or pronouncement) of Mark 10:9 and Matt 19:6: "let not man put asunder" (*mē chōrizetō*). It is true that in the middle-passive *chōrizein* does occasionally mean "depart," but this can hardly be taken as the basis of translating *mē chōristhēnai* as "let her not desert."[56] I have already discussed the problem of the aorist passive infinitive above, but what is stressed here is that the verb should properly be translated "be divorced."

Of the man, Paul uses the expression *gynaika mē aphienai* (7:11), "should not divorce his wife" (*RSV*). Again, this verb *aphienai* is used for "divorce" in Greek writers of the classical and Hellenistic periods (e.g., Herodotus, *Hist.* 5.39; Euripides, *Andromache* 973; Plutarch, *Pomp.* 44), but it apparently has not turned up in the papyri and is unattested in the LXX.[57]

In the dominical saying preserved in the Synoptics the verb is always *apolyein* (Mark 10:11–12; Luke 16:18; Matt 5:32; 19:9). It is, moreover, the same verb that Matthew uses in the infancy narrative to express Joseph's first decision about Mary (1:19, "to divorce her" because of suspected unchastity during the engagement—cf. Deut 22:20–21). With the meaning of "divorce," *apolyein* is found in Hellenistic writers such as Dionysius of Halicarnassus (*Rom. Ant.* 2.25,7) and Diodorus Siculus (*Libr. hist.* 12.18,1–2). Bauer-Arndt-Gingrich say of it: "This [use] is in accord not w. Jewish . . . , but w. Greco-Roman custom,"[58] even though they cite an instance of the sense used by Josephus (*Ant.* 15.7,10 §259).[59] Indeed, an attempt has been made to interpret the first part of the Lucan form of the dominical saying as if *apolyein* did not really mean "divorce" at all, because it lacks the pronouncement-story details of Mark and Matthew. In this view, it would mean rather "leave" and be understood in the light of Jesus' other sayings about discipleship which entail the "hating" of wife and children (14:26) or the "leaving" of house or wife (18:29). Thus Luke 16:18 would mean nothing more than "He who would [for the sake of being Jesus' disciple] leave his wife [without divorcing her] and marries another commits adultery." It is then maintained that this sense of the logion was lost in time and that it was subsequently interpreted as a saying against divorce itself.[60] Aside from the far-fetched nature of this explanation of Luke 16:18a, the word *apolyein* has now turned up in the clear sense of "divorce" in a Greek document of remarriage from Palestine. It occurs in a text from Murabbaᶜat Cave 2 from the Bar Cocheba period and should put to rest any hesitation about whether the Greek verb *apolyein* could have meant "divorce" in the Greek of Palestine in the period in question. The document attests the remarriage of the same two persons, who had been divorced, and it is dated to A.D. 124. The crucial lines read (Mur 115:3–4): *Ep<ei> pro tou synebē tō autō Elaiō Simōnos appallagēnai kai apolyein Salōmēn Iōanou Galgoula,* "since it happened earlier to the same Elaios (son) of Simon to become estranged and to divorce Salome (daughter) of John Galgoula. . . ."[61] The two verbs, *appallagēnai kai* *apolyein,* are probably an attempt to render into Greek the two Aramaic verbs customarily used in Jewish writs of divorce; these are attested in another Murabbaʿat document (Mur 19:2–4, dated A.D. 111): *šābeq wamĕtārek min rĕʿūtī yômāʾ dĕnāh ʾānāh Yĕhôsep bar Naqsan . . . lĕkī ʾintî Miryam bĕrat Yĕhônātān,* "I, Joseph son of Naqsan, repudiate and divorce you, my wife, Miriam, daughter of Jonathan."[62] The significance of this use of *apolyein,* then, should not be missed, since Moulton and Milligan were unable to give any instances of its use in the sense of "divorce" in the Greek papyri on which they based their famous study of New Testament Greek vocabulary.[63] Finally, it should be noted that whereas Mark 10:4, Matt 5:32, and Matt 19:7 quote Deut 24:1, as if the Greek translation of the latter had the verb *apolyein,* it is not found in our present-day Greek texts of Deuteronomy, which rather have *exapostelei,* "he shall send (her) away," translating exactly the Hebrew *wĕšillĕhāh.*[64]

Now, against the background of these preliminary remarks, we may turn to the material from the Qumran scrolls and related texts which shed some first-century Palestinian light on the New Testament divorce texts and on those of Matthew in particular.

II. *The Qumran Material*

The usual impression that one gets from commentaries and discussions of the New Testament divorce texts is that Jesus was making a radical break with the Palestinian tradition before him, and this is used in a variety of ways to bear on various details mentioned in the preliminary remarks. I shall cite only one modern author who has formulated such an impression:

> . . . Jesus' absolute prohibition of divorce is something quite new in relation to the view of marriage which prevailed in contemporary Judaism. Neither in the O.T., the rabbinic literature nor the Qumran documents do we find any condemnation of divorce as such. Thus Jesus was not influenced in his view of divorce by any Jewish group.[65]

So writes a modern author. His impression may seem to be confirmed by an ancient writer too; for in presenting a summary of Mosaic legislation, Josephus interprets Deut 24:1–4 (*Ant.* 4.8,23 §253) and openly acknowledges that a man "who desires to be divorced (*diazeuch-thēnai*) from the wife who is living with him for whatsoever cause (*kath' hasdēpotoun aitias*)—and with mortals many such may arise—must certify in writing that he will have no further intercourse with her." Again, in telling the story of the divorce initiated by Salome, the sister of Herod the Great, in separating from Costobarus, whom Herod had appointed governor of Idumea, he stressed that she sent him a writ dissolving their marriage (*apolyomenē ton gamon*), "which was not in accordance with Jewish law (*ou kata tous Ioudaiōn nomous*), for it is (only) the man who is permitted by us to do this" (*Ant.* 15.7,10 §259).[66] Here Josephus clearly admits the possibility of divorce in accordance "with the laws of the Jews," although his main concern was the question of a Jewish woman's right to divorce her husband.[67]

Over against this rather widespread impression one has to consider two Qumran texts which bear on the topic. One was only recently made known, and the interpretation of it is not difficult; the other has been known for a long time and is difficult to interpret, but the light that is now shed on it by the more recently published text tips the scales toward one particular interpretation often proposed in the past.

The first text is found in the Temple Scroll from Qumran Cave 11, a lengthy Hebrew document—longer than the scroll of the complete Book of Isaiah from Qumran Cave 1 (1QIsa[a])—which was discovered by Ta'amireh Bedouin in 1956. It is believed to have been in the possession of Kando, the quondam Syrian cobbler of Bethlehem, who had been the go-between for the sale of the original seven scrolls of Qumran Cave 1, from 1956 until the time of the Six-Day War (1967), when Israel occupied the west bank of the Jordan and gained control of the Old City of Jerusalem. In some mysterious, as yet not wholly revealed, way the Temple Scroll came into the possession of the Department of Antiquities in Israel and was entrusted to Y. Yadin for publication. The full text of the scroll, dating to the end of the second century B.C., has now been published; but Yadin had released a preliminary report on it[68] and had published a few lines of it which bear on texts in the Qumran corpus that are well known and controverted.[69] He had also revealed that the Temple Scroll deals in general with four topics: (1) halakic regulations about ritual cleanness, derived from the Pentateuch, but presented with many additions, deletions, and variations; (2) a list of sacrifices and offerings to be made according to different feasts; (3) details for the building of the Jerusalem temple—the longest part, occupying more than half of the 28-foot scroll, from which the name of it has accordingly been derived; and (4) statutes for the king and the army.[70] God is depicted in the scroll speaking in the first person singular and issuing decrees, and Yadin concluded that the author of the text wanted his readers to consider it virtually as Torah. The fourth section of the scroll, setting forth the statutes, begins with a direct quotation of Deut 17:14–17, the passage which instructs Israel to set up as king over it one "whom the Lord your God will choose, one from among your brethren" and which ends with the prohibition, "He shall not multiply wives for himself lest his heart turn away; nor shall he greatly multiply for himself silver and gold" (17:17, *RSV*).

Now among the statutes for the king is the prohibition both of polygamy and of divorce. The text (11QTemple 57:17–19) reads as follows:

> [17]*wlw² yqḥ ʿlyh ²šh ²ḥrt ky* [18]*hy²h lbdh thyh ʿmw kwl ymy ḥyyh w²m mth wnś²* [19]*lw ²ḥrt mbyt ²byhw mmšpḥtw.*

> And he shall not take in addition to her another wife, for she alone shall be with him all the days of her life; and if she dies, he shall take for himself another (wife) from his father's house, from his clan.[71]

The first regulation clearly precludes polygamy (probably echoing Deut 17:17), but the reason that is further added makes it clear that the king is not to divorce his wife, "for she alone (*lĕbaddāh*) shall be with him *all* the days of her life." Thus the Temple Scroll goes beyond Deut 17:17, which forbids polygamy, and proscribes divorce as well. It may be objected that this is a regulation for the "king" (*melek* of Deut 17:14) and that it does not envisage the commoner. But the principle behind such legislation is—to paraphrase an ancient dictum—*quod non licet Iovi, non licet bovi;* and it has been invoked apropos of other texts by other writers.[72] Moreover, as we shall see below, what was legislated for the king in Deut 17:17 is explicitly applied by extension to a non-regal authority-figure in the Qumran community. Again, if Yadin's opinion cited above about the intention of the author of the Temple Scroll, that he wanted it to be regarded virtually as Torah, is valid, then the regulations in it were undoubtedly to be normative for all for whom it was a virtual Torah.

Here, then, we find a clear prohibition of divorce in a first-century Palestinian Jewish text. True, it may reflect the ideas of the sectarian Jews who formed the Qumran community, normally regarded as Essenes.[73] It may also be a view that was in open opposition to what is usually regarded as the Pharisaic understanding of the matter. To this I shall return later.

Another text which bears on the same topic is the much-debated passage in the *Damascus Document* (CD 4:12b—5:14a). It has been known for a long time, having first come to light among the fragments which S. Schechter recovered from the Genizah of the Ezra Synagogue of Old Cairo in 1896 and which he published in 1910.[74] It has at times been used in the discussion of the NT divorce texts[75] and has been considered of little help. But now, because of the above-cited passage of the Temple Scroll, it needs to be discussed anew.

Fragments of the *Damascus Document,* as it is commonly called today because of the regulations that it contains for community camps in "Damascus," have been found in various Qumran caves; some of these have been published, but the vast majority of them (from Qumran Cave 4) still await publication. Some of these fragments make it clear that earlier forms of the *Damascus Document* existed and that it has a considerable literary and compilatory history. The form to which we are accustomed, in MSS of the tenth and twelfth centuries A.D., is obviously a composite document. Fragments of cols. 4 and 5 are preserved in the Qumran Cave 4 material, but unfortunately none of them contains the lines in which the controverted text from the Cairo Genizah is found. This is merely the result of the poor state of preservation of the Cave 4 fragments, and there is no reason to think that cols. 4 and 5 read any differently in the Qumran texts than they do in the copy from the Cairo Genizah.[76]

The text of the *Damascus Document* in which we are interested forms part of a section (CD 2:14—6:1) that has been labeled by J. Murphy-O'Connor as an Essene missionary document.[77] This section seems to have existed independently at one time, before it became part of the conflated text that we know today. It is an admonition or exhortation addressed to Palestinian Jews who were not members of the Essene community.[78] It seeks to explain God's attitude toward mankind as revealed in history, to extol the role of the privileged remnant to which the writer belonged (the community of the New Covenant [cf. Jer 31:31; CD 6:19]), and to hold out both a promise and a threat to Jews to consider joining the community. The warning is part of the immediately preceding context of the passage in which we are interested. In this passage the author looks at the current orthodoxy in Palestinian Judaism and levels against it a harsh indictment. It is ensnared in various traps of Belial. The part of the "missionary document" in which we are interested (CD 4:12b—5:14a) runs as follows:

And in all those years [13]Belial will be unleashed against Israel; as God said through the prophet Isaiah, son of [14]Amoz, *"Terror and pit and snare are upon you, O inhabitant*   Isa 24:17 *of the Land."* The interpretation of it: (These are) [15]the three nets of Belial about which Levi, son of Jacob, spoke, [16]in which he (Belial) has ensnared Israel. He set them ⟨be⟩fore them as three kinds of [17]"righteousness": the first is unchastity; the second, wealth; the third, [18]defilement of the sanctuary. Whoever rises out of one gets caught in another; whoever is delivered from one gets caught [19]in another.

The builders of the wall, who have *gone after Vanity*—(now) "Vanity" is a preacher, [20]of whom He said, *"They only preach"*— have been caught in unchastity in two ways: by taking [21]two wives in their lifetime, whereas the principle of creation (is) *"Male and female he created them;* [5:1]and those who entered (Noah's) ark, *"two (by) two went into the ark."* And concerning the prince (it is) written: [2]*"He shall not multiply wives for himself."*	Ezek 13:10; Hos 5:11; Mich 2:6
	Gen 1:27
	Gen 7:9
	Deut 17:17

Now David did not read the sealed book of the Law, which was [3]in the ark (of the covenant); for it was not opened in Israel since the day when Eleazar, [4]Yehoshua', Joshua, and the elders died, when they (i.e., the Israelites) began to serve Ashtoreth. It remained hidden ⟨and⟩ was ⟨not⟩ [5]revealed, until Zadok arose. And the deeds of David mounted up (like a holocaust to God), with the exception of the blood of Uriah; [6]and God left them to him (for merit).

Moreover, they defile the sanctuary, since they do not keep [7]separate according to the Law, but lie with her who sees *the blood of her flux.*

And they take (as wives), [8]each one (of them), the daughter of his brother and the daughter of his sister, whereas Moses said, *"You shall not* [9]*approach* (sexually) *your* mother's sister; she is your mother's kin."* The regulation for incest [10]is written for males, but it applies equally to women; so if a brother's daughter uncovers the nakedness of [11]her father's brother, whereas she is his kin. . . .[79]

Lev 15:19
Lev 18:15

Of the three nets of Belial in which Israel is said to be ensnared, only two are explained: "unchastity" (*hazzĕnût*) and "defilement of the sanctuary" (*ṭammē³ hammiqdāš*); the net of "wealth" (*hahôn*), is completely passed over, although it seems to be an allusion to Deut 17:17b. Moreover, two instances of *zĕnût* are given: (*a*) "by taking two wives in their lifetime" (4:20–21—the controverted clause, to which I shall return); and (*b*) "and they take (as wives), each one (of them), the daughter of his brother, and the daughter of his sister" (5:7–8). These two instances explain the word *bštym*, "in two ways," of 4:20. C. Rabin was apparently the first commentator to notice the relevance of this word and the relation that it has to the rest of the text.[80] In more recent times he has been followed by others in what is almost certainly the correct understanding of the text.[81]

The explanations of the two nets are accompanied by Old Testament passages which cite the prohibitions of the conduct characteristic of the current orthodoxy in Israel which has disregarded them. The "defilement of the sanctuary" is explained by the failure to avoid intercourse with the woman considered unclean in Lev 15:19. The two forms of "unchastity" are likewise illustrated by Old Testament passages: (a) "the taking of two wives in their lifetime" is seen to be contravening Gen 1:27, 7:9, and Deut 17:17—but note that this is now extended from the "king" of Deut 17:14 to the "prince" (*nāśîʾ*, i.e., *něśî kol hāʿēdāh*, "the prince of the whole congregation" [CD 7:20][82]); (b) the taking as wives "the daughter of his brother, and the daughter of his sister" is seen to be a contravention of Lev 18:13, which prohibits marriage within certain degrees of kinship.

Now two things above all are to be noted in this text. First, the controverted meaning of the first form of *zěnût:* "taking two wives in their lifetime" (*laqaḥat šětê nāšîm běḥayyêhem*). The text is controverted because the pronominal suffix -*hem* on the word for "lifetime" is masculine, and ever since Schechter first published the text of the *Damascus Document* the meaning of the clause has been debated. Three main interpretations of it have been proposed:[83] (a) It proscribes both polygamy and marriage after divorce. (b) It proscribes polygamy alone. (c) It proscribes any second marriage. The first is the majority opinion;[84] the second has been ably argued by G. Vermes in a recent article;[85] and the third has been defended by J. Murphy-O'Connor.[86] It was to offset the third interpretation that Yadin published in preliminary form the few lines of the Temple Scroll that I have cited above. The last line of it makes it perfectly clear that "if she dies, he shall take for himself another (wife)." Consequently, a second marriage after the death of the first wife was not forbidden; hence a prohibition of this should not be read into CD 4:21.[87] But the writers who defend the second interpretation usually point out that the suffix on "lifetime" should be feminine if divorce were being proscribed (i.e., "in their [feminine] lifetime"); the same argument, however, has been used against the interpretation that it refers merely to polygamy. But now that 11QTemple 57:17–19 speaks out not only against polygamy but also against divorce, the most natural interpretation of CD 4:20–21 is that the masculine pronominal suffix is used to refer to both the man and the woman who are joined in marriage. This is the normal way that one would express such a reference in Hebrew to the two sexes.[88] Hence the first form of *zěnût* should be understood here as an ensnarement in either polygamy or divorce—"by taking two wives in their lifetime," i.e., while both the man and the women are alive, or by simultaneous or successive polygamy. The text from the Temple Scroll is thus seen to support the first (or majority) interpretation of CD 4:19–21.

Second, the controversy that has surrounded the interpretation of the first form of *zĕnût* has normally obscured the recognition that in this text we have a clear reference to marriage within degrees of kinship proscribed by Lev 18:13, labeled indeed precisely as *zĕnût*. In the Old Testament *zĕnût* is used both of harlotry (e.g., Jer 3:2, 9; Ezek 23:27) and of idolatrous infidelity (Num 14:33). In the LXX it is translated by *porneia* (e.g., Jer 3:2, 9). Whatever one might want to say about the nuances of the word *zĕnût* in the Old Testament, it is clear that among the Jews who produced the *Damascus Document* the word had taken on further specific nuances, so that polygamy, divorce, and marriage within forbidden degrees of kinship could be referred to as forms of *zĕnût*. Thus, in CD 4:20 and 5:8–11 we have "missing-link" evidence for a specific understanding of *zĕnût* as a term for marriage within forbidden degrees of kinship or for incestuous marriage; this is a specific understanding that is found among Palestinian Jews of the first century B.C. and A.D.

III. Consequences for the Marcan and Matthean Passages

Now if the interpretation of these two Qumran passages just discussed is correct, two further important conclusions may be drawn from them.

First, there is clear first-century Palestinian support for an interpretation of *porneia* in Matt 5:32 and 19:9 in the specific sense of *zĕnût* as an illicit marital union between persons of close kinship. Matthew, therefore, would be making an exception for such marital situations for Gentile Christians who were living in a mixed community with Jewish Christians still observing Mosaic regulations. As we have already noted, this interpretation of *porneia* is not new, but the evidence that was often used in the past to support it came from rabbinic literature of a considerably later period.[89] The fact that such a meaning of *zĕnût* is also found in that literature merely strengthens the data presented here, because it would show that the understanding was not confined to the Essene type of Judaism.

Second, the prohibition of divorce by the Qumran community would show that there were at least some Jews in first-century Palestine who did proscribe it. Several writers have pointed out that at least some Qaraites of later centuries prohibited divorce; and the relation of the medieval Qaraites to the Essenes of Qumran is a matter of no little interest and research.[90] Though we do not know how such an attitude toward divorce would fit in with what Josephus has called "the laws of Jews" (*Ant.* 15.7,10 §259), which permitted it, it at least seems to give the lie to what one reads in Strack-Billerbeck's *Kommentar:* "dass es in der mischnischen Periode keine Ehe im jüdischen Volk gegeben hat, die nicht kurzerhand vom Manne in völlig legaler Weise durch Aushändigung eines Scheidesbriefes hätte gelöst werden können."[91]

But if some Palestinian Jews did prohibit divorce, then the whole question of the *Sitz im Leben* for the debate of Jesus with the Pharisees must be reconsidered; for the Qumran legislation furnishes precisely the Palestinian background needed to explain how the question attributed to the Pharisees in Mark 10:2 is comprehensible. B. Vawter has said that "neither the story as Mark tells it (a question over the licitness of divorce in principle) nor the *logion* as he has formulated it [i.e., Mark 10:11–12] (envisaging the possibility of a woman's divorcing her husband) fits into the Palestinian scene presupposed in the life of Jesus and the conflict-stories of the Gospels."[92] Similarly, D. L. Dungan has stated:

> In view of the overwhelming evidence that *nothing whatever in the Law suggests that divorce is illegal* [his italics], any commentator who proposes to defend the primitive historical character of Mark's version of the Pharisees' question, that it is more original than Matthew's, has no alternative, it seems to me, but to search for ulterior and sinister motives on the part of the Pharisees for putting such an obviously phony question to Jesus. . . . The fact is, Mark's version of the question is inconceivable in a Palestinian Pharisaic milieu. This is, of course, simply another way of saying that this is not where it arose. On the other hand, if we simply transpose the whole story in Mark into the setting of the early Hellenistic Church, everything immediately fits perfectly.[93]

Now, in the light of the statute for the king in the Temple Scroll, which directly forbids polygamy (as does Deut 17:17) and goes beyond that to give a reason which at least implies the prohibition of divorce, the question put by some Pharisees to Jesus in Mark 10:2, "Is it lawful for a man to divorce his wife?" is not as "inconceivable" in a Palestinian milieu as might be supposed. Knowing about the Essene prohibition of divorce, a Pharisee could easily have posed the question to see where Jesus stood in the matter: Do you side with the Essenes or with the Pharisees? The Qumran evidence supplies at least an intelligible matrix for the question as posed in Mark, and the priority of the Marcan passage over the Matthean is not an impossible position. The form of the question as it is found in Matt 19:3 ("Is it lawful to divorce one's wife *for any cause?*") represents merely that evangelist's reformulation of the question in terms of an inner-Pharisaic dispute, between the schools of Hillel and Shammai, perhaps even reflecting a church-synagogue controversy otherwise manifest in the First Gospel.

Now if there is any validity to the interpretation of these divorce texts in the light of the Qumran material, we see that it does not support the position that the pronouncement-story and the dominical saying, as they are found in Matthew 19, represent a more primitive form than that in Mark 10. In my opinion, it merely serves to accord to the Two-Source Theory its merited place as the most plausible solution to the Synoptic Problem.[94]

IV. *Theological Implications*

There are further implications in all of this—implications for the present-day debate about divorce; for the process of gospel-composition, as we are aware of it today, reveals that the prohibition of divorce which is recorded in the New Testament writings has gone through various stages of development. On the basis of form criticism and redaction criticism it is possible to isolate two sayings about divorce that may plausibly be regarded as traceable to Jesus himself: "What therefore God has joined together, let not man put asunder" (the pronouncement, Mark 10:9, Matt 19:6) and "Everyone who divorces his wife and marries another commits adultery, and he who marries a divorced woman commits adultery" (the dominical saying, best preserved in Luke 16:18a–b). The Marcan additional material (10:12a–b), the Matthean exceptive phrases (5:32b, 19:9b), and even the Pauline formulation of the prohibition from the standpoint of the woman (1 Cor 7:10c—if *choristhēnai* really = intransitive "separate" [see above]) are seen to be developments best explained in terms of the contexts in which the prohibition was repeated.

The Matthean exceptive phrases are particularly of interest. Though they scarcely make adultery a basis for divorce between Christians, as we have argued above, the exception for an illicit union (or for a marital situation that should not have been entered into to begin with) may be said not to render the prohibition of divorce less absolute.

What is striking in the modern study of the Gospels and of the divorce passages in particular is the number of commentators who trace back to Jesus in some form or other a prohibition of divorce, and usually in an absolute form. If the sort of analysis in which I have engaged above has any validity, it leads one to the conclusion of the absolute prohibition of divorce as coming from Jesus himself. When one hears today of commentators analyzing gospel texts with the principles of form criticism or redaction criticism, one more or less expects to learn from them some more radical or even "liberating" interpretation. But in this case it has not worked that way. Judged form-critically, the New Testament divorce texts yield as the most primitive form of the prohibition one that is absolute or unqualified.

For modern Christians who are inclined to identify as normative for Christian life and faith only that which Jesus said or did, this logion on divorce would have to be understood absolutely. But a form of fundamentalism would thus be associated with it—not the usual fundamentalism of the biblical *text*, but an even more naive sort which surrounds what he might be imagined to have said or done. And that raises the further problem about "which Jesus" stands behind that norm. But in reality the norm for Christian life and conduct cannot be other than the historical Jesus in tandem with the diverse pictures of him in the New Testament writings.[95] Yet that diversity has to be respected with all its complexity, and the New Testament tradition about the prohibition of divorce is a good example of the complexity, since we have not only the attestation of an absolute prohibition (e.g., in Paul, Luke, Mark) but also the exceptive phrases in Matthew, the Marcan modification of the prohibition with respect to the woman, and the further exception that is introduced by Paul in 1 Cor 7:15, permitting the Christian "brother or sister" to marry after being divorced by an "unbelieving partner." Even though these exceptions do not stem from Jesus of Nazareth himself—and Paul stresses that explicitly in 7:12—they do stand in the inspired writings of the New Testament, in the inspired portraits of Jesus enshrined there. They may not have the authority of *ipsissima verba Iesu*, but they do have the authority of Scripture.

Now these exceptions and modifications, being found in such an inspired record of early Christianity's reaction to Jesus, raise the crucial question: If Matthew under inspiration could have been moved to add an exceptive phrase to the saying of Jesus about divorce that he found in an absolute form in either his Marcan source or in "Q," or if Paul likewise under inspiration could introduce into his writing an exception on his own authority, then why cannot the Spirit-guided institutional church of a later generation make a similar exception in view of problems confronting Christian married life of its day or so-called broken marriages (not really envisaged in the New Testament)—as it has done in some situations.[96] The question here is whether one looks solely at the absolute prohibition, traceable to Jesus, or at "the process of understanding and adaptation" which is in the New Testament itself and "with which the modern Church can identify only by entering into the process and furthering it."[97]

Because one of the Matthean divorce texts (5:31–32) is found in the Sermon on the Mount, that saying has often been subjected to an interpretation to which the Sermon as a whole has also been submitted. Thus, we are told that the prohibition of divorce in the New Testament is proposed as an ideal toward which Christians are asked to strive, when in reality it is realized that it is not always achieved. "Jesus established a moral *ideal,* a counsel, without constituting it a legal norm."[98] This, of course, is an ingenious solution. But it is substantiated only by means of a certain exposition of the Sermon on the Mount as a whole that once had some vogue. The history of the exegesis of that Sermon has run through an entire gamut of interpretations, and one of them is the Theory of the Impossible Ideal—a blueprint for utopia.[99] And the question has always been whether that theory measures up to the radical program of Christian morality proposed by the Matthean Jesus. Alas, it appears to be as ephemeral as many of the others. This means that distinctions of this sort between "ideal" and "legal norm," born of considerations extrinsic to the texts themselves, stand little chance of carrying conviction. The Matthean Jesus' words appeal beyond Mosaic legislation and any ideal to the divine institution of marriage itself.

A still further theological question may be asked, about why Jesus himself might have assumed such an attitude toward divorce as seems to be enshrined in his prohibition. Here I find myself attracted by a solution proposed by A. Isaksson, whose interpretation about the primitivity of the Matthean pericope I otherwise cannot accept. His explanation of Jesus' attitude is by no means certain, but it is nevertheless plausible and intriguing. He presents Jesus' view of marriage as indissoluble as an extension of an Old Testament attitude towards members of the priestly families who were to serve in the Jerusalem temple. "They shall not marry a harlot or a woman who has been defiled; neither shall they marry a woman divorced from her husband (*gĕrûšāh mē'îšāh,* lit., "driven out from her husband"), for the priest is holy to his God" (Lev 21:7; cf. Ezek 44:22). Isaksson sees this as the motivation for the prohibition of divorce: "Jesus taught his disciples they were chosen for and consecrated to the service of God."[100] His suggestion fits in with other considerations of the Christian community as the temple in a new sense (2 Cor 6:14–7:1; 1 Cor 3:16–17; Eph 2:18–22)—a theme not unknown either to the Qumran community or to the early church.[101] And one might want to add the further implication of the general priestly character of Christian disciples (Rev 1:6).[102]

On the other hand, there may be a still further nuance. If it is true that what is legislated for the king is legislated for the commoner, the prohibition of divorce for the king in 11QTemple 57:17–19 and for the "prince" of the community in CD 4:20–21 may suggest a kingly reason for the prohibition as well. Here 1 Pet 2:5, 9 comes to mind: "Like living stones be yourselves built into a spiritual house, to be a holy priesthood. . . . You are a chosen race, a royal priesthood, a holy nation, God's own people. . . ."[103] Such ideas may have been in the minds of the early Christians, ideas derived from their Old Testament background, but also influenced by such Palestinian Jewish thinking as we have cited in this paper. Whether we can attribute all of it to the thinking of Jesus of Nazareth will forever remain a problem.[104]

NOTES

* Originally published in *TS* 37 (1976) 197–226.
[1] A good bibliography on the divorce texts can be found in A. Myre, "Dix ans d'exégèse sur le divorce dans le Nouveau Testament," *Le divorce: L'Eglise catholique ne devrait-elle pas modifier son attitude séculaire à l'égard de l'indissolubilité du mariage?* (Montreal: Fides, 1973) 139–63, esp. pp. 156–63.
[2] See R. Bultmann, *The History of the Synoptic Tradition,* 27.
[3] To be noted, however, are the two prohibitions of divorce in Deut 22:13–19, 28–29.
[4] See A. Oepke, *"Gynē,"* *TDNT* 1 (1964) 776–89, esp. p. 788. Cf. H. Baltensweiler, *Die Ehe im Neuen Testament: Exegetische Untersuchungen über Ehe, Ehelosigkeit und Ehescheidung* (Zürich: Zwingli, 1967) 239–41; R. L. Saucy, "The Husband of One Wife," *BSac* 131 (1974) 229–40.
[5] Ibid., 233–34. Cf. J. Murray, "Divorce," *WTJ* 11 (1948–49) 105–22; M.-J. Lagrange, *Saint Paul: Epître aux Romains* (Paris: Gabalda, 1931) 161; K. Haacker, "Ehescheidung und Wiederverheiratung im Neuen Testament," *TQ* 151 (1971) 28–38, esp. p. 28.
[6] For the significance of this formulation, see my discussion in *Pauline Theology: A Brief Sketch* (Englewood Cliffs, NJ: Prentice-Hall, 1967) 13. Cf. D. M. Stanley, "Pauline Allusions to the Sayings of Jesus," *CBQ* 23 (1961) 26–39; D. L. Dungan, *The Sayings of Jesus in the Churches of Paul: The Use of the Synoptic Tradition in the Regulation of Early Church Life* (Philadelphia: Fortress, 1971) xxx–xxxi; H. Baltensweiler, *Die Ehe* (n. 4 above), 189.
[7] H. Lietzmann (*An die Korinther I–II* [HNT 9; 4th ed.; Tübingen: Mohr (Siebeck), 1949] 31) says this precisely: "Das *chōristhēnai* muss parallel dem *aphienai* v. 11 die aktive Handlung der Scheidung bedeuten." Similarly, J. Dupont (*Mariage et divorce dans l'Evangile: Matthieu 19,3–12 et parallèles* [Bruges: Desclée de Brouwer, 1959] 59) translates *chōristhēnai* as a middle "se séparer," but he does not justify this interpretation of an aorist passive as middle. In some MSS (A, D, G, etc.) the present infinitive *chōrizesthai* is found, which could be taken as middle. But the better reading is the aorist passive. See further K.

Aland, *Studien zur Überlieferung des Neuen Testaments und seines Textes* (ANTF 2; Berlin: de Gruyter, 1967) 153 (on the reading of 1 Cor 7:10–11 in P[11]).

[8] *Die Ehe* (n. 4 above), 187–91.

[9] *A Commentary on the First Epistle to the Corinthians* (Philadelphia: Fortress, 1975) 120. Cf. E.-B. Allo, *Saint Paul: Première épître aux Corinthiens* (2d ed.; Paris: Gabalda, 1956) 165.

[10] *The Sayings of Jesus* (n. 6 above), 91. The italics are his in this and the following quotations.

[11] Ibid., 92.

[12] Ibid., 93.

[13] The different terms used by Paul in his counsels in 1 Corinthians 7 are important and should be noted: "I wish" (7:7, 32); "I say" (7:8, 35); "my opinion" (7:25, 40); "I order" (7:17); the Lord "charges" (7:10, 25). On these terms, see H. Baltensweiler, *Die Ehe* (n. 4 above), 188; cf. W. Schrage, *Die konkreten Einzelgebote in der paulinischen Paränese* (Gütersloh: Mohn, 1961) 241–49.

[14] See B. Schaller, "Die Sprüche über Ehescheidung und Wiederheirat in der synoptischen Überlieferung," *Der Ruf Jesu und die Antwort der Gemeinde: Exegetische Untersuchungen Joachim Jeremias zum 70. Geburtstag gewidmet von seinen Schülern* (ed. E. Lohse et al.; Göttingen: Vandenhoeck & Ruprecht, 1970) 245. Schaller notes that the penalty threatened in the usual casuistic form is missing here. See further K. Haacker, "Ehescheidung" (n. 5 above), 30.

[15] For my understanding of the "Q" source, see pp. 16–23 above.

[16] H. Baltensweiler, *Die Ehe* (n. 4 above), 60–64.

[17] See also F. Neirynck, "De Jezuswoorden over echtscheiding," *Mislukt huwelijk en echtscheiding: Een multidisciplinaire benadering* (ed. V. Heylen; Louvain: Leuven University, 1972) 127–41, esp. p. 133. The principle of multiple attestation is being used here.

[18] Ibid.

[19] Ibid., 132.

[20] For the relation of Matt 5:32 to Luke 16:18, see J. Dupont, *Les Béatitudes: Le problème littéraire—Les deux versions du Sermon sur la Montagne et des Béatitudes* (new ed.; Louvain: Nauwelaerts, 1958) 117–18.

[21] E.g., G. Delling, "Das Logion Mark. X 11 [und seine Abwandlungen] im Neuen Testament," *NovT* 1 (1956–57) 263–74, esp. pp. 265–67.

[22] In the LXX Deut 24:1 runs thus: *Ean de tis labē gynaika kai synoikēsē autē, kai estai ean mē heurē charin enantion autou, hoti heuren en autē aschēmon pragma, kai grapsei autē biblion apostasiou kai dōsei eis tas cheiras autēs kai exapostelei autēn ek tēs oikias autou . . .* , "If someone takes a wife and lives with her, and it happens that (lit., if) she does not find favor before him, because he (has) found in her (some) disgraceful deed (*or* thing), and he writes her a writ of divorce and puts it into her hands and sends her out of his house . . ." (A. E. Brooke and N. McLean, *The Old Testament in Greek* (Cambridge: University Press) I/iii (1911) 630; A. Rahlfs, *Septuaginta* [8th ed.; Stuttgart: Württembergische Bibelanstalt 1965], 1. 329). The newly discovered Greek version of Deuteronomy, dating from pre-Christian times (Papyrus Fuad 226, frg. 36) has unfortunately only a few words of Deut 24:1 and they are identical with the reading in Christian copies of the LXX. See F. Dunand, *Papyrus grecs bibliques (Papyrus F. Inv. 266): Volumina de la Genèse et du Deutéronome* (Cairo: Imprimerie de l'institut français d'archéologie orientale, 1966), textes et planches, 105.

²³ H. Greeven ("Ehe nach dem Neuen Testament," *NTS* 15 [1968–69] 365–88, esp. pp. 382–85) argues for Matt 5:32 as the more primitive form of the sayings than Luke's, but his arguments seem forced and are not convincing.

²⁴ Compare the similar use of two passages of Genesis (1:27 and 7:9) in the *Damascus Document*, to be treated below; cf. *NTS* 7 (1960–61) 319–20; *ESBNT*, 36–38.

²⁵ This is not the place to engage in a lengthy discussion of these variants; see H. Baltensweiler, *Die Ehe* (n. 4 above), 66–67. It may be noted, however, that the *UBSGNT* lists no variants for this verse, nor does B. M. Metzger (*A Textual Commentary on the Greek New Testament*) discuss it.

²⁶ Mss Θ, W, some minuscles of the Lake family, and the Syriac versions. This evidence, however, is not very significant. See further V. Taylor, *Mark* (p. 33 above) 420–21.

²⁷ Cf. G. Delling, "Das Logion Mark. X 11" (n. 21 above), 270.

²⁸ See W. Kunkel, "Matrimonium," PW 14/2 (1930) 2259–86, esp. cols. 2275–81; T. Thalheim, "Ehescheidung," PW 5/2 (1905) 2011–13; F. Raber, "Divortium," *Der kleine Pauly: Lexikon der Antike* (ed. K. Ziegler and W. Sontheimer; Stuttgart: Druckenmüller) 2 (1957) 109–10; J. Dauvillier, "L'Indissolubilité du mariage dans la nouvelle Loi," *Orient-Syrien* 9 (1964) 265–89.

²⁹ *AP* 15:22–23 reads: "Should Miptahiah rise up in an assembly tomorrow [or] some other [da]y and say, 'I divorce (lit., I hate) my husband Eshor,' the divorce fee is on her head. . . ." See my commentary on this text, "A Re-Study of an Elephantine Aramaic Marriage Contract (*AP* 15)," *Near Eastern Studies in Honor of William Foxwell Albright* (ed. H. Goedicke; Baltimore: Johns Hopkins University, 1971) 137–68; reprinted, *WA*, 243–71. See further *BMAP* 2:9; 7:25; cf. *AP* 9:8.

³⁰ An attempt has been made by E. Bammel ("Markus 10:11f. und das jüdische Eherecht," *ZNW* 61 [1970] 95–101) to gather evidence that a Jewish woman had a right to divorce her husband. There is a text in Josephus (*Ant.* 15.7,10 §259) which mentions a case of it, and we shall return to it below. The restoration of Mur frg. 20:6 [DJD 2, 110–13] proposed by J. T. Milik is highly questionable, as even Bammel recognizes; it cannot really be used for evidence.

³¹ The twofold occurrence of the prohibition of divorce in the Matthean Gospel is a good example of a "doublet" in the Synoptic tradition (see pp. 20–21 above); Matt 5:32 is derived from "Q," and Matt 19:3–9 from the Marcan source. See E. von Dobschütz, "Matthäus als Rabbi und Katechet," *ZNW* 27 (1928) 338–48, esp. p. 340.

³² The modification consists mainly in the admission of private sources which both Matthew and Luke had, usually designated "M" and "L", either oral or written (see pp. 28, 39 above).

³³ E.g., R. H. Charles, *The Teaching of the New Testament on Divorce* (London: Williams and Norgate, 1921) 19–31; B. H. Streeter, *The Four Gospels* (p. 30 above), 259; J. Jeremias, *Jesus als Weltvollender* (Gütersloh: Bertelsmann, 1930) 65; M. R. Lehmann, "Gen 2:24 as the Basis for Divorce in Halakhah and New Testament," *ZAW* 72 (1960) 263–67; A. Isaksson, *Marriage and Ministry in the New Temple: A Study with Special Reference to Mt 19,13–12 [sic] and I. Cor. 11,3–16* (Lund: Gleerup, 1965) 70–74; B. Vawter, "The Biblical Theology of Divorce," *PCTSA* 22 (1967) 223–43, esp. pp. 233–34.

³⁴ E.g., D. L. Dungan, *The Sayings of Jesus* (n. 6 above), 103–31. Cf. his article, "Mark—The Abridgement of Matthew and Luke," *Jesus and Man's Hope* (p. 30 above), 1. 51–97.

[35] See J. Dupont, *Mariage et divorce* (n. 7 above), 28. For parallels to "for any reason," see the Greek formulas in Josephus, *Ant.* 4.8,23 §253 (*kath' hasdēpotoun aitias*), and Philo, *De spec. leg.* 3.5 §30 (*kath' hēn an tychē prophasin*).

[36] See further F. Neirynck, "De Jezuswoorden" (n. 17 above), 136.

[37] G. Delling, "Das Logion" (n. 21 above), 270.

[38] Some MSS (B, D, the Freer and Lake families of minuscules) read *parektos logou porneias* in 19:9, but that is obviously the result of harmonization with 5:32. For an attempt to defend a different form of the Matthean text, see J. MacRory, "The Teaching of the New Testament on Divorce: A Critical Examination of Matt. xix. 9," *ITQ* 6 (1911) 74–91; "Christian Writers of the First Three Centuries and St. Matt. xix. 9," ibid., 172–85. Cf. H. Crouzel, *L'Eglise primitive face au divorce* (Théologie historique, 13; Paris: Beauchesne, 1971) 29–34; J. P. Arendzen, "Ante-Nicene Interpretations of the Sayings on Divorce," *JTS* 20 (1919) 230–41.

[39] Tortuous attempts to read these phrases as other than "exceptive" have to be recognized for what they really are, subterfuges to avoid the obvious. B. Vawter ("The Divorce Clauses in Mt 5,32 and 19,9," *CBQ* 16 [1954] 155–67, esp. 160–62, 163–64) has supplied a list of such attempts and discussed the problems inherent in them. Cf. G. Delling, "Das Logion" (n. 21 above), 268–69; J. Dupont, *Mariage et divorce* (n. 7 above), 96–106; H. Baltensweiler, *Die Ehe* (n. 4 above), 89–91.

[40] E.g., A. Schlatter, *Der Evangelist Matthäus: Seine Sprache, sein Ziel, seine Selbstständigkeit* (Stuttgart: Calwer Verlag, 1929) 568; H. G. Coiner, "Those 'Divorce and Remarriage' Passages (Matt. 5:32; 19:9; 1 Cor 7:10–16)," *CTM* 39 (1968) 367–84; A. Isaksson, *Marriage and Ministry* (n. 33 above) 75–152; J. Schniewind, *Das Evangelium nach Matthäus übersetzt und erklärt* (NTD 2; Göttingen: Vandenhoeck & Ruprecht, 1962) 64.

[41] See J. Dupont, *Mariage et divorce*, 88 n. 2.

[42] See E. von Dobschütz, "Matthäus als Rabbi" (n. 31 above), 339–40, 344; R. Bultmann, *History of the Synoptic Tradition*, 148; J. Dupont, *Mariage et divorce*, 89.

[43] This is the conclusion of many New Testament interpreters today—in fact, of so many that it is useless to try to document it; see G. Delling, "Das Logion" (n. 21 above), 274; H. Greeven, "Zu den Aussagen des Neuen Testaments über die Ehe," *Zeitschrift für evangelische Ethik* 1 (1957) 109–25.

[44] BAG, 699.—This is not the place to deal with the question raised by B. Malina, "Does *Porneia* Mean Fornication?" *NovT* 14 (1972) 10–17, whose answer has oversimplified the matter. For criticisms of Malina's views, see J. J. O'Rourke, "Does the New Testament Condemn Sexual Intercourse outside Marriage? *TS* 37 (1976) 478–79; J. Jensen, "Does *Porneia* Mean Fornication? A Critique of Bruce Malina," *NovT* 20 (1978) 161–84; cf. M. Zalba, "Declaratio de quibusdam quaestionibus ad sexualem ethicam spectantibus (*AAS* 68 [1976] 77–96)," *Periodica* 66 (1977) 72–115, esp. pp. 96–97. Nor am I happy with Malina's approval of K.-G. Kuhn's interpretation of *zěnût* in CD 4:19ff. (see "The Epistle to the Ephesians in the Light of the Qumran Texts," *Paul and Qumran* [ed. J. Murphy-O'Connor; Chicago: Priory, 1968] 115–31, esp. p. 121), as will be made clear in part II of this essay.

[45] Rom 1:29 and Gal 5:19 might also be involved, but there are text-critical problems involved in these passages.

[46] For the variants on these passages in different MSS, see H. Baltensweiler, *Die Ehe* (n. 4 above), 92; B. M. Metzger, *A Textual Commentary on the Greek New Testament*, 429–35.

[47] See E. Haenchen, *The Acts of the Apostles: A Commentary* (Philadelphia: Westminster, 1971) 449; Str-B, 2. 729–39; F. Hauck and S. Schulz, *"Pornē*, etc.," *TDNT* 6 (1968) 593; H. Richards, "Christ on Divorce," *Scripture* 11 (1959) 22–32; H. Baltensweiler, *Die Ehe,* 92–103.

[48] So, e.g., F. Hauck and S. Schulz, *"Pornē*, etc.," *TDNT* 6 (1968) 592; E. Klostermann, *Das Matthäusevangelium* (4th ed.; Tübingen: Mohr [Siebeck], 1971) 46 (quoting B. Weiss); M. Dibelius, *From Tradition to Gospel* (New York: Scribner, n.d.) 249; M.-J. Lagrange, *Evangile selon saint Matthieu* (4th ed.; Paris: Gabalda, 1927) 105 ("Le sens est donc: 'mis à part le cas d'adultère'"); M.-E. Boismard, *Synopse des quatre évangiles en français 2: Commentaire* (Paris: Cerf, 1972) 308 ("l'adultère de la femme").

[49] See K. Bornhäuser, *Die Bergpredigt* (Gütersloh: Bertelsmann, 1923) 82; A. Fridrichsen, "Excepta fornicationis causa," *SEA* 9 (1944) 54–58, esp. p. 55 n. 2. T. L. Thompson ("A Catholic View on Divorce," *JES* 6 [1969] 53–67, esp. p. 58 n. 22) calls the distinction between *porneia* and *moicheia* "groundless and the result of a very mechanical, almost mathematical idea of language." But that is a sciolist approach to the whole problem.

[50] See J. L. McKenzie, "The Gospel according to Matthew," *JBC,* art. 43, §38.

[51] What it comes to in the long run is whether one is going to use the Pauline meaning of *porneia* in Matthew or the Lucan meaning from Acts 15. Given the nature of the community that Matthew is addressing, the latter seems more appropriate.

[52] E.g., W. K. L. Clarke, "The Excepting Clause in St. Matthew," *Theology* 15 (1927) 161–62; F. Gavin, "A Further Note on *Porneia,*" *Theology* 16 (1928) 102–5; F. W. Green, *The Gospel according to Saint Matthew* (2d ed.; Oxford: Clarendon, 1945) 220; H. Baltensweiler, *Die Ehe* (n. 4 above), 87–102; "Die Ehebruchs-klausel bei Matthäus: Zu Matth. 5, 32; 19, 9," *TZ* 15 (1959) 340–56; M. Thurian, *Marriage and Celibacy* (London: SCM, 1959) 28.—In Roman Catholic circles this interpretation has been mainly associated with the name of J. Bonsirven, *Le divorce dans le Nouveau Testament* (Paris: Desclée, 1948); "'Nisi ob fornicationem': Exégèse primitive," *Mélanges offerts au R. P. Ferdinand Cavallera* (Toulouse: Bibliothèque de l'Institut Catholique, 1948) 47–63; "'Nisi fornicationis causa': Comment résoudre cette 'crux interpretum'?" *RSR* 35 (1948) 442–64. It had, of course, been proposed by several others before him, but he popularized the interpretation. A lengthy list of those who use it can be found in J. Dupont, *Mariage et divorce,* 106–7 nn. 2–3. Some who have adopted it more recently are: J. Schmid, *Das Evangelium nach Matthäus* (RNT 1; 5th ed.; Regensburg, Pustet, 1965) 104; R. Pesch, "Die neutestamentliche Weisung für die Ehe," *BibLeb* 9 (1968) 208–21, esp. p. 211; R. Schnackenburg, "Die Ehe nach dem Neuen Testament," *Theologie der Ehe* (ed. G. Krems and R. Munn; Regensburg: Pustet, 1969) 9–36, esp. pp. 17–18.

[53] I am passing over other meanings that have been proposed at times, e.g., the interpretation of *porneia* as intercourse on the part of an engaged girl (see Deut 22:20–21), proposed by A. Isaksson, *Marriage and Ministry* (n. 33 above), 135–42; or the figurative interpretation of *porneia* as pagan unbelief, or "something unseemly [in the eyes of God]," as proposed by A. Mahoney, "A New Look at the Divorce Clauses in Mt 5,32 and 19,9," *CBQ* 30 (1968) 29–38, esp. pp. 32–35; or the interpretation that it refers to "all offences short of adultery," because the dissolubility of marriage for adultery permitted in the Old Testament was implicitly admitted by Jesus," proposed by R. H. Charles, *The Teaching* (n. 33 above), 21–22.

[54] For further discussion of the destination of the Matthean Gospel to a mixed but predominantly Jewish-Christian community, see my note, "Anti-semitism and the Cry of 'All the People' (Mt 27:25)," *TS* (1965) 667–71, esp. pp. 670–71.

[55] See MM, 696. Also other papyrus texts such as *PSI* §166.11–12; *P. Rylands*, 2. 154:25 (A.D. 66; LCL, *Select Papyri*, 1. 15; *BGU* §1101:5; §1102:8; §1103:6 (13 B.C.; LCL, 1. 22–23).

[56] See the tortuous attempts of R. H. Charles to translate the verb in this way (*The Teaching* [n. 33 above], 43–61).

[57] Possibly it occurs in Josephus, *Ant.* 15.7,10 §259, but the reading is not textually certain.

[58] BAG, 96. Cf. D. Daube, "The New Testament Terms for Divorce," *Theology* 47 (1944) 66.

[59] Cf. also Esdras A (LXX) 9:36.

[60] So B. K. Diderichsen, *Den markianske skilsmisseperikope: Dens genesis og historiske placering* (Copenhagen: Gyldendal, 1962) 20–47, 347. See A. Isaksson, *Marriage and Ministry* (n. 33 above), 94–96; H. Baltensweiler, *Die Ehe* (n. 4 above), 64 n. 63; F. Neirynck, "De Jezuswoorden" (n. 17 above), 130.

[61] See P. Benoit et al., *Les grottes de Murabbaʿat* (DJD 2), 248. A. Isaksson (*Marriage and Ministry*, 95) wrongly refers to this document as a "divorce certificate found at Qumran." It has nothing to do with Qumran. See further E. Lövestamm, "*Apolyein* en gammalpalestinensisk skilsmässoterm," *SEA* 27 (1962) 132–35.

[62] See P. Benoit et al., *Les grottes de Murabbaʿat* (DJD 2), 105. This document is technically known as a *Doppelurkunde*, "double document," because the same text of the contract was written twice, and the upper form of it (*scriptura interior*) was folded over and officially sealed, whereas the lower form (*scriptura exterior*) was left visible for ready consultation. In case of a dispute over the wording, the seals of the upper part could be broken and the texts compared to make sure that the *scriptura exterior* had not been tampered with. In this instance the *scriptura interior* contains the identical formula (lines 13–15).

[63] MM, 66–67. The word turns up in this sense in later Greek literature.

[64] See n. 22 above.

[65] A. Isaksson, *Marriage and Ministry* (n. 33 above), 145. See further B. Vawter, "Biblical Theology" (n. 33 above), 232; A. Finkel, *The Pharisees and the Teacher of Nazareth* (Leiden: Brill, 1964) 164–65. Not even the strictures against divorce in Mal 2:14–16 were interpreted in the sense of prohibition.

[66] The text continues, ". . . and not even a divorced woman may marry again on her own initiative unless her former husband consents." See further R. Marcus, "Notes on Torrey's Translation of the Gospels," *HTR* 27 (1934) 220–21.

[67] It is, of course, quite unclear what precedent this divorce of Salome constitutes in Palestinian Judaism of the time; Josephus regards it as an illegal exception. Part of the problem is that Idumeans are involved, people who were often regarded as "half-Jews."

[68] "The Temple Scroll," *BA* 30 (1967) 135–39; reprinted, *New Directions in Biblical Archaeology* (ed. D. N. Freedman and J. C. Greenfield; Garden City, NY: Doubleday, 1969) 139–48, esp. p. 141. Cf. "Un nouveau manuscrit de la Mer Morte: Le rouleau du Temple," *CRAIBL* 1968, 607–16. Yadin has now published the *editio princeps* in a modern Hebrew publication, *Mgylt-hmqdš* [The Temple Scroll] (3 vols.; Jerusalem: Israel Exploration Society, Archaeological Institute of the Hebrew University, Shrine of the Book, 1977).

Cf. J. Maier, *Die Tempelrolle vom Toten Meer übersetzt und erläutert* (Munich/Basel: E. Reinhardt, 1978); A. Caquot, "Le rouleau du temple de Qoumrân," *ETR* 53 (1978) 443–500; Y. Yadin, "Temple Scroll," *Encyclopedia Judaica* (Jerusalem: Keter; New York: Macmillan, 1971), 15. 996–98.

[69] The main article in which we are interested is "L'Attitude essénienne envers la polygamie et le divorce," *RB* 79 (1972) 98–99. Two other short articles also supply texts that bear on other matters in the Temple Scroll: "Pesher Nahum (4QpNahum) Reconsidered," *IEJ* 21 (1971) 1–12 (treating of 11QTemple 64:6–13 [see pp. 132–33 below]); "The Gate of the Essenes and the Temple Scroll," *Qadmoniot* 5 (1972) 129–30 [in Hebrew]; *Jerusalem Revealed: Archaelogy in the Holy City 1968–1974* (Jerusalem: Israel Exploration Society, 1975) 90–91.

[70] "The Temple Scroll," *New Directions* (n. 68 above), 142.

[71] A fuller, detailed discussion of the Hebrew text of these lines and of the passage to be cited below from the *Damascus Document* has been published by me in an article, "Divorce among First-Century Palestinian Jews," *H. L. Ginsberg Volume* (Eretz-Israel, 14; Jerusalem: Israel Exploration Society, 1978) 103*–10*.

[72] See, e.g., G. Vermes, *The Dead Sea Scrolls in English* (Baltimore: Penguin, 1970) 37. See further, D. Daube, *The New Testament and Rabbinic Judaism* (London: University of London, 1956) 86. Daube calls attention to the fact that CD 7:16–17 quotes Amos 5:26 and interprets the "king" of the Amos passage as "the congregation" (*qhl*).

[73] Josephus makes no mention of this tenet of the Essenes.

[74] *Documents of Jewish Sectaries* (2 vols.; Cambridge: University Press, 1910; reprinted in the Library of Biblical Studies with a prolegomenon by me, New York: Ktav, 1970), 1. xxxv–xxxvii, 21, (67)–(69), (114)–(115). Schechter's text has to be used with caution. The best edition of the *Damascus Document* today is that of C. Rabin, *The Zadokite Documents 1: The Admonition; 2. The Laws* (Oxford: Clarendon, 1954) 16–19. Cf. S. Zeitlin, *The Zadokite Fragments: Facsimile of the Manuscripts in the Cairo Genizah Collection in the Possession of the University Library, Cambridge, England* (Philadelphia: Dropsie College, 1952) pls. iv–v.

[75] Most of the older discussions have been surveyed and commented on by H. Braun, *Qumran und das Neue Testament* (2 vols.; Tübingen: Mohr [Siebeck], 1966), 1. 40–42; 2. 103–4.

[76] From Qumran Cave 4 have come seven, possibly eight, fragmentary copies of the text. Further fragments were found in Caves 5 and 6; the latter have been published: 5QD (or 5Q*12*), corresponding to CD 9:7–10; 6QD (or 6Q*15*), corresponding to CD 4:19–21; 5:13–14; 5:18–6:2; 6:20–7:1. In the Cave 6 fragments one finds a bit that corresponds to the text of CD 4:19–21, in which we are interested here; but what is there is identical with the text of the medieval copy. See M. Baillet et al., *Les 'Petites Grottes' de Qumrân* (DJD 3; Oxford: Clarendon, 1962) 181 and 128–31. Cf. *RB* 63 (1956) 513–23.

[77] "An Essene Missionary Document? CD II, 14—VI,1," *RB* 77 (1970) 201–29.

[78] See further J. Murphy-O'Connor, "The Essenes and Their History," *RB* 81 (1974) 215–44.

[79] The translation which I give here differs slightly from that used in an earlier article in which this passage was quoted in part, "The Use of Explicit Old Testament Quotations in Qumran Literature and in the New Testament," *ESBNT*, 37. I now take *bznwt* more closely with the three preceding words; for further discussion of this matter, see the article mentioned in n. 71 above.

[80] *The Zadokite Documents,* 17 n. 2 (on line 20).

[81] E.g., E. Cothenet, "Le Document de Damas," *Les textes de Qumran traduits et annotés* (2 vols.; Paris: Letouzey et Ané, 1961), 2. 162; L. Moraldi, *I manoscritti di Qumrân* (Turin: Unione tipografica, 1971) 236; J. Murphy-O'Connor, "An Essene Missionary Document?" (n. 77 above), 220.

[82] This identification of the "prince" is taken from C. Rabin, *Zadokite Documents* (n. 74 above), 18 n. 3 (on line 1).

[83] G. Vermes ("Sectarian Matrimonial Halakhah in the Damascus Rule," *JJS* 25 [1974] 197–202; reprinted, *Post-Biblical Jewish Studies* [SJLA 8; Leiden: Brill, 1975] 50–56) says that there have been four, but he wrongly ascribes to R. H. Charles an interpretation that the latter did not hold.

[84] Besides Schechter, it has been so interpreted by, among many others, D. Daube, P. Winter (for a survey of opinions, see his article "Sadoqite Fragments IV 20, 21 and the Exegesis of Genesis 1:27 in Late Judaism," *ZAW* 68 [1956] 71–84), A. Dupont-Sommer, E. Cothenet, L. Moraldi, G. Vermes (in "The Qumran Interpretation of Scripture in Its Historical Setting," *ALUOS* 6 [1969] 85–97, esp. p. 94), J. Dupont (?).

[85] "Sectarian Matrimonial Halakhah" (n. 83 above), 197–202. Others who so interpret the text are H. Braun, J. Carmignac, C. Rabin, F. Neirynck.

[86] "An Essene Missionary Document?" (n. 77 above), 220. Before him it was so interpreted by J. Hempel, *ZAW* 68 (1956) 84; and possibly by M. Burrows, *More Light on the Dead Sea Scrolls* (New York: Viking, 1958) 98–99. Murphy-O'Connor remains skeptical about Yadin's interpretation of CD 4:20–21 in the light of the clear evidence from 11QTemple 57:17–19; see his 'Remarques sur l'exposé du Professeur Y. Yadin," *RB* 79 (1972) 99–100. But his remarks are unconvincing and represent a reluctance to give up a position taken before the new evidence came along.

[87] However, it might be permitted to relate this passage from 11QTemple to Rom 7:4, where Paul speaks about the married woman who is free to marry again after the death of her husband.

[88] G. Vermes ("Sectarian Matrimonial Halakhah" [n. 83 above], 202) has also recognized this interpretation of the suffix.

[89] The most extensive treatment of this material is given by J. Bonsirven, *Le divorce* (n. 52 above), but his treatment is scarcely a model of clarity; see J. Dupont, *Mariage et divorce* (n. 7 above), 108 n. 1.

[90] This matter is not entirely clear, but it is not beyond the realm of possibility that the Qaraite Jews who differed strongly with the rabbinic interpretation of the Torah were influenced by Essene views. It has even been suggested that they might have discovered some of the scrolls themselves and used them as the basis for their own interpretations. The prohibition of divorce is ascribed to them by H. Cazelles, "Marriage," *DBS* 5 (1957) 905–35, esp. col. 927; M.-J. Lagrange, "La secte juive de la nouvelle alliance au pays de Damas," *RB* 9 (1912) 213–40, esp. pp. 332–35. Cf. L. Nemoy, *Karaite Anthology: Excerpts from the Early Literature* (New Haven: Yale University, 1952) 334; A. Büchler, "Schechter's 'Jewish Sectaries,'" *JQR* 3 (1912–13) 429–85, esp. pp. 433–34; N. Wieder, *The Judean Scrolls and Karaism* (London: East and West Library, 1962) 131–135.

[91] *Kommentar zum Neuen Testament,* 1. 319–20: ". . . that in the Mishnaic period there was no marriage among the Jewish people which could not be dissolved abruptly by the husband in a fully legal way by the delivery of a writ of divorce."

[92] "The Biblical Theology of Divorce" (n. 33 above), 233.
[93] *The Sayings of Jesus* (n. 6 above), 233. See further R. H. Charles, *The Teaching* (n. 33 above), 29 ("an unhistorical question").
[94] See further H. Baltensweiler, *Die Ehe* (n. 4 above), 83–84.
[95] And in the Roman Catholic view of things, coupled with genuine dogmatic tradition. For further discussion of "the historical Jesus in tandem with the diverse pictures of him in the New Testament," see my article, "Belief in Jesus Today," *Commonweal* 101 (1974) 137–42.
[96] E.g., in the so-called Petrine privilege. See J. McGrath, "Marriage, Canon Law of: 13. Favor of Faith Cases," *New Catholic Encyclopedia* (New York: McGraw-Hill, 1967), 9. 289–90.
[97] G. W. MacRae, S.J., "New Testament Perspective on Marriage and Divorce," *Divorce and Remarriage in the Catholic Church* (ed. L. G. Wrenn; New York: Newman, 1973) 1–15, esp. p. 3. See further G. Schneider, "Jesu Wort über die Ehescheidung in der Überlieferung des Neuen Testaments," *TTZ* 80 (1971) 65–87, esp. p. 87; B. Byron, "1 Cor 7:10–15: A Basis for Future Catholic Discipline on Marriage and Divorce?" *TS* 34 (1973) 429–45.
[98] V. J. Pospishil, *Divorce and Remarriage: Towards A New Catholic Teaching* (New York: Herder and Herder, 1967) 37. Whatever else is to be said about the merits or demerits of this book, the treatment of the biblical passages in it is unspeakably bad. That a book on such a touchy issue could appear as late as 1967, treating the biblical passages dealing with it, and basing that treatment solely on such writers as W. R. O'Connor, F. E. Gigot, F. Prat, J. MacRory, and R. Yaron, is indicative of the quality of the proposal being made.

Others who propose the prohibition of divorce merely as an ideal: W. J. O'Shea, "Marriage and Divorce: The Biblical Evidence," *Australasian Catholic Record* 47 (1970) 89–109, esp. pp. 106–8; J. A. Grispino, *The Bible Now* (Notre Dame: Fides, 1971) 95–107, esp. p. 106; D. Crossan, "Divorce and Remarriage in the New Testament," *The Bond of Marriage: An Ecumenical and Interdisciplinary Study* (ed. W. W. Bassett; Notre Dame, IN: University of Notre Dame, 1968) 1–40.
[99] See A. M. Hunter, "The Meaning of the Sermon on the Mount," *ExpTim* 63 (1952) 176–79; J. Jeremias, *The Sermon on the Mount* (Philadelphia: Fortress, 1963) 1–12. Cf. A. M. Ambrozic, "Indissolubility of Marriage in the New Testament: Law or Ideal?" *Studia canonica* 6 (1972) 269–88.
[100] *Marriage and Ministry* (n. 33 above), 147.
[101] See B. Gärtner, *The Temple and the Community in Qumran and the New Testament: A Comparative Study in the Temple Symbolism of the Qumran Texts and the New Testament* (SNTSMS 1; Cambridge: University Press, 1963).
[102] See E. S. Fiorenza, *Priester für Gott: Studien zum Herrschafts- und Priestermotiv in der Apokalypse* (NTAbh ns 7; Münster: Aschendorff, [1972]).
[103] See J. H. Elliott, *The Elect and the Holy: An Exegetical Examination of I Peter 2:4–10 and the Phrase basileion hierateuma* (NovTSup 12; Leiden: Brill, 1966).
[104] See the comments of B. Vawter on the original form of this article, "Divorce and the New Testament," *CBQ* (1977) 528–42, esp. pp. 529–34. Now that the Temple Scroll has been fully published (see n. 68 above), one can verify Yadin's reading of 11QTemple 57:17–19 easily enough. His preliminary publication of the lines did not lead us astray; hence my dependence on him has not turned out to be as "precarious" as Vawter would lead his readers to understand. Moreover, I stick to my guns in the interpretation of the passage in

CD in terms of polygamy *and* divorce. Vawter tries to fault my interpretation of CD 4:20–21 by referring to another passage in that document (13:17–19) and saying that I failed to mention its stipulation "that the 'Essenes' should seek the permission of their *mĕbaqqēr* (bishop) before divorcing their wives" (p. 534 n. 9). True, I said nothing of that passage in CD in the original form of this article, because I had treated it *in extenso* in the article mentioned in n. 71 above, which was not yet published when Vawter wrote, but which had been submitted for publication long before. As a matter of fact, that passage in CD *has nothing to do with divorce,* save in Rabin's questionable translation of it, which Vawter has uncritically followed. For further details, see "Divorce among First-Century Palestinian Jews," *H. L. Ginsberg Volume,* 109*–10*.

See further R. Trevijano Etcheverría, "Matrimonio y divorcio en Mc 10, 2–12 y par.," *Burgense* 18 (1977) 113–51; A. Stock, "Matthean Divorce Texts," *BTB* 8 (1978) 24–33; A.-L. Descamps, "Les textes évangéliques sur le mariage," *RTL* 9 (1978) 259–86; 11 (1980) 5–50; J. J. Kilgallen, "To What Are the Matthean Exception-Texts (5,32 and 19,9) an Exception?" *Bib* 61 (1980) 102–5; J. R. Mueller, "The Temple Scroll and the Gospel Divorce Texts," *RevQ* 10 (1980–81) 247–56.

Four

ARAMAIC KEPHA² AND PETER'S NAME IN THE NEW TESTAMENT *

AMONG THE MANY problems surrounding the figure of Peter in the New Testament are the meaning of his name and the significance attached to the change of it.[1] Some of them involve the relation between Symeon and Simon as used of him; some of them the relation between Cephas and Peter. In this sort of discussion it is surprising how little attention has been paid to a striking occurrence of the Aramaic name *Kephā²*, and I should like to draw the attention of New Testament scholars to it.

At the outset we may be permitted to set the context for this discussion of Peter's name by recalling the various names that are given to him and the problems they raise. In this way we shall be able to see better the relation to them of the Aramaic material to be discussed.

First of all, we may recall that he is given the name Symeon or Simon.[2] The Semitic form of the name, Symeon or *Šimĕ'ōn,* is reflected in the Greek of Acts 15:14—at least so it is intended in the Lucan text as we have it. James refers thus to Peter, who has just spoken in 15:7–11. This is the only time that Peter is so named in Luke–Acts; elsewhere he is always referred to as Simon, a similar-sounding Greek name (*Simōn*),[3] or as Peter (*Petros*),[4] or as Simon Peter.[5] The use of Symeon in 15:14 for Peter is striking and has given rise to one of the classic problems in that chapter (often used as an important piece of evidence that Luke is here depending on a source—which he may not have completely understood).[6] The name Symeon is likewise attested for him in some MSS of 2 Pet 1:1, but even there it is not uniformly attested.[7] In any case, the use of both Symeon and Simon reflects the well-known custom among Jews of that time of giving the name of a famous patriarch or personage of the Old Testament to a male child along with a similar-sounding Greek/Roman name. This use of Symeon can be compared with Luke 2:25,

34; 3:30 and with the names of Joseph or Jacob. The Old Testament background for Symeon is undoubtedly to be sought in Gen 29:33. Used of this disciple of Jesus, it stands in contrast to that of other disciples like Philip or Andrew, who bear Greek names.

Second, in addition to the use of Symeon/Simon for him, the New Testament has recorded the recollection of Jesus having changed Simon's name: "Simon whom he surnamed Peter" (Mark 3:16; cf. Matt 4:18; 10:2; Luke 6:14; Acts 10:5). This change of name is preserved in an even more explicit way in the Gospels of Matthew and John. In the Matthean form of the episode at Caesarea Philippi, after Simon has stated, "You are the Christ, the Son of the living God," Jesus says to him, "Blessed are you Simon Bar-Jona! . . . I tell you, you are Peter, and on this rock I will build my church" (Matt 16:17–18, *RSV*): *Sy ei Petros, kai epi tautē tē petra oikodomēsō*. . . . In the Johannine Gospel, Andrew finds his brother Simon and brings him to Jesus, who says to him, " 'So you are Simon the son of John? You shall be called Cephas' (which means Peter)" (1:42, *RSV*): *Sy ei Simōn ho huios Iōannou; sy klēthēsē Kēphas ho hermēneuetai Petros.* Cephas is not used again in the Fourth Gospel, where the Greek name Peter rather prevails. Aside from the translation of Cephas that is given in 1:42, which removes any hesitation about the way in which one part of the early church understood the change of the name from Simon to Cephas, little is otherwise told in the Johannine Gospel about the significance of the change. A significance of the new name, however, is found in the Matthean passage, at least if one grants that there is a wordplay involved and that the underlying Aramaic substratum involved a similar wordplay.

Reasons for the change of Simon's name have often been proposed. Today we smile at the relation seen between Greek *Kēphas* and Latin *caput* by some patristic writers, who assumed a connection between *Kēphas* and *kephalē*. Thus Optatus of Milevis once wrote (ca. A.D. 370): ". . . omnium apostolorum caput, Petrus, unde et Cephas est appellatus. . . ."[8] How much was made of this connection and its unsophisticated medieval exploitation need not detain us here.[9] In a similar way we may treat the theorizing about the alleged tendency of Jews at the turn of the Christian era to avoid the use of the Hebrew name Symeon or the Greek name Simon either because it was supposedly forbidden to them by the Roman occupiers of Palestine on account of its hyperpatriotic associations with famous bygone military figures or because it was regarded as too sacred a name for normal use by nationalistic Jews.[10] Such speculation has had to yield to the fact that Symeon/Simon was among the most widely used names for Palestinian male children of the period.[11] Such an avoidance of the name is scarcely the reason for the change from Simon to Cephas/Peter.

Much more frequently the reason for the change of the name has been explained by relating it to the change of names of rather prominent persons in the Old Testament in view of roles that they were to play in the history of the people of Israel: Abram/Abraham (Gen 17:5); Jacob/Israel (Gen 32:28); etc. Against such a background the wordplay of Matt 16:18b has been understood. It is not my purpose to rehearse here all the details of the long debate over that wordplay— whether "this rock" refers to the faith of Peter, to the confession of Peter, to Peter himself, or to Jesus.[12] There are rather some aspects of the question that have been somewhat neglected and some philological evidence that should be brought to bear on the names Cephas and Peter.

I. *The Greek Name* Kēphas *and Its Aramaic Counterpart*

The name *Kēphas* is found in the New Testament, outside of the Johannine passage (1:42), only in the Pauline writings (Gal 1:18; 2:9, 11, 14; 1 Cor 1:12; 3:22; 9:5; 15:5).[13] Paul, however, never uses of him the name Simon/Symeon, and he uses *Petros* only in Gal 2:7–8, in a context in which *Kēphas* otherwise predominates.

Either on the basis of the early church's interpretation of *Kēphas* as *Petros* (John 1:42) or for other reasons, modern commentators usually identify the Cephas of Galatians with Peter. However, there has always been a small group of commentators who have sought to identify the Cephas of Galatians 1–2 with someone other than Simon Peter. Eusebius quotes the fifth book of the *Hypotyposes* of Clement of Alexandria to the effect that the "Cephas concerning whom Paul says 'and when Cephas came to Antioch I withstood him to the face' [Gal 2:11] was one of the seventy disciples, who had the same name as the apostle Peter."[14] More sophisticated reasons for hesitating about the identity of Cephas and Peter in Galatians have been found in modern times.[15] In antiquity it was often a question of the supposed relative positions of Peter and Paul in the church; in recent times it is the peculiar shift from Cephas to Peter. Though the majority of modern commentators agree that Cephas and Peter are the same person in Galatians 1–2, the shift has been explained by postulating that Paul is "quoting an official document"[16] in vv. 7–8, whereas he has elsewhere used the name Cephas which he otherwise preferred for him. Another aspect of the problem is that whereas the manuscript tradition is constant in 1 Corinthians in reading *Kēphas,* there is fluctuation between *Kēphas* and *Petros* in the manuscripts of Galatians.[17] In any case, though we take note of this minority opinion about the identity of Cephas and Peter in Galatians 1–2, we cannot consider it seriously.

The translation of *Kēphas* by *Petros* in John 1:42 and the wordplay in Matt 16:18 between *Petros* and *petra* have been explained from time immemorial by an appeal to the Aramaic background of the name Cephas. *Kēphas* is regarded as a grecized form of the Aramaic word *kephā',* assimilating it to masculine nouns of the first declension (cf. *Ioudas, -ou*).[18] The Hebrew noun *kēph* is found in Jer 4:29; Job 30:6; Sir 40:14. To illustrate the Aramaic use, one has often appealed to later rabbinic writings, Syriac, and Christian Palestinian Aramaic.[19] However, there is now some better Aramaic evidence that can be used, coming from earlier or contemporary sources.

The common noun *kephā'* appears twice in the targum of Job from Qumran Cave 11. A fragmentary phrase containing it is preserved in 11QtgJob 32:1: *y'ly kp',* "wild goats of the crag," translating Hebrew *ya'alê sela'* (Job 39:1), "mountain goats" (*RSV*).[20] It also occurs in 11QtgJob 33:9: *[b]kp' yškwn wyqnn [   ],*[21] "[On] the crag it (i.e., the black eagle[22]) dwells, and it nests [   ]," translating Hebrew *sela' yiškōn* (Job 39:28), "(On) the rock he dwells" (*RSV*). It is further found several times in the newly published texts of Aramaic Enoch from Qumran Cave 4: *[w'mr' s]lq lr['š k]p ḥd rm,* "[and the sheep] climbed to the sum[mit of] a certain high [cr]ag" (4QEn^e 4 iii 19 [= *1 Enoch* 89:29]);[23] *[b]tnyn' wslq lr'š kp' dn,* "climbed up [again for] a second time to the summit of that crag" (4QEn^c 4:3 [= *1 Enoch* 89:32]);[24] *[wlm]drk 'l 'prh w['']l [kp]yh l' tškḥwn mn [ḥmth],* "[and] you are not able [to tr]ead upon the dirt or upon the [roc]ks on account [of the heat]" (4QEn^a 1 ii 8 [= *1 Enoch* 4]).[25] In all of these passages the word seems to have the sense of a "rock" or "crag," a part of a mountainous or hilly region. Coming from Aramaic texts that were used in Palestine in pre-Christian times, this evidence is of no little value.

But does *kp'* occur in pre-Christian writings as a proper name? T. Zahn, in his commentary on Matt 16:18, implied that the word was so used, but he provided no examples of it.[26] O. Cullmann, who notes Zahn's lack of documentation, stated that *kp'* "is not, as one might suppose, attested as a proper name in Aram."[27] Indeed, this lack of attestation of *kp'* as a proper name has been seen as one of the major difficulties in viewing the occurrence of *Petros* and *petra* in Matt 16:18 as a reflection of an Aramaic wordplay. In answering an objection which O. Immisch[28] had brought against his interpretation of Matt 16:17–

19,[29] A. Dell argued that Jesus could not have used the wordplay, because the Greek could not have been a translation from an Aramaic *Vorlage,* since that would imply that *kpʾ* was a proper name. "Nun ist aber *kypʾ* kein Eigenname."[30] And in John 1:42, argued Dell, *Petros* is a translation of *Kēphas,* not of a proper name, but of a description (*Bezeichnung*). The main thrust of Dell's argument, then, was that since *kpʾ* is unknown as a proper name, there could have been no wordplay involved.

Now, aside from the fact that, as we noted above, Paul uses the grecized form of *kpʾ* properly as a name for Peter—which reflects a very early use of it as a proper name (certainly prior to the composition of Matthew)—there does exist an instance of the Aramaic name which should be introduced into the discussion.

Though the text in which it appears has been known since 1953, when it was first published, it has scarcely been noticed; as far as I know, it has not been introduced into the discussion of the *Kēphas/Petros* problem. However, *kpʾ* does occur as a proper name in an Aramaic text from Elephantine (*BMAP* 8:10) dated to the eighth year of Darius the King (= Darius II, 424–402 B.C.), hence to 416 B.C.[31] The name is found in a list of witnesses to a document in which a certain Zakkur gives or transfers a slave, named Yedaniah, to a certain Uriah. Nine lines of the document spell out the details of the transfer, and the last three give the names of the witnesses, the first of which runs as follows:

10 *śhdyʾ bgw ʿtrmlky br qlqln, snkšr br šbty; śhd ʿqb br kpʾ.*

Witnesses hereto (are): ʿAtarmalki, son of QLQLN; Sinkishir, son of Shabbetai; witness: ʿAqab, son of Kephaʾ.

The Uriah to whom the slave is given in the text is identified as an "Aramean of Syene" (*ʾrmy zy swn*). This is not the place to discuss in detail the meaning of *ʾrmy* over against *yhwdy* as designations of Jewish individuals in Elephantine texts.[32] Suffice it to say that many Jews and persons with Jewish names figured in the fifth-century military colony on the island of Elephantine and in the town of Syene (= modern Assuan), on the east bank of the Nile opposite the island, and have been given these gentilic designations in the papyri discovered there. The persons mentioned in these Aramaic texts bore not only Northwest Semitic names (Hebrew, Aramaic, or Phoenician), but also Babylonian, Egyptian, and Persian names. Indeed there was a mixture of these names too, even within families, as other names in line 10 show: Sinkishir, a Babylonian name for a son of Shabbetai, an (almost certainly) Hebrew name (used of a Jew in Ezra 10:15; Neh 8:7; 11:16).

This mixture of names in the Elephantine texts raises a question about the patronymic in *BMAP* 8:10. The *br* that precedes it makes it clear the *kp᾽* is a proper name; so it can no longer be maintained that the name is unattested. But is it clearly an Aramaic name, one that would underlie *Kēphas* in the New Testament? When E. G. Kraeling first published this Elephantine text, he translated the name of the last witness on line 10 simply as "'Akab b. *Kp᾽*,'" setting the transliterated consonants of the patronymic in italics, as he did elsewhere for names about which he was uncertain or for which he had no real explanation.[33] His note on 8:10 explains the son's name thus:

> the perf. (or part.) of the same verb that appears in the impf. in *yᶜqb*, Jacob. In both cases we have hypocoristica—the full name must have been something like ᶜ*qbyh* (on a 3d century B.C. inscription from Alexandria; see *RES*, 2. No. 79) or ᶜ*qbnbw*, Aqab-Nebo, in *AP* 54:10. . . .[34]

Concerning the patronymic, Kraeling wrote:

> The name *kp᾽* must also have a deity for a subject; J. A. *kp᾽*, "overthrows." Or may one compare *kf᾽*, Ranke, *ÄP*, 344:15?[35]

That the name *kp᾽* is a hypocoristicon is most probable, even though we have no clear instance of a fuller form of the name. That it has anything to do with Aramaic *kp᾽*, "overthrow," is quite problematic, in my opinion, since that root more properly means "to bend, curve."

The name *kp᾽* resembles other proper names which end in *aleph* in Aramaic documents from Egypt, such as *Bs᾽* (*BMAP* 11:2), *Ṣḥ᾽* (*AP* 18:4), *Pms᾽* (*AP* 73:13), *Ky᾽* (*AP* 2:19), *Tb᾽* (*RES* 1794:18), etc. The problem is to suggest real Egyptian equivalents for such short names in these Aramaic texts. In a name like *Ḥrtb᾽* (*CIS* 138B:3) an Egyptian equivalent has been suggested, *Ḥr-(n)i-ßibʒ-t* (= Greek *Artbōs*), where the *aleph* of the Aramic form may reflect a real *aleph* in an Egyptian word, *bʒ.t*, "tree": "Horus of the tree." But in some of the short names there are also variants, such as *Kyh* (*RES* 1297:2), or *Ṣhh*, which suggest that the final *aleph* of the Aramaic form is a vowel letter. In the last instance, the name *Ṣḥʒ*, though often explained as Egyptian,[36] is in reality an Aramaized form, and the Akkadian transcription of it as *Ṣi-ḥa-a* argues in favor of the final *aleph* as a vowel letter. Compare also *Pms᾽* (*AP* 73:13) and *Pmsy* (*AP* 44:7). All of this may not be making out an air-tight case; yet it does at least suggest that the best explanation for *kp᾽* is that it is not an Egyptian name, but rather an Aramaic name. In that case, it represents *Kephā᾽*.

It has, at any rate, been so interpreted by no less an authority in things Aramaic than W. Baumgartner. He listed it under the Hebrew word *kēph*, "Fels," in *Hebräisches und aramäisches Lexikon zum Alten Testament*,[37] identifying it as a masculine proper name and equating it, without further question, with "*Kēphas* NT." P. Grelot similarly toyed with the equation of the *BMAP* form and the New Testament name,[38] but he was obviously hesitant about it, since he mentions two other explanations: a hypocoristicon derived from *kpp*, "bend, bow down" (yet he gives no plausible fuller form of the name with which it could be compared); or the Egyptian *kf₃* (an explanation which he simply borrows from Kraeling). But, as Baumgartner has rightly seen, the only plausible explanation of the *BMAP* is that it is an Aramaic name, related to Hebrew *kēph* and the Aramaic common noun *kephā*ʾ.

If one had to justify the existence of such an Aramaic name in the fifth century B.C., the best explanation of it would be that it is a hypocoristicon which has lost some theophoric element. In itself, it would be no more enigmatic as a name than the Hebrew *Ṣûr*, "Rock," borne by one of the sons of Jeiel and Maacah of Gibeon (1 Chr 8:30; 9:36) and by one of the kings or leaders of the Midianites (Num 25:15; 31:8; Josh 13:21).[39] This name is rendered in the *RSV* as Zur, but it is a hypocoristicon of such names as *Ṣûrîʾel* (Num 3:35) or *Ṣûriṥadday* (Num 1:6; 2:12).

The least one can say is that *kp*ʾ is not unknown as a proper name and that Peter is not the first person to have borne it. That it was otherwise in use among Jews of Palestine remains, of course, to be shown. The existence of it as a proper name at least makes more plausible the suggestion that a wordplay in Aramaic was involved. On the other hand, it may take away some of the uniqueness of the name which was often seen in the conferral of it on a disciple by Jesus.

The Aramaic substratum of Matt 16:17–18 (at least for those phrases mentioned at the beginning of this essay) might have been something like the following:[40]

> ʾantāh hûʾ mĕšîḥāʾ, bĕrēh dî ʾĕlāhāʾ . . . ṭûbayk, Šimʿôn bar Yônāh . . . ʾantāh hûʾ Kephāʾ wĕʿal kephāʾ dēnāh ʾebnêh . . . .

The wordplay that emerges from such an Aramaic substratum of the Matthean verse could be the key to the role that Simon is to play: He or some aspect of him is to be a crag/rock in the building of the *ekklēsia*. The further connotations of this image can be explored by others.

One further aspect of the philological consideration of the Matthean verse needs to be explored, viz., the relation of Aramaic *kp*ʾ to Greek *Petros*. This brings us to the second part of this essay.

II. *The Greek Name* Petros

The problem that confronts one is to explain why there is in the Matthean passage a translation of the Aramaic substratum, which is claimed to have the same word *kp'* twice, by two Greek words, *Petros* and *petra*. In John 1:42, *Petros* is given as the equivalent of Aramaic *Kephā'* (grecized as *Kēphas*); this is quite understandable. But if the underlying Aramaic of Matt 16:18 had *kephā'* twice, then we should expect *sy ei Petros kai epi toutō tō petrō oikodomēsō. . . .* Because of this problem, two different conclusions have been drawn: (1) A. Dell has concluded that v. 18 cannot be a translation of an underlying Aramaic saying of Jesus ("kein Jesuswort"), but must rather be the creation of Greek-speaking Christians.[41] (2) P. E. Hughes, in studying the pair *Petros/petra*, "for which a suitable Semitic equivalent is not available," infers rather that "Jesus actually spoke in Greek on this occasion."[42] It is hard to imagine two more radically opposed conclusions!

Part of the problem comes from the nature of the languages involved. Both *petros* and *petra* are at home in the Greek language from its earliest periods; and though the words were at times used with slightly different nuances, it is clear that "they are often used interchangeably."[43] On the other hand, G. Gander has shown how Hebrew *'eben, selaʿ, and ṣûr* are all rendered by *kephā'* in Syriac (i.e., Aramaic of a later period).[44] So perhaps we are dealing with an Aramaic term which was used with different nuances. When translated into Greek, the masculine form *petros* would lend itself as a more likely designation of a person (Simon), and a literary variant, the feminine *petra*, for an aspect of him that was to be played upon.

Another aspect of the problem is that *Petros* has not yet turned up in Greek as a proper name prior to its occurrence for Simon in the New Testament. The impression has been given that it does indeed occur. The first two occurrences of *Petros* in D. Foraboschi's *Onomasticon alterum papyrologicum*,[45] suggest that there is a contemporary extrabiblical occurrence or a nearly contemporary one: in SB 6191,[46] which Foraboschi dates to the first century;[47] and in *P.Oxy.* 2235, which Foraboschi dates to the second century.[48]

Neither of these references is accurate. The text in SB 6191 is most likely late Roman or Byzantine. It is listed under *"christliche Grabsteine"* and comes from Antinoe.[49] So Foraboschi's date for it in the first century A.D. is erroneous. Similarly, his second-century date for *P.Oxy.* 2235 is not correct; the editor of the text says of it, *"Circa A.D. 346."*[50] The list of occurrences of the name *Petros* in F. Preisigke's *Namenbuch*[51] contains no names that are clearly pre-Christian. In Christian usage after the New Testament the name *Petros* is, of course, found. It is even found as the name of a pagan in Damascius, *Vita Isidori* 170 (fifth-sixth centuries A.D.), and as the name of the *praeses Arabiae* (A.D. 278–79), Petrus Aurelius.[52]

These, then, are the philological considerations that I have thought worth proposing in the matter of the names, Cephas/Peter. Even if what is presented here stands up under further scrutiny, we should still have to admit that "not all the problems connected w. the conferring of the name Cephas-Peter upon Simon . . . have yet been solved."[53]

NOTES

* Originally published in *Text and Interpretation: Studies in the New Testament Presented to Matthew Black* (ed. E. Best and R. M. Wilson; Cambridge: University Press, 1979) 121–32.

[1] Modestly tucked away in an otherwise informative article on *Petros* in BAG, 660 is the admission: "Not all the problems connected w. the conferring of the name Cephas-Peter upon Simon . . . have yet been solved."

[2] Ibid., 758, 785.

[3] Luke 4:38; 5:3, 4, 5, 8, 10; 22:31; 24:34.

[4] Luke 8:45, 51; 9:20, 28, 32, 33; 12:41; 18:28; 22:8, 34, 54, 55, 58, 60, 61; Acts 1:13, 15; 2:14, 37, 38; 3:1, 3, 4, 6, 11, 12; 4:8, 13, 19; 5:3, 8, 9, 15, 29; 8:14, 20; 9:32, 34, 38, 39, 40; 10:5, 9, 13, 14, 17, 19, 21, 25, 26, 34, 44, 45, 46; 11:2, 4, 7; 12:3, 5, 6, 7, 11, 14, 16, 18; 15:7.

[5] Luke 5:8; cf. in addition to Acts 10:5 cited in n. 4 above, 10:18, 32; 11:13.

[6] To some commentators it has seemed that the Jewish-Christian James would naturally use the Semitic form "Symeon" in speaking of Peter; so O. Cullmann, *Peter: Disciple, Apostle, Martyr: A Historical and Theological Study* (2d ed.; Philadelphia: Westminster, 1962) 19 n. 3. Others, aware of the compilatory nature of Acts 15, raise the question whether vv. 13–29 may not have been derived from a source different from that from which Luke derived the information in vv. 4–12. In this hypothesis, the name Symeon may have referred originall/ to another person (e.g., Symeon Niger of Acts 13:1; see S. Giet, "L'Assemblée apostolique et le décret de Jérusalem: Qui était Siméon?" *RSR* 39 [1951] 203–20; cf. *JBC*, art. 46, §32–34; art. 45, §72–77). In any case, as the text of Acts stands today, "Symeon" is to be understood as referring to Peter (for Luke has undoubtedly "telescoped" accounts of two originally separate and distinct Jerusalem decisions).

[7] See B. M. Metzger, *A Textual Commentary on the Greek New Testament,* 699: "The weight of external support for the two readings is almost equally divided." "The Committee was agreed that transcriptionally it is more likely that *Simōn* is a correction of *Symeōn* than vice versa. . . ."

[8] CSEL, 26. 36 (ed. C. Ziwsa, 1893). Similarly, Isidore of Seville, *Etym.* 7.9,3 (PL, 82. 287); cf. W. M. Lindsay, *Isidori hispalensis episcopi etymologiarum sive originum libri xx* (2 vols.; Oxford: Clarendon, 1957).

[9] See Y. M.-J. Congar, "Cephas—Céphalè—Caput," *Revue du moyen âge latin* 8

(1952) 5–42; cf. J. A. Burgess, *History of the Exegesis of Matthew 16:17–19 from 1781 to 1965* (Ann Arbor, MI: Edwards, 1976) 58–59, 89.

[10] See C. Roth, "Simon-Peter," *HTR* 54 (1961) 91–97.

[11] See my reply to C. Roth, "The Name Simon," *HTR* 56 (1963) 1–5, with further discussion in *HTR* 57 (1964) 60–61. It has all been reprinted in *ESBNT*, 104–12.

[12] For a recent survey of these opinions, see J. A. Burgess, *A History of the Exegesis* (n. 9 above), passim.

[13] The name Cephas further appears in *1 Clem.* 47.3. The antiquity of the name is established by the Pauline use of it. One can only speculate about his seeming preference for it.

[14] *Hist. eccl.* 1.12,2 (GCS, 2/1. 82).

[15] See K. Lake, "Simon, Cephas, Peter," *HTR* 14 (1921) 95–97; A. M. Völlmecke, *Jahrbuch des Missionshauses St Gabriel* 2 (1925) 69–104; 3 (1926) 31–75; D. W. Riddle, "The Cephas-Peter Problem, and a Possible Solution," *JBL* 59 (1940) 169–80; N. Huffman, "Emmaus among the Resurrection Narratives," *JBL* 64 (1945) 205–26, esp. pp. 205–6 n. 1; C. M. Henze, "Cephas seu Kephas non est Simon Petrus!" *Divus Thomas* 35 (1958) 63–67; J. Herrera, "Cephas seu Kephas est Simon Petrus," ibid., 481–84.

[16] O. Cullmann, "*Petros*," *TDNT* 6 (1968) 100 n. 6; *Peter* (n. 6 above), 20. Cf. G. Klein, "Galater 2, 6–9 und die Geschichte der Jerusalemer Urgemeinde," *ZTK* 57 (1960) 275–95, esp. p. 283; reprinted, *Rekonstruktion und Interpretation: Gesammelte Aufsätze zum Neuen Testament* (Munich: Kaiser, 1969) 99–128 (mit einem Nachtrag), esp. pp. 106–7.

[17] *UBSGNT*[3], 650–51, makes no mention of this fluctuation, probably considering it not serious enough to note. According to E. Nestle's *apparatus criticus*, *Petron* is read in 1:18 by D, G, the Koine text-tradition, *pl*, latt, sy[h]; in 2:9 P[46] reads *Iakōbos kai Petros*. But MSS D, G, it, Marcion, Origen, and Ambrosiaster invert the order of these names; in 2:11 *Petros* is read by the Koine text-tradition, D, G, *pm*, s[h], Marcion; in 2:14 *Petrō* is read by the same MSS as in 1:18.—Cf. J. T. Clemons, "Some Questions on the Syriac Support for Variant Greek Readings," *NovT* 10 (1968) 26–30.

[18] See BDF §53(1).

[19] See, e.g., A. Dell, "Matthäus 16, 17–19," *ZNW* 15 (1914) 1–49, esp. pp. 14–17. For an interesting comparison of the nuances of *kephā'* in Syriac as a translation of Greek *petros, petra, lithos* or of Hebrew '*eben, selaʿ*, and *ṣûr*, see G. Gander, "Le sens des mots: *Petros-petra/Kiphâ-kiphâ/Kyp'-kyp'* dans Matthieu xvi:18a," *RTP* 29 (1941) 5–29; but some of his reasoning is strange. Cf. A. F. J. Klijn, "Die Wörter 'Stein' und 'Felsen' in der syrischen Übersetzung," *ZNW* 50 (1959) 99–105.

[20] See J. P. M. van der Ploeg and A. S. van der Woude, *Le targum de Job de la grotte xi de Qumran* (Koninklijke nederlandse Akademie van Wetenschappen; Leiden: Brill, 1971) 74.

[21] Ibid., 76.

[22] On the "black eagle," see my remarks in "The Contribution of Qumran Aramaic to the Study of the New Testament," *NTS* 20 (1973–74) 382–407, esp. p. 396; reprinted, *WA*, 85–113, esp. p. 95.

[23] See J. T. Milik, *The Books of Enoch: Aramaic Fragments of Qumran Cave 4* (with the collaboration of Matthew Black) (Oxford: Clarendon, 1976) 243–44. Note the use of the adjective *rm*, "high," in this passage.

[24] Ibid., 204–5.

[25] Ibid., 146–47. Here [kp]yh, "rocks," stands in parallelism with ʿprh, "dirt." The Aramaic preposition ʿl is interesting, as a background for the Matthean epi. One should also note the meaning of the verb tškhwn, "you are able"; for the problem on which it bears, see my commentary, The Genesis Apocryphon of Qumran Cave 1 (BibOr 18A; 2d ed.; Rome: Biblical Institute, 1971) 150.

[26] Das Evangelium des Matthäus (Kommentar zum Neuen Testament, 1; 4th ed.; Leipzig: Deichert, 1922) 540.

[27] "Petros, Kēphas," TDNT 6 (1968) 100 n. 6. Cf. R. E. Brown, The Gospel According to John (i–xii): Introduction, Translation, and Notes (AB 29; Garden City, NY: Doubleday, 1966) 76: "Neither Petros in Greek nor Kēphâ in Aramaic is a normal proper name; rather it is a nickname. . . ." Brown has a similar statement in his article, "Peter," IDBSup, 654. See further J. Schmid, "Petrus 'der Fels' und die Petrusgestalt der Urgemeinde," Begegnung der Christen: Studien evangelischer und katholischer Theologen (ed. M. Roesle and O. Cullmann; Stuttgart: Evangelisches Verlagswerk; Frankfurt: J. Knecht, 1959) 347–59, esp. pp. 356–57; H. Rheinfelder, "Philologische Erwägungen zu Matth 16,18," BZ 24 (1938–39) 139–63, esp. p. 153 n. 1; H. Clavier, "Petros kai petra," Neutestamentliche Studien für Rudolf Bultmann (BZNW 21; Berlin: Töpelmann, 1954) 94–109, esp. p. 106; J. Lowe, Saint Peter (New York/Oxford: Oxford University, 1956) 7.

[28] "Matthäus 16, 18: Laienbemerkungen zu der Untersuchung Dells, ZNW xv, 1914, 1ff," ZNW 17 (1916) 18–26 (see n. 19 above).

[29] "Matthäus 16, 17–18," ZNW 15 (1914) 1–49. On the value of Dell's interpretation, see R. Bultmann, "Die Frage nach dem messianischen Bewusstsein Jesu und das Petrus-Bekenntnis," ZNW 19 (1919–20) 165–74, esp. p. 170 n. 2.

[30] "Zur Erklärung von Matthäus 16, 17–19," ZNW 17 (1916) 27–32. See further P. Lampe, "Das Spiel mit dem Petrusnamen—Matt. xvi. 18," NTS 25 (1978–79) 227–45, esp. p. 229 ("Auch kyp/kypʾ lässt sich bislang in vorchristlicher Zeit nicht als Eigenname auffinden").

[31] E. G. Kraeling, The Brooklyn Museum Aramaic Papyri: New Documents of the Fifth Century B.C. from the Jewish Colony at Elephantine (New Haven: Yale University, 1953; reprinted, New York: Arno, 1969) 224–31 (+ pl. VIII). The text is actually dated to the 6th of Tishri by the Babylonian calendar (= 22 October) and to the 22d of Paoni by the Egyptian calendar (= 22 September), but there seems to be an error in the text; see Kraeling's note, p. 228.

[32] See B. Porten, Archives from Elephantine: The Life of an Ancient Jewish Military Colony (Berkeley/Los Angeles: University of California, 1968) 3–27 (and the literature cited there); P. Grelot, Documents araméens d'Egypte: Introduction, traduction, présentation (Littératures anciennes du Proche-Orient; Paris: Cerf, 1972) 33–47.

[33] E. G. Kraeling, BMAP, 227.

[34] Ibid., 230. Note, however, the occurrence of the name ʿAqqûb in Neh 8:7, along with Shabbetai.

[35] Ibid.; H. Ranke (Die ägyptischen Personennamen [Glückstadt: Augustin, 1935], 1. 344) gives as the meaning of kfʒ, " 'der Hintere'(?)."

[36] See further my article, "A Re-Study of an Elephantine Aramaic Marriage Contract (AP 15)," Near Eastern Studies in Honor of William Foxwell Albright (ed. H. Goedicke; Baltimore: Johns Hopkins University, 1971) 137–68, esp. p. 147;

reprinted, *WA,* 243–71, esp. p. 250. What is said there about *Ṣḥ⁾* being "Egyptian" needs the more proper nuance that is now being stated here. I am indebted to Professor Thomas O. Lambdin, of Harvard University, for advice on this matter of Egyptian names appearing in Aramaic texts, especially for the treatment of *aleph* in the short names. The formulation of the matter given above, however, is my own; and I alone am responsible for any possibly unfortunate wording.

³⁷ W. Baumgartner, *Hebräisches und aramäisches Lexikon zum Alten Testament* (Leiden: Brill, 1974), 2. 468. I am indebted to J. A. Burgess for calling this reference to my attention.

³⁸ P. Grelot, *Documents araméens d'Egypte* (n. 32 above), 476. Strangely enough, Grelot writes the New Testament form with *epsilon* instead of with *ēta*. The spelling [*K*]*ephas* (with a short *e*) turns up in the Coptic *Acts of Peter and the Twelve Apostles* 1:2 (see M. Krause and P. Labib, *Gnostische und hermetische Schriften aus Codex II und Codex VI* (Glückstadt: Augustin, 1971) 107.

³⁹ Note that Koehler-Baumgartner, *Lexicon in Veteris Testamenti libros* (Leiden: Brill, 1958) 800, even compares Hebrew *Ṣûr,* the proper name, with Aramaic *kyp⁾.*

⁴⁰ If I attempt to retrovert the words of Matt 16:18 here, I am implying only the pre-Matthean existence of such a tradition in Aramaic.

⁴¹ A. Dell, "Zur Erklärung," 29–30.

⁴² P. E. Hughes, "The Languages Spoken by Jesus," *New Dimensions in New Testament Study* (ed. R. N. Longenecker and M. C. Tenney; Grand Rapids, MI: Zondervan, 1974) 127–43, esp. p. 141. I am extremely skeptical about the preservation of any Greek sayings of Jesus; see *WA,* 37.

⁴³ *"Petra,"* *TDNT* 6 (1968) 95. For another view of this matter, see P. Lampe, "Das Spiel" (n. 30 above), 240–45.

⁴⁴ G. Gander, "Le sens des mots" (n. 19 above), 15–16.

⁴⁵ *Onomasticon alterum papyrologicum: Supplemento al Namenbuch di F. Preisigke* (Testi e documenti per lo studio dell'antichità, xvi, serie papirologica, ii; Milano/ Varese: Ist. editoriale cisalpino, 1967–71), fasc. 4, p. 256. I am indebted to my colleague, F. T. Gignac, S.J., for help in checking these Greek texts, and especially for this reference to Foraboschi.

⁴⁶ See F. Preisigke and F. Bilabel, *Sammelbuch griechischer Urkunden aus Ägypten* (Berlin/Leipzig: de Gruyter, 1926) 28.

⁴⁷ D. Foraboschi, *Onomasticon alterum,* 256.

⁴⁸ Ibid. Cf. E. Lobel et al., *The Oxyrhynchus Papyri, Part XIX* (London: Egypt Exploration Fund, 1948) 101.

⁴⁹ F. Preisigke and F. Bilabel, *Sammelbuch* (n. 46 above) 28. Cf. G. Lefebvre, "Egypte chrétienne," *ASAE* 15 (1915) 113–39, esp. pp. 131–32 (§839). Lines 4– 6 date the inscription to "the month of Pachon, 16th (day), beginning of the 13th indiction."

⁵⁰ E. Lobel et al., *The Oxyrhynchus Papyri, Part XIX* (n. 48 above), 101.

⁵¹ F. Preisigke, *Namenbuch* (Heidelberg: Privately published, 1922; reprinted, Amsterdam: A. M. Hakkert, 1967) 321.

⁵² The attempts to cite *Petron* as a reading in one MS of Josephus (*Ant.* 18.6,3 §156) have long been recognized as useless. The best reading there is *Prōton.*

The name *Petros* is not found in such lists as those given in the following places: F. Bechtel, *Die historischen Personennamen des Griechischen bis zur Kaiserzeit* (Halle: Niemeyer, 1917; reprinted, Hildesheim: Olms, 1964) (should be on pp.

370–71); L. Robert, *Noms indigènes dans l'Asie Mineure gréco-romaine: Première partie* (Bibliothèque archéologique et historique de l'institut français d'archéologie d'Istanbul, 13; Paris: A. Maisonneuve, 1963) (should be on p. 563). The entry on *Petros* in W. Pape and G. Benseler, *Wörterbuch der griechischen Eigennamen* (Braunschweig: Vieweg, 1911; reprinted, Graz: Akademische Druck- und Verlagsanstalt, 1959) 1187–88, gives only Christian names, or those of pagans of the Christian period.

[53] See n. 1 above.—See further J. K. Elliott, "*Kēphas: Simon Petros: ho Petros:* An Examination of New Testament Usage," *NovT* 14 (1972) 241–56.

Five

CRUCIFIXION IN ANCIENT PALESTINE, QUMRAN LITERATURE, AND THE NEW TESTAMENT*

IN WRITING to the Corinthians, Paul summed up his Christian message thus: "Jews demand signs and Greeks seek wisdom, but we preach Christ crucified, a stumbling block to Jews and folly to Gentiles, but to those who are called, both Jews and Greeks, Christ the power of God and the wisdom of God" (1 Cor 1:22–24). This familiar Pauline statement, culminating in a rhetorical abstraction of Christ as the power and the wisdom of God, contains nevertheless the succinct Pauline formulation, "we preach Christ crucified." As E. E. Ellis once pointed out, the words "cross" and "crucify" appear in the New Testament outside of the Gospels almost exclusively in the Pauline literature,[1] and there they are used primarily as theological concepts. He continues,

> This is not to say that the historical event of the crucifixion has become less important, much less that the theological concept has displaced it. In accordance with Paul's thought generally the theological meaning arises out of and remains united with the historical occurrence, the "salvation history," to which it refers.[2]

However one wants to explain the relation of the theology of the cross to the historical occurrence, the cross and the crucifixion of Jesus of Nazareth are at the heart of Christian faith. Hence, the phenomenon of crucifixion in first-century Palestine will always be of interest to Christians, and new data that come to light about it will always evoke relationships previously unsuspected. Some new evidence of crucifixion in Palestine and some texts from Qumran that bear on the question have recently been published, and it seems good to review the matter to see what bearing this material has on a cardinal tenet of Christianity and the central affirmation of Paul, "we preach Christ crucified."

I propose to take up three pieces of information and shall discuss the topic under three headings: (1) Ossuary remains from Giv'at ha-Mivtar; (2) Mention of crucifixion in two Qumran texts; and (3) The bearing of this material on certain New Testament passages.

I. *Ossuary Remains from Giv'at ha-Mivtar*

To the northeast of Jerusalem, in the vicinity of the Nablus Road and slightly north of Mt. Scopus, three tombs were discovered in an area called Giv'at ha-Mivtar (or Ras el-Masaref) in June of 1968. They were excavated by V. Tzaferis, of the Israeli Department of Antiquities and Museums, and his report was published in 1970.[3] The tombs belonged to "a vast Jewish cemetery of the Second Temple period, extending from Mount Scopus in the east to the Sanhedriya tombs in the northwest."[4] They were rock-cut family tombs with burial chambers and loculi reached by a forecourt. Two ossuaries found in Tomb I are of particular interest to us. Whereas, in general, the pottery found in these tombs can be dated chronologically to the Late Hellenistic period (end of the second century B.C.) and the destruction of the Second Temple in A.D. 70, Tzaferis limits that of Tomb I to the first century A.D.

The five inscribed ossuaries from Giv'at ha-Mivtar were published by Joseph Naveh.[6] Ossuary 1 was inscribed with *Smwn bnh hklh* (on the broad side) and with *Smwn/bn' hklh* (on the narrow side): "Simon, builder of the Temple."[7] Of this ossuary Tzaferis says:

> The Temple mentioned here is certainly the Temple built by Herod and his successors, and it is clear that this Simon died sometime after the building of the Temple had commenced, i.e., after 20 B.C. The building of the Temple was not finished until a short time before its destruction in A.D. 70, and it is within this period that the death of Simon must be dated.[8]

Ossuary 4 of Tomb I was inscribed on its broad side with two inscriptions:

(a) *Yhwhnn*   "Yehohanan"
(b) *Yhwhnn bn hgqwl*   "Yehohanan son of HGQWL."[9]

Naveh found no satisfactory explanation of *hgqwl*.

Ossuary 4 of Tomb I, however, is precisely the one that is intriguing, since in it were found the bones of an adult male and of a child. The lowest parts of the adult leg bones (*tibiae* and *fibulae*) had been broken, and the heel bones (*calcanei*) had been pierced by an iron nail. Tzaferis comments:

> This is undoubtedly a case of crucifixion. . . . Mass crucifixions in Judea are mentioned under Alexander Janneus, during the revolt against the census of A.D. 7 and again during the Jewish revolt which brought about the final destruction of the Second Temple in A.D. 70. Individuals were also crucified occasionally by the Roman procurators.

> Since the pottery and ossuaries found in Tomb I exclude the period of Alexander Janneus for this crucifixion, and since the general situation during the revolt of A.D. 70 excludes the possibility of burial in Tomb I, it would seem that the present instance was either of a rebel put to death at the time of the census revolt in A.D. 7 or the victim of some occasional crucifixion. It is possible, therefore, to place this crucifixion between the start of the first century A.D. and somewhere just before the outbreak of the first Jewish revolt.[10]

The skeletal remains of the Giv‘at ha-Mivtar ossuaries were further examined by Dr. N. Haas, of the department of anatomy of the Hebrew University and Hadassah Medical School,[11] on whose report the comments of Tzaferis depend. Haas reported: "Both the heel bones were found transfixed by a large iron nail. The shins were found intentionally broken. Death caused by crucifixion."[12] At the end of Haas's article a more extended treatment of the bones is given, along with drawings, photos, and attempts to reconstruct or depict the mode of crucifixion.[13]

The bones were those of an adult male, aged 24–28, about 5′5″ tall. The marks of violence found on the bones were limited to the nailed *calcanei*, to both bones of the left calf (*tibia* and *fibula*), which had been broken in a simple, oblique line, and to the right *tibia*, which had suffered a comminuted (or splintering) fracture. According to Haas, the *calcanei* had been fixed to the upright of the cross by an iron nail that had first been driven through a small plaque of acacia or pistacia wood, then through the heel-bones, and through the upright of olive wood; the point of the nail was finally bent over, apparently behind the upright. Haas described the position of the crucified thus:

> The feet were joined almost parallel, both transfixed by the same nail at the heels, with the legs adjacent; the knees were doubled, the right one overlapping the left; the trunk was contorted; the upper limbs were

stretched out, each stabbed by a nail in the forearm. A study of the nail itself, and of the situation of the calcanean bones between the head and the top of this nail, shows that the feet had not been securely fastened to the cross. This assumption requires the addition of the traditional "sedecula" . . . intended to provide a secure seating for the buttocks of the victim, to prevent collapse and to prolong agony.[14]

Haas also concluded that the leg bones were broken by a *coup de grâce.* The fracture of the right tibial bone was produced by a single, strong blow and had repercussions on the left ankle-bones. "The percussion, passing the already crushed right calf bones, was a harsh and severing blow for the left ones, attached as they were to the sharp-edged wooden cross."[15] The situation was such that when the body was removed from the cross, it was impossible to withdraw the nail and there was a post mortem amputation of the feet—the cut being made only after several abortive attempts had been made to extract the nail. Such are the gruesome details recovered from the evidence of the crucifixion of a Palestinian Jew of the first century A.D., named Yehohanan.

The enigmatic inscription on the ossuary was further studied by Y. Yadin, who suggested a connection between the meaning of it and the way in which the adult had died.[16] The puzzling word in the second inscription is the father's name, which Naveh gave as *hgqwl.* Yadin recalled a story told in the Talmud[17] about a *ḥāsîd* who dreamt about a deceased tax-collector who was tormented in the after-life by being hanged upside down over a river without being able to reach its water with his tongue. In the *Baraitha de-Masseket Niddah,* however, the tax-collector's position is described thus: "He saw the son of Theodorus the tax-collector *ʿqwl* by his legs, and his tongue barely touching the water."[18] Now one of the priestly blemishes mentioned in the Mishnah is *ʿyql* (*ʿiqqēl*), i.e., "bow-legged," "one whose soles come together and whose knees do not touch."[19] Hence, the son of Theodorus was seen hanging upside down with his legs positioned like the *ʿiqqēl*, "soles together, knees apart." In view of this, Yadin suggested that one should rather read line *b* of the ossuary inscription as *Yhwḥnn bn hʿqwl,* in which the *he* is really the definite article: "Yehohanan, son of the *ʿqwl* (= the one hanged with his knees apart)."[20] Thus line *a* of the inscription would refer to the crucified man himself, Yehohanan, and line *b* to his son, Yehohanan, the son of the *ʿqwl,* explaining the child's bones buried in the same ossuary.

Yadin also called in question the mode of crucifixion. He contests Haas's interpretation that the heels and the acacia-wood plaque, pierced by the nail, were affixed to the upright of olive wood, the upright of the cross. Rather, according to him, the heels were pierced and fixed together to be attached to two plaques of wood, acacia near the end of the nail, and olive near its point, and the nail was then bent backwards to secure the attachment. The man then was fixed to the cross by being hung by his parted legs over the top of the cross—the legs with knees apart but with heels securely fastened together to form a loop over the top to prevent the body from sliding down.

Yadin's interpretation is thus quite different from that originally proposed by either Haas (for the crucifixion) or Naveh (for the inscription). Though Yadin's interpretation of the skeletal remains may possibly be better than Haas's, the defense that he attempts to offer for the reading of *hgqwl*, with the *ghimel* as a badly written *ʿayin,* is far from convincing, and, frankly, even calls in question the proposed mode of crucifixion. The mode seems to be proposed to explain the questionable philological explanation of the inscription.

In any case, the evidence brought to light by this Israeli excavation is precious, indeed; and coming from Christian and non-Christian teamwork, it cannot be thought to be conditioned or prejudiced.

It might also be well to recall here the words of Josephus who described the crucifixion of Jews at the time of the Fall of Jerusalem (A.D. 70):

> The soldiers out of rage and hatred amused themselves by nailing their prisoners in different postures; and so great was their number that space could not be found for the crosses nor crosses for the bodies.[21]

Though this evidence of crucifixion from ossuary 4 of Tomb I of Givʿat ha-Mivtar is unrelated to the crucifixion of Jesus of Nazareth, it is nevertheless of value in giving us evidence of such a first-century Palestinian execution. In other words, the evidence for the practice is no longer solely literary in extrabiblical writings, but now archaeological as well.[22]

II. *Mention of Crucifixion in Two Qumran Texts*

One of the Qumran texts in which mention is made of crucifixion has been known for some time, the pesher on Nahum of Qumran Cave 4,[23] but it has been the subject of renewed discussion because of a passage in the Temple Scroll of Qumran Cave 11, which was published not long ago. The pesher on Nahum (4QpNah) has been fully published by J. M. Allegro as 4Q*169*.[24] The relevant passage in it is found on frgs. 3–4, col. i, lines 1–11, esp. lines 7–8. It forms part of a commentary on Nah 2:12–14, in which the prophet describes in poetic fashion the plundering of the treasures of Nineveh and the terror caused for its Assyrian inhabitants as a result of the opposition that the Lord of Hosts assumed toward that rapacious city. It fell in 612 B.C. The author of the Qumran commentary applies the sense of Nahum's words rather to events in the history of Judea to present its own interpretation of what God has done to certain elements in that people. The text of the part of the pesher that interests us reads as follows:

1]מדור לרשעי גוים אשר הלך אריה לבוא שם גור ארי

2 [ואין מחריד פשרו על דמי]טרוס מלך יון אשר בקש לבוא ירושלים בעצת דורשי החלקות

3 [ולא השלים אל אותה   ביד מלכי יון מאנתיכוס עד עמוד מושלי כתיים ואחר תרמס

4]ארי טורף בדי גוריו מחנק ללביותיו טרף

5]פשרו[על כפיר החרון אשר יכה בגדוליו ואנשי עצתו

6]וימלא טרף[חירה ומעונתו טרפה פשרו על כפיר החרון

7 [אשר מצא חטא חטא משפט] מות בדורשי החלקות אשר יתלה אנשים חיים

8 [על העץ כי כן נעשה] בישראל מלפנים כי לתלוי חי על העץ ויק[רא הנני אלי]כה[

9 נא[ם יהוה צבאות והבערתי בעשן רובכ]ה וכפיריכה תאכל חרב והכרתי מארץ ט[רפה

10 ולא י[שמע עוד קול מלאככה   פש]רו רובכה הם גדודי חילו א[שר בירושלי]ם וכפיריו הם

11 גדולי[ו   ] וטרפו הוא ההון אשר קב[צו כוה]ני ירושלים אשר

12 וי[תנוהו ע[   ]

[1[Jerusalem shall become] a dwelling-place for the wicked among the Gentiles. *Where the lion went to enter (and where) the lion's cubs (were)* [2][*with none to disturb (them)*. The interpretation of it concerns Deme]trius, the king of Greece, who sought to enter Jerusalem at the advice of the Seekers-after-Smooth-Things, [3][but God did not deliver it] into the hand of the kings of Greece from Antiochus (IV Epiphanes) until the appearance of the rulers of the Kittim. Later on she will be trodden down [4][   ]. *The lion tears enough for its cubs (and) strangles* prey *for its lionesses.* [5][

The interpretation of it] concerns the Lion of Wrath, who strikes by means of his nobles and his counsellors [6][*and he fills with prey] his cave and his dens with torn flesh.* The interpretation of it concerns the Lion of Wrath [7][who has found a crime punishable by] death in the Seekers-after-Smooth-Things, whom he hangs as live men [8][on the tree, as it was thus done] in Israel from of old, for of one hanged alive on the tree (Scripture) re[ads]. *Behold, I am against [you]*, [9]*say[s Yahweh of Hosts, and I will burn in smoke your abundance]; and the sword shall devour your young lions. And [I] will cut off [from the land] its [p]rey,* [10]*and no [longer] sh[all the voice of your messengers be heard.* The inter]pretation of it: "Your abundance" means his warrior-bands wh[o are in Jerusal]em; and "his young lions" are [11]his nobles

[   ] and "his prey" is the wealth which [the prie]sts of Jerusalem have amas[sed], which [12]they will give t[o   ][25]

It is not possible to discuss this text here in great detail.[26] But the following three points in it should be noted.

(1) Surprising, indeed, is the virtually unanimous agreement among commentators on this text that it contains an allusion to the Seleucid ruler, Demetrius III Eucerus (95–78 B.C.).[27] Enemies of the bellicose Sadducee high priest, Alexander Janneus (in office 103–76 B.C.), had invited Demetrius to come to their assistance in Jerusalem.[28] In this text the enemies are called the "Seekers-after-Smooth-Things" and are generally identified as Pharisees.[29] Demetrius III Eucerus did come, indeed, to the aid of Alexander Janneus' enemies. He encamped at Shechem in 88 B.C., where a fierce battle between his troops and the forces of Alexander Janneus eventually took place. Even though he was the victor in the battle, he had to leave the country in a short time, having lost the support of most of the Jews who had invited him in the first place. As a result he never succeeded in entering Jerusalem—a fact to which 4QpNah 3–4 i 2–3 alludes quite clearly. But Alexander Janneus eventually managed to regain Jerusalem and brought back to it many of the enemy Jews who had caused him so much trouble. Josephus tells us how he then "did a thing that was as cruel as could be: While he feasted with his concubines in a conspicuous place, he ordered some eight hundred of the Jews to be crucified, and slaughtered their children and wives before the eyes of the still living wretches."[30] This is the fact to which 4QpNah 3–4 i 7–8 refers, even though the exact interpretation of these lines is not perfectly clear.

(2) Ever since the first publication of this column by Allegro in 1956, it has been recognized that *kpyr hḥrwn*, "the Lion of Wrath" (lines 5, 6), refers to Alexander Janneus.[31] The reason for this designation is not clear, but it fits the pattern of the cryptic names that are otherwise used in this (and other) Qumran text(s), such as the "Seekers-after-Smooth-Things," the "Kittim," "Ephraim," etc.

(3) The crucial passage in this column, which has received varied interpretations, is found in lines 7–8. After the lacuna in line 7 Allegro originally understood the first word *mwt* as "death,"[32] an interpretation that he subsequently abandoned in the *editio princeps,* where he regarded the three consonants rather as the end of the word [*nq*]*mwt*, "vengeance" (*nĕqāmôt*).[33] Y. Yadin has, however, more plausibly suggested that one should read *mšpṭ mwt*, an allusion to Deut 21:22,[34] which in this context would mean "a verdict of death." Yadin made no effort to restore the rest of the lacuna, but I should propose, following up his

suggested allusion to Deut 21:22, that one read [*'šr mṣ' ḥṭ' mšpṭ*] *mwt bdwršy hḥlqwt,* "[who has found a crime punishable by] death in the Seekers-after-Smooth-Things," which is closely dependent on the wording of that verse of Deuteronomy.

At the beginning of line 8 the lacuna has been restored in various ways, as Yadin has already pointed out.[35] But in these various restorations one idea has been common: the horror that the sect was expressing at such crucifixion (resembling that of Josephus himself quoted above). The various proposed ways of restoration are the following:

(a) *'šr l' y'šh,* "[which was never done] before in Israel";[36]
(b) *'šr lw' 'šh 'yš,* "[which no man did] before in Israel";[37]
(c) *'šr lw' hyh,* "[which never took place] before in Israel."[38]

More recently Yadin has proposed a different interpretation of the passage and one that is almost surely correct.[39] According to him, the sect did not condemn Alexander Janneus for his actions; although it did not approve of them, it nevertheless recognized in them an expression of God's wrath against the Seekers-after-Smooth-Things, the Pharisees. Consequently, Yadin restores the beginning of line 8 thus: Either [*'l h'ṣ ky z't htwrh*] *byśr'l mlpnym,* "[on the tree, as this is the law] in Israel as of old" or [*'l h'ṣ ky kn hmšpṭ*] *byśr'l mlpnym* (same translation).[40] Yadin explains the "law in Israel" by referring to Josh 8:23–29, the execution of the king of Ai, and to Deut 21:22, as used in the Temple Scroll. Yadin's restoration is certainly acceptable, but the one that I have proposed above expresses the same basic idea, without saying whether it was "law" or not, [*'l h'ṣ ky kn n'šh*] *byśr'l mlpnym.*[41]

No little part of the reason for so interpreting 4QpNah comes from a passage in the Temple Scroll, to which we now turn. This text was acquired at the time of the Six-Day War in 1967 by Y. Yadin for the Shrine of the Book (through support from the Wolfson Foundation).[42] The passage, which is related to 4QpNah, is found in col. 64, lines 6–13 and reads as follows:

כי	6
יהיה איש רכיל בעמו ומשלים את עמו לגוי נכר ועושה רעה בעמו	7
ותליתמה אותו על העץ וימת על פי שנים עדים ועל פי שלושה עדים	8
יומת והמה יתלו אותו ‹על› העץ כי יהיה באיש חטא משפט מות ויברח אל	9
תוך הגואים ויקלל את עמו ואת בני ישראל ותליתמה גם אותו על העץ	10
וימות ולוא תלין נבלתמה על העץ כי קבור תקוברמ{ה} ביום ההוא כי	11
מקללי אלוהים ואנשים תלוי על העץ ולוא תטמא את האדמה אשר אנוכי	12
נותן לכה נחלה	13

[6] . . . If [7]a man has informed against his people and has delivered his people up to a foreign nation and has done evil to his people, [8]you shall hang him on the tree and he shall die. On the evidence of two witnesses and on the evidence of three witnesses, [9]he shall be put to death, and they shall hang him ⟨on⟩ the tree. If a man has committed a crime punishable by death and has fled to [10]the midst of the Gentiles and has cursed his people and the children of Israel, *you shall hang him* too *on the tree* [11]*and he shall die. Their bodies shall not pass the night on the tree, but you shall indeed bury* them *that very day, for what is* [12]*hanged upon the tree is accursed by God* and men; *and you shall not defile the land which* I am [13]*giving to you for an inheritance.* . . .

Once again, we cannot discuss this text here in great detail, but the following three points should be noted.[43]

(1) There is no doubt that the text is providing a halakic interpretation of Deut 21:22–23. Since this is a pre-Christian Jewish interpretation—even though it may stem from a particular type of Judaism—it is important to see what was being made of the text of Deuteronomy itself at this period. Two crimes are specified as being covered by Deut 21:22–23: (*a*) treason, i.e., the passing on of information to an enemy, the delivering of one's people to a foreign nation, and the doing of evil to one's people;[44] (*b*) evading the due process of law in a case of capital punishment, i.e., by fleeing to a foreign country, and cursing one's people and the children of Israel.[45] These are clearly developments of the Deuteronomic text itself, specifying the crimes for execution.

Yadin is of the opinion that the specific crimes mentioned here, to which Deut 21:22 is being applied, allude to the historic incident of Demetrius III Eucerus and Alexander Janneus.[46] I think that he is right, but there is scarcely any way of really proving it, and he admits this himself.

(2) The text is not clear about what the punishment for the crimes is to be. In the case of treason it says, first, "you shall hang him on the tree and he shall die," but then it adds, on the testimony of witnesses, "he shall be put to death, and they shall hang him ⟨on⟩ the tree" (lines 8–9). The first sounds like crucifixion; Yadin, however, understands the punishment that "such a man should be hanged alive, dying as a result."[47] But the second statement could mean that such a man should be put to death by some other means and then should be hung on a tree. It is possible, of course, to understand the second statement in the light of the first. In any case, the punishment in the crime of evasion of due process is clearly stated as a hanging of the criminal on the tree alive so that he will die (lines 10–11). This could be understood as crucifixion.

This understanding of the verb *tlh* in the text has been questioned by J. M. Baumgarten, who maintains that the "hanging" which is mentioned in 11QTemple is not crucifixion, but rather one of the four classic modes of capital punishment in Jewish law (stoning, burning, decapitation, and strangulation).[48] "Hanging" here would be a form of *heneq*, "strangulation." Baumgarten admits that in 4QpNah *ytlh 'nšym ḥyym* refers to crucifixion because it explicitly mentions the hanging of "men alive" on the tree, whereas 11QTemple does not. Moreover, Baumgarten notes that "talmudic exegetes have recognized that it [strangulation] lacks any pentateuchal basis and rests ultimately only on the authority of tradition (*b. Sanhedrin* 52b–53a)."[49]

From the use of *ytlh 'nšym ḥyym* in 4QpNah 3–4 i 7 and of *ltlwy ḥy 'l h'ṣ* in line 9 with its allusion to the story in Josephus about Alexander Janneus,[50] who uses the Greek verb *anastauroun,* there can be no doubt that *tlh* in this text refers to crucifixion. It seems to me that 11QTemple is seeking precisely a pentateuchal basis for the "hanging" of which it speaks in the crimes mentioned. Moreover, Yadin is correct in pointing out that in two instances it reverses the order of the verbs, and that this reversal means hanging men alive, "dying as a result," even though the text does not explicitly mention their being "alive." 4QpNah with its allusion to Deut 21:22–23 and its use of *tlh* meaning "crucify" makes it plausible that 11QTemple, which also alludes to Deut 21:22–23, understands *tlh* in the same sense, even without the mention of living persons. Why should *tlh* in this scroll be interpreted by the meaning that it might possibly have in another Jewish tradition, viz., rabbinic— and of a later date? That *ṣlybt qys',* "hanging on a tree,"[51] came to be substituted for *ḥnq* in the list of classic rabbinic modes of execution is beyond doubt—at least for that tradition which made use of the *Tg. Ruth.*[52] Baumgarten maintains that "the term *ṣlybt qys'* refers to hanging, not to crucifixion."[53] But this, in my opinion, is far from certain, and even in his footnote he admits that *ṣlb* "in Aramaic usage . . . was used to designate a variety of forms of execution: impalement, hanging, *as well as crucifixion*" (my italics).[54] The upshot of this is that I think that Yadin's interpretation of 11QTemple is basically correct; but I should interpret *tlh* in it in the light of the use of that verb in 4QpNah, viz., of crucifixion. In this I remain within the literature of the Qumran community for the interpretation and see no reason to understand *tlh* in either of these texts in terms of the rabbinic tradition, as Baumgarten has done.

(3) Deut 21:22–23, which refers to the hanging up of the corpse of an executed criminal exposed as a deterrent to crime, is clearly alluded to in lines 11–13. It refers to a practice that was tolerated in Israel, but which had its limits—and this is the reason for the injunction of burial before sundown. In the MT the reason is *ky qllt 'lhym tlwy* "for a hanged

person is accursed by God." This becomes in 11QTemple 64:12 *ky mqwlly ʾlwhym wʾnšym tlwy ʿl hʿṣ,* "for what is hanged upon the tree is accursed by God and men."[55] The author has thus modified the biblical text and insured its interpretation. Whether this was a deliberate modification to offset the modes of interpretation of Deut 21:23 that became current in the later rabbinic tradition is hard to say. But the debate whether *ky qllt ʾlhym tlwy* means "the hanged is something accursed of God" or "the cursing (= the curser) of God (is) hanged"[56] is clearly excluded. In the course of the rabbinic debate blasphemy and idolatry were considered as "the cursing of God."

If Yadin is right in seeing a connection between 4QpNah and 11QTemple—and I think that he is—and if *tlh* in both does refer to crucifixion, then it would seem to imply that not only Romans in Palestine had made use of this mode of execution. It would also give the lie to a comment made by G. Vermes that the "furious young lion" adopted "a form of execution unknown to the Jewish Law."[57] Whether it was admitted in Jewish Law or not is one thing; whether it was practiced by some Jews is another. Josephus has attributed it to the Hasmonean ruler, Alexander Janneus, and 11QTemple 64:6–13 seems to envisage it as the Essene punishment for the crimes of treason and evasion of due process, as discussed above.

Now the material from these Qumran texts has nothing *per se* to do with the evidence of crucifixion now available from the Palestine ossuary of the Givʿat ha-Mivtar tomb discussed in the first part of this paper. We have no idea of the crime for which Yehohanan suffered the fate that he did. Yet there are details both in the new archaeological evidence and in the Qumran texts that shed some light on certain New Testament texts, to which I should now like to turn.

III. *The Bearing of This Material on Certain New Testament Passages*

In an otherwise enlightened and interesting discussion of "Quotations in St. Paul," B. Lindars discusses the use of Deut 21:23 in *m. Sanh.* 6:4 and in a footnote says, "The interesting reference to this passage in 1QpNahum [*sic,* read 4QpNahum] has no relevance to the New Testament material."[58] This is an astounding assertion, but it illustrates the kind of interpretation of both the Qumran literature and the New Testament that one meets from time to time. It is well, then, that we consider some of the New Testament passages to which this archaeological and literary evidence is certainly relevant.

An allusion to the nailing of Jesus to the cross is found in Col 2:14 in the reference to the cancelling of the bond which stood out against us with its legal demands: "This he set aside, nailing it to the cross" (*RSV*, *proselōsas auto tō staurō*). The implication is that the bond was nailed to the cross together with Jesus himself. There is a further allusion to it in Acts 2:23b, *prospēxantes aneilate*, which the *RSV* translates simply as "(this Jesus) you crucified and killed," but which should more properly be translated as "you fastened to (the cross) and did away with." Cf. also John 20:25. The Colossians' passage has been illustrated by a reference to one in Josephus, which tells of the action of the procurator Gessius Florus (A.D. 64–66), who "ventured that day to do what none had ever done before, viz., to scourge before his tribunal and nail to the cross (*staurō proselōsai*) men of equestrian rank, men who, if Jews by birth, were at least invested with that Roman dignity." The heel bones pierced with an iron nail in the ossuary from Givʿat ha-Mivtar now adds concrete archaeological evidence of the practice of nailing human beings to a wooden cross as an instrument of execution such as is mentioned in these New Testament passages. The evidence for it is no longer purely literary.

The bones from that ossuary, however, illustrate yet another passage in the New Testament, viz., John 19:32: "So the soldiers came and broke the legs of the first, and of the other who had been crucified with him; but when they came to Jesus and saw that he was already dead, they did not break his legs." The Fourth Gospel sees passover-lamb typology in the act, but the fractured, splintered right *tibia* of Yeho-hanan, and his broken left shin bones, which N. Haas interpreted as the *coup de grâce*, give again concrete evidence of the practice to which the Fourth Gospel refers. Cf. *Gos. Pet.* 4:14.

Of course, the main New Testament verses which speak of the crucifixion of Jesus (Mark 15:24, *kai staurousin auton;* Matt 27:35, *staurōsantes de auton;* Luke 23:33, *estaurōsan auton;* and John 19:18, *hopou auton estaurōsan*) are the ones on which this archaeological evidence chiefly bears.

But the evidence from 4QpNah interests us still more. Several points in it should be noted in this connection. Though H. H. Rowley, in his reaction to the wild interpretations of the text given by his quondam student, J. M. Allegro, once called in question whether there was a reference to crucifixion in this column of the pesher,[59] there is today virtually unanimous agreement about the interpretation of that text as referring to the actions of Alexander Janneus against his Jewish enemies. The result is that this text supplies the missing-link in the pre-Christian Palestinian evidence that Jews did regard crucifixion practiced in that period as a form of the "hanging" to which Deut 21:22–23 could be referred. That crucifixion could have been regarded as a form of "hanging on a tree" was often explained by citing the way in which the crime of *perduellio* was punished in the Roman world by a statutory penalty of crucifixion, "caput obnubito, arbori infelici suspendito."[60] That crucifixion was practiced in Roman Palestine—by the Romans themselves and even by the Hasmonean Alexander Janneus before them—has never been doubted. But the application of Deut 21:22–23 to it has been puzzling, even though always taken for granted as customary exegesis. The pesher on Nahum now provides precisely the extrabiblical documentation for such an interpretation.

As is well known, the death of Jesus is described in various New Testament writers as a hanging on a/the tree. In Acts 5:30 Peter, summoned with John before the *synedrion* which had forbidden them to preach in Jesus' name, replies that he must obey God rather than men and continues, "The God of our fathers raised Jesus whom you killed by hanging on a tree" (*hon hymeis diecheirisasthe kremasantes epi xylou*). Or again, in Acts 10:39 Peter, speaking on the occasion of Cornelius' conversion, proclaims, "They put him to death by hanging him on a tree" (*hon kai aneilan kremasantes epi xylou*). Indirectly, another allusion to it is made in Acts 13:29, when Paul, preaching in the synagogue of Antioch in Pisidia, says, "When they had fulfilled all that was written of him, they took him down from the tree (*kathelontes apo tou xylou*) and laid him in a tomb." Similarly, the crucifixion of Jesus, associated with a tree, is spoken of in 1 Pet 2:24, "He himself bore our sins in his body on the tree (*hos tas hamartias hēmōn autos anēnenken en tō sōmati autou epi ton xylon*), that we might die to sin and live to righteousness." In this instance, some commentators have preferred to translate the text, "he himself carried our sins up onto the tree." And there is, of course, the earliest passage of all (Gal 3:13), which alludes explicitly to Deut 21:23, to which I shall return shortly. At the moment we are noting only those New Testament writers who speak explicitly of Jesus' crucifixion as a "hanging on a/the tree."[61] Paul, Acts, and 1 Peter know of this mode of expression, and commentators have generally referred in their explanations to Deut 21:22–23.

Haenchen's comment on Acts 5:30 is interesting in this regard. He says, "The Old Testament expression *kremasantes epi xylou* alludes to Deut 21.22f. LXX, which *the Christians* applied to the crucifixion of Jesus."[62] If by that Haenchen means that Christians were the first to apply Deut 21:22–23 to crucifixion, then the relevance of this Old Testament passage in 4QpNah and 11QTemple to the discussion of such New Testament texts, as we have just mentioned, is obvious. The pesher makes it clear that among at least some Palestinian Jews of the first century B.C. or A.D. the text of Deut 21:22–23 had already been associated with crucifixion. But the anarthrous Pauline and Lucan phrase (*epi xylou*, Gal 3:13; Acts 5:30; 10:39) may well have been influenced by the Greek Old Testament of Deut 21:22.

The New Testament passage that interests us above all in the light of the Qumran material is Gal 3:13. It is part of the first of four midrashic developments of the Abraham story in Genesis which is being used by Paul in chaps. 3–4 as part of his proof for justification by faith.[63] The first midrashic development is found in Gal 3:6–15, and its starting-point is Gen 15:6, from which Paul concludes that people of faith are the real children of Abraham, the ones who inherit the blessings of Abraham. By contrast, however, "all who rely on works of the Law are under a curse, for it is written, 'Cursed be everyone who does not abide by all the things written in the book of the law or do them.'" Paul quotes Deut 27:26 to show that the Mosaic law itself uttered a curse against those who were to live by it. He argues that this "curse of the law" has been removed by Christ Jesus, who became himself a "curse " of the law: "Christ redeemed us from the curse of the law, by becoming a curse for us—for it is written, 'Cursed be every one who hangs on a tree'" (and Deut 21:23 is quoted by him; but his quotation omits "by God" and adds "on a tree," which is not found in the MT, but in the LXX). Judged by the canons of Aristotelian logic, his argument is defective indeed. If it were put into a syllogism, it would clearly have four terms, because the "curse of the law" (referring to Deut 27:26 does not have the same sense (or "comprehension") as the "curse" which Jesus became by being hanged on the tree (Deut 21:23). In this passage Aristotelian logic has to yield to what may be called "rabbinic" logic—a type of interpretation of Old Testament texts which relies on catchword bonds or free associations. I hesitate to identify it simply with the type of Jewish interpretation called *gĕzērāh šāwāh*.[64] In a generic sort of way it may be related to that type of interpretation, because it does interpret one word in the Old Testament by the same word in a different passage, but it does not exactly do with it what is otherwise done. In any case, Paul makes his point when he says that Christ Jesus became a "curse" (in one sense) in redeeming us from "the curse of the law" (in another sense). It is a way of describing one of the effects of the Christ-event.

The Qumran texts, however, help in the understanding of this Pauline passage in the following way. First, they reveal a pre-Christian understanding of crucifixion as a "hanging on a tree" and provide a link for Paul's argumentation. This is especially true of 4QpNah (*pace* B. Lindars). Second, they reveal an analogous extension of the

Deuteronomic text, of which Paul makes use. As mentioned earlier, Deut 21:22–23 really deals with the exposure or "hanging" of the corpse of an executed criminal. The Temple Scroll shows the extension of the text to two specific crimes, treason (which Yadin has related to the prohibition in Lev 19:16)[65] and evasion of due process. Though flight to the Gentiles is not specifically condemned in the Old Testament, the cursing of one's people associated with it is probably an allusion to the prohibition of Exod 22:27 [Engl. 22:28].[66] Paul, of course, does not allude to either of these Old Testament passages, but in an analogous way he has related Deut 27:26 to Deut 21:22–23. His vicarious, soteriological use of Deut 21:23 and its "hanging" applied to Jesus is a Christian theologoumenon, which we would not expect to find in a Qumran text. Third, commentators have often pointed out that when Paul applies Deut 21:23 to Jesus, he modifies the quotation, writing simply *epikataratos pas ho kremamenos epi xylou*. The Greek Old Testament reads, *kekatēramenos hypo theou pas kremamenos epi xylou*, "cursed by God is every one who is hanged on a tree." This reflects the Hebrew of the MT, *qllt ᵓlhym tlwy*, although the Hebrew lacks the counterpart of *epi xylou* in this part of the verse. The omission of "by God" in Paul's use of Deut 21:23 is said to represent the delicacy of Paul who could not bring himself to say of Jesus that he was *qllt ᵓlhym*, "cursed by God." The same omission is, however, found in 4QpNah 3–4 i 8, and the omission did not escape the notice of Allegro, when he first published the column, ascribing it to the author's "pietistic reasons."[67] Whatever may be the reason for the failure to quote the text of Deut 21:23 in full here, this use of it is at least similar to Paul's.

Moreover, in the Temple Scroll the modified form of the curse-formula is to be noted. In the MT the formula runs *qllt ᵓlhym tlwy*, but in 11QTemple 64:12 it is *mqwlly ᵓlwhym wᵓnšym tlwy*, "accursed by God and men." A second *nomen rectum* has been introduced into the construct chain. The addition may be midrashic, as M. Wilcox suggests,[68] but it clearly precludes a misunderstanding of the Hebrew *qllt ᵓlhym* as blasphemy or a "cursing of God." In another way it provides an interesting illustration of the derision of Jesus by passers-by, chief priests, and scribes (Mark 15:29–32a; Matt 27:39–43).

Finally, it is very questionable, indeed, whether any of the new material in these Qumran texts helps solve the age-old problems about the death of Jesus and reponsibility for it raised by the four canonical Gospels. J. M. Ford has tried to use this Qumran material to support "the historicity of the Gospels and Acts, and Paul's placing of the death of Jesus precisely within the context of the Jewish law."[69] But she has not coped sufficiently with the redaction of many of the passages involved in her discussion and has not allowed for the *Tendenz* that is present in many of them.[70]

Similarly, I have not attempted to relate the various ways in which Deut 21:22–23 is understood in the later targums to this Qumran and New Testament material.[71] At times they have further testimony to the traditions discussed here, but they are later witnesses to this traditional material, perhaps confirming it, but scarcely influencing either the Qumran or the New Testament writers.[72]

NOTES

* Originally published in *CBQ* 40 (1978) 493–513.

[1] "Christ Crucified," *Reconciliation and Hope: New Testament Essays on Atonement and Eschatology Presented to L. L. Morris on His 60th Birthday* (Grand Rapids: Eerdmans, 1974) 69–75, esp. p. 69.

[2] Ibid.

[3] "Jewish Tombs at and near Givʿat ha-Mivtar, Jerusalem," *IEJ* 20 (1970) 18–32.

[4] Ibid., 30.

[5] Ibid., 20.

[6] "The Ossuary Inscriptions from Givʿat ha-Mivtar," *IEJ* 20 (1970) 33–37.

[7] Ibid., 33; see pl. 11.

[8] "Jewish Tombs," 31. The inscription on this ossuary thus helps to date the contents of the tomb.

[9] "The Ossuary Inscriptions," 35; see pl. 13.

[10] "Jewish Tombs," 31. The mass crucifixions under Alexander Janneus are known from Josephus, *Ant.* 13.14,2 §380–81; *J.W.* 1.4,6 §97; for those during the revolt prior to A.D. 70, see Josephus, *Life* 75 §420; *J.W.* 2.14,9 §306–8; 3.7,33 §321; 5.6,5 §289; 5.11,1 §449–51. For crucifixion by Roman governors, prefects, or procurators, see Josephus. *J.W.* 2.5,2 §129. Crucifixion of Jews was also practiced by Antiochus IV Epiphanes; see Josephus, *Ant.* 12.5,4 §256.

[11] "Anthropological Observations on the Skeletal Remains from Givʿat ha-Mivtar," *IEJ* 20 (1970) 38–59.

[12] Ibid., 42. Cf. J. W. Hewitt, "The Use of Nails in the Crucifixion," *HTR* 25 (1932) 29–45.

[13] *IEJ* 20 (1970) pls. 19–24.

[14] Ibid., 58.

[15] Ibid., 57.

[16] "Epigraphy and Crucifixion," *IEJ* 23 (1973) 18–22.

[17] See *j. Hag.* 2,2 (77d); M. Schwab, *Le Talmud de Jérusalem* (6 vols.; Paris: G.-P. Maisonneuve, 1960), 4. 278; cf. *b. Sanh.* 44b; I. Epstein, *The Babylonian Talmud: Seder Nezikin V: Sanhedrin I* (London: Soncino, 1935) 292 and n. 6.

[18] See C. M. Horowitz, *Bāraytāʾ dē-Masseket Niddāh* (*Sēper Tōsĕpātāʾ ʿattîqātāʾ*: Uralte Tosefta's [Borajta's] 5; Frankfurt: Horowitz, 1890), 15, 66–68.

[19] *m. Bek.* 7:6 (see P. Blackman, *Mishnayoh, Volume V: Order Kodashim* (2d ed.; New York: Judaica, 1964), 5. 278. Cf. H. Danby, *The Mishnah Translated from the Hebrew with Introduction and Brief Explanatory Notes* (London: Oxford, 1933) 538–39.

[20] "Epigraphy," 19. Yadin devotes a whole paragraph here to the problem of the *ghimel* instead of an ʿ*ayin.*

[21] *J.W. 5.11,1* §451.

[22] See further J. F. Strange, "Crucifixion, Method of," *IDBSup,* 199–200. Cf. H.-W. Kuhn, "Zum Gekreuzigten von Givʿat ha-Mivtar: Korrektur eines Versehens in der Erstveröffentlichung," *ZNW* 69 (1978) 118–22; "Der Gekreuzigte von Givʿat ha-Mivtar: Bilanz einer Entdeckung." *Theologia crucis— Signum crucis: Festschrift für Erich Dinkler zum 70. Geburtstag* (ed. C. Andresen and G. Klein; Tübingen: Mohr [Siebeck], 1979) 303–34.

[23] See J. M. Allegro, "Further Light on the History of the Qumran Sect," *JBL* 75 (1956) 89–95, esp. 90–93 (+pl. 1). Cf. "More Unpublished Pieces of a Qumran Commentary on Nahum (4QpNah)," *JSS* 7 (1962) 304–8. See also *Scrolls from the Wilderness of the Dead Sea* (Smithsonian Institution Exhibit Catalogue; Cambridge, MA: American Schools of Oriental Research, 1965) 17, 26–27.

[24] *Qumran Cave 4, I (4Q158-4Q186)* (DJD 5; Oxford: Clarendon, 1968) 37–42 (+pls. XII [upper right and lower frgs.], XIII, XIV [upper frgs.]. For most of the literature on the preliminary publications up to late 1968, see my article, "A Bibliographical Aid to the Study of the Qumran Cave IV Texts 158–186," *CBQ* 31 (1969) 59–71. For other literature, especially more recent discussions of 4QpNah, see G. Jeremias, *Der Lehrer der Gerechtigkeit* (SUNT 2; Göttingen: Vandenhoeck & Ruprecht, 1963) 131–35; A. Dupont-Sommer, "Observations sur le Commentaire de Nahum," *RB* 71 (1964) 298–99; D. Flusser, "Pharisees, Sadducees and Essenes in Pesher Nahum," *Sēper zikkārôn liGĕdalyāhû ʾAlôn: In Memory of Gedaliahu Alon: Essays in Jewish History and Philology* (Tel Aviv: Hqwbs hmʾwhd, 1970) 133–60; A. Dupont-Sommer, "Résumé des cours de 1969–70," *L'Annuaire du Collège de France* 70 (1970–71) 399–414; Y. Yadin, "Pesher Nahum (4QpNahum) Reconsidered," *IEJ* 21 (1971) 1–12 (+pl. 1); A. Dupont-Sommer, "Observations nouvelles sur l'expression 'suspendu vivant sur le bois' dans le *Commentaire de Nahum* (4QpNah ii 8) à la lumière du *Rouleau du Temple* (11QTempel [sic] Scroll lxiv 6–13)," *CRAIBL* 1972, pp. 709–20; J. M. Ford, "'Crucify Him, Crucify Him' and the Temple Scroll," *ExpTim* 87 (1975–76) 275–78; L. Díez Merino, "La crucifixión en la antigua literatura judía (periodo intertestamental)," *EstEcl* 51 (1976) 5–27; "El suplicio de la cruz en la literatura judía intertestamental," *SBFLA* 26 (1976) 31–120; M. Wilcox, "'Upon the Tree'—Deut 21:22–23 in the New Testament," *JBL* 96 (1977) 85–99; M. P. Horgan, *Pesharim: Qumran Interpretations of Biblical Books* (CBQMS 8; Washington: Catholic Biblical Association of America, 1979) 158–90.

[25] Since no attempt has been made here to mark doubtful or probable readings, one should consult the *editio princeps.* See n. 24 above.

[26] Note, however, the following problems: (a) The meaning of the last two words of line 3 is obscure, because of the following lacuna at the beginning of line 4. (b) The crucial phrase "on the tree" is admittedly restored at the beginning of line 8, but it seems to be demanded not only by the foregoing context, but also by the phrase later on in line 8. (c) The word [*yq*]*rʾ* is a possible restoration. Yadin notes that it could also be restored as [*qw*]*rʾ*. As he does, I

understand it to refer to Scripture (preferably niph. impf.); it could also be translated, "(Scripture) is read." This is to be referred to the allusion to Deut 21:22–23 in the preceding material. It does not introduce the quotation Nah 2:13 in lines 8–10.

[27] H. H. Rowley ("4QpNahum and the Teacher of Righteousness," *JBL* 75 [1956] 188–93) opposed this view; however, that was not only at a period when Qumran research was still primitive, but Rowley was reacting against some of the exaggerated claims that Allegro was basing on lacunae in the text (see *Time* Magazine, 2 April 1956, p. 71). Though he does not say so explicitly, M. Wilcox ("'Upon the Tree,'" 88) seems to query it.

[28] Josephus, *Ant.* 13.14,2 §380; cf. *J.W.* 1.4,5–6 §93–98.

[29] See J. T. Milik, *Ten Years of Discovery in the Wilderness of Judaea* (SBT 26; Naperville: Allenson, 1959) 73. Cf. J. Amusin [Amoussine], "Éphraïm et Manassé dans le Pésher de Nahum (4 Q p Nahum)," *RevQ* 4 (1963–64) 389–96; D. Flusser, "Kt mdbr yhwdh whprwšym (The Judean Desert Sect and the Pharisees)," *Molad* 19 (1962) 456–58.

[30] *Ant.* 13.14,2 §380; cf. *J.W.* 1.4,5–6 §93–98. Cf. P.-E. Guillet, "Les 800 'Crucifiés' d'Alexandre Jannée," *Cahiers du Cercle Ernest Renan* 100 (1977) 11–16.

[31] "Further Light," 92.

[32] Ibid., 91.

[33] 4Q*169* (DJD 5, 38), but he gives no justification for it.

[34] "Pesher Nahum," 11.

[35] Ibid., 4.

[36] So J. M. Allegro, "Further Light," 91; similarly, G. Vermes, *The Dead Sea Scrolls in English* (Pelican Books; Baltimore: Penguin, 1970) 232 ("a thing never done"); T. H. Gaster, *The Dead Sea Scriptures in English Translation* (2d ed.; Garden City: Doubleday, 1964) 240; J. Carmignac, "Interprétation de Nahum," *Les textes de Qumran traduits et annotés* (ed. J. Carmignac and P. Guilbert; 2 vols.; Paris: Letouzey et Ané, 1961, 1963), 2. 86.

[37] So A. Dupont-Sommer, "Le commentaire de Nahum découvert près de la Mer Morte (4QpNah): Traduction et notes," *Sem* 13 (1963) 55–88, esp. pp. 57–58.

[38] So A. M. Habermann, *Megilloth midbar Yehuda: The Scrolls from the Judaean Desert* (Jerusalem: Machbaroth Lesifruth, 1959) 153.

[39] "Pesher Nahum," 10–12.

[40] Ibid.

[41] See also Josh 10:26.

[42] See further pp. 92–93 above.

[43] Several problems of minor character should be pointed out: (a) Yadin compares the informer of 1. 7 with Lev 19:16–18 and 1QS 7:15–16. (b) On "a foreign nation," see CD 14:15. (c) The prep. "on" is my editorial addition, 1. 9. (d) In lines 12–13 God speaks in the first person; contrast the MT of Deut 21:23.

[44] It should be noted that the conjunction w- used in lines 7–8 (and also perhaps the first one in line 10) could be translated as "or," thus making it possible to interpret these lines as various instances of the crimes of "treason" and of "evasion."

[45] Yadin notes ("Pesher Nahum," 7) that the scribe wrote in secondarily the *waw* before "the children of Israel." It presents a problem; how should it be interpreted? Does it equate "the children of Israel" with "his people," or does

it mean that "his people" would refer to the Essene community of Qumran and "the children of Israel" would refer to the larger community of Israel? See L. Díez Merino, "La crucifixión," 14.

[46] "Pesher Nahum," 9.

[47] Ibid. Yadin studiously avoids the use of the term "crucifixion" in this article.

[48] "Does *TLH* in the Temple Scroll Refer to Crucifixion?" *JBL* 91 (1972) 472–81. Cf. *m. Sanh.* 7:1 (H. Danby, *The Mishnah Translated from the Hebrew with Introduction and Brief Explanatory Notes* [London: Oxford, 1933] 391; S. Krauss, *Sanhedrin (Hoher Rat)—Makkōt (Prügelstrafe): Text, Übersetzung und Erklärung* [Die Mischna, IV/4–5; Giessen: Töpelmann, 1933] 207).

[49] "Does *TLH*," 478.

[50] *Ant.* 13.14,2 §380; *J.W.* 1.4,6 §97 (*anastaurōsas en mesē tē polei*); cf. *J.W.* 1.5,3 §133. One should also recall the passage in Josephus, where he reports that in the murder of Ananus and a certain Jesus by Idumeans they went so far as to cast out the corpses without burial, whereas, "the Jews are so careful about funeral rites that even malefactors who have been sentenced to crucifixion are taken down and buried before sunset" (*hōste kai tous ek katadikēs anestaurōmenous pro tou dyntos hēliou kathelein te kai thaptein, J.W.* 4.5,2 §317). From this one can conclude that it was not just people like Alexander Janneus who practiced crucifixion in Palestine.—Note also that Josephus (*Ant.* 2.5,3 §73) interprets the decapitation and hanging (*wĕtālāh*) of the chief baker (Gen 40:19) in the Joseph story as crucifixion (*anestaurōse*). Similarly, the eunuchs of Esth 2:23 who were hanged (*wayyitālû*) in the MT become "crucified" in Josephus' form of the story (*Ant.* 11.6,4 §208). Contrast the LXX version of both incidents: *kai kremasei se epi xylou* (Gen 40:19); *kai ekremasen autous* (Esth 2:23). See further Josephus, *Ant.* 11.6,10–13 §246, 280, 289; 12.5,4 §256 (= 1 Macc 1:44).

[51] This phrase is found in *Tg. Ruth* 1:17: *ʾyt ln ʾrbʿ mwtʾ lḥyybyʾ, rgymt ʾbnyn wyqydt nwrʾ wqtylt syypʾ wṣlybt qysʾ*, "We have four death penalties for the guilty: the throwing of a stone, burning by fire, death by the sword, and hanging on a tree" (E. Levine, *The Aramaic Version of Ruth* [AnBib 58; Rome: Biblical Institute, 1973] 22). In *m. Sanh.*, the four modes of execution are: *slyqh śrph hrg wḥnq*, "stoning, burning, beheading, and strangling." In *Tg. Ruth*, *wḥnq* has become *wṣlybt qysʾ*. The problem is whether the latter means that one is to regard it as a form of "strangling" or whether it was a mode deliberately substituted for it.—Cf. A. Büchler, "Die Todesstrafen der Bibel und der jüdisch-nachbiblischen Zeit," *MGWJ* 50 (1906) 664–706.

[52] E. Levine says in his commentary on this verse (p. 60), "The targum violates the unanimous rabbinic sources, in perfect accord with sectarian tradition." While this may be true, it should be noted that a variant reading of *Tg. Ruth* 1:17 is found in the MS de Rossi 31, which has *wḥnyqt swdrʾ*, "choking with a scarf," instead of *wṣlybt qysʾ*. See S. Speier, "'Wṣlybt qysʾ,' trgwm Rwtʾ:yz," *Tarbiz* 40 (1970–71) 259 (see also p. x). In my opinion, the de Rossi MS is simply making the targum conform to the classic modes of execution. Cf. E. Bammel, "Crucifixion as a Punishment in Palestine," *The Trial of Jesus* (SBT 2/13; ed. E. Bammel; London: SCM, 1970) 162–65.—See further L. Rosso, "Deuteronomio 21,22 contributo del rotolo del tempio alla valutazione di una variante medievale dei settanta," *RevQ* 34 (1977) 231–36; J. Le Moyne, *Les Sadducéens* (EBib; Paris: Gabalda, 1972) 241.

[53] "Does *TLH*," 474.

[54] Ibid., n. 9. J. Levy (*Wörterbuch über die Talmudim und Midrashchim* [2d ed.;

rev. L. Goldschmidt; Berlin/Vienna: B. Harz, 1924], 4. 189) defines both Hebr. and Aram. *ṣlb* "aufhängen, kreuzigen." Similarly, J. Levy, *Chaldäisches Wörterbuch über die Targumim und einen grossen Theil des rabbinischen Schrifttums* (Cologne: J. Melzer, 1850), 2. 325. M. Jastrow (*A Dictionary of the Targumim, the Talmud Babli and Yerushalmi, and the Midrashic Literature* [New York/Berlin: Choreb, 1926] 1282) gives the meaning as "to hang, impale," yet he refers to *m. Yeb.* 16:3, *wṣlwb ʾl-hṣlybh*, and translates it, "nailed to the stake." Cf. K. H. Rengstorf, *Jebamot (Von der Schwagerehe): Text, Übersetzung und Erklärung* (Die Mischna, III/1; Giessen: Töpelmann, 1929) 202–3. For other negative reactions to Baumgarten's interpretation, see L. Díez Merino, "La crucifixión," *EstEcl* 51 (1976) 15; J. Heinemann, "Early Halakah in the Palestinian Targumim," *JJS* 25 (1974) 114–22, esp. p. 121 n. 46; M. Hengel, "Mors turpissima crucis: Die Kreuzigung in der antiken Welt und die 'Torheit' des 'Wortes vom Kreuz,'" *Rechtfertigung: Festschrift für Ernst Käsemann zum 70. Geburtstag* (ed. J. Friedrich et al.; Tübingen: Mohr [Siebeck]; Göttingen: Vandenhoeck & Ruprecht, 1976) 125–84, esp. p. 177 n. 159; cf. *Crucifixion* (Philadelphia: Fortress, 1977) 84 n. 2.

[55] Though the subject (*tlwy*) is singular, the predicate ptc. is plural (*mqwlly*).

[56] See the discussion in *m. Sanh.* 6:4 (H. Danby, *The Mishnah*, 390).

[57] *The Dead Sea Scrolls in English* (Pelican Books; Baltimore; Penguin, 1962) 61; see also p. 231, "a sacrilegious novelty." Cf. P. Winter, *On the Trial of Jesus* (Studia Judaica, 1; rev. ed. T. A. Burkill and G. Vermes; New York/Berlin: de Gruyter, 1974) 90–96.

[58] *New Testament Apologetic: The Doctrinal Significance of the Old Testament Quotations* (London: SCM, 1961) 233 n. 2.

[59] "4QpNahum and the Teacher of Righteousness," *JBL* 75 (1956) 188–93, esp. pp. 190–91.

[60] See Cicero, *Pro C. Rabirio perduellionis reo*, 4.13: "Namque haec tua [verba], quae te hominem clementem popularemque delectant, 'I lictor, conliga manus,' non modo huius libertatis mansuetudinisque non sunt sed ne Romuli quidem aut Numae Pompili; Tarquini, superbissimi atque crudelissimi regis, ista sunt cruciatus carmina quae tu, homo lenis ac popularis, libentissime commemoras: '*Caput obnubito, arbori infelici suspendito,*' quae verba, Quirites, iam pridem in hac re publica non solum tenebris vetustatis verum etiam luce libertatis oppressa sunt."—"Now those [words] of yours which you, a merciful man and a friend of the people, are so fond of, 'Lictor, go tie his hands,' not only do not belong to this liberty and clemency (of Romans), but not even to Romulus or Numa Pompilius. Those [words] of Tarquinius, the most haughty and cruel of tyrants, provide the chants for the torture-chamber which you, a gentle soul and friend of the people, delight to recall: 'Veil his head; hang him on the tree of shame." These words, my fellow citizens, have long since been done away with in this state of ours, suppressed not only by the darkness of antiquity, but also by the light of liberty."

In this passage Cicero implies that the verdict of crucifixion derives from pre-Republican times. The same idea seems to be present in Livy (1.26,6–7; 1.26,11).

Some classical scholars understand the phrase *arbori infelici suspendito* to refer to crucifixion (e.g., H. C. Hodge, *Cicero: Speeches* [LCL; Cambridge: Harvard University, 1927] 448). But others think that neither crucifixion nor hanging was meant, but rather that the criminal was fastened to a tree and scourged to death. See W. A. Oldfather, "Livy 1, 26 and the supplicium de more maiorum," *Transactions of the American Philological Association* 39 (1908) 49–72. But how widespread is the latter interpretation? Cf. M. Hengel, "Mors turpissima crucis," 145–66; *Crucifixion*, 33–45; J. Schneider, "*Stauros*, etc.," *TDNT* 7 (1971) 572–84. Indeed, in the context of the speech itself, Cicero makes reference to punishment by a cross ("crucem ad civium supplicium defigi et constitui iubes," 4.11; cf. 10.28).

[61] What should be noted is the use of the article in the New Testament phrases about "hanging on a/the tree." The definite article is found in Acts 13:29 and 1 Pet 2:24; otherwise the phrase is anarthrous. In Deut 21:22 no article is used in the MT; in Deut 21:23, when reference is made to the corpse hanging "on the tree," the article is present. But, significantly, at the end of the verse when it tells of what is "cursed of God" it mentions only "the person hanged," without a reference to the gibbet. The LXX introduces a reference to the tree: *pas kremamenos epi xylou*, as do 4QpNah 3–4 i 8 [so restored at the beginning too] and 11QTemple 64:8, 9, 10, 11. The question arises, then, whether the mention of "the tree" might not have by this time taken on a specific connotation, "hanging on *the* tree" as = crucifixion.

[62] *The Acts of the Apostles: A Commentary* (Philadelphia: Westminster, 1971) 251. And n. 4 adds: "As Gal. 3.13 and Acts 10.39 also attest."

[63] See my commentary, "The Letter to the Galatians," *JBC*, art. 49, §21 (p. 241).

[64] See H. L. Strack, *Introduction to the Talmud and Midrash* (New York: Atheneum, 1969) 94.

[65] Lev 19:16 reads, *l' tlk rkyl b'myk*, "you shall not go as a slanderer (or informer) against your people." Yadin also explains the doing of evil to one's people in a "military sense" (see 2 Kgs 8:12).

[66] Exod 22:27 reads *'lhym l' tqll wnsy' b'mk l' t'r*, "you shall not revile God nor curse a ruler of your people" (*RSV*).

[67] "Further Light," 91 note o-o, where he ascribes such an interpretation to D. N. Freedman and F. M. Cross.

[68] " 'Upon the Tree,' " 89. Wilcox is certainly correct in his interpretation of Paul's use of *epikataratos* instead of the *kekateramenos* of the LXX as an "assimilation" of this quotation to the words of Gal 3:10 (p. 87).

[69] "Crucify Him,' " 278.

[70] For instance, to understand the cursing of the fig tree (Mark 11:12–14, 20–25; Matt 21:18–22) as an instance of Jesus "cursing his people (Temple Scroll line 10)" (ibid., 277) and to suggest that "originally the cursing of the fig tree may have been an important contributing cause of Jesus' death" (ibid.) is just asking too much.

[71] This later material has been discussed in part by M. Wilcox (" 'Upon the Tree,' " 86–99) and even more extensively by L. Díez Merino ("La crucifixión," 16–24), who also discusses the targumic forms of Num 25:4; Lev 19:26; and Ruth 1:17. The extent to which these targumic paraphrases belong to what he calls "periodo intertestamental" (in the title of his article) is precisely the difficulty. In this connection it would be interesting to speculate a bit. Num 25:4 tells of Yahweh's instruction to Moses to put to death the chiefs of the people to expiate the corporate guilt of Israel because of its apostasy in yoking itself to the Moabite Baal of Peor: " 'Take all the chiefs of the people, and hang (*whwq'*) them in the sun before the LORD, that the

fierce anger of the LORD may turn away from Israel." The paraphrase in *Tg. Neofiti* reads: "Take all the chiefs of the people and set them up in a Sanhedrin before YYY and let them become judges. Everyone who is sentenced to death they shall fix to a cross (*kl mn dmṭḥyyb qṭlh yṣlbwn ytyh ʿl ṣlybh*), and bury their corpse with the setting of the sun. In this way the vehement anger of YYY will withdraw from Israel." (See A. Díez Macho, *Neophyti 1, Targum palestinense: MS de la Biblioteca Vaticana, Tomo IV Números. . . .* [Textos y estudios, 10; Madrid: Consejo superior de investigaciones científicas, 1974] 245). Now if this targum were representative of the intertestamental period, then we would have a very interesting recognition of the right of a Jewish Sanhedrin not only to put a criminal to death, but even to crucify him. But that is precisely a big "if"!

[72] This article represents a reworked form of one of the Speaker's Lectures given at Oxford University in May 1975. In a revised form it was delivered at the fortieth annual meeting of the Catholic Biblical Association, University of Detroit, MI, 17 August 1977.

Part II

PAULINE TOPICS

Six

THE GOSPEL
IN THE THEOLOGY OF PAUL*

IT IS WIDELY admitted today that long before the four canonical Gospels took shape there existed a growing tradition in the early church about what Jesus did and said, about who and what he was. Why that came to be regarded as a "gospel" tradition is not immediately clear. Nor is it perfectly evident why the literary narrative accounts about him eventually composed came to be called "Gospels." Indeed, the word *euangelion* is neither used very often in the Gospels themselves nor in the New Testament outside of the Pauline corpus (see 1 Pet 4:17; Rev 14:6). This situation stands in contrast to the abundant Pauline use of the term. It raises, moreover, a question about the relationship of the Pauline *euangelion* not only to the use of it elsewhere in the New Testament but to the literary form that came to be known as a "gospel."

It seems rather obvious, however, that *euangelion* in the first verse of the earliest Gospel was a factor in the development of the title for the four canonical accounts: "The beginning of the good news of Jesus Christ, the Son of God" (Mark 1:1). *Euangelion* is not used there as a title of the literary form being introduced, as the noun came to be used later on; hence the translation, "good news." But within the Synoptic tradition neither Matthew nor Luke follow Mark in so introducing their accounts: Matthew uses *biblos*, "a book," and Luke, *diēgēsis*, "a narrative account." (If one were to look for a comparable designation in the Fourth Gospel, it would have to be *martyria*, "testimony," 1:19). The sense of *euangelion* in Mark 1:1, however, is found elsewhere in this early Gospel (see 1:14, 15; 8:35; 10:29; 13:10; 14:9 [also 16:15]): the message about God's new mode of salvific activity on behalf of human beings made present in Jesus Christ, his Son.

One detects at least a Matthean reluctance to use *euangelion* as often as did Mark, but much more significant is the avoidance of the term by Luke in his Gospel (see, however, Acts 15:7; 20:24) and by John. The contrast is intensified when one considers the related verb *euangelizesthai:* Mark never uses it, neither does John, and Matthew has it only once (11:5). Luke, however, uses it frequently in both the Gospel (10 times) and Acts (15 times) but almost always merely in the generic sense of "preaching" (like *kēryssein* or *lalein*).[1]

By way of contrast, both the noun and the verb appear frequently in the Pauline corpus. This is significant not only because of the abundant use of the terms in these earliest New Testament writings, but also because of their role in Pauline teaching. Are they factors in the use of *euangelion* in Mark or in the apparent hesitancy of the other evangelists to pick it up? If, as is usually held, the Marcan Gospel came into being only about A.D. 65,[2] most of the Pauline corpus was already in existence—certainly at least those uncontested Pauline writings, in which the noun occurs most frequently.[3] To try to show what the relation of the Pauline use of *euangelion/euangelizesthai* to the gospel tradition might have been, one has to consider various aspects of "gospel" in Pauline theology. My discussion of the Pauline notion of gospel, therefore, will fall into three parts: (1) The Pauline use of *euangelion/euangelizesthai;* (2) The main characteristics of the Pauline gospel; (3) The origin and background of the Pauline gospel.

I. *The Pauline Use of* Euangelion/Euangelizesthai

Paul uses the noun *euangelion* 56 times in his letters (and it occurs four times in the Pastorals); the verb *euangelizesthai* appears 21 times (and never in the Pastorals).[4] In general, *euangelion* serves as a label to express in summary fashion the message that Paul, "the servant of Jesus Christ, called to be an apostle" (Rom 1:1), announced to the world of his day—and, through his letters, to human beings of all ages since then.

Paul sometimes used the noun *euangelion* to express his activity of evangelization (Gal 2:7; Phil 4:3, 15; 1 Cor 9:14b, 18b; 2 Cor 2:12; 8:18). In this sense he often used the verb *euangelizesthai* absolutely (Gal 1:8–9, 16; 4:13; 1 Cor 1:17; 9:16a, b, 18; 15:2; 2 Cor 10:16; Rom 1:15; 15:20). But in the vast majority of passages *euangelion* denotes the content of his apostolic message—what he preached, proclaimed, announced, or talked about.[5] That content, succinctly stated, is "the gospel of Christ" (1 Thess 3:2; Gal 1:7; Phil 1:27; 1 Cor 9:12; 2 Cor

2:12; 9:13; 10:14; Rom 15:19), "the gospel of our Lord Jesus" (2 Thess 1:8), or "the gospel of his Son" (Rom 1:9), wherein the genitive is normally understood as objective, i.e., the good news about Christ. In some of these instances, however, one can also detect the nuance of Christ as the originator of the gospel (e.g., Rom 15:18–19). More specifically, the gospel is "the good news of the *glory* of Christ" (2 Cor 4:4), i.e., a message about the risen Christ: "It is not ourselves that we preach, but Christ Jesus as Lord" (2 Cor 4:5). Here Paul uses of Christ the title *par excellence* for his risen status, "Lord." At times, however, the content of the gospel can also be expressed as "the faith" (Gal 1:23, in a content-sense), or as "the unfathomable riches of Christ" (Eph 3:8).

Another synonym for the gospel in the Pauline letters is "the word" (1 Thess 1:6) or "the word of God" (2 Cor 2:17). Often enough, when he is discussing the gospel, he refers to it by these synonyms (see 2 Cor 4:2; Phil 1:12–14; 1 Thess 2:13). What is implied in "God's gospel" thus finds expression in a more traditional term, borrowed from the Old Testament itself (1 Chr 17:3 [Hebr.]).[6]

But "gospel" is *par excellence* Paul's *personal* way of summing up the significance of the Christ-event, the meaning that the person, life, ministry, passion, death, resurrection, and lordship of Jesus of Nazareth had and still has for human history and existence. "Christ did not send me to baptize, but to preach the gospel" (1 Cor 1:17). This is why Paul speaks at times of "my gospel" (Rom 2:16; 16:25), "the gospel that I preach" (Gal 2:2; cf. 1:8, 11), or "our gospel" (1 Thess 1:5; 2 Thess 2:14; 2 Cor 4:3; cf. 1 Cor 15:1).

Though "my gospel" emphasized Paul's personal awareness about the special nature of the commission given to him by God to preach his Son among the Gentiles (Gal 1:16), he did not mean thereby that he was announcing a message wholly peculiar to himself or different from that preached by others "who were apostles before me" (Gal 1:17). For he insisted, "whether it was I or they, so we preach and so you came to belief" (1 Cor 15:11). He knew of only one gospel (Gal 1:6) and called down an anathema on anyone who would seek to proclaim a different one (Gal 1:8). Involved in this mode of speaking about the gospel was Paul's own struggle to be recognized in the early Christian church as an apostle and as an authentic preacher of "the gospel," as the first part of Galatians (1:1–2:10) and isolated passages in other of his letters (e.g., 1 Cor 9:1–2; 2 Cor 11:4–6) make clear. He was only too keenly conscious of the special grace of apostolate which had been given to him and which enabled him to announce the good news of Christ Jesus.

Paul realized, of course, that he was preaching a message which had its origin in God himself, "God's gospel" (1 Thess 2:2, 8–9; 2 Cor 11:7; Rom 1:1; 15:16). Just as Christ in his person and ministry brought God's salvific bounty to human beings in a new way, so now, as object of the gospel that is preached, his work is carried on, and the gospel brings that salvific bounty in its way. In it God accosts human beings, soliciting from them a response of "faith working through love" (Gal 5:6). Because of its origin in God himself, it manifests its character as "gift" and "grace" (cf. 2 Cor 9:14–15).

Obviously, what Paul preached about Christ was phrased by him at times in other ways. Synonyms for "the gospel" reveal some aspects of that notion. They are found in such affirmations as "we preach Christ crucified" (1 Cor 1:23; cf. 15:12; 2 Cor 1:19; Phil 1:15, 17) or in phrases like "the story of the cross" (1 Cor 1:18), "the word of faith" (Rom 10:8), or simply "Jesus" (2 Cor 11:4). Indeed, the last cited passage clearly implies an identity of "the gospel" and "Jesus." In all of these formulations, however, Paul plays on nuances of the Christ-event itself. That one essential in his thinking he viewed in various ways and expressed the effects thereof under various images.[7] In all, however, he sought to proclaim a message about "Jesus our Lord, who was handed over for our transgressions and raised for our justification" (Rom 4:25), about him who became "the source of life" for human beings, "Christ Jesus, whom God made our wisdom, our uprightness, sanctification, and redemption" (1 Cor 1:30). Paul never told his "story of the cross" in the form of stories about what Jesus did and said. Yet even before those stories took final shape he had presented his "gospel," his interpretation of the Christ-event.

II. *The Main Characteristics of the Pauline Gospel*

The above survey reveals in a superficial way the various modes in which Paul spoke of the "gospel," but it is now necessary to probe a little more deeply into the characteristics or aspects of that gospel. We may single out six of them.

(1) The first characteristic that we should consider is the *revelatory* or *apocalyptic* nature of the gospel. For it is the means whereby God's salvific activity toward human beings is manifested in a new way, involving specifically the lordship of Jesus Christ. The thesis of Romans makes this immediately clear, since the aspect of God, which is at the root of that salvific activity, viz., "the righteousness of God," is revealed in the gospel (1:17). This is why it is "good news," because

it makes known the reality of the new age, the reality of the *eschaton*. (Cf. Eph 3:3–6.) Paul is also aware that his gospel can be veiled; but it is so only for the blinded minds of unbelievers, "hindered from seeing the light of the gospel of the glory of Christ who is the likeness of God" (2 Cor 4:4).

(2) A very important characteristic of the gospel for Paul is its *dynamic* character. Though the evangelists' stories about what Jesus did and said may be a more vivid and less abstract way of presenting the Christ-event and its effects, Paul's use of abstractions, such as we have quoted above—including "the gospel"—should not obscure this very important aspect of it. In announcing the thesis of Romans, Paul begins by insisting that he is not ashamed of the gospel, because it is "the power of God (*dynamis theou*) for the salvation of everyone who has faith, for the Jew first and also the Greek" (1:16). In other words, he views the gospel not merely as an abstract message of salvation or as a series of propositions about Christ (e.g., "Jesus is Lord") which human beings are expected to apprehend and give assent to, but rather as a salvific force unleashed by God himself in human history through the person, ministry, passion, death, and resurrection of Jesus, bringing with it effects that human beings can appropriate by faith in him. That is why it is "God's gospel," though in the human words of Paul.[8] That is why Paul could maintain that he proclaims a Son whom God has raised from the dead, Jesus, who "*is delivering* us from the coming wrath" (1 Thess 1:10) and that his gospel came to the Thessalonians "not in words only, but with power (*en dynamei*) and the Holy Spirit, and with much conviction" (1 Thess 1:5). In his earliest letter Paul thus hints that the power associated with the gospel is somehow related to the Spirit of God himself (see further Eph 1:13). That is why he can speak of "the word of God, which is at work (*energeitai*) among you who believe" (1 Thess 2:13).

(3) Another characteristic of the Pauline gospel is its *kerygmatic* relationship. This is expressed not only by the verbs associated with it, mentioned above in part I, which emphasize its proclamatory character, but also in the association of the gospel with a pre-Pauline tradition. For Paul has embedded elements of a primitive proclamation in 1 Cor 15:1–7; indeed, he makes use of language that implies dependence on a prior tradition ("the gospel, which you received . . . ; I passed on to you above all what I received," 15:1–2). To be noted in this passage is his reference to the "form" or "terms" (*tíni logō*) in which he "evangelized" them (15:2). This seems even to suggest that the primitive kerygma or gospel had already taken a somewhat fixed shape in the

pre-written tradition. Moreover, what appears in that embedded fragment is merely another way of formulating what Paul calls his "gospel": "that Christ died for our sins in accordance with the scriptures, that he was buried, that he was raised on the third day in accordance with the scriptures, and that he appeared to Cephas, then to the twelve. Then he appeared to more than five hundred at one time. . . . Then he appeared to James, then to all the apostles. . . . Last . . . he appeared to me."[9] This relation of the Pauline gospel to the primitive kerygma is what enabled Paul to affirm, "Whether it was I or they, so we preach and so you came to belief" (1 Cor 15:11).

In the New Testament *kērygma* can denote either (a) the content of Christian preaching (Rom 16:25; 1 Cor 1:21), as in 1 Cor 15:1–7 cited above, or (b) the activity of proclaiming (1 Cor 2:4; 15:14), or (c) the role or task given to a preacher or herald (Titus 1:3). Martin Kähler, in a reaction against exaggerated efforts of the *Leben-Jesu-Forschung* of the last century, insisted that "the real Jesus is the preached Jesus."[10] This is truly part of the kerygmatic aspect (*Botschaftscharakter*) of the Pauline gospel, since its purpose is to re-present Jesus to human beings of all ages, ever since he first appeared in human history, as one who confronts them with God's new mode of salvific activity to be appropriated by faith working itself out through love. This kerygmatic aspect is not independent of the gospel's dynamic character discussed above; it merely presents it in a different light. It needs to be emphasized, even though one cannot divest either the kerygma or the gospel in Pauline thinking of a content sense, as C. H. Dodd saw years ago.[11] For an essential part of the Pauline gospel is its backward glance—what Christ Jesus *did* "once and for all" (Rom 6:10) for human beings. That immediately says "content," even though the effort to re-present that "what" is equally important. Both of the aspects constitute the proclamatory or kerygmatic character of the gospel.[12]

Yet another aspect of the kerygmatic character of the gospel has to be considered, viz., the implication that the gospel (as content) and evangelization (as activity) are related to an emergent official process in the Christian community. As the structures of the church begin to appear in the Pauline letters, one detects an awareness of those who are official gospel-heralds (*euangelistai* [not to be confused, of course, with "evangelists" in the modern sense of Gospel-authors]). This provision in church structure is born of the corporate appreciation of Easter faith: To say "Jesus is Lord," there have to be gospel-preachers as well as gospel-hearers (Rom 10:8–17). The gifts and services listed in 1 Cor 12:8–12, 28–30 or Rom 12:6–8 eventually come to include the *euangelistai* (Eph 4:11).[13] But, if this implication is truly present, it must be rightly understood and in two ways: (*a*) Hidden in it is the logical priority of the gospel over the structured community (or "church"); it is the gospel that calls the church into being, as it were. (*b*) The kerygmatic character of the gospel relates the communal faith-reaction to it only because of a Spirit-guided process of tradition: No one, individual or community, can react to the proclaimed gospel and identify himself/herself/itself with other Christians in confessing that "Jesus is Lord" unless empowered by the Spirit (1 Cor 12:3). That, ultimately, is why Paul reminded the Christian community of the "form" or "terms" in which he had originally "evangelized" them. He appeared among them as *euangelistēs,* a gospel-herald with a Spirit-empowered challenge, accosting them from an already existent tradition and representing an emerging, structured community.

These diverse, yet related, aspects of the kerygmatic character of the gospel lead to yet another characteristic of it.

(4) A significant characteristic of the gospel in Pauline thinking is its *normative* role. For there is a sense in which the gospel stands critically over Christian conduct, church officials, ecclesiastical teaching, and even the written Scriptures themselves. This role emerges from various ways in which Paul treats of "the gospel."

In Gal 1:6–9 Paul makes it clear that the gospel that he has preached to the Galatian churches tolerates no rival. There is simply no "other gospel" (1:7). This was said in a context of the Judaizing problem in the early church in which certain Jewish practices were being imposed on Gentile Christians (circumcision, dietary regulations, and the celebration of certain feasts in a Jewish calendar). Though Paul was anxious to "share" his gospel with others (1 Thess 2:8), he never tolerated its adulteration or contamination, because he recognized its sovereignty and unmanipulability.

In preaching the gospel, Paul insisted that human beings were expected to listen to it (Eph 1:13), welcome it (2 Cor 11:4), even obey it (2 Thess 1:8; Rom 10:16). In short, they were to "believe" or "put faith" in Christ Jesus preached in it (Rom 1:5, 17; 10:16). Their hearing of it (*akoē*) was not to stop short of a personal commitment to it (*hypakoē,* Rom 10:16–17; 1:5; 16:26). Thus, the gospel is understood to exercise a certain authority over human beings, playing a normative role linked to its kerygmatic character. It accosts them, challenging them to conform to its proclamation.

With regard to Christian conduct, Paul sees the gospel as an inspiration and guide for it: "Let your manner of life be worthy of the gospel of Christ, so that whether I come and see you or am absent, I may hear of you that you stand firm in one spirit, with one mind striving side by side for the faith of the gospel" (Phil 1:27). Here Paul sees the united testimony of Christians governed by the gospel itself and not by any allegiance to him.

Though we may look in vain in the Pauline letters for a passage in which he discusses explicitly the relationship of the church to the gospel, we can detect some of his thinking about this relationship when we recall the famous Antioch incident (Gal 2:11–14). There he rebuked Cephas, one of the "pillars" of the church (2:9), when he saw that he was not "walking straight according to the truth of the gospel" (2:14). Regardless of how one interprets the respective roles of Cephas and Paul in the early chapters of Galatians,[11] it is clear that Paul considered the gospel as a norm: its "truth" was the gauge of the conduct even of an important church-official. And the implication is that the gospel is above him.

But "norm," almost by definition, seems to imply restriction, boundary, or limit. Yet the gospel, especially as it has been historically understood ever since Marcion, who sought to separate law and gospel as two antitheses,[15] has seemed rather to be liberating or open. This idea seems to be founded in yet another place in Galatians itself; in 2:5 Paul speaks of "the truth of the gospel," mentioning it in a context of "the freedom which we have in Christ Jesus" (2:4), which has to be preserved in the face of the "false brothers" who were seeking to undermine it. The freedom of which Paul speaks there was being endangered in the Judaizing problem, when Christians, who should have understood the role of the liberating gospel in Christian life, were seeking to impose forms of a man-made legalism on other Christians. One may see a dialectic here in the Pauline notion of gospel, which is normative but liberating. It plays a *liberating* role vis-à-vis the restrictions of man-made legalism, whereas it plays a *normative* role because of its God-based origin. If one wants to accept the new mode of salvation offered to humanity in Christ Jesus, one has to accept its demands. In the long run the irony exists in that the very "truth of the gospel" according to which Paul was asking Cephas to walk was itself a liberation of him from a man-made contamination of the gospel itself.

The gospel can also be understood as an entity that even plays a normative role over the Scriptures themselves. All through this discussion of the Pauline notion of gospel, we have been regarding it as "the good news of Jesus Christ," dealing with it as the "word" (1 Thess 1:6) in a pregnant sense, as "the word of God" (2 Cor 2:17), as a reality that existed prior to the written Gospels and even prior to Paul's preaching of Christ. But the Scriptures—those of the New Testament—came into being only several decades after the gospel or the word of God had already been dynamically and kerygmatically at work. The New Testament writings in all their diversity, record a distillation of that dynamism and kerygma—in a privileged form, to boot, that no subsequent church teaching or dogmatic formulation can rival—but they still remain a reflection, an inspired reflection, of the gospel reality. And as such, the gospel acts as a norm even for the written Scriptures.[16] Herein one would find at least one aspect of the relation of the gospel (in the Pauline sense) to the written Gospels.[17]

(5) Still another characteristic of the Pauline gospel is its *promissory* nature. In the very opening formula of the Letter to the Romans, Paul speaks of God's gospel, "which he promised beforehand through his prophets in the holy scriptures" (1:2). The gospel, then, is looked on as a concrete realization of God's promises of old. This is, however, the only place in Romans where Paul brings "the gospel" into close relationship to "the promise." This may seem strange in view of his explicit quotation of the prophetic words of Isa 52:7, about the beautiful feet of those who announce good news, quoted in 10:15 in the context of the need of Christian heralds so that human beings may come to faith. Though the notion of God's promise of old plays an important role in Paul's treatment of Abraham in Rom 4:13–21; 9:4–13 and in Gal 3:14–29; 4:21–31, where it is pitted against "the law," in none of these passages is the gospel explicitly introduced or brought into relationship with the promise. However, in the Epistle to the Ephesians the two ideas are closely joined (cf. 1:13; and especially 3:6).[18]

(6) The preceding characteristic, especially as it is presented in Eph 3:6, introduces yet another; the *universal* character of the gospel in Pauline thinking. This aspect of the gospel is proposed in the thesis of Romans, where it is described as the power of God for salvation "to every one who has faith, to the Jew first and also to the Greek" (1:16). Indeed, the word that is preached and that seeks to elicit faith in view of salvation is announced to all, "for there is no distinction between Jew and Greek; the same Lord is Lord of all" (Rom 10:12). Paul recognized that he had been entrusted with the gospel for the uncircumcised, just as Peter had been entrusted with it for the circumcised (Gal 2:7). If Paul admitted a priority in the matter to the Jews, as he did in Romans 1:16 (cf. 2:10), that is simply because of the relation of the gospel to the promise mentioned above and because of the prerogatives that he, even as a Christian apostle, always admitted about his former co-religionists (see Rom 3:1–2); "to them belong . . . the promises"

(Rom 9:4). But, he insisted, "God shows no partiality" (Rom 2:11). Thus the salvific bounty made available to human beings in the Christ-event was destined for Jew and Gentile, for everyone.

III. *The Origin and Background of "Gospel"*

The foregoing survey of the use of *euangelion/euangelizesthai* and of its various characteristics in Pauline theology reveal that it was a notion of no little importance to the Apostle. How did he come to express his interpretation of the Christ-event in terms of it?

The initial survey of the use of *euangelion/euangelizesthai* in the Gospels and Acts in the introduction to this paper revealed how rarely these terms were used by the evangelists in contrast to Paul. Though one may want to debate the question, the data in Mark and Matthew are such that one cannot conclude with certainty that Jesus himself made much use of the terms or of the Aramaic counterpart of *euangelion*. The Greek noun appears on his lips in Mark 1:15; 8:35; 10:29; 13:10; 14:9; [16:15].[19] But in the Matthean parallels to the first three of these sayings it is absent. Moreover, though the great commission of the risen Christ in the Marcan appendix (16:15) is phrased in terms of it (in keeping, as it were, with a theme in the Gospel itself), the commission in Matthew avoids all reference to it (28:18–20). Hence the question is raised whether the use of it in Mark 13:10 and 14:9 (on which Matt 24:14 and 26:13 depend) is to be attributed to Marcan formulation or not. If it were to be, then further questions arise. Willi Marxsen is of the opinion that Mark introduced the term *euangelion* into the material of the Synoptic tradition, and that Paul's understanding of "gospel" is the presupposition of the Marcan usage, even though one may not assume direct dependence.[20] This may be an acceptable interpretation of the evidence,[21] but it raises the further question about how Paul came to use the term so frequently and significantly.

The noun *euangelion* had already been in use in Greek literature and inscriptions long before Paul. In Homer's *Odyssey* it denotes a "reward given to a herald of good news" (14.152, 166). In the sense of "good news" or even simply of "news" it is often found in Hellenistic writings.[22] A religious connotation was associated with the word when it came to designate a "sacrifice" offered to gods "for good news."[23] A still more significant use of the word is found on the Calendar Inscription from Priene (in Asia Minor), first published in 1899. It had been set up as part of the introduction of the use of the Julian Calendar into the Roman province of Asia, making New Year's day coincide with the emperor Augustus' birthday, 23 September: "And [the birthday] of the god (= Augustus, the *divi filius*) was for the world the beginning of the good tidings owing to him (*ērxen de tō kosmō tōn di' autou evangeli[ōn hē genethlios] tou theou*).²⁴ Here a beneficial, even sacral, connotation of the plural *euangelia* is recognized to be present.

Yet despite this considerable Greek evidence of the use of *euangelion* in the contemporary world, recent students and commentators have been reluctant to ascribe the Pauline use of *euangelion* solely to this background, because *euangelizesthai* occurs in the Greek Old Testament in a far closer religious sense (e.g., Ps 68:12; 96:2; Nah 2:1; Isa 52:7; cf. *Ps. Sol.* 11:1).²⁵ It is often the translation of the Hebrew noun *běśôrāh*, "good news" (announced by a herald). The sole dependence of the Pauline usage on that in the contemporary emperor cult is, indeed, simply not that evident. There exists a notable difference between the eschatological connotation of Pauline *euangelion* and its beneficial connotation in that cult. Moreover, the fact that Paul deliberately quotes Isa 52:7 in Rom 10:15, precisely in a context in which he is speaking of the preaching of "the gospel" (10:16), shows that his notion of *euangelion* is heavily dependent on the Old Testament idea of God's herald and his message.

It is, of course, not impossible that the Christian kerygma was already cast in terms of *euangelion* prior to Paul—1 Cor 15:1–2 may even suggest that—but we cannot be sure. Yet, in any case, it seems as though the Christian use of *euangelion* as the good news about the risen Jesus as Lord and the new mode of salvation available to human beings in him may have emerged quite independently of the so-called sacral or beneficial use of *euangelion* in the contemporary emperor cult in the eastern Mediterranean lands.

If we are right in relating the Pauline use of *euangelion* to that in the Old Testament writings of the postexilic period, then we can appreciate better the nuance of Paul's reference to the "gospel promised aforetime through his prophets" (Rom 1:2) and the promissory character of the gospel that Paul himself preached.

That Paul's use of *euangelion* is related to the New Testament Gospels is thus rather likely, even though he never uses the word in the sense of a literary composition. We have seen above that his use of the term may have been the presupposition of the Marcan introduction of the term into his account of what Jesus did and said. From there it would have spread as a Christian word to designate the other "Gospels" (canonical and apocryphal). The distinctive Christian use of the term is seen when one considers that Greek *euangelion* was not translated into Latin as *nuntius bonus* (as it might have been), but was rather simply transcribed as *evangelium* because of the distinctive religious content-sense that it carried. Having entered Latin as *evangelium,* it spread to the romance languages as *évangile, vangelo, evangelio.*

NOTES

* Originally published in *Interpretation* 33 (1979) 339–50.

¹ An exception would have to be made for the etymological sense of the verb in Luke 4:18, where he so uses it in a quotation from Isa 61:1. Also in Luke 7:22, which alludes to these passages.

² It should be recalled, however, that some interpreters would date Mark after A.D. 70. Yet, if one were to prefer to go along with J. A. T. Robinson (*Redating the New Testament* [Philadelphia: Westminster, 1976] 352) and date all the New Testament writings before A.D. 70, one should note that even for him the *entire* Pauline corpus antedates Mark. See my review, *Int* 32 (1978) 309–13.

³ Since the use of *euangelion* in 2 Thessalonians, Colossians, and Ephesians is so similar to that of the uncontested Pauline letters, I shall include data from them in this survey, considering only the Pastorals as Deutero-Pauline.

⁴ See R. Morgenthäler, *Statistik des neutestamentlichen Wortschatzes* (Zürich: Gotthelf, 1958) 101; K. Aland, *Vollständige Konkordanz zum griechischen Neuen Testament* (Berlin: de Gruyter, 1978), 2. 118–19.

⁵ With the noun *euangelion,* Paul uses various verbs: *euangelizesthai* (Gal 1:11; 1 Cor 15:1; 2 Cor 11:7); *lalein* (1 Thess 2:2); *kēryssein* (1 Thess 2:9; Gal 2:2); *katangellein* (1 Cor 9:14); *gnōrizein* (Eph 6:19). See further E. Molland, *Das paulinische Euangelion: Das Wort und die Sache* (Avhandlinger utgitt av Det Norske Videnskaps-Akademie i Oslo, II. Hist.-Filos. Klasse, 1934, No. 3; Oslo, J. Dybwad, 1934) 11–12, 41–42.

⁶ See further Col 1:5, "The word of truth, the gospel"; Eph 1:13, "the word of truth, the gospel of your salvation." Cf. 2 Cor 6:7. See R. Bultmann, *Theology of the New Testament* (2 vols.; London, SCM, 1952), 1. 188–89.

⁷ For further discussion of these effects of the Christ-event, see pp. 163–64 below.

⁸ See H. Schlier, *"Euangelion im Römerbrief,"* *Wort Gottes in der Zeit: Festschrift Karl Hermann Schelkle zum 65. Geburtstag dargebracht* (ed. H. Feld and J. Nolte; Düsseldorf: Patmos, 1973) 127–42.

⁹ The last phrase in v. 7 is a Pauline addition to the kerygmatic fragment. For further discussion of this passage, see R. E. Brown et al. (eds.), *PNT,* 33–36. Paul has also embedded further fragments of the kerygma into other parts of his letters (e.g., Rom 1:3–4; 1 Thess 1:9–10).

¹⁰ See *Der sogenannte historische Jesus und der geschichtliche, biblische Christus* (Leipzig: A. Deichert, 1892) 22 (new edition by Ernst Wolf; Munich: Kaiser, 1953, 44).

¹¹ *The Apostolic Preaching and Its Developments* (London: Hodder and Stoughton, 1944) 7–17; *The Gospel and the Law of Christ* (London: Longmans, Green, 1947) 5; *History and the Gospel* (New York: Scribner's Sons, 1938) 7.

¹² For further discussion of the kerygmatic character of the gospel, see my article, "The Kerygmatic and Normative Character of the Gospel," *Evange-*

lium—Welt—Kirche: Schlussbericht und Referate der römisch-katholisch/evangelisch-lutherischen Studienkommission "Das Evangelium und die Kirche", 1967–1971, Auf Veranlassung des Lutherischen Weltbundes und des Sekretariats für die Einheit der Christen (ed. H. Meyer; Frankfurt am M.: O. Lembeck; J. Knecht, 1975) 111–28, esp. pp. 118–21.

[13] See also Acts 21:8; 2 Tim 4:5.

[14] For various possibilities of interpretation, see *PNT*, 27–32.

[15] Tertullian (*Adv. Marc.* 1.19) wrote of him: "Separatio legis et evangelii proprium et principale opus est Marcionis" (see also 1.21; 4.1 [CSEL, 47.314, 318, 423]).

[16] The normative role of the gospel vis-à-vis the Old Testament is seen in Paul's attitude toward it, viewing some of its essential teachings in the light of the Christ-event (see Rom 4:23–24; 15:4).

[17] For some comments on the gospel as a canon-critical principle (discussed by Käsemann), see the article mentioned in n. 12, p. 124.

[18] It may cause some surprise that it is only in the Epistle to the Ephesians that gospel and promise are really brought into explicit relationship. For those who regard Ephesians as Deutero-Pauline it may create something of a difficulty; but it should be kept in mind in view of the emphasis put on these notions over against law at the time of the Reformation.

[19] In Mark 1:1, 14 it occurs in a remark of the evangelist.

[20] *Mark the Evangelist: Studies on the Redaction History of the Gospel* (Nashville: Abingdon, 1969) 146.

[21] Marxsen seeks to explain further differences that Mark introduced beyond the Pauline conception (e.g., a certain identification of Jesus with the gospel [see 8:35; 10:29, "for my sake and that of the gospel"] with the result that in Marcan usage Jesus is both the subject and the object of the gospel; see pp. 126–50). On this explanation, see Georg Strecker, "Literarkritische Überlegungen zum *euangelion*-Begriff im Markusevangelium," *Neues Testament und Geschichte: Historisches Geschehen und Deutung im Neuen Testament: Oscar Cullmann zum 70. Geburtstag* (Zürich: Theologischer Verlag; Tübingen: Mohr [Siebeck], 1972) 91–104.

[22] E.g., Plutarch, *Sertor.* 11.4; Appian, *Bell. civ.* 3.93 §384; 4.20 §78; Josephus, *J.W.* 2.17,4 §420; 4.10,6 §618. The profane use of *euangelion/euangelia* can also be found in the Greek OT: 2 Sam 4:10; 18:20, 22, 25, 27; 2 Kgs 7:9; Jer 20:15.

[23] E.g., Diodorus Siculus 15.74,2; Plutarch, *Sertor.* 26.3.

[24] See W. Dittenberger, *Orientis graeci inscriptiones selectae* (2 vols.; Leipzig, S. Hirzel, 1903–05; reprinted, Hildesheim, G. Olms, 1970) sec. 458, pp. 40–41. Cf. Hennecke-Schneemelcher, *NTA*, 1. 71–75.

[25] The background of the Pauline usage has been well worked out by P. Stuhlmacher, *Das paulinische Evangelium: I. Vorgeschichte* (FRLANT 95; Göttingen: Vandenhoeck & Ruprecht, 1968).

Seven

RECONCILIATION IN PAULINE THEOLOGY*

IN CHRISTIAN THEOLOGY reconciliation has always played an important role.[1] The doctrine of reconciliation is rooted in biblical teaching, but it has also been developed in various ways through the course of the centuries, as theologians wrestled with the concept in their explanations of the ways of God with man. The Christian doctrine of the reconciliation of sinful man is rooted in the Old Testament as well as in the New Testament, and an adequate discussion of the biblical treatment of the topic would demand a monograph. But one of the main proponents of reconciliation in the Bible is the Apostle Paul, and since the role of reconciliation in his theology has recently been called in question,[2] there is reason to reconsider it. My purpose, then, is to discuss the notion of reconciliation in Pauline theology.

Before we examine the idea of reconciliation itself, however, it might be wise to situate it in a general way in Pauline theology as a whole. As the first Christian theologian, Paul left us in his letters many teachings, and among them are the various ways in which he interpreted the Christ-event. In reflecting on what Christ Jesus accomplished for mankind and what his effect was on human history, different writers of the early Christian community summed up his words, his deeds, and his personal impact in various ways. Paul showed little interest in the earthly life of Jesus or in what he actually did and said—in what is for so many Christians of today a thing of no little importance. Paul did learn indeed of some of the sayings of Jesus and of his teachings, as a number of passages in his letters reveal.[3] But because most of his letters were composed prior to the composition of the earliest Gospel, it is understandable that he did not echo much of what we know of today as the gospel-tradition.[4] Paul's dominant interest was in what Jesus accomplished for humanity in his passion, death, burial, resurrection, exaltation, and heavenly intercession. This complex of the last phases of Christ's earthly career can be referred to as "the Christ-event," even though Paul himself never so expressed it; it is a convenient modern way of labelling that about which he preached and wrote. Some writers call it the "whole work of Christ."[5] It has also been termed the "objective redemption," i.e., that aspect of the redemption of human beings wrought in Christ Jesus which he accomplished "once for all" (*ephapax*, Rom 6:10) and which is wholly independent of our cooperation. It consequently underlines its gratuitous character. In this view, it stands in contrast to our attempt to appropriate or apprehend the effects of the Christ-event through faith (and baptism), which is often then regarded as the "subjective redemption." This terminology, actually born of a later problem, is not biblical or Pauline; but it does help at least to sharpen the aspects of the Christ-event about which we are talking.

Looked at in this way, it is not difficult to single out the various ways in which Paul objectively viewed the Christ-event, because in many instances he himself employed abstractions which enable us to grasp what he had in mind. As labels for the effects of the Christ-event, Paul used a series of abstract nouns and also some verbal forms. We can cull at least nine of them from his letters. Thus, as Paul looked back at the Christ-event, he interpreted its effects as (1) "justification" (*dikaiōsis, dikaiosynē, dikaioun*), an acquitting of human beings, whereby they may stand before God's tribunal or judgment-seat innocent, upright, or righteous (Gal 2:16; Rom 3:26–28; 4:25; 5:18)—to this effect goes the pride of place;[6] (2) "salvation" (*sōtēria, sōzein*), a restoration of human beings to safety, health, wholeness, or integrity from a state of danger, sickness, corruption, or sin (2 Cor 7:10; Rom 1:16; 10:10; 13:11;[7] (3) "expiation" (*hilastērion*), a wiping away of human sin[8] by the blood of the crucified Christ, who is now the new "mercy seat," superseding the *kappōret* of old (Rom 3:25);[9] (4) "ransom/redemption" (*apolytrōsis*), an emancipation or manumission of human beings bringing about their liberation through a ransom, whereby God acquires a people in a new sense (1 Cor 1:30; Rom 3:24; 8:32; cf. Eph 1:14);[10] (5) "sanctification" (*hagiasmos, hagiazein*), a dedication of human beings to God's service, thus removing them from the profane (1 Cor 1:2, 30; 6:11);[11] (6) "freedom" (*eleutheria, eleutheroun*), a liberation of human beings which gives them new rights (as citizens of a heavenly commonwealth) and an outlook freed of the anxiety of Self, Sin, Death, and Law (Gal 5:1, 13; Rom 8:1–2, 21; 2 Cor 3:17);[12] (7) "transformation" (*metamorphōsis*), a gradual reshaping of human beings by the glory of God reflected in the face of Christ; it is the effect of the Creator God, who through Christ shines light anew into human life (2 Cor 3:18; Rom 12:2; cf. Eph 4:22–24);[13] (8) "new creation" (*kainē ktisis*), a creating of a new life and of a new humanity, of which Christ is the head as the Adam of the *eschaton* through his life-giving Spirit (Gal 6:15; 2 Cor 5:17; Rom 6:4; 1 Cor 15:45);[14] and (9) "reconciliation" (*katallagē, katallassein*), a restoring of humanity (and the world [*kosmos*]) to a status of friendship with God and fellowmen (2 Cor 5:18–20; Rom 5:10–11; 11:15; cf. Col 1:20–22; Eph 2:16)—this effect is listed last only because we shall treat it more extensively in the rest of this essay.[15] These are, then, the main ways in which Paul characterized or described the effects of what Christ Jesus did for humanity in his proclamation of "the story of the cross."

It is important to note, however, that when Paul refers to the Christ-event in these ways, he is applying to it various images or figures derived from his background, Jewish or Hellenistic. For instance, his view of the Christ-event as justification can only be explained from his Jewish or Old Testament background; or his view of it as redemption cannot be adequately accounted for without some reference to modes of emancipation in the Hellenistic world of his time. For in his interpretation of the whole work of Christ he applies to it figures which have definite connotations, and these have to be respected. In certain developments of later Christian theology these figures were eventually erected into propositions, with all sorts of baneful results. But the effort to depict Paul's understanding of any one of the figures must treat them for what they are.

Reconciliation is one of these figures, and my concern here is to comment (1) on the figure and its background or origin; (2) on Paul's use of it; (3) on problems in the modern interpretation of it; and (4) on the pertinence of it to modern life.

I. *The Figure of Reconciliation and Its Background*

The basic idea that is conveyed by the figure of reconciliation is the restoration of men and women to a status of friendship and intimacy. The Greek words, *katallagē, apokatallassō, diallassō, katallassō*, are all compound forms of a root meaning "other" (*all-*) and denote a "making otherwise."[17] The words are abundantly used in the literature of the Greeks, both in a secular sense and a religious sense.[18] In the secular sense, they denote a change or alteration of relations between individual persons or groups of persons (e.g., nations); it is a change from anger, enmity, or hostility to love, friendship, or intimacy. The words do not express primarily a change of feelings or a psychological reaction. This may be present, but the essential change is rather in the relationship or situation vis-à-vis another. It is a change of relationship in the social or political realm. This secular use of the word is even found in the Bible. In translations of Judg 19:2–3 we read of a Levite who took to himself a concubine, who eventually became angry with him and went home; the Levite went to talk to her "to reconcile her to himself,"[19] i.e., to restore a relationship with her (lit., "to cause her to return," the hiphil infinitive of *šûb*, "return"—Hebrew has no verb for "reconcile"). And in the Sermon on the Mount Jesus teaches, "If you are offering your gift at the altar, and there remember that your brother has something against you, leave your gift there before the altar and go; first be reconciled (*diallagēthi*) to your brother, and then come and offer your gift" (Matt 5:23–24; cf. 1 Cor 7:11). These are instances of the secular use of the word. In the religious sense, the words are used in Greek literature of the reconciliation of gods and humans (e.g., Sophocles, *Ajax*, 744).[20] This use is likewise found in the Greek Old Testament. In 2 Macc 1:5 the Jews of Jerusalem and Judea write to their brethren in Egypt and pray, "May he [God] hear your prayers and be reconciled to you" (*katallageiē hymin*). See further 7:33; 8:29. Similarly, the Jewish historian Josephus tells of Samuel the prophet who learned that God had repented of having made Saul the king: "Samuel was quite disturbed and all night long undertook to entreat God to be reconciled (*katallattesthai*) to Saul and not to be angry with him" (*Ant.* 6.7,4 §143). What is noteworthy here in these two instances of Jewish authors who wrote in Greek is the use of the verb *katallassein* in the passive of God; God is expected to be reconciled with men. What should also be noted, however, is that in Greek writings the verb plays no essential role in the propitiatory rites of the Greek and Hellenistic religion, for in these rites "the relation between divinity and humanity does not have this personal nearness."[21] Since Hebrew lacks a specific term for "reconcile," and it begins to appear in Hellenistic Jewish writings, such examples suggest that Paul derived this figure for the Christ-event from the Greco-Roman world,[22] even though he makes his own use of it. Before we try to describe his use of the figure, there is one further remark that must be made about it, and that concerns the relation of reconciliation to atonement.

Fundamentally, reconciliation as we have described it above is the same as atonement. But the history of the use of the latter term has loaded it with connotations that are not part of the Pauline figure.

"Atonement" is, in fact, a peculiarly English word, lacking any real counterpart in other modern European languages. It really means at-one-ment and denotes the setting of two or more persons at one with each other, implying the restoration of them to a mutually shared relationship after a period of estrangement. The word was so used in English in a secular sense. But it also developed a theological sense, and the *Oxford English Dictionary* says of it: "As applied to the redemptive work of Christ, *atonement* is variously used by theologians in the senses of *reconciliation, propitiation, expiation,* according to the view taken of its nature."[23] Now it is precisely the confusion of reconciliation with "expiation" (the wiping away of human sins by the crucified Christ who is now the new "mercy seat," superseding the *kappōret* of old)[24] and with "propitiation" (the appeasing of an angry God by rites and sacrifices) that creates the difficulty in interpreting Paul's use of the figure of reconciliation. As we examine the texts in which he speaks of reconciliation, we shall see that for him reconciliation can be understood as atonement (= at-one-ment), but that it is not the same as expiation, and has, practically speaking, nothing to do with propitiation. So much for the idea of reconciliation and its background.

II. *The Pauline Use of the Figure of Reconciliation*

Paul describes the status of human beings without Christ as one of hostility with God. "If, while we were enemies, we were reconciled to God by the death of his Son, much more, now that we are reconciled, shall we be saved by his life. Not only so, but we also rejoice in God through our Lord Jesus Christ, through whom we have now received our reconciliation" (Rom 5:10–11). This is said by Paul in a passage in Romans in which he has just finished setting forth his thesis on the justification of man by faith in Christ Jesus and apart from what he calls "the works of the Law" (1:16–4:25). He sees the situation of human beings vis-à-vis God as having been basically changed by what Christ did; if they are now justified in the sight of God because of the Christ-event, then their relationship has been radically altered, and not merely in a legalistic, juridical sense that the figure of justification connotes, but in the fundamental way of reconciliation. Similarly, in writing to the Colossians,[25] to a congregation that was made up largely of Gentile Christians, Paul says of their former relation to God: "You . . . once were estranged (*apēllo-triōmenous*) and hostile in mind . . . " (Col 1:21). This is, then, the situation of mankind without Christ according to Paul, a situation of hostility or estrangement. This is but another way of describing the human condition that Paul spoke about in Rom 1:18–3:20, mankind without the gospel.

Wherein lies the cause of this hostility or estrangement, as Paul sees it? In 2 Cor 5:19 he cites human "trespasses" as the root of the difficulty. In Rom 8:5–7 he probes more deeply and shows that it is human preoccupation with "flesh" (*sarx*): "Those who live according to the flesh set their minds on the things of the flesh. . . . To set the mind on the flesh is death, but to set the mind on the Spirit is life and peace. For the mind that is set on the flesh is hostile to God; it does not submit to God's law." One must understand what Paul means by "flesh" in such a passage, especially in its contrast to the Spirit. On the one hand, it has the Old Testament connotation of *bāśār*, meaning "flesh" as opposed to blood, or, in a collective sense, "man," "mankind," "humanity."[26] On the other hand, it often has for Paul a pejorative connotation, meaning the humdrum, non-elevating condition of human existence in its down-trodden, earth-oriented propensities. It represents all in human beings that makes them close in on themselves and refuse openness to the Spirit, to God, and to one's fellowman. In this sense, Paul says, "To set the mind on flesh is death." By contrast, the spirit is that aspect of human nature that makes one open to God's Spirit. Hence, the mind that is set on flesh does not submit to the law of God and is actually hostile to God. As Paul sees it, human beings left to themselves cannot help but set their minds on flesh and cannot help but be alienated and estranged from God. This is why Paul lists "enmity" among the "works of the flesh" in Gal 5:20.

Paul also finds another cause for the hostility, when he addresses Gentile Christians and refers to their former condition as pagans as a separation from Israel; in this he finds another source of alienation from God. "You were at that time separated from Christ, alienated from the commonwealth of Israel, and strangers to the covenants of promise" (Eph 2:12). This estrangement implied the very futility of their existence: "They are darkened in their understanding, alienated from the life of God because of the ignorance that is in them, due to their hardness of heart" (Eph 4:18). Thus Paul writes, as he exhorts the Gentile Christian recipients of his letter to realize that they must "no longer live as the Gentiles do, in the futility of their minds" (4:17). These may sound like harsh words, but Paul's view of the condition of pagans in his day is otherwise well known to us (Rom 1:18–32). These, then, are the two main causes of the hostility between mankind and God, "trespasses," coming from minds set on flesh, and the estrangement of pagans.

How has God remedied this situation, or brought about the reconciliation of hostile, alienated human beings? Paul never says that God is reconciled (in the passive) to them, as did the author of 2 Maccabees or Josephus.[27] He rather sees God actively taking the initiative and bringing about the reconciliation of mankind through his Son, Jesus of Nazareth. True, Paul invites human beings to be reconciled to God (2 Cor 5:20), but that is an invitation to appropriate or apprehend the effect of the Christ-event for themselves (the aspect of subjective redemption). What Christ Jesus did is actually the restoration of the relationship of friendship, love, and intimacy. Once human beings react to the invitation and accept it through faith in Christ Jesus, they are introduced into the realm of reconciliation; one is no longer *echthros,* "hostile," *asebēs,* "impious," *asthenēs,* "weak," or *hamartōlos,* "a sinner." These are the adjectives that Paul uses of human beings in their enmity in Rom 5:6–8. Moreover, the change of status is not just a legal fiction; it is a genuine renewal of human life, a radical altering of humanity's relation with God.

Paul attributes this reconciliation of mankind with God especially to the death of Jesus. "We were reconciled to God by the death of his Son . . . now that we are reconciled, we shall be much more saved by his life" (Rom 5:10). Here the figure of reconciliation is associated closely with the death of Christ, whereas that of salvation is associated with the risen life of Christ (i.e., with the influence of the risen Lord on Christian life and conduct). Sometimes, instead of speaking of the "death" of Christ, Paul will refer reconciliation to his "blood," i.e., the blood shed in his passion and death. Thus, "you [Gentiles] who were once far off have been brought near in the blood of Christ"; this is said in the context of reconciliation in Eph 2:13. Or again, "he has now reconciled [you] in his body of flesh by his death, in order to present you holy and blameless and irreproachable before him [God]" (Col 1:22). "For in him [Christ] all the fulness of God was pleased to dwell, and through him to reconcile to himself all things, whether on earth or in heaven, making peace by the blood of the cross" (Col 1:19–20).

There are two other aspects of Paul's reflection on the Christ-event as reconciliation which call for comments. The first is his calling Christ "our peace," ascribing to him in an abstract way the very effect of reconciliation that he has brought into human lives. Paul sees this as a breaking down of barriers, between Jew and Greek, and between man and God—or, if I might so put it, as a horizontal and a vertical reconciliation.

> [11]Therefore remember that at one time you Gentiles in the flesh, called the uncircumcision by what is called the circumcision, which is made in the flesh by hands—[12]remember that you were at that time separated from Christ, alienated from the commonwealth of Israel, and strangers to the covenants of promise, having no hope and without God in the world. [13]But now in Christ Jesus you who once were far off have been brought near in the blood of Christ. [14]For he is our peace, who has made us both one, and has broken down the dividing wall of hostility, [15]by abolishing in his flesh the law of commandments and ordinances, that he might create in himself one new man in place of the two, so making peace, [16]and might reconcile us both to God in one body through the cross, thereby bringing the hostility to an end. [17]And he came and preached peace to you who were far off and peace to those who were near; [18]for through him we both have access in one Spirit to the Father (Eph 2:11–18).

Thus Paul sees the Christ-event as having achieved reconciliation, peace, at-one-ment for Jews and Greeks alike and for both with God through faith in Christ Jesus. In a similar way he writes in Rom 5:1, "We have peace with God through our Lord Jesus Christ."[28]

The other aspect of Paul's reflection is the cosmic dimension of Christ's reconciliation. In the earliest passage in which he discusses reconciliation (2 Cor 5:18–21) he introduces it thus: "All this is from God, who through Christ reconciled us to himself and gave us the ministry of reconciliation; that is, in Christ God was reconciling the world to himself. . . ." Now "the world" (*kosmos*) may seem at first to mean the world of human beings,[29] but it is probably to be understood in the sense of the universe of creation, since that is what is implied in Col 1:20, where Paul speaks of God reconciling to himself through Christ "all things, whether on earth or in heaven." In this view of things, Paul sees reconciliation as having not merely an anthropological dimension, but also a cosmic dimension; it affects not only the relation of human beings to God, but also that of the created universe. It thus recasts in terms of reconciliation what Paul wrote about in Rom 8:19–23, where he saw material creation, subjected to futility because of human sinfulness, now sharing in the hope that is born of the Christ-event: "Creation itself will be set free from its bondage to decay and obtain the glorious liberty of the children of God" (8:21). In Romans the figure used was freedom, in 2 Corinthians and Colossians it is rather reconciliation.

This, then, is a brief description of the main elements of Paul's use of the figure of reconciliation to describe an effect of the Christ-event. What is striking is the absence of any allusions to expiation, propitiation, or even sacrifice in any of the passages which deal with the notion of reconciliation.[30] Paul clearly says that the reconciliation was effected by the death of Christ, by his blood, or the blood of the cross; yet he does it without importing these nuances. And with that we may now pass to another phase of our discussion.

III. *Problems in the Modern Interpretation of Reconciliation*

From the foregoing survey of Pauline passages dealing with reconciliation we can see that the figure being used is derived from the sociological or political spheres of life. The notions of enmity, hostility, estrangement, and alienation, as well as their counterparts, reconciliation, atonement, friendship, and intimacy are derived from social intercourse of human persons or from the relations of ethnic and national groups, such as Jews and Greeks, Palestinians and Romans. There is nothing in the Pauline passages that suggests a cultic or liturgical background to the figure, and even less a sacrificial origin. By contrast, expiation (used by Paul only in Rom 3:25) does have a cultic or liturgical background, since it is derived from the *Yôm Kippûr* ceremony of Leviticus 16. In saying that Christ himself has been proposed as the *hilastērion*, "the means of expiation" or the "mercy seat," Paul sees the blood of Christ achieving what the ritual sprinkling of the mercy seat in the Holy of Holies on the feast of *Yôm Kippûr* was supposed to achieve. That was a yearly rite, a cultic act; and Paul's figurative use of expiation reflects that background. But it is a distinct figure, having nothing to do with reconciliation.[31]

A few years ago E. Käsemann, contributing an article to Bultmann's third Festschrift, *Zeit und Geschichte,* penned some "Erwägungen zum Stichwort 'Versöhnungslehre im Neuen Testament.'"[32] His purpose was to show that "the whole soteriology of the New Testament" could not be summed up as a doctrine of atonement, as he sees it done "in the Anglo-Saxon theological world in particular." Though he names no Anglo-Saxon authors and refers only to "a large number of theological textbooks," his critical finger is not entirely misdirected. Though he speaks of the "Versöhnungslehre im Neuen Testament," he finds that "the motif [of reconciliation] appears only in the general realm of Paulinism, though without having any significant meaning for Pauline theology as a whole."[33] And he concludes that "there is no such thing as a doctrine of reconciliation which is regulative for the whole New

Testament. It does not exist even in Paul, who only occasionally makes use of the motif, however important it becomes in the context of 2 Cor 5.18ff."[34] The bulk of Käsemann's subsequent discussion is devoted to the Pauline passages.

Though he may be right in castigating the Anglo-Saxon theological world for thinking of atonement as the summation of New Testament soteriology, I am not sure that he rightly understands the role of reconciliation in the Pauline writings or that one can write it off as having no significant meaning for Pauline theology. Part of the difficulty is Käsemann's understanding of Pauline theology. It is not until the next-to-last page of the article that one learns that "to Paul the doctrine of justification is the heart of the Christian message; it establishes the legitimacy and sets the limits of all varieties and even interpretations of NT teaching."[35] Let us grant for a moment—*dato, non concesso*—that for Paul the doctrine of justification is the heart of the Christian message, does that mean that since reconciliation is not the same as justification, it plays no significant role in Pauline theology as a whole?

Käsemann arrives at this understanding of reconciliation in Pauline writings by deciding initially that reconciliation "acquires terminological significance in Rom. 5.10f.; 11.15; and—here only with theological emphasis!—II Cor. 5.18ff.," whereas "it appears as a catchword in the hymnic fragments in Col. 1.20,22 and Eph. 2.16."[36] Now this is a subtle way of writing off unwanted evidence, since we are never told just what the acquiring of terminological significance in the two passages in Romans and the one in 2 Corinthians really means, or what having "theological emphasis" in 2 Corinthians implies. How can a motif acquire terminological significance or theological emphasis "without having any significant meaning for Pauline theology as a whole?" And who decides that?

Käsemann further confuses the issue by associating *katallassein* and *hilaskesthai*; he writes, "The exegete can, strictly speaking, find the New Testament speaking of 'reconciliation' only in those passages in which *katallassein* and *hilaskesthai* and their derivatives occur."[37] Then he asks "to what extent the translation 'reconciliation' ought to take the place of (the surely more appropriate) 'expiate'."[38] By this association and this query, he falls into the same trap that has bedevilled Anglo-Saxon theology for the last four hundred years. In associating *katallassein* and *hilaskesthai*, he does what Paul has never done, and this enables him to attribute to the figure of reconciliation a cultic nuance and a liturgical background which it does not have. Again, when he says that "eschatological reconciliation does not exist apart from the 'means of expiation' mentioned in [Rom] 3.25, which is the dying Christ himself, or apart from his vicarious mediation,"[39] he implies the same confusion. For though it is true that no effect of the Christ-event (described under any of the nine figures mentioned earlier) can exist apart from the event itself, it does not mean that reconciliation is expiation or that *hilastērion* and *katallagē* are the same figure, having the same connotation or origin.

When we look at Käsemann's treatment of the Pauline passages in which reconciliation is mentioned, there are further problems in his discussion. He finds the phrase "the reconciliation of the world" in Rom 11:15 to be used without any preparation and to be obviously a formula that "can only be explained on the grounds of a fixed tradition."[40] Since this is the passage in which Paul discusses the so-called rejection of Israel and finds that in God's providence the reaction of the Jews to the Christian gospel has opened it up to the Gentiles *de facto*, he reflects on how wonderful it will be when they too accept it: "For if their rejection means the reconciliation of the world, what will their acceptance mean but life from the dead?"[41] "Reconciliation of the world" is here used as a tag, without any preparation indeed; that it is part of a "fixed tradition" is quite plausible. But does that mean that it is not Paul's own? Why could it not be echoing Rom 5:1–11 or, better still, 2 Cor 5:19, "in Christ God was reconciling the world to himself." Again, the problem is how to decide that a formulaic expression is echoing something other than Pauline teaching, and not an important element in his theology.

When Käsemann turns to Rom 5:9–10, he finds that reconciliation is used "in a non-cultic sense and means bringing hostility to an end."[42] This is accurate enough; but when he continues that reconciliation takes place "by his blood" (Rom 5:9) or "by the death of his Son" (Rom 5:10) and "for us" (*hyper hēmōn*, 5:8), he immediately decides that these phrases "have a liturgical colouring."[43] But is this clearly so? The "cultic associations" in these phrases are not *per se* evident, and they could just as easily express social or political associations of interpersonal, intergroup relationships quite independently of cult.

The real question in Romans 5 is whether Paul has introduced the motif of reconciliation to heighten the concept of *justificatio impiorum,* viz., by the assertion of *justificatio inimicorum.*[44] There is no doubt that justification and reconciliation are related in Romans 5; but the real question is, what is the nature of that relation? Is reconciliation subordinated to justification? In Rom 5:1 Paul says, "Having been justified . . . , we have peace with God." As I read that verse, it suggests that justification takes place in view of something, viz., reconciliation, so that reconciliation does not "sharpen and point up the doctrine of justification" in Pauline thought. It is rather the other way round. Further involved in this issue is the subtle question of the relation of Romans chaps. 1–4 to Romans chaps. 5–8, and indeed the place of Romans 5 in the whole of chaps. 1–8.[45] No matter how one decides this question, it seems to me to be clear that the climax of chaps. 1–8 is not in chap. 4, for as Paul begins chap. 5 he moves from justification to the manifestation of God's love in Christ and through the Spirit (chap. 8), so that the latter is the climax of it all. If so, justification is only a part of the process and a stage in the development of his thesis in Romans chaps. 1–8—and then justification finds a more adequate expression in reconciliation; indeed, "reconciliation" becomes the better way of expressing that process.

When Käsemann takes up 2 Cor 5:18–21, he finds that it is most likely a piece of tradition which was handed down to Paul and that Paul is there echoing a Jewish-Christian tradition, with vss. 19–21 being "a pre-Pauline hymnic fragment."[46] But if Paul has indeed "taken up and used motifs from earlier forms of the Christian proclamation," does that mean that they do not become part of Pauline theology? And the same question has to be asked about the "hymnic fragments in Col. 1.20, 22 and Eph. 2.16."[47] Once we ascertain that there is pre-Pauline material in Paul's writings, does that mean that it is not really part of his thinking or that it cannot be considered a part of his theology?

The extreme to which this sort of analysis of Pauline writings is carried is found in Käsemann's discussion of the relation between what he calls anthropological and cosmological reconciliation. It is the question that we mentioned earlier in terms of cosmic reconciliation over against the reconciliation of human beings to God. For Käsemann the anthropological reconciliation presupposes cosmological reconciliation; the latter is especially prominent in the "two deutero-Pauline texts" of Col 1:20 and Eph 2:16.[48] Käsemann argues thus:

> We have already seen in Rom. 5.10f. the goal and result of the reconciling act to be peace; similarly these texts [Colossians and Ephesians] are clearly concerned with cosmic peace, the revelation of which is dreamed of as early as Vergil's Fourth Eclogue. This peace is thought of as the eschatological state of salvation, not as a psychological attitude, something in which the NT is very rarely interested. In this situation of peace what was formerly separated becomes solidly united, i.e., the heavenly is united with the earthly, just as warring earthly camps are united with one another. Even religious antipathies now become irrelevant, as may be seen in a radical way in the antithesis between Israel and the Gentile world. The world is made peaceful, as under the *pax romana*, in that it is everywhere subjected to its new Lord, Christ, as Cosmocrator.[49]

Now in this paragraph Käsemann has caught up beautifully some of the Pauline or Deutero-Pauline nuances of reconciliation, and his paraphrase of them leaves little to be desired. And again,

> Though the world may not yet know of the transformation that has taken place, the Christian community does. Its message is characterized by the open proclamation of the seizure of power by God and his appointed Savior and by the verification of that proclamation in the union of both Jews and Gentiles in the Christian church.[50]

The difficulty is that Käsemann sees the affirmation of cosmic reconciliation as something that precedes anthropological reconciliation and understands both Col 1:20–22 and 2 Cor 5:19–20 implying a "transition from a cosmological to an anthropological message of reconciliation."[51] He seems to mean that Paul or the author of the Deutero-Paulines only came to the idea of the reconciliation of mankind from the notion of the reconciliation of the world (or the All), and that this was a notion current in the Hellenistic world of the time, as is dreamed of in Vergil's Fourth Eclogue.[52]

There are several comments that are in order in this regard. First, one may concede that there is a vague idea of reconciliation in the Fourth Eclogue. In it Vergil sings of the *ultima aetas,* when "a new generation descends from heaven on high" and "a golden race springs up throughout the world," putting an end to "the iron brood." As it begins in Pollio's consulship, "lingering traces of our guilt shall become void and release the earth from its continual dread." And the child to be born "shall have the gift of divine life, shall see heroes mingled with gods, and shall himself be seen of them, and shall sway a world to which his father's virtues have brought peace." And the untilled earth shall pour forth its bounty of flowers and plants and vegetables, while "the herds shall not fear huge lions" (*Eclogues* 4.4–22). I regard the idea of reconciliation that may be contained in this Eclogue as vague because it is really dealing with another matter, the birth of the Golden Age, when all will be blissful and bountiful. To compare such a view of cosmic progression with the cosmic reconciliation of Pauline or Deutero-Pauline writings is somewhat farfetched. What they have in common is only a rosy, utopian view of a future age; but all the details are remarkably different.

Second, it seems to me that the prime analogate in the Pauline writings that deal with reconciliation is anthropological reconciliation, and that the transition is from mankind to the world, or to the All, not the other way round. Cf. Rom 8:21–23 for the progress of his thought (under another image, to be sure).

Third, it is difficult to understand how a notion that Käsemann generally relegates to Deutero-Pauline writings, cosmic reconciliation in Colossians and Ephesians, can be considered the source of something that is found in the authentic Pauline writings themselves, anthropological reconciliation.

These are, then, some of the difficulties that I have with the Käsemann interpretation of the role of reconciliation in Pauline theology. Despite them I have recognized that there are some excellent paragraphs in the article on the consequences of this notion for Christian life and conduct. And this brings me to the last point of my discussion.

IV. *The Pertinence of Pauline Reconciliation to Modern Life*

Having reflected on the figure of reconciliation that Paul uses to describe one of the effects of the Christ-event and that emphasizes the gratuitous initiative taken by God to bring humanity closely into a sphere of friendship and intimacy with himself, we can see that this idea has to be proclaimed anew by Christians of today. Ours is a world in which we have struggled to put an end to war, not merely because we fear the consequences of a Third World War of atomic- or hydrogen-bomb dimensions, but because people of varying religious backgrounds, Judeo-Christian or other, have come to a stage of cosmic or worldwide awareness that simply as human beings we can no longer act that way with one another. "Jamais plus la guerre," said Paul VI, addressing the United Nations. For Christians in particular the motivation for this is found in the Apostle's idea of reconciliation, in the breaking down of the barriers between human beings (and by implication, between nations).

On another level of dealings between groups and individuals within a given national or ethnic society there is need for further reflection on the Pauline message of reconciliation. There is a feeling abroad that our human society is sick—for all sorts of reasons. One aspect of it is precisely the alienation of men and women from those things or those persons with which they have been intimately identified in the past. To such as are estranged and alienated the Pauline message of reconciliation addresses itself ever anew: "For as many of you as were baptized into Christ have put on Christ; there is neither Jew nor Greek, there is neither slave nor free, there is neither male nor female; for you are all one in Christ Jesus." This Paul wrote in another context (Gal 3:27–28), but it supplies the background to his thinking on reconciliation or at-one-ment. The Christian, regardless of his/her ethnic origin, social status, or sexual identity, is expected to meet the challenge of putting on Christ, of donning his outlook on life. If he is "our peace" and has made us both one (Eph 2:14), then in him the Christian finds the remedy to the alienation that besets him/her in the society in which he/she lives.

In the earliest passage in which Paul deals with reconciliation, he speaks of himself as having been given "the ministry of reconciliation" (2 Cor 5:18) and of being an "ambassador for Christ" (5:20). In this, as in some other passages (cf. Col 1:24), Paul did not hesitate to depict himself as having the task of extending, in a sense, one of the effects of the Christ-event. Paul would never have substituted himself for Christ, implying that anything that he would do would replace or substitute for the Christ-event itself. But he could speak of himself as a "minister of reconciliation," proclaiming to the world the message of reconciliation, announcing the effect of the Christ-event, and striving to get more and more of mankind to appropriate to itself the benefits thereof. So, as ambassador for Christ, he extends the ministry of reconciliation.

Paul's teaching about reconciliation obviously has something of the idyllic about it. We look at other Christians who surround us, and we see all the forms of estrangement and alienation among them as among many others who are not Christian. We wonder why it is that such an effect of the Christ-event has not taken root and manifested itself in the lives of such persons, if faith in Christ Jesus and baptism into his life really mean all that they are supposed to mean. This is a real problem, and it has often been called the problem of the integration of Christian life. How does a Christian become aware that his outlook and life are to be dominated by the person of Christ and all that he stood for and taught? Paul was not unaware of this himself. Writing in a context that did not deal with reconciliation as such, he said, "I have been crucified with Christ; it is no longer I who live, but Christ who lives in me; and the life I now live in the flesh (*kata sarka*) I live by faith in the Son of God" (Gal 2:20). The ontological reality of Christ-in-me has somehow or other to be brought to the level of psychological awareness. This is the problem of the integration of Christian life: "Be what you are." You are in Christ; you have entered a state of reconciliation with God and with your fellowmen through your faith and baptism into Christ Jesus. Let them influence your existence, life, and conduct. The challenge is thus given to men and women of all ages and generations to be what they are.

By extension of the last two points that have been made, it would not be false to say that the Christian of today shares in a sense in that "ministry of reconciliation" of which Paul spoke. The role of the Christian in the twentieth century would be to manifest that reconciliation to others, to other Christians, to his/her Jewish brother or sister, to other members of the human race who are not part of the Judeo-Christian heritage.

There is obviously a greater problem here today than that envisaged by Paul. His horizons were limited to the Christian message that he was explaining to the Christians to whom he wrote, whether they came from a Jewish or a Gentile background. He found the reconciliation of them in Christ Jesus, who is "our peace." Today the role of the Christian is to be faithful to his/her own Christian heritage, yet so manifest his/her love and friendship as to include even those who are not of his/her own immediate Christian circle. If the Roman poet Terentius could write, "Homo sum; humani nihil a me alienum puto" (*Heaut.* 1.1,25: "I am a human being; I consider nothing human to be foreign from me"), the Christian could also boast, "Christianus sum; christiani nihil a me alienum puto." That Christian challenge would be at once a loyalty to one's own heritage and an openness to and love of what is not of it.

In Paul's ken the reconciliation of Jew and Greek of which he spoke was envisaged as an at-one-ment brought about between them through faith and baptism in Christ Jesus—through the conversion of both Jews and Greeks to Christianity. This is Paul's sole perspective. Today we have all witnessed in one way or another the alienation of Christian and Jew. It is an age-old problem of a barrier that exists between us, born of what Paul calls "their rejection." This stern word, used of his former co-religionists, was likewise associated with his sorrow about that barrier (see Rom 9:2–3). But as we ponder the implications of his teaching about the reconciliation of all human beings in Christ, we cannot be blind to the problems that that teaching has created and can still create. For Christian theologians have never yet been able to explain satisfactorily why it is that the God that they worship has in his providence continued to favor a people which nourishes itself on a great deal of the same Scriptures that feed our Christian lives and yet have not accepted the reconciliation that is at hand in Christ Jesus. Christian theologians have no adequate theology of Israel. This is the enigma that the Pauline theology of reconciliation proposes.

If I was somewhat critical of Käsemann earlier in this paper, I should like to end by making my own some of his comments on an aspect of reconciliation. Without buying all the connections which he establishes between the New Testament hymns and "the unbridled enthusiasm . . . of the earliest Hellenistic community and the beginnings of its world mission," I can agree that the Pauline teaching on reconciliation could be viewed too enthusiastically and with too rosy a hue, so that an "individual Christian will understand the salvation he experiences as devoid of temptation and consequently cease looking toward the future and giving himself to the service of others. So it is no accident that the anthropological statements about reconciliation occur in a parenetic context, portraying existence as still hanging in the balance. The message of reconciliation is not an eschatological myth, as in Vergil's Fourth Eclogue. It is actualized between the indicative of the gift of salvation and the imperative of the duties of salvation, i.e., in the historical realm, the realm of concrete daily life and corporate community. Cosmic peace does not settle over the world, as in a fairy tale. It takes root only so far as men in the service of reconciliation confirm that they have themselves found peace with God."[53]

In concluding this discussion of the theological notion of reconciliation, I should like to stress that I have sought merely to situate it in Pauline theology as a whole and to restore it to its merited relation to justification. I have not tried to say that it is in Pauline theology more important than justification or that the essence of Pauline theology can be summed up by it. It expresses an aspect of the Christ-event that justification does not, and it is really impossible to say which is more important. In certain discussions of Paul (e.g., Romans 5) one may debate, as I have above, whether justification is not subordinated to reconciliation, but that still leaves the question open about the place of reconciliation in Pauline theology as a whole.[54]

NOTES

* Originally published in *No Famine in the Land: Studies in Honor of John L. McKenzie* (ed. J. W. Flanagan and A. W. Robinson; Missoula, MT: Scholars Press, for the Institute for Antiquity and Christianity, Claremont, 1975) 155–77.

[1] See F. Büchsel, "*Allassō*, . . . ," *TDNT* 1 (1964) 251–59; R. Bultmann, *Theology of the New Testament* (London: SCM, 1956), 1. 285–87; T. R. Clark, *Saved by His Life: A Study of the New Testament Doctrine of Reconciliation and Salvation* (New York: Macmillan, 1959) 179–83; J. Dupont, *La réconciliation dans la théologie de Saint Paul* (*ALBO* 3/32; Bruges: Desclée de Brouwer, 1953); L. Goppelt, "Versöhnung durch Christus," *Christologie und Ethik: Aufsätze zum Neuen Testament* (Göttingen: Vandenhoeck & Ruprecht, 1968) 147–64; E. Käsemann, *An die Römer* (HNT 8a; Tübingen: Mohr, 1973) 129; "Erwägungen zum Stichwort 'Versöhnungslehre im Neuen Testament'," *Zeit und Geschichte: Dankesgabe an Rudolf Bultmann zum 80. Geburtstag* (ed. E.

Dinkler; Tübingen: Mohr, 1964) 47–59; "Some Thoughts on the Theme 'The Doctrine of Reconciliation in the New Testament'," *The Future of Our Religious Past: Essays in Honour of Rudolf Bultmann* (ed. J. M. Robinson; New York: Harper & Row, 1971) 49–64; A. F. N. Lekkerkerker, "Dialectisch spreken over de verzoening," *Nederlands theologische Stemmen* 1 (1946–47) 212–32; W. Michaelis, *Versöhnung des Alls: Die frohe Botschaft von der Gnade Gottes* (Gümligen/Bern: Siloah, 1950) 23–30, 122–51; J. Michl, "Die 'Versöhnung' (Kol 1,20)," *TQ* 128 (1948) 442–62; A. Nygren, *Die Versöhnung als Gottestat* (Studien der Luther-Akademie, 5; Gütersloh: Bertelsmann, 1932); E. Percy, *Die Probleme der Kolosser- und Epheserbriefe* (Acta regiae societatis humaniorum litterarum Lundensis, 39; Lund: Gleerup, 1946) 85–92, 271–73; A. Ritschl, *Die christliche Lehre von der Rechtfertigung und Versöhnung* (3 vols.; 3d ed.; Bonn: Adolf Marcus, 1888–89); V. Taylor, *Forgiveness and Reconciliation: A Study in New Testament Theology* (2d ed.; London: Macmillan, 1948) 70–108; B. N. Wambacq, "Per eum reconciliare . . . quae in caelis sunt," *RB* 55 (1948) 35–42; D. E. H. Whiteley, "St. Paul's Thought on the Atonement," *JTS* ns 8 (1957) 240–55; *The Theology of St. Paul* (Oxford: Blackwell, 1964) 130–54. G. Wiencke, *Paulus über Jesu Tod: Die Deutung des Todes Jesu bei Paulus und ihre Herkunft* (Beiträge zur Förderung christlicher Theologie, 2/42; Gütersloh: Bertelsmann, 1939) 69–78; G. W. H. Lampe, *Reconciliation in Christ* (Maurice Lectures 1955; London: Longmans, Green, 1956); J. Denney, *The Christian Doctrine of Reconciliation* (London: J. Clarke, 1959).

[2] By E. Käsemann, "Some Thoughts."

[3] E.g., 1 Thes 4:2, 15; 1 Cor 7:10 [cf. 7:25]; 9:14; 13:2; Rom 12:14; 13:9; 16:19. See further W. D. Davies, *Paul and Rabbinic Judaism: Some Rabbinic Elements in Pauline Theology* (London: S.P.C.K., 1948) 136–41; B. Gerhardsson, *Memory and Manuscript: Oral Tradition and Written Transmission in Rabbinic Judaism and Early Christianity* (ASNU 22; Lund: Gleerup, 1961) 302–06; D. M. Stanley, "Pauline Allusions to the Sayings of Jesus," *CBQ* 23 (1961) 26–39; D. L. Dungan, *The Sayings of Jesus in the Churches of Paul: The Use of the Synoptic Tradition in the Regulation of Early Church Life* (Philadelphia: Fortress, 1971); F. F. Bruce, "Paul and the Historical Jesus," *BJRL* 56 (1974) 317–35.

I do not mean that Paul did not know the words or the teaching of Jesus or that his interpretation of the Christ-event was wholly derived from his conversion-experience or something similar. His mention of his visit to Jerusalem (*historēsai Kēphan*, Gal 1:18) was almost certainly intended to suggest that he had obtained some information about Jesus from Cephas. See further R. E. Brown et al., *PNT*, 23–24. One can also debate the meaning of 2 Cor 5:16, his knowing Christ according to the flesh. But whatever one wants to say about his knowledge of the earthly Jesus, the fact still remains that he is much more interested in the interpretation of the Christ-event for Christians who had never witnessed the earthly ministry of Jesus of Nazareth.

[4] Most of the letters of the Pauline corpus were composed prior to the composition of the earliest Gospel (Mark, ca. A.D. 65).

[5] E.g., D. E. H. Whiteley, *The Theology of St. Paul*, 130.

[6] See E. Käsemann, " 'The Righteousness of God' in Paul," *New Testament Questions of Today* (Philadelphia: Fortress, 1969) 168–82; "Justification and Salvation History in the Epistle to the Romans," *Perspectives on Paul* (Philadelphia: Fortress, 1971) 60–78; P. Stuhlmacher, *Gerechtigkeit Gottes bei Paulus*

(FRLANT 87; Göttingen: Vandenhoeck & Ruprecht, 1965); K. Kertelge, *"Recht-fertigung" bei Paulus: Studien zur Struktur und zum Bedeutungsgehalt des paulinischen Rechtfertigungsbegriffs* (NTAbh ns 3; Münster in W.: Aschendorff, 1967); J. A. Fitzmyer, "Pauline Theology," *JBC*, art. 79, §94–97; J. A. Ziesler, *The Meaning of Righteousness in Paul: A Linguistic and Theological Enquiry* (SNTSMS 20; Cambridge: University Press, 1972); D. Lührmann, "Rechtfertigung und Versöhnung: Zur Geschichte der paulinischen Tradition," *ZTK* 67 (1970) 436–52.

[7] See F. Amiot, *The Key Concepts of St. Paul* (New York: Herder and Herder, 1962); S. Lyonnet, "The Terminology of 'Salvation,' " *Sin, Redemption, and Sacrifice: A Biblical and Patristic Study* (ed. S. Lyonnet and L. Sabourin; AnBib 48; Rome: Biblical Institute, 1970) 63–78; W. Foerster and G. Fohrer, "Sōzō, sōtēria, . . . ," *TDNT* 7 (1971) 964–1024.

[8] In this instance one can ask whether Paul is using the word *hilastērion* as an adjective or as a noun; in the interpretation which I prefer it would be a concrete noun, best translated as "a means of expiation," with an allusion to the *kappōret* of Exod 25:17–20, which is translated in the LXX at first as *hilastērion epithema*, but consistently thereafter as simply *hilastērion*. See further my article, "The Targum of Leviticus from Qumran Cave 4," *Maarav* 1 (1978–79) 5–23, esp. pp. 15–17.

[9] See my "Pauline Theology," §83–89; S. Lyonnet, "The Terminology of 'Expiation' in the Old Testament," "The Terminology of 'Expiation' in the New Testament," *Sin, Redemption, and Sacrifice*, 120–66; D. E. H. Whiteley, *The Theology of St. Paul*, 145–47. Contrast L. Morris, "The Biblical Use of the Term 'Blood,' " *JTS* ns 3 (1952) 216–27. See further L. Moraldi, *Espiazione sacrificale e riti espiatori nell'ambiente biblico e nell'Antico Testamento* (AnBib 5; Rome: Biblical Institute, 1956).

[10] See my "Pauline Theology," §90–93 (Redemptive Liberation); S. Lyonnet, "The Terminology of 'Liberation,' " *Sin, Redemption, and Sacrifice*, 79–119; D. E. H. Whiteley, *The Theology of St. Paul*, 137–45. I prefer today to separate *eleutheria* from *apolytrōsis;* the former is certainly derived from Paul's Hellenistic background, whereas the latter may be influenced by both the Hellenistic and Jewish (OT) backgrounds.

[11] See O. Procksch and K. G. Kuhn, *"Hagios, hagiazō, . . . ," TDNT* 1 (1964) 88–115; L. Cerfaux, *Christ in the Theology of St. Paul* (New York: Herder and Herder, 1959) 296–315.

[12] See H. Schlier, *"Eleutheros, eleutheroō, . . . ," TDNT* 2 (1964) 487–502; H. D. Betz, "Spirit, Freedom, and Law: Paul's Message to the Galatian Churches," *SEA* 39 (1974) 145–60; D. Nestle, *Eleutheria: Studien zum Wesen der Freiheit bei den Griechen und im Neuen Testament* (Hermeneutische Untersuchungen zur Theologie, 16; Tübingen: Mohr [Siebeck], 1967); R. Schnackenburg, "Freedom in the Thought of the Apostle Paul," *Present and Future: Modern Aspects of New Testament Theology* (Notre Dame: University of Notre Dame, 1966) 64–80.

[13] In this instance the abstract noun is not found in Paul's writings, but he does use the verb *metamorphoun*. See J. Dupont, "Le chrétien, miroir de la gloire divine, d'après II Cor. 3,18," *RB* 56 (1949) 392–411; W. C. van Unnik, " 'With Unveiled Face,' an Exegesis of 2 Corinthians iii 12–18," *NovT* 6 (1963) 153–69; reprinted in *Sparsa collecta: The Collected Essays of W. C. van Unnik* (NovTSup 29; Leiden: Brill, 1973) 194–210; I. E. Friesen, *The Glory of the Ministry of Jesus Christ: Illustrated by a Study of 2 Cor. 2:14–3:18* (Theologische Dissertationen,

7; Basel: F. Reinhardt, 1971); D. M. Stanley, *Christ's Resurrection in Pauline Soteriology* (AnBib 13; Rome: Biblical Institute, 1961) 131–34; S. Schulz, "Die Decke des Moses," *ZNW* 49 (1958) 1–30.

[14] See W. Foerster, "*Ktizō, ktisis, . . . ,*" *TDNT* 3 (1965) 1000–35, esp. pp. 1033–35. Cf. E. Sjöberg, "Neuschöpfung in den Toten-Meer-Rollen," *ST* 9 (1955) 131–36.

[15] On this figure, see the literature cited in n. 1 above.

[16] One further figure might be added, viz., "forgiveness" (*aphesis*), a remitting of the debt implied in the sins of mankind. However, since this figure is found only in the Captivity Letters of the Pauline corpus (Col 1:14; Eph 1:7; cf., however, Rom 4:7 [quoting Ps 32:1]), some might prefer to consider it a Deutero-Pauline figure, which is closer to the Lucan way of viewing the Christ-event. In any case, one would have to discuss here the very problematic word *paresis* in Rom 3:25, which may be nothing more than a synonym for *aphesis*.

[17] See F. Büchsel, "*Allassō, . . . ,*" *251*.

[18] There is no need to rehearse this evidence here, since it has been adequately presented by J. Dupont, *La réconciliation*, 7–15. An interesting additional example of the secular use of the Greek expression comes from a papyrus contract of remarriage found in one of the Murabbaʿat caves in Palestine. It is dated to the year A.D. 124 (the seventh year of Hadrian, in the consulate of Manius Acilius Glabrio and Bellicius Torquatus) and bears witness to the remarriage of Eleaios, son of Simon, of the village of Galoda, to Salome, daughter of John Galgoula. The crucial part of the text reads: "Since it happened earlier to the same Eleaios (son of) Simon to become estranged and divorce (*appallagēnai kai apolyein*) Salome (daughter) of John Galgoula [. . .] for the sake of living together (?), now the same Eleaios agrees anew (*ex ananeōseōs*) to reconcile and to take to himself (*katallaxai k[ai] proslabesthai*) the same Salome (daughter of) John Galgoula as wedded wi[fe] with dowry of 200 denarii, which make 50 Tyrian (shekels)" (Mur 115:3–5). Here one finds not only the use of *apolyein* in the sense of "divorce" (see pp. 90–91 above), but also *katallassein* in a secular sense. What is interesting is the active use of the verb with an object (to reconcile Salome). P. Benoit, who published the Greek text, translates it, however, differently: "est d'accord pour se réconcilier à nouveau et reprendre la même Salomé." See *Les grottes de Murabbaʿat* (DJD 2; Oxford: Clarendon, 1961) 250.

[19] So at least reads the LXX MS A (the purpose infinitive *diallaxai* in MS A has as its counterpart in MS B the infinitive *epistrepsai*); the MT has an infinitive, *lhśybw*, which is vocalized as *lahăśîbāw*. Since the latter makes no sense in the context, emendations have been suggested. As far as our discussion is concerned, it seems rather obvious that the exact nuance in *diallassein/katallassein* is not rooted in the Hebrew scriptural tradition and that Greek translators have introduced the idea of "reconciliation" which is otherwise well attested in Hellenistic writers. I am aware that compounds of *allassein* are used in the LXX to translate various Hebrew words; but the question is whether the Hebrew words so translated actually denoted what the Greek words did or whether the Greek words have introduced a further Hellenistic (if not Hellenic) nuance.

[20] It should be noted, however, in this instance that we are not told how Ajax was reconciling himself with the gods. J. Dupont (*La réconciliation*, 13) speaks of his doing this "au moyen de purifications rituelles." This may be involved, but

Sophocles does not even hint at them; and it seems more likely in view of the fundamental thrust of the play that what is meant is that Ajax has gone to reconcile himself to the gods by his own death. The extent to which anyone can read a cultic or ritual sense into Sophocles' expression in *Ajax* 744 is questionable. See further pp. 171–73 above.

[21] Büchsel, "*Allassō, ...*," 254.

[22] This is also the conclusion of Dupont, *La réconciliation*, 28. He rightly admits that Paul invests the figure with certain nuances derived from his Jewish background. But I am not sure that the figure of reconciliation has "le caractère essentiellement juridique" which he associates with it.

[23] See *The Compact Edition of the Oxford English Dictionary* (New York: Oxford University, 1971), 1. 135.—The first instance of the verb "atone" is cited from Shakespeare (*Richard the Second*, 1.i, 202). One will find its use there is in the secular sense. The *OED* continues: "*Atone* was not admitted into the Bible in 1611, though *atonement* had been in since Tindale."

[24] See nos. 7–8 above.

[25] In this discussion of Pauline passages dealing with reconciliation, I am treating ten letters of the corpus as authentic (1–2 Thes, Gal, Phil, 1–2 Cor, Rom, Phlm, Col, Eph). If one prefers to regard 2 Thes, Col, and Eph as Deutero-Pauline, even though not in the same sense as the Pastorals, it would require but a slight adjustment to speak of the author of these letters rather than of Paul. In any case, they belong to a Pauline circle and reflect a view of the Christ-event that it represented in the early Christian church. The interpretation of the Christ-event as reconciliation that one encounters in Colossians and Ephesians is so similar to that in 2 Corinthians and Romans that it is almost impossible to distinguish a Pauline and a Deutero-Pauline view of this matter. See further my remarks on Käsemann's treatment of the Pauline material above, pp. 173–75, who does not radically separate them from the authentic Pauline corpus.

[26] See further R. Bultmann, *Theology of the New Testament*, 1.232–38; J. A. Fitzmyer, "Pauline Theology," §119.

[27] See p. 165 above; cf. J. Dupont, *La réconciliation*, 10–18.

[28] Here one could add further Pauline passages that deal with the peace of Christ. He is "the peace of God" that surpasses all understanding and that will keep your hearts and your minds in Christ Jesus" (Phil 4:7). Or "let the peace of Christ rule in your hearts, to which indeed you were called in one body" (Col 3:15). Cf. 2 Thes 3:16. Moreover, "peace" is not to be understood in this connection merely as the absence of war or enmity, for it carries with it the Old Testament nuances of *šālôm*, the wholeness or perfection of bounty that can come only from God himself.

[29] As in Rom 3:6; 5:12. But Paul also used *kosmos* in the sense of the created universe; see Rom 1:20; 1 Cor 3:22; cf. Eph 1:4. See R. Bultmann, *Theology of the New Testament*, 1. 254–59.

[30] J. Dupont (*La réconciliation*, 39–42) associates reconciliation with both sacrifice and propitiation. In this I have to disagree. It is not that Paul did not consider the death of Christ a sacrifice (cf. Eph 5:2), but rather whether in the passages in which he deals with reconciliation he uses the expressions, "his death," "the blood of the cross," or "the blood of Christ" with the sacrificial connotation. No one will deny that the saying of Lev 17:11 ("for the life of the flesh is in the blood; and I have given it for you upon the altar to make expiation

for yourselves; for it is the blood that makes expiation") underlies Paul's use of "blood" in Rom 3:25, where it is closely associated with *hilastērion.* That meaning of blood is thus clearly related to expiation. But in Romans 3 Paul does not introduce the figure of reconciliation.

I cannot help but think that D. E. H. Whiteley ("St. Paul's Thought on the Atonement," 240–55, esp. pp. 247–49) comes closer to Paul's sense when he relates the mention of blood in the reconciliation passages to "covenant blood" (cf. Exod 24:3–8): "The Apostle means that through his death Christ constituted a relationship with all things analogous to that established in the Old Testament by means of the blood of the covenant" (249). Cf. his *Theology of St. Paul,* 140. Lührmann ("Rechtfertigung und Versöhnung," 438–40) speaks of the use of blood in Rom 3:24–26 as also related to "Bundestheologie." In a footnote he recognizes the connection with Leviticus 16 and the similar use of material in Qumran literature. To my way of thinking, the primary reference in Romans 3 is to Leviticus 16—and only thereafter possibly a reference to "Bundestheologie." The reason is that only in Romans 3 are "blood" and *hilastērion* associated, whereas elsewhere the "blood" or "death" of Christ (e.g., when related to reconciliation) could have the covenant reference more directly.

[31] What is curious is to recall that English-speaking Jews translate *Yôm hak-Kippûrîm* as the "Day of Atonement." See *The Torah: The Five Books of Moses* (Philadelphia: Jewish Publication Society, 1962) 226 (Lev 23:27). This name is undoubtedly influenced by the translation of Christian English Bibles. In French the Hebrew expression is more accurately translated as "Jour de l'Expiation." The JPS *Torah* uses, however, the noun "expiation" in Lev 16:6, 10, 11, 17; 17:11 (where the *RSV* has "atonement"; but cf. Lev 16:34 in the JPS *Torah*). Apparently, English-speaking Jews have never used any other translation for the Hebrew name of this feast-day; at least so I have been informed by Prof. Harry M. Orlinsky and Dr. Philip Goodman, the compiler of *The Yom Kippur Anthology* (Philadelphia: Jewish Publication Society of America, 1971). To both of these gentlemen I owe my thanks.

[32] See n. 1 above for details. The article was translated under the title "Some Thoughts on the Theme 'The Doctrine of Reconciliation in the New Testament,' " but in view of the article's starting-point it would have been better to render "Versöhnungslehre" as "the doctrine of Atonement," for this is the term more properly used in the Anglo-Saxon theological world, which Käsemann criticizes.

[33] "Some Thoughts," 51. Käsemann considers Colossians and Ephesians to be Deutero-Pauline; but in reality this distinction means little in his discussion. Hence my position; see n. 25 above.

[34] Käsemann continues: "In the deutero-Paulines [presumably Colossians and Ephesians] it also characterizes only very limited contexts, specifically the liturgical tradition contained in two passages" [presumably Col 1:20, 22; Eph 2:16]. But the fact that the image is used in a text of "liturgical tradition" does not mean that the image itself is of a liturgical background; liturgy does use figures and language drawn from other contexts and relationships.

[35] "Some Thoughts," 63. I can understand how one might say that the doctrine of justification establishes the legitimacy and sets the limits of *Pauline* teaching, but "of [presumably, all] NT teaching"? How does Paul become a norm for John, or Pauline theology a criterion of, say, Lucan theology?

D. Lührmann ("Rechtfertigung und Versöhnung," 446) likewise asserts that reconciliation has "keine eigenständige Bedeutung" in Paul's theology, but is subordinated to the "Hauptthema seiner Theologie, das in der Antithese von Glaube und Gesetz zu beschrieben ist." Though Lührmann tries to refine Käsemann's position somewhat, he is still operating with the basic presupposition of the latter. He breaks with Käsemann, when the latter describes "Versöhnung" as only one soteriological variant among others that were taken up in early Christianity, especially in those circles in which Christ was hailed as the cosmic victor. But he still derives the whole idea of anthropological reconciliation from cosmic reconciliation, as does Käsemann.

[36] "Some Thoughts," 50.

[37] Ibid.

[38] Ibid. This is not merely a problem of the English translation of Käsemann's article, to which I referred above in n. 32, but it is even true of the German original: "Blickt man von da aus auf die um *hilaskesthai* kreisende Wortgruppe, muss sofort gefragt werden, ob und wie weit die Übersetzung 'versöhnen' überhaupt an die Stelle des sicher angemesseneren 'sühnen' treten darf" ("Erwägungen," 48). The problem is by what right one can say that the *katallassein*-words belong to the orbit of *hilaskesthai* in Pauline thinking. *Sühnen*/expiate has cultic, liturgical, and even sacrificial overtones; but does *versöhnen*/reconcile imply any of that? Moreover, Paul never uses the two together in the same passage. That atonement, reconciliation, expiation, and even propitiation, came to imply all that is part of the history of the doctrine of the atonement. But is it so in Pauline theology?

[39] "Some Thoughts," 52. To show that *hilaskesthai* and words related to it designate "an event in the cultic realm," Käsemann cites Rom 3:25; Heb 2:17; 8:12; 9:5; 1 John 2:2; 4:10. Then he adds, confusing the issue still more, "to which may be added the ransom-sayings in Mark 10.45 and 1 Tim 2.6" (p. 50). But the image in *lytron* (or *antilytron*) is distinct. The mere fact that Paul links both *apolytrōsis* and *hilastērion* in Rom 3:24–25 does not necessarily mean that they have the *same* background or, for that matter, share a cultic background, let alone the *same cultic* background. That *hilastērion* has a Palestinian Jewish cultic background can be readily admitted; but if one were to insist rather on its Hellenistic background (e.g., on its derivation from propitiatory rites in the Greco-Roman world), it could also be of cultic origin. But it is not at all clear that the figure involved in *apolytrōsis* is necessarily cultic. Here one would have to discuss the extent to which the (fictive) emancipation of a slave or a prisoner at the shrine of a god in the ancient eastern Mediterranean world was really considered to be an act of worship or cult. And if it were, would that imply the same cultic background that the Hellenistic origin of *hilaskesthai* might?

[40] "Some Thoughts," 51.

[41] The phrase, "life from the dead," is very difficult to interpret and has been understood in many ways; for my preferred understanding of it, see the commentary on Romans in *JBC*, art. 53, §112.

[42] "Some Thoughts," 51.

[43] Ibid., 52.

[44] Ibid. Käsemann's starting-point was a criticism of Anglo-Saxon theology and its use of the doctrine of atonement as a summation of New Testament soteriology. Given all the overloading of the term "reconciliation" or "atonement" with the nuances of expiation, propitiation, satisfaction, penal substitu-

tion, etc., that ensued in that "theological world," Käsemann was rightly critical. But when he employs the tag *justificatio impiorum* in the context of a discussion of Pauline theology and fashions another in imitation of it, *justificatio inimicorum* (thereby subordinating reconciliation to justification), he runs the risk of importing into Pauline theology nuances born of a later problematic. For that Latin abstract phrase, though based on Rom 4:5 (*dikaiounta ton asebē*), is not found precisely in Paul's writings—and I do not mean simply that Paul did not write in Latin. The abstraction with the *genitive plural* is not his way of putting it; in using it, Käsemann betrays a later theological stance.

⁴⁵ For a brief summary of the discussion about the relation of chap. 5 to the whole of Romans, see my commentary in *JBC,* art. 53, §49 and the literature cited there. Cf. U. Luz, "Zum Aufbau von Röm. 1–8," *TZ* 25 (1969) 161–81. As for the relation of reconciliation and justification, it might be well to recall the treatment of J. Weiss, *The History of Primitive Christianity* (ed. F. C. Grant; New York: Wilson-Erickson, 1937), 2. 496–504, esp. p. 497: "The most common and comprehensive expression for the event which Paul had experienced, and which all Christians must experience, is undoubtedly 'reconciliation'. . . ."

⁴⁶ "Some Thoughts," 53.

⁴⁷ Ibid., 50. Obviously, it would not be part of it if one insists on the Deutero-Pauline character of these hymnic fragments in Colossians and Ephesians.

⁴⁸ Actually cosmic reconciliation is not found in Eph 2:11–22. Since it is found in Col 1:20–22, it may be called Deutero-Pauline. But it should be remembered that it is explicitly mentioned in 2 Cor 5:18–19 and is echoed in Rom 11:15. Hence it cannot be simply written off as a Deutero-Pauline motif, as Käsemann implies in his discussion of the idea in *An die Römer* (HNT 8a; Tübingen: Mohr, 1973) 129.

⁴⁹ "Some Thoughts," 54.

⁵⁰ Ibid., 55.

⁵¹ Ibid.

⁵² Ibid.

⁵³ Ibid., 55–56.

⁵⁴ See P. T. O'Brien, "Colossians 1,20 and the Reconciliation of All Things," *Reformed Theological Review* 33 (1974) 45–53; J. I. Vicentini, " 'Déjense reconciliar con Dios': Lectura de 2 Corintios 5, 14–21," *RevistB* 36 (1974) 97–104; A. Stöger, "Die paulinische Versöhnungstheologie," *TPQ* 122 (1974) 118–31; V. P. Furnish, "The Ministry of Reconciliation," *CurTM* 4 (1977) 204–18; E. Lohse, " 'Das Amt, das die Versöhnung predigt,' " *Rechtfertigung: Festschrift für Ernst Käsemann zum 70. Geburtstag* (ed. J. Friedrich et al.; Tübingen: Mohr [Siebeck]; Göttingen: Vandenhoeck & Ruprecht, 1976) 339–49; J. Milgrom, "Atonement in the OT," *IDBSup,* 78–82; P. Garnet, *Salvation and Atonement in the Qumran Scrolls* (WUNT 2/3; Tübingen: Mohr [Siebeck], 1977).

Eight

PAUL AND THE LAW*

As I begin this discussion of Paul and the Law with members of the Canon Law Society, I cannot help but recall the famous words of the Apostle, "I am speaking to those who know the law" (Rom 7:1). Such a realization did not deter him, however, from devoting no little space to the subject in his writings, and in this I take courage.

Paul's treatment of law is found for the most part in two letters: in Gal 2:16–6:13 and in Rom 2:12–8:7. Though there are scattered remarks about it elsewhere (e.g., in 1 Cor 9:20; 15:56; 2 Cor 3:17–18; Rom 9:31; 10:4–5; 13:8–10; Eph 2:15 [cf. 1 Tim 1:8–9]), it is well to recall at the outset that his main discussion is found in polemical contexts. The Judaizing problem in the early Church called forth his remarks on the subject; this was a threat to his fundamental understanding of the Christ-event, and he reacted vigorously against it.[1] But it would be a mistake to think that Paul's teaching about law occupies the center of his theology. To regard it in this way would be to commit the same error which has plagued much of Christian thinking since the Reformation which identified the essence of his theology solely with justification.[2] We have finally come to recognize that the Pauline view of Christ lies as much in the "new creation" brought about in Christ and through the Spirit, as God initiated a new phase of salvation-history. Similarly we have learned that Paul viewed this Christian condition in terms of justification mainly because of the context of the Judaizing problem. Even though his teaching about law is, therefore, somewhat time-conditioned and polemical, nevertheless it has in all parts of it aspects which are relevant and pertinent to our situation today.

Likewise at the outset it is necessary to mention one further minor problem. It concerns the literal and figurative sense of *nomos* used by Paul as well as his use of the noun with and without the article. In a number of instances Paul will make statements such as these: the

Gentiles "are a law to themselves" (Rom 2:14); or "in my members another law at war with the law of my mind" (Rom 7:23); or, as he makes use of oxymoron, "the law of the Spirit of life" (Rom 8:2), "the law of Christ" (Gal 6:2), or "the law of faith" (Rom 3:27). In all such instances the use of *nomos* is figurative, and its prime analogate is the Mosaic law. These figurative expressions attempt to describe pagan or Christian counterparts of the Mosaic law in a term that is frankly borrowed from it. But aside from such clearly figurative expressions Paul otherwise speaks only of the Mosaic law, "the religious system under which the Jews had lived since the time of Moses."[3] He speaks only of it, and makes no distinction between its cultic, ritual, or ethical demands.[4] It may be that he sometimes extends it, designating by *nomos* the whole of the Old Testament and not just the Torah or Pentateuch (cf. Rom 3:19 and the quotations cited in the preceding context). But it is useless to try to distinguish his statements according to the use of the article or the lack of it.[5] If we emphasize this at the outset, it is only to avoid a misunderstanding; for Paul does not really talk about "law as such." Not even the verse quoted at the beginning of this paper (Rom 7:1) refers to anything but the Mosaic law, as the verses in the immediately following context show.[6] However, it is true that some statements are couched in terms which are generic and lend themselves by extension to other legal systems than that of Moses; for this reason it is not difficult to apply them to other types of law, Christian or otherwise, and find that they are still relevant.

With such preliminary remarks we may turn to the discussion itself, which will have three parts: (1) Paul's view of the law and the anomaly which it presents in human life; (2) his explanation of the anomaly; and (3) his solution of the anomaly.

I. *Paul's View of the Law and Its Anomaly*

We can best describe Paul's view of the law by making five observations about it.

(1) Paul personifies *nomos,* just as he does *hamartia* ("sin") and *thanatos* ("death").[7] This is especially true in the letter to the Romans. Like *Thanatos* and *Hamartia, Nomos* is depicted as an actor playing a role on the stage of human history (see Rom 5:20).

To understand its role, we must recall Paul's view of salvation-history. His conception of it is based on the unilinear view of world history which he inherited from the Pharisaic tradition. Early rabbis maintained that the duration of the world would be 6000 years, divided into three phases: (a) the period of *Tōhû-wā-bōhû* ("Chaos," see Gen 1:2), lasting from Adam to Moses when there was no law; (b) the period of *Tôrāh* ("Law"), lasting from Moses to the Messiah when the law ruled human existence; (c) the period of the Messiah, when either the law would cease (according to some rabbis), or the Messiah would perfect it by giving it a new interpretation (according to others).[8] Paul employs a similar threefold division of history: (a) From Adam to Moses the period was law-less; human beings did evil or sinned, but there was no imputation of transgressions (Rom 5:13).[9] "For the law brings wrath; but where there is no law, there is no transgression" (Rom 4:15). (b) From Moses to Christ the law reigned and sins were imputed as transgressions of it; "the law brings wrath" (Rom 4:15). (c) The Messianic Age began with Christ Jesus, who is "the end of the law" (Rom 10:4).

Paul apparently followed that view which regarded the law as coming to its end in the period of the Messiah.[10] For him Jesus himself is "the end of the law" (*telos nomou*), not only in the sense that it was aimed at him as its consummation, its goal, or its *finis* (Gal 3:24), but also in the sense that, as the *Christos* (or "Messiah"), he put an end to it. For he "abolished in his flesh the law with its commandments and ordinances" (Eph 2:15). Through him "we are discharged from the law" (Rom 7:6).[11] Upon us "the ends of the ages have met" (1 Cor 10:11 [my translation]), i.e., the last end of the age of the Torah and the first end of the age of the Messiah. In the latter there reigns instead *ho nomos tou Christou*, "the law of the Messiah" (Gal 6:2).

Thus all of human history has become a stage; and the actors who come upon it to influence this condition are Death, Sin, and the Law.

(2) When Paul describes the actor *Nomos* for us, we learn that he is good: "The law is holy, and the commandment is holy and righteous and good" (Rom 7:12; see also 7:16). Indeed, it is even said to be "spiritual" (*pneumatikos,* Rom 7:14), i.e., belonging to the sphere of God and not of earthbound humanity. For it is "the law of God" (Rom 7:22, 25; 8:7; cf. 1 Cor 7:19), since it ultimately came from God and was destined to lead human beings to "life," i.e., to communion with God. It was "the very commandment whose purpose was life" (*hē entolē hē eis zōēn,* Rom 7:10). In a broad sense it could even be said to be "the oracles of God" (Rom 3:2), for it manifested to human beings God's word and his will. In Gal 3:12 Paul quotes Lev 18:5 and is constrained to admit that "he who does them [i.e., the prescriptions of the law] shall live by them," i.e., shall find life through them. Even though the law was

secondary and inferior when compared to the promises made to Abraham by God (Gal 3:21), it was certainly not a contradiction of them. It enjoyed, therefore, a fundamental goodness by which the saints of the Old Dispensation were to achieve their destiny, a life of uprightness in the sight of God.

(3) This character *Nomos* constituted one of the privileges of Israel. Paul frankly lists it among the prerogatives enjoyed by his kinsmen by race: "They are Israelites, and to them belong the sonship, the glory, the covenants, the giving of the law . . ." (Rom 9:4). They were privileged in that they possessed a God-given means of seeking their justification. And everything that the law says is addressed to those who are under its authority and who acknowledge it (Rom 3:19).

But Paul turns the coin, precisely in this regard. For it does little good for a Jew to boast of his possession of the law and of hearing it read every Sabbath in the synagogue, if he does not obey it (Rom 2:17–24). As a prerogative of Israel, the law set Paul's kinsmen by race apart from those who were *a-nomoi* and *hamartōloi*, "law-less" and "sinners" (seeing that they were without the law). But Paul emphasizes the obligation which lay on Israel to observe that law, and to observe it in its entirety (Gal 5:3), if it is recognized as a norm for life.

(4) In spite of all this, *Nomos* is depicted as incapable of producing the uprightness which it was destined to achieve. Though it was "holy and righteous and good," came from God, and was Israel's prerogative, yet it did not bring "life" to men. Paul is severe in his judgment, as he makes a daring addition to Ps 143:2, "No human being will be justified in the sight of God—*by observing the law*" (lit., "from the deeds of the law" [my translation]). The last phrase, boldly added by Paul to the Psalm in Rom 3:20, amounts to a devastating accusation which formulates the anomaly which the character *Nomos* brings into human existence. *Nomos* was supposed to bring life, as Lev 18:5 had promised; but in reality it brought just the opposite. Thus Paul describes the *negative role* of the law: its inability to give life, because it is nothing more than an external norm. It tells people what they must do without giving them the *dynamis* ("the force") to do it. And so, the law was not a dynamic force for life (unlike the gospel [see p. 153 above]).

To prove his point, Paul appeals to the *de facto* situation of the Jews who are just as much subject to God's wrath, even though they possess the law, as the heathen who do not obey it because they do not know it.[12] Indeed, his accusation implies that the Jews *cannot* really obey it. As proof he cites the Old Testament itself in the words of Hab 2:4, "the upright person shall live by faith" (see Rom 1:17; Gal 3:12); but faith has nothing to do with the law. This, then, is the negative role of *Nomos:* it fails to give human beings the ability to fulfill the obligations which it imposes on them.

(5) But *Nomos* also plays a positive role by multiplying or enhancing sin and by levelling a curse on human beings. And herein we find the real anomaly which Paul sees in the law. Good though it was, the law really multiplied sin. Paul teaches this explicitly: "It was added [to the promises made to Abraham] for the sake of transgressions" (Gal 3:19); "the law came in to increase the transgression" (Rom 5:20 [my translation]).

These Pauline statements must be understood in terms of the periods of salvation-history mentioned above. Arriving on the stage of human history in the second period, *Nomos* became the tool and the instrument of *Hamartia.* In fact, it became the very *"dynamis* of Sin" itself (1 Cor 15:56). While supplying to human beings no *dynamis* of its own whereby they might find "life," it ironically enough became the henchman of *Hamartia;* and thus it unleashed on humanity God's wrath: "for the law brings wrath" (Rom 4:15). Though it was not sin itself, it contributed to sin: "What then shall we say? That the law is sin? By no means! Yet, if it had not been for the law, I would not have known sin" (Rom 7:7). And the reason is that in the absence of law "sin was dead" (Rom 7:8).

This positive role of *Nomos* is played in three ways: (*a*) The law acts as an occasion (*aphormē*) for sin. It instructs human beings in the material possibility of sinning, either by forbidding what is indifferent (e.g., the eating of unclean animals, Lev 11:2–47; Deut 14:4–21), or by exciting desires in annoying the conscience by the imposition of an external, positive regulation against "forbidden fruit." This aspect of law, however, as an occasion of sin, is for Paul only secondary; he alludes to it briefly in Rom 7:5, 8, 11, but otherwise makes very little of it.[13]

(*b*) Much more important is the role which *Nomos* plays as a moral informer. For *Nomos* gives human beings "a real and profound knowledge of sin" (*epignōsis* [not just *gnōsis*] *hamartias,* Rom 3:20). This deep awareness of the true character of moral disorder shows sin up to be a rebellion, a transgression, an act against a personal God, and an infidelity to the covenant relation and stipulations formulated in the Decalogue. This is why Paul could say, "Sin indeed was in the world before the law was given; but sin is not counted (*ouk ellogeitai*) where there is no law" (Rom 5:13). Paul would not deny that human beings were evil during the period from Adam to Moses (during the "law-less" period of Chaos). But he insists that their sinfulness did not have the character of open rebellion and transgression because the Mosaic law had not yet been given. Men sinned, but it was not "like the transgression of Adam" (Rom 5:14), who violated a command of God (Gen 2:17; 3:6, 11). Again, "where there is no law there is no transgression" (Rom 4:15), or "apart from the law sin lies dead; I was once alive apart from the law, but when the commandment came, sin revived and I died" (Rom 7:8b–9a).

(c) In addition to being an occasion for sin and a moral informer about the real nature of sin, *Nomos* also played its positive role by laying a curse on human beings. This stern view of the law, which modern Christians may be inclined to tone down, is derived by Paul from Deut 27:26, which he quotes in Gal 3:10, "Cursed be every one who does not abide by all things written in the book of the law and do them." This shows, as Paul argues, that the law itself cursed the very human beings on whom it imposed its obligations. It brought them under "condemnation" (Rom 8:1), and thus it became a "ministry of condemnation" (2 Cor 3:9) and a "dispensation of death" (2 Cor 3:7). And this is the height of the anomaly of human existence in the period of Torah. Understanding it all in this way, Paul can only exclaim, "Did that which is good, then, bring death to me?" (Rom 7:13). Did the God-given *Nomos* in the service of *Hamartia* bring humanity into the clutches of *Thanatos*? His answer is "yes," and it happened that the true colors of *Hamartia* might be shown up: "that sin might be shown to be sin" (Rom 7:13). But could this be? How could such a thing happen? To answer this brings us to our second point, Paul's explanation of the anomaly.

II. *Paul's Explanation of the Anomaly*

Paul not only recognized and described the anomaly that *Nomos* brought into human life, but he also tried to explain how it could have come about. His explanation is twofold, differing according to his letters. In his earlier letter to the Galatians Paul gives an extrinsic explanation, setting forth the temporary role of the law: "Now before faith came, we were confined under the law, kept under restraint until faith should be revealed. So that the law was our custodian (*paidagōgos*) until Christ came, that we might be justified by faith" (Gal 3:23–24). Here in Galatians *Nomos* is depicted as a slave who in the Hellenistic world accompanied the school-age boy to and from classes, kept him in tow, and supervised his studies. Thus the law schooled and disciplined humanity in preparation for Christ, "the end of the law."[14] But this was only a temporary disposition of God, permitted until mankind reached the maturity in which it could do without the *paidagōgos* and respond to Christ, who came in the fulness of time, with an adult and personal commitment which is faith. Thus the law played a temporary role in salvation-history, disciplining God's people that it might gradually come of age to learn of Christ.

Paul stresses its temporary, provisional character by pointing out that it was added to Israel's promised heritage four hundred and thirty years after the original promises made to Abraham. Paul's chronology may be off by several centuries, but in any case the law came in *later*. This shows that it was in reality inferior to the promises and could in no way annul them. Its inferiority was also manifest in that it was promulgated by angels and through the mediation of Moses (see Gal 3:19–20). Whatever Paul may have thought about the angels, he certainly relegated them to the same category as the Mosaic law as far as Christians were concerned.[15] He chides the fickle Galatians, warning them that to adopt *any* of the Judaizers' practices would be a return to the worship of "the elements of the world" (Gal 4:3, 9). As heathens, they were once enslaved to such elements or primitive rudiments; but to adopt any of the material observances of the Judaizers would be tantamount to a return to such slavery. Such is the pejorative view of the law and its worth that Paul finally developed. Now that Christ's rule has replaced that of spirits and angels, their role in human history is over; and thus their identification with the law reveals its inferior and temporary status as well.

This explanation of the anomaly of the law was apparently not very satisfactory even for Paul, being in effect quite extrinsic. For it did not really come to grips with the problem of human incapacity to obey the God-given law. So when Paul composed Rom 7:13–24, he abandoned that explanation and sought a more intrinsic, philosophical explanation. Paul finally realized that the difficulty was not with the Mosaic law as such, but rather with human beings in their earthbound condition of *sarx*, "flesh," alienated from God and dominated by *Hamartia*. In Romans 7 Paul explains the anomaly of the law from the fact that human beings are *sarkinoi*, "made of flesh," i.e., composed of a principle which ties their whole personal existence, outlook, and mentality to earth and to a material mode of existence which distracts them from any consideration of God. Here we must let Paul speak for himself:

> Did that which was good, then, bring death to me? By no means! It was sin, working death in me through what is good, in order that sin might be shown to be sin, and through the commandment might become sinful beyond measure. We know that the law is spiritual; but I am carnal (*sarkinos*), sold under sin. I do not understand my own actions. For I do not

do what I want, but I do the very thing I hate. Now if I do what I do not want, I agree that the law is good. So then it is no longer I that do it, but sin which dwells in me. For I know that nothing good dwells in me, that is, in my flesh; I can will what is right, but I cannot do it, for I do not do the good I want, but the evil I do not want is what I do. For if I do what I do not want, it is no longer I that do it, but sin which dwells in me.

So I find it to be a law that when I want to do right, evil lies close at hand. For I delight in the law of God, in my inmost self, but I see in my members another law at war with the law of my mind and making me captive to the law of sin which dwells in my members. Wretched man that I am! Who will deliver me from this body of death? (Rom 7:13–24)

It is the evil force introduced into the world by Adam's transgression, Sin (with a capital S), which keeps human beings in bondage and slavery. Even if they want to obey God's law, they cannot do so because the earthbound self (*sarx*) is dominated by *Hamartia*. Paul even goes so far as to call, figuratively indeed, this indwelling sin a "law"; it is "the law of sin" (Rom 7:25), an appositional genitive.

At the end of chap. 7 in Romans Paul can only exclaim, "Wretched man that I am! Who will deliver me from this body of death?" And his answer to his own question yields the solution to the anomaly of the law. It also provides us with our third point.

III. *Paul's Solution of the Anomaly*

Paul's solution is, "Thank God! It is done through Jesus Christ our Lord" (Rom 7:25 [my translation]), an answer that is as remarkable as it is simple.[16] He continues, "There is therefore now no condemnation for those who are in union with Christ Jesus. For the law of the Spirit of life in Christ Jesus has freed me from the law of sin and death" (Rom 8:1–2). It has often been pointed out how in that short answer Paul introduces his great insight into the meaning of the Christ-event for humanity (viz., freedom from the law, from sin, and from death) and succinctly summarizes the entire second part of the doctrinal section of Romans. For Rom 8:2 is a brief résumé of chaps 5, 6, and 7: "The law of the Spirit of life in Christ Jesus had freed me from the law of sin and death." The three key-words, law, sin, and death, are significantly juxtaposed.

With a slightly different nuance the same message is the burden of the letter to the Galatians, which is Paul's "Charter of Christian Liberty." In it he almost had to thrust his ideas of liberty on reluctant Gentile-Christian neophytes, who seemed to prefer bondage and restraint in Judaizing practices. To those who did not want to be free of the law he could only exclaim: "For freedom Christ has set us free" (Gal 5:1). And these words sum up his whole message of Christian liberty.[17] In the same context he brands the law of Moses as a "yoke of slavery." "I testify again to every man who receives circumcision that he is bound to keep the whole law" (5:3).

We must specify further the sense in which Paul can say that Christ has freed human beings from the law. For it is also obvious that the freedom he preached did not mean a throwing off of all restraint, an invitation to license. Even Paul insisted, "For you were called to freedom, brethren; only do not use your freedom as an opportunity for the flesh" (Gal 5:13). Even in the letter, which is his "Charter of Christian Liberty," Paul inserts the catalogues of vices and virtues which he inherited from the catechesis of the primitive church. Here as in other letters they serve as norms of *Christian* conduct. For instance, in Gal 5:19–21 he lists "the works of the flesh" as "fornication, impurity, licentiousness, idolatry, sorcery, enmity, strife, jealousy, anger, etc." and ends with the warning, "those who do such things shall not inherit the kingdom of God." To put it more bluntly, Paul for all his talk about Christ's abolition of the law still seems to have in the hortatory sections of his letters elaborate lists of *do's* and *don't's*. Moreover, he seems to regard them as fundamental to Christian community life. It might seem, then, that Paul has simply done away with the Mosaic law with its Pharisaic interpretation and casuistry only to set up his own code.

To understand his attitude, we must try to see what he meant by saying that Christ "abolished in his flesh the law of commandments and ordinances" (Eph 2:15), or that Christians "have died to the law through the body of Christ" (Rom 7:4). For it is noteworthy that Paul in his letters ascribes this freedom from the law or death to the law precisely to the crucifixion and death of Christ himself. The explanation of this facet of Pauline theology is found in one of the most difficult verses of the Pauline corpus: "Through the law I died to the law, that I might live for God; I have been crucified with Christ" (Gal 2:19–20).[18] In these words Paul means that the Christian identified with Christ through baptism shares in his death by crucifixion. As Christ by his death put an end to the law, so the Christian has died to the law; it no longer has any claim on him. But how did this death (of Christ and the Christian) take place "through the law"? Paul almost certainly means "through the pernicious effects of the law," or, as we might say today, "through legalism." For Paul implies that it is the attitude of mind fostered by the Mosaic law itself in those who crucified Jesus (cf.1 Thess 2:14–15). He was undoubtedly thinking of the formalism and legalism of the traditions that he knew as a Pharisee which made it impossible for his "kinsmen by race" (Rom 9:3) to accept Jesus of

Nazareth as Messiah. So it was "through the law" that the Christian has died to the law (by his con-crucifixion with Christ, *synestaurōmai*) that he/she might live for God.

This liberty from the law brought about by the death of Christ is still further explained in Galatians 3. In that and the following chapter Paul develops an elaborate midrash on the Abraham story of Genesis; he shows how God, foreseeing the justification of the Gentiles by faith, announced in effect the gospel aforetime to Abraham in blessing all nations in him. But by contrast, Paul argues, the law, which came in after these promises made to Abraham, levels a curse on all who would live by it: "Cursed be every one who does not abide by all the things written in the book of the law, and do them" (Deut 27:26). But Christ *by his death* has removed this curse from humanity.

To show how this was done Paul indulges in a little "rabbinic" logic.[19] His argument is not marked by Aristotelian logic, and any attempt to reduce it to a syllogism fails, for there are actually four terms in the argument. Christ has removed the curse of Deut 27:26 from humanity because he became the "curse of the law" in the sense of Deut 21:23, and by dying he blotted it out. When he died as "the curse of the law," in one sense, the curse of the law in another sense died with him: "Christ redeemed us from the curse of the law, having become a curse for us—for it is written, 'Cursed be everyone who hangs upon a tree' " (Gal 3:13). Here Paul cites the curse of Deut 21:23, levelled against the exposed dead body of an executed criminal. It was customary to hang it up as a deterrent to crime, but it was not allowed to remain beyond sundown, for it would defile the land; in this sense it was accursed. In Roman times, when punishment by crucifixion became frequent in Palestine, the verse was applied to this form of capital punishment. Paul, knowing that Jesus died by this manner of death, realizes that the curse of the law materially applied to him. So by a free association he maintains that Jesus, the "curse of the Law" (in the sense of Deut 21:23) blotted out by his death the curse levelled against humanity (by Deut 27:26). Thus Christ "abolished the law" (Eph 2:15). Thus he "cancelled the bond that stood against us with its legal demands; this he set aside, nailing it to the cross" (Col 2:14). Thus he became "the end of the Law" (Rom 10:4).

Instead there now reigns the "law of the Spirit of life" (Rom 8:2), which is in reality no "law" at all,[20] but is given that appellation by Paul through oxymoron. The Christian who has been baptized into Christ lives a new life, a symbiosis of himself with Christ. Having grown together with Christ, the Christian can now only think as Christ thinks and conduct his life only for God. "I live, now not I, but Christ lives in me" (Gal 2:20). For the Christian is now motivated, energized, and vitalized by the Spirit of the Risen Jesus; it frees him from his condition as *sarx;* it is what later theology calls "grace."[21] "For God has done what the law, weakened by the flesh, could not do: sending his own Son in the likeness of sinful flesh and for sin, he condemned sin in the flesh, in order that the just requirement of the law might be fulfilled in us, who walk not according to the flesh but according to the Spirit" (Rom 8:3–4). The principle of Christian activity is no longer merely an external list of *do's* and *don't's,* but rather the internal whispering of the dynamic Spirit which enables the Christian to cry, "Abba, Father," and which testifies to him that he/she is a child of God (Gal 4:6; Rom 8:15). For the Christian is "led by the Spirit" (Rom 8:14); it has become for him/her a *nomos,* principle, a figurative "law." He/she is no longer earthbound *sarx* when so activated, but is now *pneumatikos,* "spiritual." Living thus for God, and being so captivated with Christ that he/she is even his "slave" (*doulos,* 1 Cor 7:22),[22] the Christian has nothing to do with sin, evil, disorder, or transgression. For Paul it is inconceivable that a human being identified with the death, burial, and resurrection of Christ in baptism could ever again think of sin and evil. "How can we who died to sin still live in it?" (Rom 6:2); just "as Christ was raised from the dead by the glory of the Father, so we too must walk in the newness of life" (Rom 6:4). In other words, for the Christian there is no need of a legal system such as was the Mosaic law, especially as understood in the Pharisaic tradition with its 613 commands and prohibitions.

How explain, then, Paul's insistence on the catalogues of vices and virtues mentioned earlier? True, Paul does not hesitate to exhort his Christian communities to the practice of virtue. But his norms for individual conduct are now subsumed all under one notion: under love, under concern for others, under the dynamic demand of Christian communal living. In Rom 13:8–10 he makes it explicit:

> Owe no one anything, except to love one another; for he who loves his neighbor has fulfilled the law. The commandments, "You shall not commit adultery, You shall not kill, You shall not steal, You shall not covet," and any other commandment, are summed up in this sentence, "You shall love your neighbor as yourself." Love does no wrong to a neighbor; therefore love is the fulfilling of the law. (See also Gal 5:14.)

Love is the fulfilment of the law, not because it replaces the Mosaic law with another external norm of conduct, but because it is itself a dynamic force impelling human beings to seek the good of others, energizing their faith in Christ Jesus (Gal 5:6: *pistis di' agapēs energoumenē,* "faith working itself out through love"). For Paul what does not express love does not lead to life.[23]

It is in this sense that Paul speaks of "the law of Christ." For this Pauline expression is obviously a "take-off" on the expression, the law of Moses. When, however, we look at the context in which the expression is used in Gal 6:2, it is obviously that of brotherly love, and specifically of fraternal correction. "Brethren, if a person is overtaken in any violation, you who are spiritual should restore him in a spirit of gentleness; but look to yourself, lest you too be tempted. Bear one another's burdens, and so fulfill the law of Christ."[24] The example which Paul uses here should obviously be understood as precisely that, an example; for if the "law of Christ" is to be understood in terms of love, as the passage suggests, it is not to be restricted to that form of love which would manifest itself only in fraternal correction.

When one sees how Paul does away with the Mosaic law and its legalism and substitutes for it the "law of the Spirit of life" and the principle of love, one cannot help but ask how Paul, the former Pharisee, could ever have come to such a view of the Old Testament. But, to my way of thinking, it is precisely his background which has brought him to this reaction.[25] We must remember that Paul's attitude toward the Old Testament is at least double. For if he is very severe in speaking of the Old *Law,* nevertheless he frequently quotes the Old Testament, appeals to it as the source of the promises made to Abraham (Rom 4:13), as "the oracles of God" (Rom 3:2), and sees in it "the book written for our instruction" (1 Cor 10:11; cf. Rom 4:23–24; 15:4). But his negative attitude toward the Old Testament is undoubtedly due to the "traditions of the Fathers" (Gal 1:14) which surrounded and encrusted it and in which he had been schooled. How often he looked on it as "law," and how infrequently he thinks of it as "covenant"! This notion, which looms so large in modern interpretation of the Old Testament and in a sense sums it up, is somewhat slighted in Paul's letters.[26] This may well be owing to his dependence on the Old Testament in the Greek translation of the LXX, where the Hebrew word *bĕrît,* "covenant," was rendered by *diathēkē,* a word which in Hellenistic Greek often bore the connotation of "last will, testament" (see Gal 3:15). This Greek translation colored the Old Testament covenant with the connotation that it was an expression of God's will; and this aided the tendency to exploit it legalistically and casuistically. It obscured the covenant as "pact," which might have been more appropriately translated as *synthēkē.* The result was a preoccupation with the Old Testament as an expression of God's will that had to be carried out by Israel and as a legal system which had to be interpreted to the extreme of casuistry.

Finally, we conclude our remarks on the subject by referring to one verse which we have not considered so far. It is found in the Pastoral Epistles, but since Paul did not write these letters himself, we have been reluctant to introduce it into the main discussion. Whether it is authentically Pauline or not, it forms a fitting conclusion to it. For it sums up succinctly what has been said—in a way, however, not said above: "Now we know that the law is good, if one uses it as law should be used, understanding this, that the law is not laid down for the just but for the lawless and disobedient, for the ungodly and sinners . . ." (1 Tim 1:8–9 [my translation]). This statement fits in perfectly with what Paul wrote about the law, about its fulfillment in love, about the Spirit as the principle of the "new creation" (Gal 6:15), and about the complete incompatibility of the Christian with what is evil and sinful.

In summary, then, Paul's teaching is a reaction to the Mosaic law, on the one hand, abolished by Christ Jesus who has now enabled man through his own Spirit to transcend the earthbound condition of *sarx,* and, on the other, summed up and fulfilled in the dynamic principle of love. The grace and favor of Christ enables human beings to be truly Christian. The norm, however, for the Christian's conduct is no longer an external list of *do's* and *don't's;* such a thing exists for "the lawless and the disobedient." Instead, Paul's specific exhortations and recommendations express not so much a code or a norm to be exploited and interpreted casuistically as examples of the Christian principle of love reacting to communal situations. If my presentation of Paul's reaction to law has stressed the Mosaic over against any generic consideration, it is because this is in fact the perspective from which he viewed and treated it. But it is well to repeat here one phrase that he did write. "The commandments, 'You shall not commit adultery, You shall not kill, You shall not steal, You shall not covet,' *and any other commandment,* are summed up in this sentence, 'You shall love your neighbor as yourself' " (Rom 13:9).[27]

NOTES

* Originally published under the title, "Saint Paul and the Law," in *The Jurist* 27 (1967) 18–36.

[1] So strong was his reaction to this problem that it did not take long for a doctrine of "separatio legis et evangelii" to emerge in the early church; see pp. 156, 161 above.

[2] See, e.g., E. Käsemann's remarks quoted above, p. 171; also his articles cited in n. 6, p. 179. Cf. K. Stendahl, "The Apostle Paul and the Introspective

Conscience of the West," *HTR* 56 (1963) 199–215; reprinted, *Paul among the Jews and Gentiles and Other Essays* (Philadelphia: Fortress, 1976) 78–96. See also Stendahl's reaction to Käsemann's criticism of the foregoing article, pp. 129–32.

[3] L. Cerfaux, *Christ in the Theology of St. Paul* (New York: Herder and Herder, 1959) 147. Cf. H.-H. Esser, "Law, Custom, Elements," *The New International Dictionary of New Testament Theology* (3 vols.; ed. C. Brown; Grand Rapids, MI: Zondervan, 1975, 1976, 1978), 2. 436–51, esp. pp. 444–45.

[4] See R. Bultmann, *Theology of the New Testament* (2 vols.; London: SCM, 1956), 1. 259–60; cf. C. Haufe, "Die Stellung Paulus zum Gesetz," *TLZ* 91 (1966) 171–78.

[5] See the extensive treatment of the question in P. Bläser, *Das Gesetz bei Paulus* (NTAbh 19/1–2; Münster in W.: Aschendorff, 1941) 1–30, esp. p. 24. Cf. W. Gutbrod, *"Nomos," TDNT* 4 (1967) 1022–91, esp. pp. 1069–71; G. B. Winer, *Grammatik des neutestamentlichen Sprachidioms* (8th ed.; Göttingen: Vandenhoeck & Ruprecht, 1894) § 19, 13h.

[6] At first sight it may seem that Paul is referring to the famous Roman law in making this statement, which actually lacks the definite article in the Greek text, "for I am speaking to those who know what law is" (*ginōskousin gar nomon lalō*). A number of commentators have so understood it (e.g., B. Weiss, A. Jülicher). Some others think that Paul understands *nomon* here as law in general (e.g., M.-J. Lagrange, S. Lyonnet, Sanday-Headlam, E. Käsemann). But the majority of commentators argue from the immediately following context to the Mosaic law (so H. Lietzmann, J. Huby, P. Althaus, H. W. Schmidt, P. Bläser et al). See the remarks of F. Leenhardt, *The Epistle to the Romans: A Commentary* (London: Lutterworth, 1961) 177–78; O. Kuss, *Der Römerbrief* (Regensburg: Pustet, 1963), 2. 435; C. E. B. Cranfield, *A Critical and Exegetical Commentary on the Epistle to the Romans* (2 vols.; ICC; Edinburgh: Clark, 1975, 1979), 1. 332–33.

[7] See P. Benoit, "La loi et la croix d'après Saint Paul (Rom. VII, 7–VIII,4)," *RB* 47 (1938) 481–509, esp. pp. 484–85; reprinted, *Exégèse et théologie* (3 vols. Paris: Cerf, 1961, 1961, 1968), 2. 9–40, esp. pp. 12–13. Cf. L. Cerfaux, *Christ*, 227. As is evident, I am heavily indebted to P. Benoit in this essay.

[8] See *b. Sanh.* 97b; *b. Abod. Zar.* 9b; *Ep. Barn.* 15:4. The Torah was expected to cease in the messianic age according to *b. Šabb.* 151b or *b. Nid.* 61b; but in *Tg. Isa* 12:3 and *Midr. Qoh* 2:1; 12:1 it is expected that the Messiah will promulgate a new Torah. See W. D. Davies, *Torah in the Messianic Age and/or the Age to Come* (SBLMS 7; Philadelphia: Society of Biblical Literature, 1952) 50–94; *Paul and Rabbinic Judaism: Some Rabbinic Elements in Pauline Theology* (London: SPCK, 1948) 72–73. This difference of rabbinic opinion about the relation of the Messiah to the law may be reflected in the different treatment of the Mosaic law in Paul, for whom it is abolished, and in Matthew, for whom it is to be perfected (5:17). See, however, A. Díez Macho, "¿Cesará la 'Torá' en la edad mesiánica?" *EstBib* 12 (1953) 115–58; 13 (1954) 1–51.

[9] In viewing history in this way, Paul prescinds completely from the biblical account of the Flood and the generation of classic sinners associated with it. To introduce them into the discussion of Rom 5:13 is a distraction, *pace* S. Lyonnet in J. Huby, *Saint Paul: Epître aux Romains* (rev. ed.; VS 10; Paris: Beauchesne, 1957) 554 n. 6.

[10] Differently from Matt 5:17 (see n. 8 above); cf. W. D. Davies, *The Setting of the Sermon on the Mount* (Cambridge: University Press, 1964) 334–36.

[11] In both passages the verb *katargein* is used, which suggests that what Christ Jesus did rendered the law "ineffective" for human beings henceforth. C. E. B.

Cranfield, however, attempts to show that for Paul "the law is not abolished by Christ" ("St. Paul and the Law," *SJT* 17 [1964] 42–68, esp. pp. 54–65). He analyses a number of Pauline passages (Rom 3:21; 6:14b; 7:4, 8:2; 2 Cor 3:7–17; Gal 3:15–25; Col 2:14; Eph 2:15) in this sense; but his discussion is scarcely convincing. In effect, he eliminates the anomaly which most readers of Paul's letters have always sensed in his treatment of the law. Cf. O. Kuss, "Nomos bei Paulus," *MTZ* 17 (1966) 173–227.

[12] Care must be had in the interpretation of Rom 2:14. This verse certainly does not imply that "Gentiles who do not possess the [Mosaic] law" carry out by nature or instinct (*physei*) *all* that "the law requires." The phrase *ta tou nomou* must mean something like "some of the things of the law." Nor can it be used without further ado to support a thesis about the "natural law." See further C. H. Dodd, "Natural Law in the New Testament," *New Testament Studies* (Manchester: University Press, 1953) 129–42; J. L. McKenzie, "Natural Law in the New Testament," *BR* 9 (1964) 1–13; O. Kuss, *Der Römerbrief*, 1. 72–75; F. Flückiger, "Die Werke des Gesetzes bei den Heiden (nach Röm. 2, 14ff.)," *TZ* 8 (1951) 17–42. —The teaching about the natural law in the Christian tradition must be considered as the *sensus plenior* of Paul's statement in Rom 2:14, not the primary sense of his words.

[13] See P. Benoit, "La loi" (n. 7 above), 485–86.

[14] See G. Salet, "La loi dans nos coeurs," *NRT* 79 (1957) 449–62, 561–78, esp. pp. 577–78; L. Cerfaux, *The Christ*, 148.

[15] See B. Reicke, "The Law and This World according to Paul," *JBL* 70 (1951) 259–76.

[16] The interpretation of this verse is not without its difficulties. The *RSV* takes the whole of the first member of the verse as a doxology, as do a number of commentators (e.g., M.-J. Lagrange, P. Althaus, C. K. Barrett, C. E. B. Cranfield, E. Käsemann). But there is another possibility, which separates *dia Iēsou Christou*, "through Jesus Christ," from the thanks expressed to God and understands it as an abridged answer to the question of v. 24b. See my commentary in *JBC*, art. 53 §78; I am now more inclined to accept this understanding of the phrase, which I once called "awkward." Even if this interpretation were to be inadequate, Paul's answer to the question in 7:24 is given in 8:1–4.

[17] See J. Cambier, "La liberté chrétienne selon saint Paul," *SE II*, 315–53; in a shorter form in *Lumière et vie* 61 (1953) 5–40.

[18] See especially P. Bonnard, *L'épître de Saint Paul aux Galates* (CNT 9; Neuchâtel: Delachaux et Niestlé, 1953) 55–57; H. Schlier, *Der Brief an die Galater* (MeyerK 7; 12th ed.; Göttingen: Vandenhoeck & Ruprecht, 1962) 98–103. Cf. H. D. Betz, *Galatians: A Commentary on Paul's Letter to the Churches in Galatia* (Hermeneia; Philadelphia: Fortress, 1979) 122; J. B. Lightfoot, *The Epistle of St. Paul to the Galatians* (Grand Rapids, MI: Zondervan, 1957) 118. No little part of the problem in this verse is caused by the lack of a definite article before the word for law (*dia nomou nomō apethanon*).

[19] On this whole passage, see my comments on pp. 138–39 above.

[20] See F. Prat, *The Theology of Saint Paul* (Westminster, MD: Newman, 1956), 2. 318–21. It is this aspect of Paul's teaching which guarantees it against any "breakdown of moral responsibility." On this point, see S. Lyonnet, "St. Paul: Liberty and Law," *The Bridge* 4 (1962) 229–51, esp. pp. 241–43.

[21] Later theology, of course, was careful to distinguish the created gift

("grace") from the uncreated gift ("the Spirit"). What is meant here is that if one looks in Pauline writings for the basis of "sanctifying grace," one has to look to his teaching on the Spirit, and not simply on *charis,* by which Paul expresses much more the "favor" of God himself in granting the gift.

[22] The word "slave" is applied analogously to the Christian in such a situation, just as "law" is applied to the Spirit and to Christ.

[23] See A. Descamps, "La charité, résumé de la Loi," *Revue diocésaine de Tournai* 8 (1953) 123–29; A. Viard, "La charité accomplit la Loi," *VSpir* 74 (1946) 27–34; A. Feuillet, "Loi ancienne et morale chrétienne d'après l'épître aux Romains," *NRT* 42 (1970) 785–805; A. van Dülmen, *Die Theologie des Gesetzes bei Paulus* (SBM 5; Stuttgart: Katholisches Bibelwerk, 1968) 173.

It should be noted in passing that not even Paul, for all his insistence on the summation of the law and its commandments in love could dispense entirely with regulations of a positive nature within the Christian community. Though the vast majority of his exhortations concern matters of basic morality, there is the notorious example of his positive prescription in an indifferent matter, viz., the regulations for hairdo of men and women in liturgical assemblies (1 Cor 11:2–16; see now J. Murphy-O'Connor, "Sex and Logic in 1 Corinthians 11:2–16," *CBQ* 42 [1980] 482–500), possibly for the silence of women in similar assemblies (if the passage is not a gloss). His teaching in such matters is obviously time-conditioned; we would love to know what his reaction would have been if someone confronted him with his own principle of "love" in this very matter.

[24] The phrase *ho nomos tou Christou* occurs only in Gal 6:2; in 1 Cor 9:20 there is a kindred adjectival phrase, *ennomos Christou,* demanded by the context in which Paul contrasts it with *anomos:* people who are "free" and "enslaved," "lawless" and "under the law (of Christ)." Even in the latter passage the expression has the connotation of brotherly love: "To those outside the law I became as one outside the law—not being without law toward God but under the law of Christ (*ennomos Christou*)—that I might win those outside the law." —For a different interpretation of the "law of Christ" in Gal 6:2, see J. G. Strelan, "Burden-bearing and the Law of Christ: A Re-examination of Galatians 6:2," *JBL* 94 (1975) 266–76. Cf. H. D. Betz, *Galatians,* 300.

[25] Here one should have to cope with the thesis of E. P. Sanders, *Paul and Palestinian Judaism: A Comparison of Patterns of Religion* (Philadelphia: Fortress, 1977). But that is a task too vast to undertake here.

[26] Passing allusion is made to "covenant" in Rom 9:4 (actually in the plural!); 2 Cor 3:14; Gal 3:17 (the covenant of promise made with Abraham, not that of Sinai); 4:24; Eph 2:12. In this matter one may consult H. J. Schoeps, *Paul: The Theology of the Apostle in the Light of Jewish Religious History* (London: Lutterworth, 1959), chap. 5 (to be used with caution).

[27] See further W. Grundmann, "Gesetz, Rechtfertigung und Mystik bei Paulus: Zum Problem der Einheitlichkeit der paulinischen Verkündigung," *ZNW* 32 (1933) 52–65; S. Lyonnet, "Liberté chrétienne et loi de l'Esprit selon Saint Paul," *Christus* 4 (1954) 6–27; R. Bring, "Die Erfüllung des Gesetzes durch Christus: Eine Studie zur Theologie des Apostels Paulus," *KD* 5 (1959) 1–22; G. E. Ladd, "Paul and the Law," *Soli Deo gloria: New Testament Studies in Honor of William Childs Robinson* (ed. J. M. Richards; Richmond, VA: John Knox, 1968) 50–67.

Nine

"TO KNOW HIM AND THE POWER OF HIS RESURRECTION" (Phil 3:10)*

IN THE COURSE of his letter to the Christians of the young church of Philippi the Apostle Paul composed one of his more significant statements on the meaning of Christ's resurrection for the life and destiny of every Christian. It is a statement that is fully appreciated only when understood in the light of Paul's complex and total view of the resurrection of Jesus. It also reflects an understanding the early church had of the mystery and an aspect of it that must vitalize the modern appreciation of Christian life.

Many writers have stressed the importance of Christ's resurrection in Pauline soteriology.[1] My purpose is not to repeat what they have presented so well, much less to gainsay it, but rather to bring into clearer focus a perspective of Pauline theology of the resurrection that might be overlooked. Though my remarks are centered about Phil 3:10, which gives formal expression to the perspective in which I am interested, the discussion will go farther afield. For it is concerned with the phrase, "the power of his resurrection," and its implications in Pauline theology.

I. *The Philippian Context*

The verse on which our attention immediately focuses is found in the third chapter of Paul's letter to the Philippians. As a whole, it is the most charming of his letters, one written to a cherished and fervent community, and filled with counsels of love and joy. As a whole, it reads like a letter of gratitude. Paul thanks his Philippian converts for the material aid sent to him on several occasions: while he was laboring in Macedonia, and now that he is imprisoned (see Phil 4:16; 1 Thess 2:9; cf. Acts 17:1–9). Modern interpreters of Philippians have pointed out the abrupt joining of paragraphs and the lack of a real transition in certain parts of the letter (2:19; 3:2; 4:4, 10). For a variety of reasons Philippians seems to be a composite letter, made up of several notes that Paul once wrote to the church of Philippi. Composed on different occasions, they were joined together subsequently, perhaps when the Pauline corpus was being fashioned toward the end of the first century.[2] This plausible analysis of the canonical letter to the Philippians allows us to reckon with the following division of it:

Letter A:
1:1–2; 4:10–20 (Paul's note of thanks for the aid sent by the Philippians)
Letter B:
1:3–3:1; 4:4–9, 21–23 (Personal news and a report about Epaphroditus and Timothy)
Letter C:
3:2–4:3 (A warning to the Philippians).

The verse that interests us, Phil 3:10, is part, then, of the warning that Paul sends to the Philippian Christians, cautioning them against certain enticements of "Judaizers." These Christians were apparently advocating the adoption of circumcision, and he seems to have learned about their presence in Philippi. Writing from an imprisonment—possibly in Ephesus, *ca.* A.D. 56—he admonishes his favorite community against the deceptions latent in these enticements. This he does with an unwonted vehemence, and in a surprising tone (when it is compared with the rest of Philippians): "Look out for the dogs, look out for those evil workers, and look out for those who mutilate the flesh" (3:2). The boast implicit in the attitude of those opponents, that Paul found so incomprehensible, causes him to counterpoise the real foundation of his Christian confidence. Rather than set his hope on a mark in the flesh, Paul bases his hope on knowing Christ Jesus. This foundation is greater than all else: "Whatever gain I had, I counted as loss for the sake of Christ" (3:7). "Indeed", he exclaims, "I count everything as loss because of the surpassing worth of knowing Christ Jesus my Lord" (3:8). In this affirmation Paul acknowledges his faith in the *Kyrios,* his risen Lord, giving him the title that denoted par excellence the primitive church's belief in Christ as the instrument of the Father's plan of salvation. To know Jesus as *Kyrios*—the summation of Christian faith—is the basis of his hope and his "boast."

Consequently, Paul continues:

> [8]For his sake I have suffered the loss of all things and count them as refuse, in order that I may gain Christ [9]and be found in him, not having a righteousness of my own, based on law, but that which is through faith in Christ, a righteousness from God that depends on faith; [10]that I may know him and the power of his resurrection, and may share his sufferings, becoming like him in his death, that if possible I may attain the resurrection from the dead (3:8–10).

Having come to "know" Christ Jesus as *Kyrios* through faith, Paul's hope is to "gain Christ," i.e., to be associated with him in the future, or "to attain the resurrection from the dead." The implication is that somehow through faith in Christ Jesus the power of the risen *Kyrios* brings it about that Paul—and every Christian—will be "found in him," to share a glory that is his. This immediately raises the question about the nature of that "power of his resurrection."

II. *The Power of His Resurrection*

A facile way of explaining the "power of the resurrection" in Phil 3:10 would be to invoke the divinity of Christ. Since Jesus is the Son of God and himself rose from the dead as "the firstborn from among the dead" (Rev 1:5), he will bring about the resurrection of the righteous by his own divine power. Such an explanation, while true when formulated in terms of the later Chalcedonian definition of christology, goes beyond the Pauline conception and fails to reckon with either its primitive formulation or the complex notion involved in Paul's theology of the resurrection.

To understand the phrase, "the power of his resurrection," in Pauline theology, one should recall a few basic tenets of the Apostle's teaching about Christ's resurrection. First of all, Paul almost always ascribes it to the Father. To cast it in terms of Aristotelian causality, God (or the Father) would be the efficient cause of Jesus' resurrection. In 1 Thess 4:14 Paul speaks of the resurrection intransitively: "Since we believe that Jesus died and rose again (*anestē*), even so, through Jesus, God will bring with him those who have fallen asleep." He is referring here to the parousia of Jesus and to the resurrection of Christian dead that is to take place at that event. But this is the only place in his writings where he uses the intransitive *anestē* of Jesus' resurrection. It stands in significant contrast to 1 Thess 1:10, where Paul also refers to the parousia of the "Son," "whom he [i.e., God] raised (*ēgeiren*) from the dead, Jesus who delivers us from the wrath to come."

On occasion, Paul uses the passive form of the verb *egeirein* to express Jesus' resurrection (e.g., Rom 4:25; 6:4,9; 7:4; 8:34; 2 Cor 5:15). It would seem to mean that Jesus "was raised." But grammarians of Hellenistic and New Testament Greek have often pointed out that the aorist passive form, unlike its use in the classical period, was being used more often in a deponent sense—though passive in form, it was becoming active in meaning.[3] Consequently, it is sometimes argued that when Paul or other New Testament writers[4] use the aorist passive of *egeirein*,[5] it may not mean "was raised" but simply "rose," and be a synonym of *anestē*. Indeed, to support this argument, appeal is often made within the New Testament itself to such passages as Mark 2:12 ("and he rose") or Luke 7:14 ("arise," to be compared with the active in 8:54).[6] In such passages the only suitable meaning is admittedly the intransitive "rose."

Yet aside from the fact that most of the passages to which appeal is thus made have nothing to do with resurrection from the dead in the same sense as the resurrection of Jesus, there are many places in Paul's letters where he uses the active, transitive form of the verb *egeirein* with *ho theos*, "God," as the subject and Jesus or Christ as the object. Thus at the beginning of his earliest letter, in the passage referred to above, Paul reminds the Thessalonians how they turned from idols "to serve a living and true God, and to wait for his Son from heaven, whom he raised from the dead, Jesus who delivers us from wrath to come" (*hon ēgeiren ek tōn nekrōn*, 1 Thess 1:10). Similarly in 1 Cor 15:15 he says, "We are even found to be misrepresenting God, because we testified of God that he raised (*ēgeiren*) Christ, whom he did not raise if it is true that the dead are not raised."[7] In the light of such texts that clearly attribute Jesus' resurrection to the Father (or to God) in the active sense, one should prefer the passive meaning of the aorist (and perfect) forms to the deponent usage, at least in Paul's letters, and elsewhere as well, when there is a trace of a similar primitive tradition.[8] This is to respect the specifically primitive Pauline nuance in speaking of Jesus' resurrection, a nuance undoubtedly inherited from the early Christians who preceded him.

Another minor issue ought also to be mentioned in this connection, viz., that of the so-called theological passive.[9] To avoid the mention of God's name, Palestinian Jews out of reverence often cast a sentence in the passive voice.[10] This practice seems to have been adopted by early Jewish Christians too. The former Jew and Pharisee, Paul, would not be expected to differ from them in this regard. This practice explains the lack of a prepositional phrase with the passive forms that would formally express the agency (*hypo tou theou* or *hypo tou patros*), e.g., in Rom 4:25; 1 Cor 15:4.

Second, for Paul the God who raised Jesus from the dead was a God of power. This view of God reflects his inherited Jewish understanding of the might and power of Yahweh in the Old Testament.[11] Paul refers to this understanding in Rom 1:20, when he speaks of God's *aïdios dynamis*, "eternal power," in parallelism with his *theiotēs*, "divinity," that pagans should have come to recognize and reverence. It is the *dynamis* of Yahweh, the personal God of Israel, and not merely of some nature god such as was commonly venerated in lands surrounding Israel, much less some magic force. It represents the personal power of Yahweh, the creator, who fashioned for himself a people; it is his life-giving power which manifested itself on various occasions in Israel's behalf, particularly at the Exodus from Egypt and the passage of the Reed Sea (see Exod 15:6; 32:11; Josh 4:23–24; Ps 77:15; Isa 40:26). It is the power of Yahweh that Israel celebrated in its prayers, "Yours, O Yahweh, is the greatness, and the power, and the glory, and the victory, and the majesty. . . . In your hand are power and might" (1 Chr 29:11–12).[12] That Paul thinks of such a quality of Yahweh is clear from Rom 9:17, where he cites Exod 9:16, "For the Scripture says to Pharaoh, 'I have raised you up for the very purpose of showing my power in you, so that my name may be proclaimed in all the earth.'" The life-giving quality of this power appears too in Rom 4:17–21, where Paul, commenting on the Abraham story in Genesis and the promise made to the patriarch of a numerous progeny to be born of Sarah, speaks of God as one "who gives life to the dead and calls into existence the things that do not exist" and who revitalized Abraham's body "which was as good as dead" because "God was able (*dynatos*) to do what he had promised." Abraham, consequently, became the model of the believer; and "the power of God" became the basis of Christian faith (see 1 Cor 2:5).

Third, for Paul the act of raising Jesus from the dead was not a mere restoration of him to the life that he formerly led on earth. It was not a return to the terrestrial existence Jesus had known and experienced during his ministry. Paul never speaks of Jesus' resurrection as other New Testament writers speak of the resuscitation of Lazarus, of the son of the widow of Nain, or of the daughter of Jairus.[13] Lazarus apparently had to face death again; the risen Jesus is the victor over death. Hence, the resurrection for Paul meant the endowment of Jesus by the Father with the "power" of a new life. In 2 Cor 13:4a Paul explains, "He was crucified in weakness, but lives by the power of God (*zē ek dynameōs theou*)." The precise nuance of this Greek phrase indicates that God's life-giving power became the source of the vitality of the risen Christ. This is, further, the meaning underlying the enigmatic phrase in Rom

1:4, where Paul speaks of "his [i.e., God's] Son, who was born of the line of David according to the flesh, but established[14] as the Son of God in power according to the Spirit of holiness as of (his) resurrection from the dead." The act by which the Father raised Jesus from the dead became in Paul's view an endowment of him with power as of the resurrection. It is not sufficient to explain this verse in terms of some messianic enthronement of Jesus;[15] nor is it convincing to explain away the difficult phrase *en dynamei* by construing it as a prepositional phrase modifying the participle *horisthentos*.[16] While defensible grammatically in the immediate sentence-context, it does not reckon with the nuances the phrase has when considered in its relational sense (i.e., against other Pauline passages dealing with the resurrection or the background of Paul's theology of the resurrection as a whole). In this passage, then, Paul seems to be contrasting Jesus as the Son, born into messianic, Davidic lineage, with a fuller idea of him as powerful Son "appointed, established, installed, constituted" as such as of the resurrection. Once this is understood, it is easy to grasp how Paul could even come to speak of the risen Christ as "the power of God" (1 Cor 1:24). So endowed at the resurrection, he is, abstractly expressed, the very power of God.

Paul offers a further explanation (2 Cor 13:4): "He was crucified in weakness, but lives by the power of God. For we are weak in him, but in dealing with you we shall live with him by the power of God."[17] Here Paul sees the *dynamis* of the risen Jesus as something not given for himself alone, but for human beings. What effected the resurrection of Jesus works also for the salvation of humanity. Hence Paul can say in 1 Cor 6:14, "God raised the Lord and will also raise us up by his (i.e., Jesus') power."[18] The power is ultimately derived from the Father and is life-giving; it brings about the resurrection of Jesus, and of Christians in union with him. It is not something, therefore, that is related solely to Jesus himself.

In the light of this background one must interpret the phrase, "the power of his resurrection," in Phil 3:10. Frequently enough, the phrase is explained of a power that emanates from the risen Jesus and becomes the source for the vitality of Christian life. Commentators are accustomed to insist that Paul is not thinking of the physical event of the resurrection itself,[19] but rather of the state in which the risen Jesus exists as an influence exerted on the believer. For instance, E. Osty insists that "the power of his resurrection" is "not the power which had raised Christ, but that which emanates from Christ."[20] Similarly, E. Lohmeyer, "It is not a question of God activating the process, but rather 'his resurrection' possesses the formative and perfecting 'power.'"[21] Again J. Huby displays a similar understanding of it, when he writes, "The resurrection, of which the Christian experiences the power, is not the very *act* by which Christ came forth living from the tomb, but the *term* of this action, the life of the glorified Christ.[22] M. R. Vincent also proposes this sort of explanation: "*Dynamin* is not the power by which Christ was raised from the dead (Chr., Oec.), nor as Theoph. 'because to arise is great power'; nor Christ's power to raise up believers. Like the preceding expressions, it describes a subjective experience. It is the power of the risen Christ as it becomes a subject of practical knowledge and a power in Paul's inner life. . . . The resurrection is viewed, not only as something which Paul hopes to experience after death, nor as a historical experience of Christ which is a subject of grateful and inspiring remembrance, but as a present, continuously active force in his Christian development."[23] Or again, P. Biard writes, "The power of the resurrection, then, of which Paul speaks, is certainly not a power which is exercised on Christ in order to raise him, but the powerful and glorious state of the risen Christ to which believers are assimilated (configurés)."[24] Similary, D. M. Stanley, "It is this power of his [i.e., Christ's] new supernatural life which gives the Christian the capacity for sharing in Christ's sufferings (Médebielle, Dibelius) which so unites the Christian's sufferings with Christ's that they are part of his passion."[25]

On the other hand, a writer like B. M. Ahern believes the "the activity of the Holy Spirit . . . constitutes the 'power of Christ's resurrection.'"[26] Ahern offers no explanation for this interpretation of the phrase. Perhaps he is thinking of Rom 1:4, "established as the Son of God in power according to the Spirit of holiness as of (his) resurrection from the dead." Here, however, one must be careful not to equate "the Spirit of holiness" too hastily with "the Holy Spirit," since the phrase *kata pneuma hagiōsynēs*, being parallel to *kata sarka*, seems to designate something intrinsic to the risen Christ himself in that context.[27]

It seems to me, however, that the adequate understanding of Paul's theology of the resurrection calls for a reconsideration of the phrase, "the power of his resurrection," and of a perspective that is being overlooked in such interpretations. This "power" is not limited to the influence of the risen Jesus on the Christian, but includes a reference to the origin of that influence in the Father himself. The knowledge, then, that Paul seeks to attain, the knowledge that he regards as transforming the life of a Christian and his/her sufferings, must be understood as encompassing the full ambit of that power. It emanates from the Father, raises Jesus from the dead at his resurrection, endows him with a new vitality, and finally proceeds from him as the life-giving, vitalizing force of the "new creation" and of the new life that Christians in union with Christ experience and live. It is not something simply equated with the "physical" act of raising Jesus from the dead, or with the miraculous character of that event, or with the state of the risen Jesus. It is rather the full, comprehensive power in its various phases; and the knowledge of it, emanating from Christian faith, is the transforming force that vitalizes Christian life and molds the suffering of the Christian to the pattern which is Christ. This is the basis of Paul's hope and his boast.

This interpretation may be confirmed by the (Pauline or Deutero-Pauline?) letter to the Eph 1:19–20, where the author gives thanks and prays that the Christians of Ephesus may come to know "what is the immeasurable greatness of his [i.e., God's] power in us who believe (*to hyperballon megethos tēs dynameōs autou eis hēmas tous pisteuontas*), according to the working of his great might (*kata tēn energeian tou kratous tēs ischyos autou*), which he accomplished in Christ when he raised him from the dead and made him sit at his right hand in the heavenly places." See further Eph 2:5–7; cf. 1 Pet 1:5.

This interpretation seems to underlie the very brief explanation of the phrase, "the power of his resurrection," that has been proposed by such commentators as P. Bonnard, F. W. Beare, K. Staab, and possibly G. Friedrich.[28]

When this interpretation is pondered, it can be understood as a primitive attempt to formulate the relation of the risen Son to the Father and can be seen as the Pauline basis of the later Trinitarian speculation about the relations of the Divine Persons.

III. *A Further Specification of This Power*

What precedes may seem coherent enough, but the question still has to be asked whether Paul gives any further indication of what this *dynamis* might be. My discussion began with the rejection of the idea that it can be simply explained in terms of Jesus' divinity. Is there any other way in which Paul regards it?

In Paul's theology the power of God is closely related to his glory.[29] That which brings about the glorification of Christ is not merely said to be the power of God, but even the glory (*doxa*) of the Father. The risen

Jesus is in the status of glory; he is not merely raised from the dead, but is exalted. Just as it was for Paul the God of power who raised Jesus from the dead, so it is "the Father of glory" (Eph 1:17) who has exalted him. Indeed, if it seemed that the "power" of God was the instrument whereby Jesus was raised, it is the "glory" whereby he is exalted. This indicates the close relation of God's power and glory in the resurrection.

The significance of this is seen above all in Rom 6:4, where Paul states that "we were buried with him by baptism into death, so that as Christ was raised from the dead *by the glory of the Father,* we too might walk in newness of life." Here Paul speaks of glory (*doxa*) almost in the same way he spoke of power (*dynamis*). Glory belongs to the Father, was used in raising Jesus from the dead, and results in a "newness of life" for the Christian.

The "glory of the Father" is related to the "power of God" in 2 Thess 1:9, where Paul explicitly joins the two, "the presence of the Lord and the glory of his might (*apo tēs doxēs tēs ischyos autou*). Again, in Phil 3:21 the two ideas are closely related, as Paul teaches that our commonwealth is in heaven, from which we await a Savior, the Lord Jesus Christ, "who will change our lowly body to be like his glorious body (*tō sōmati tēs doxēs autou*), by the power (*kata tēn energeian*) which enables him to subject all things to himself." This too is the background of the prayer that Paul utters in Col 1:11, "May you be strengthened with all power, according to his glorious might . . ." (*en pasē dyamei dynamoumenoi kata to kratos tēs doxēs autou*). Again, "when Christ who is our life appears, then you also will appear with him in glory" (Col 3:4). This is "our hope of sharing the glory of God" (Rom 5:2).

Just as Paul was able to refer to Jesus as "the power of God" (1 Cor 2:5), so too he called him "the Lord of glory" (1 Cor 2:8). In the latter passage the quality of the state is linked explicitly to the title of the risen Jesus, who is depicted by the Apostle as sharing the Old Testament attributes of Yahweh himself. In an analogous way the gospel that Paul preached was related by him both to the power and the glory of God and Christ; his "gospel" is the "power of God" for the salvation of everyone who believes (Rom 1:16), but it is also "the gospel of the glory of Christ, who is the likeness of God" (2 Cor 4:4).[30] (Cf. the Deutero-Pauline way of putting it in 1 Tim 1:11, "the gospel of glory of the Blessed God with which I have been entrusted.")

The richness of the Pauline concept of *doxa* as the source of the new life that the Christian enjoys can be further seen in the conclusion of Paul's midrash on an Exodus passage developed in 2 Cor 3:7–4:6. Paul alludes to and cites from Exod 34:29–35, which tells of the descent of Moses from Mt. Sinai. The "glory" (*kābôd*) of Yahweh had shone on the face of Moses as he conversed with him; when he came down from the mountain, Moses had to veil his face because Yahweh's glory reflected there frightened the Israelites. "Whenever Moses went in before the LORD to speak with him, he took the veil off, until he came out . . . ; and the people of Israel saw the face of Moses, that the skin of Moses' face shone; and Moses would put the veil upon his face again, until he went in to speak with him" (34:34–35).

In 2 Corinthians 3–4 Paul contrasts the new covenant with that of Sinai; if the old covenant were ushered in with such glory, how much more attends the new. To make his point, Paul shifts the sense of the veil. He sees it as hiding from the Israelites not that which frightened them, but the fading of the glory on Moses' face. This detail is not in the Exodus story itself; it represents a Pauline view of the passing of the covenant of old. For him it has "faded" (2 Cor 3:7, 10–11). But this is not all, for he introduces still another free association: a veil hanging before someone's face not only conceals from others what is there (and frightens) or what is not there (because it is fading away and impermanent), but it also hinders the sight of the one before whose eyes it hangs. Once again, this detail is not in the Exodus story. Paul introduces it into his midrash as he transfers the veil from Moses to his Jewish contemporaries: "Yes, to this day whenever Moses is read a veil lies over their minds" (2 Cor 3:15). With this unflattering condition Paul contrasts the lot of the Christian who has turned to the Lord—an allusion to Moses' turning to the Lord when he went in to speak with him. "When a person turns to the Lord the veil is removed. Now the Lord is the Spirit, and where the Spirit of the Lord is, there is freedom. And we all, with unveiled face, beholding the glory of the Lord, are being changed into his likeness from one degree of glory to another; for this comes from the Lord who is the Spirit" (2 Cor 3:16–18).[31] Underlying Paul's conception here is the belief that as of the resurrection Jesus became "the Lord" and a "vivifying Spirit" (1 Cor 15:45; cf. Rom 1:4). This he became as the "last Adam," i.e., the Adam of the *eschaton,* the head of a new humanity which began with the dawning of the messianic age. To this "new creation" (Gal 6:15; 2 Cor 5:17) Paul alludes at the end of the midrashic development in 2 Cor 4:4–6. He insists that he preaches the "gospel of the glory of Christ, who is the likeness of God (*eikōn tou theou*)," and explains it all by referring to the Creator, Yahweh himself. "For it is the God who said, 'Let light shine out of darkness,' who has shone in our hearts to give the light of the knowledge of the glory of God in the face of Christ" (2 Cor 4:6). Thus the source of the new

Christian life is traced back to the Creator himself. Yahweh caused his glory to shine on the face of Jesus, endowing him with a glory greater than that of Moses; this glorification and exaltation of "the Lord" made him the "image" or mirror of the Creator. He reflects the glory by degrees to the Christian who turns to him. This reflection brings about what the Greek Fathers often called the "progressive divinization of the Christian" through the influence of the risen Jesus.

The involved midrash on Exodus 34 thus spells out in its own way the relation of the glory of Yahweh to the resurrection of Jesus and to the new life that the Christian lives who is "in Christ Jesus." The Father's glory is again seen to be the origin of the life-giving power that vitalizes Christian experience. It is true that there is no reference to "the power" of God in this passage.[32] But that is because of its starting-point, the *glory* on the face of Moses. And yet, the role of glory depicted here fills out the Pauline picture of its relation to "power," used elsewhere in his letters in a similar context.

What underlies the Pauline equation of *dynamis, energeia,* or *ischys* with *doxa* with reference to the resurrection of Jesus and the new life of the Christian is the Old Testament association of these as attributes of God. We have already cited above 1 Chr 29:11–12, where these attributes of Yahweh are mentioned in prayer. Similarly one could refer to Dan 2:37 in the LXX version; also Ps 135:2; Wis 7:25; Isa 2:10, 19, 21. Perhaps more significant is Isa 40:26: "Lift up your eyes on high and see: who created these? He who brings out their host by number, calling them all by name; by the greatness of his might and because he is strong in power . . . ." Here the LXX translates the Hebrew of the last clause *mērōb 'ônîm wĕ'ammîṣ kōah* by *apo pollēs doxēs kai en kratei ischyos,* i.e., rendering *'ônîm* ("strength") by *doxa* ("glory"). G. Kittel has noted "how strongly the LXX came to sense the thought of God's power in the term *doxa.*" He compares the Greek and Hebrew of Ps 67:34; Isa 45:24 and continues, "In reality, the term [*doxa*] always speaks of one thing. God's power is an expression of the 'divine nature,' and the honour ascribed to God by man is finally no other than an affirmation of this nature. The *doxa theou* is the 'divine glory' which reveals the nature of God in creation and in His acts, which fill both heaven and earth."[33]

Though this collocation of God's power and glory is found in the Old Testament, it is not as frequent as one might expect. In contrast, the frequency of the parallelism of *kābôd* and *gĕbûrāh* (or more rarely *kōah*) in Qumran literature is striking. It reveals a development in Palestinian Jewish thinking in pre-Christian times. For example, "to God shall I say, 'My righteousness' and to the Most High, 'Founder of my welfare, source of knowledge, spring of holiness, height of glory and power of all'" (1QS 10:11–12). "Your power is [unfathomable] and your glory is immeasurable" (1QH 5:20). "There is no one besides you, there is no one with you in might; there is nothing to compare with your glory, and for your power there is no price" (1QH 10:9–10). "And I have learned that your mouth is truth, in your hand is righteousness; and in your thought all knowledge, in your might all power; and all glory is with you" *wbkwḥkh kwl gbwrh wkwl kbwd 'tkh hwʾ,* 1QH 11:7–8); ". . . a collection of glory and a spring of knowledge and powe[r]" (1QH 12:29). See also 1QS 11:6–7, 20; 1QH 4:28–29; 9:16–17, 25–26; 15:20. These examples scarcely bear directly on the meaning of the Pauline phrase in Phil 3:10; there is no direct contact here. But they at least illustrate the growing frequency of the parallelism of power and glory in more or less contemporary Jewish (Essene) writings. It makes all the more plausible the close relationship of God's "power" and "glory" in Paul's theology of the resurrection.

If this explanation of Paul's view of the role of "power" in the resurrection of Jesus has any merit, it serves to unite a number of elements in his theology that might otherwise seem disparate. It also enables one to understand the full theological meaning that is latent in the phrase of Phil 3:10, "the power of his resurrection." Paul sought to bring his Philippian converts to a deeper knowledge and awareness of this transforming power that they might better appreciate their experience of the Christ-event.

NOTES

* Originally published in *Mélanges bibliques en hommage au R. P. Béda Rigaux* (ed. A. Descamps and A. de Halleux; Gembloux: Duculot, 1970) 411–25.

[1] See D. M. Stanley, *Christ's Resurrection in Pauline Soteriology* (AnBib 13; Rome: Biblical Institute, 1961); F. X. Durrwell, *The Resurrection: A Biblical Study* (New York: Sheed and Ward, 1960); W. Künneth, *The Theology of the Resurrection* (St. Louis, MO: Concordia, 1965); A. M. Ramsey, *The Resurrection of Christ: An Essay in Biblical Theology* (2d ed.; London: G. Bles, 1956); J. Schmitt, *Jésus ressucité dans la prédication apostolique: Etude de théologie biblique* (Paris: Gabalda, 1949); R. C. Tannehill, *Dying and Rising with Christ: A Study in Pauline Theology* (BZNW 32; Berlin: Töpelmann, 1967); S. Lyonnet, "La valeur sotériologique de la résurrection du Christ selon saint Paul," *Greg* 39 (1958) 295–318; E. Schweizer, "Dying and Rising with Christ," *NTS* 14 (1967–68) 1–14; B. Vawter, "Resurrection and Redemption," *CBQ* 15 (1953) 11–23; L. Cerfaux, "La résurrection du Christ dans la vie et la doctrine de saint Paul," *Lumière et vie* 3 (1952) 61–82. E. Ruckstuhl and J. Pfammatter, *Die Auferstehung Jesu Christi:*

Heilsgeschichtliche Tatsache und Brennpunkt des Glaubens (Munich: Rex, 1968); B. Rigaux, *Dieu l'a ressucité: Exégèse et théologie biblique* (Gembloux: Duculot, 1973); W. Marxsen, *The Resurrection of Jesus of Nazareth* (Philadelphia: Fortress, 1970); X. Léon-Dufour, *Resurrection and the Message of Easter* (New York: Holt, Rinehart and Winston, 1975); R. H. Fuller, *The Formation of the Resurrection Narratives* (New York: Macmillan, 1971).

2 See further my commentary on "The Letter to the Philippians," *JBC*, art. 50 §5–8. Cf. H. Koester, "The Purpose of the Polemic of a Pauline Fragment (Philippians III)," *NTS* 8 (1961–62) 317–32.

3 See C. F. D. Moule, *An Idiom Book of New Testament Greek* (Cambridge: University Press, 1953) 26; M. Zerwick, *Biblical Greek: Illustrated by Examples* (Rome: Biblical Institute, 1963) 231; BDF, §342.3; N. Turner, in his treatment of syntax in vol. 3 of J. H. Moulton and W. F. Howard, *A Grammar of New Testament Greek* (4 vols.; Edinburgh: Clark, 1908, 1919–29, 1963, 1975), 3. 57, maintains that *egerthē* "is passive only in form and is used of the resurrection with a very active nuance. . . . There is simply no difference between this and *anestē,* where the action of the Father is assumed no more and no less. . . ." This, however, is quite debatable, and the evidence amassed above should reveal why. Cf. A. T. Robertson, *A Grammar of the Greek New Testament in the Light of Historical Research* (New York: G. H. Doran, 1914) 817, 896; G. B. Winer, *A Treatise on the Grammar of the New Testament* (3d ed.; Edinburgh: Clark, 1882) 316 n. 3. Note that BDF §313 ("Passives with intransitive meaning") includes no example of *egeirein;* nor does BDR §313.

4 Mark 16:6; Matt 17:9; 27:64; John 2:22; 21:14.

5 Although the use of the perfect passive is not in the same category, because its form is identical with the perfect middle (often used deponently), the same question can be posed about it (see 1 Cor 15:4, 12, 13, 14, 16, 17, 20 [cf. 2 Tim 2:8]). Cf. BDF §342.3.

6 See also *egerthē* in Matt 17:9 (to be compared with Mark 9:9, *anestē*); Matt 25:7; etc. Cf. the unnuanced discussion of this problem by John A. Lacy, Sr., "*Egerthē*—He Has Risen," *TBT* 36 (1968) 2532–35.

7 See also Gal 1:1; 1 Cor 6:14; 2 Cor 4:14; Rom 4:24; 8:11(bis); 10:9; Col 2:12; Eph 1:20.

8 The active usage is also found in 1 Pet 1:21; Acts 3:15; 4:10; 5:30; 10:40; 13:30. This makes it likely that the aorist passive of *egeirō* in such passages as Mark 14:28; 16:6; Matt 27:64; 28:6–7; Luke 24:6, 34 should also be translated as a real aorist passive, "he was raised." This clear and obvious conclusion is also drawn by C. F. D. Moule, *Idiom Book,* 26. The translation, "He is risen" or "He has risen," which has been in the English Bible tradition for the last four hundred years is influenced by the Latin Vulgate much more than by Hellenistic usage of the aorist passive as a mode of expressing the intransitive. In part, it also reflects a later understanding of the resurrection born of such New Testament passages as John 10:30 ("I and the Father are one") and the later realization that Jesus and the Father act as one (the common *operatio ad extra* of the Trinity).

It may be good to compare in this regard the way the New Testament refers to the ascension of Jesus. The theological passive of *analambanein* is used in Mark 16:19, "the Lord Jesus . . . was taken up into heaven" (i.e., by God). Aside from the fact that there is probably an allusion to the assumption of Elijah in 2 Kgs 2:11, the passive of *analambanein* (which is also used in Acts 1:2, 11, 22 and 1

Tim 3:16) can scarcely mean "he ascended." The intransitive verb *anabainein* is never used by Paul or Luke of Jesus' ascension. It is found in Rom 10:6, which *may* have some overtones of the ascension [?]—more likely it refers to Moses' ascent of Mt. Sinai—but even that occurs in a quotation of Deut 30:12. There may also be a covert allusion to Jesus' ascension in Acts 2:34, but in reality it denies David's ascent. The only text in which *anabainein,* "ascend," is used of Jesus' ascension is in Eph 4:8, again in an allusion to Ps 68:19. One should compare the use of the intransitive *anabainein* or *anerchesthai* in the early creeds, which reflect a more developed theology and christology. The analogous use of the passive of *analambanein* must enter into any decision about the meaning of the aorist and perfect passive forms of *egeirein* (over against the intransitive use of *anistanai*).

⁹ See M. Zerwick, *Biblical Greek,* §236; BDF §130.1; 342.1.

¹⁰ See J. Jeremias, *New Testament Theology: The Proclamation of Jesus* (New York: Scribner, 1971) 10–14.

¹¹ The Greek word that Paul uses for this notion is *dynamis* (and its cognate forms); only rarely does the word *ischys* occur (2 Thess 1:9; Eph 1:19; 6:10), which is so frequently employed in the LXX to express God's power. In reality, however, there is little difference between the use of these two words or *energeia* (see P. Biard, *La puissance de Dieu* [Travaux de l'Institut Catholique de Paris, 7; Paris: Bloud & Gay, 1960] 22–33, 138, for an attempt to determine the Old Testament and the Pauline nuances). Cf. O. Schmitz, "Der Begriff *Dynamis* bei Paulus: Ein Beitrag zum Wesen urchristlicher Begriffsbildung," *Festgabe für Adolf Deissmann* (Tübingen: Mohr [Siebeck], 1927) 139–67; S. N. Roach, "The Power of His Resurrection: Phil. III:10," *RevExp* 24 (1927) 45–55, 297–304; 25 (1928) 29–38, 176–94.

¹² See further P. Biard, *La puissance de Dieu;* W. Grundmann, *"Dynamai,* etc.," *TDNT,* 2 (1964) 290–94; *Der Begriff der Kraft in der neutestamentlichen Gedankenwelt* (BWANT 4/8; Stuttgart: Kohlhammer, 1932) 11–26; E. Fascher, *"Dynamis theou,"* *ZTK* 19 (1938) 82–108.—R. E. Murphy ("GBR and GBWRH in the Qumran Writings," *Lex tua veritas: Festschrift für Hubert Junker* [ed. H. Gross and F. Mussner; Trier: Paulinus-V., 1961] 137–43) surveys the related notion of God's power in the Qumran texts and supplies important links in the development of this notion from the Old Testament to the Pauline writings.

¹³ See my article, "Jesus the Lord," *Chicago Studies* 17 (1978) 75–104, esp. pp. 95–96.

¹⁴ The meaning of the participle *horisthentos* is debated. The Latin tradition, represented by the Vulgate, Augustine, and Pelagius understood it to mean "predestined"; but this is to give to the simple verb *horizein,* which means "limit, define, determine," the meaning of the compound *proorizein,* which it does not really have. The Greek patristic tradition understood it to mean "manifested, displayed"; Chrysostom explained it as *deichthentos, apophanthentos.* This was a meaning influenced, in part at least, by the theological discussions about the natures in Christ. In view of the use of *horizein* in Acts 10:42 and 17:31, a meaning like "appointed, installed, set up," seems preferable. See further A. Brown, "Declared or Constituted, Son of God," *ExpTim* 5 (1893–94) 308–9; E. Käsemann, *An die Römer* (HNT 8a; Tübingen: Mohr [Siebeck], 1974) 8–9; O. Kuss, *Der Römerbrief übersetzt und erklärt* (2d ed.; Regensburg: Pustet, 1963), 1. 8–9.

¹⁵ See M.-E. Boismard, "Constitué Fils de Dieu (Rom., I, 4)," *RB* 60 (1953) 5–

17; J. Trinidad, "Praedestinatus Filius Dei . . . ex resurrectione mortuorum (Rom 1,4)," *VD* 20 (1940) 145–50; W. H. Griffith Thomas, "Romans i. 4," *ExpTim* 24 (1912–13) 44–45.

[16] So W. Sanday and A. C. Headlam, *A Critical and Exegetical Commentary on the Epistle to the Romans* (5th ed.; Edinburgh: Clark, 1902) 9 ("not with *huiou theou*, . . . but rather adverbially, qualifying *horisthentos*, 'declared with might to be Son of God' "). This mode of construing the prepositional phrase regards the resurrection as a miracle, a signal manifestation of God's power. Similarly E. J. Goodspeed ("decisively declared"), the *NEB* ("by a mighty act"). The meaning of "Son of God in power," which I prefer as more consonant with Paul's understanding of the resurrection, takes the prepositional phrase as a noun-modifier; on the omission of the definite article with it, see BDF §272. Cf. E. Käsemann, *An die Römer*, 9–10.

[17] The context of this statement immediately concerns Paul's authority as an apostle in his dealings with the Corinthian church; he sees his role rooted in his close association with the risen Jesus. Implied, however, in his statement is the more radical idea that what gave life to Jesus gives vitality also to himself.

[18] The Greek text has the pronoun *autou*, which in the non-reflexive form must refer to Jesus. The result is that the Father's vivifying power, with which Jesus in his risen state is endowed, is now regarded as the means whereby the Christian will be raised. The trisyllabic form *heautou* is commonly preferred as the reflexive in Hellenistic Greek to the dissyllabic *hautou;* in fact, the latter disappears in the papyri of the first century B.C. (see BDF §64.1). Hence it is scarcely likely that *autou* is to be read as *hautou* or that it refers to the Father's power.

[19] For want of a better term I speak of the "physical event." This is preferable to the term "historical event," used by many commentators. But both have connotations which are out of place in speaking of Christ's resurrection.

[20] See *Les épîtres de saint Paul* (Paris: Cerf, 1945) 194. See also R. C. Tannehill, *Dying and Rising,* 121.

[21] *Die Briefe an die Philipper, an die Kolosser und an Philemon* (MeyerK 9; Göttingen: Vandenhoeck & Ruprecht, 1956) 138.

[22] *Saint Paul: Les épîtres de la captivité* (VS 8; 19th ed.; Paris: Beauchesne, 1947) 350. He supports his interpretation by an appeal to Suarez, *In 3 Sent.,* 56.1.

[23] *A Critical and Exegetical Commentary on the Epistles to the Philippians and to Philemon* (ICC; New York: Scribner, 1906) 104.

[24] *La puissance de Dieu,* 148.

[25] *Christ's Resurrection,* 104.

[26] "The Fellowship of His Sufferings (Phil 3,10): A Study of St. Paul's Doctrine on Christian Suffering," *CBQ* 22 (1960) 1–32, esp. p. 30.

[27] See O. Kuss, *Der Römerbrief,* 7–8; W. Charlesworth, "The Spirit of Holiness: Romans i. 4," *ExpTim* 5 (1893–94) 115; W. S. Curzon-Siggers, "Power and the Resurrection," *ExpTim* 6 (1894–95) 44.

[28] See P. Bonnard, *L'Epître de Saint Paul aux Philippiens* (CNT 10; Neuchâtel: Delachaux et Niestlé, 1950) 66; F. W. Beare, *A Commentary on the Epistle to the Philippians* (BNTC; London: Black, 1959) 122; K. Staab, *Die Thessalonicherbriefe; Die Gefangenschaftsbriefe* (RNT 7; 3d ed.; Regensburg: Pustet, 1959) 193; G. Friedrich, *Der Brief an die Philipper* (NTD 8; 13th ed.; Göttingen: Vandenhoeck & Ruprecht, 1972) 119.

[29] See A. Plé, "La gloire de Dieu," *VSpir* 74 (1946) 479–90; J. Duplacy, "La

gloire de Dieu et du Seigneur Jésus dans le Nouveau Testament," *BVC* 9 (1955) 7–21; R. Reitzenstein, *Die hellenistischen Mysterienreligionen nach ihren Grundgedanken und Wirkungen* (3d ed.; Leipzig: Teubner, 1927) 344, 355–59; A. H. Forster, "The Meaning of *Doxa* in the Greek Bible," *ATR* 12 (1929–30) 311–16; I. Abrahams, *The Glory of God* (London/New York: Oxford University, 1925); J. Edwards, "The Glorification of Christ in St. Paul," *Bellarmine Commentary* 4 (1965) 9–17.

[30] See further p. 151 above.

[31] See further J. Dupont, "Le chrétien, miroir de la gloire divine d'après II Cor., III, 18," *RB* 56 (1949) 392–411; J. Goettsberger, "Die Hülle des Moses nach Ex 34 und 2 Kor 3," *BZ* 16 (1922–24) 1–17; H. Ulonska, "Die Doxa des Mose," *EvT* 26 (1966) 378–88; P. Grech, "2 Corinthians 3,17 and the Pauline Doctrine of Conversion to the Holy Spirit," *CBQ* 17 (1955) 420–37; S. Schulz, "Die Decke des Moses: Untersuchungen zu einer vorpaulinischen Überlieferung in II Cor 3,7–18," *ZNW* 49 (1958) 1–30; D. Georgi, *Die Gegner des Paulus im 2. Korintherbrief: Studien zur religiösen Propaganda in der Spätantike* (WMANT 11; Neukirchen-Vluyn: Neukirchener-V., 1964) 265–300; R. Bultman, *Der zweite Brief an die Korinther* (MeyerK 6; 10th ed.; Göttingen: Vandenhoeck & Ruprecht, 1976) 81–112.

[32] See, however, 2 Cor 4:7, where Paul speaks of "the transcendent power belonging to God."

[33] *See* "*Dokeō, doxa*, etc.," *TDNT*, 2 (1964) 244; also A. H. Forster, "The Meaning of Power for St. Paul," *ATR* 32 (1950) 177–85 (he admits that at times "*dynamis* and *doxa* are almost identified," but fails to pursue the relation between them).

Ten

NEW TESTAMENT KYRIOS
AND MARANATHA AND THEIR
ARAMAIC BACKGROUND*

WHENEVER NEW PALESTINIAN Aramaic texts from the early centuries of Christianity are made available to the scholarly world, there is inevitably some aspect or other in them that illumines New Testament expressions and bears on the interpretation of them. Recently some material has been published which sheds light on such age-old problems as the New Testament title *kyrios* for Jesus and the phrase *maranatha* preserved in 1 Cor 16:22. Such new light has been shed on these problems in the recently published Enochic material from Qumran Cave 4.

First discovered in 1952, by both Bedouins and archaeologists, the fragments of Qumran Cave 4 are still in large part unpublished. It has been estimated that, out of the nearly 15,000 fragments found in that cave, 511 fragmentary texts have been pieced together like a jigsaw puzzle and mounted under glass in 620 plates.[1] To date, not even a hundred of these texts have been fully published.[2] Preliminary reports have been issued and partial publications of some of the texts have been made;[3] these have told us about the astounding character of the material discovered.

The bulk of the Enoch fragments is part of the lot entrusted to J. T. Milik for publication; a few of them also belong to the lot of fragments entrusted to J. Starcky. The preliminary reports issued by these scholars had warned us about the complicated picture of the Qumran fragments of this Enoch-literature now available in its Semitic original. Late in 1976 Milik published the majority of the Enochic fragments.[4] He presented the Aramaic text of seven fragmentary copies of the book that we know of as *1 Enoch* or *Ethiopic Enoch*.[5] He also published the text of four fragmentary manuscripts of Astronomical Enoch and parts of three fragmentary texts of the Enochic Book of Giants. Besides these fourteen fragmentary manuscripts Milik also identified several fragments from Qumran Caves 1, 2, and 6, which had been published earlier by others, but had either gone unidentified or had been wrongly identified.

Milik speaks of the *Books* of Enoch, because what we have normally known as *1 Enoch* is the result of a later redactional process; and it is now apparent that the Enochic literature at Qumran existed in a different form. It has been customary to speak of five parts of *1 Enoch:* (1) The Book of Watchers (chaps. 1–36); (2) The Book of Parables (*mesallê*, chaps. 37–71); (3) The Astronomical Book (chaps. 72–82); (4) The Book of Dreams (chaps. 83–90); and (5) The Epistle of Enoch (chaps. 91–108, with a possible insert in the latter [chaps. 106–7] originally separate [?] and sometimes called the Book of Noah). At Qumran, however, the "Astronomical Book" was copied separately on a scroll by itself and was much more extensive than its counterpart in the third section of *1 Enoch*. Moreover, the Book of Parables is completely missing from the form of the Book of Enoch found at Qumran. In its stead Milik has discovered a number of fragments of the Enochic Book of Giants, otherwise known from Manichean and patristic literature. In one case, part of the Book of Giants is actually copied on the same fragments as part of the Book of Enoch (4QEnGiants[a] was part of 4QEn[c]). So it seems clear that the Book of Enoch at Qumran was likewise a pentateuch, composed of (1) The Astronomical Book; (2) The Book of Watchers; (3) The Book of Giants; (4) The Book of Dreams; and (5) The Epistle of Enoch.

In publishing this Qumran Enoch-material, Milik has proposed a thesis that needs further scrutiny: that the Book of Parables, known to us as the second part of *1 Enoch,* was originally a Christian Greek composition, which was only later inserted into the Enochic literature by Christians, who for some reason replaced the Book of Giants with it—possibly because the Book of Giants was popular with the Manicheans. If Milik's thesis has any foundation, then it will have great repercussions on the debate about the New Testament title Son of Man.[6]

Milik dates these fourteen Enochic texts roughly from the end of the third century B.C. to the beginning of the first century A.D. They thus preserve for us a form of the Aramaic language that was in use in Palestine during the last two centuries B.C. and the first century A.D. Hence, in addition to their importance for the recovery of the original

Aramaic text of some of the Enoch-literature, they also preserve for us examples of this important language in which the Palestinian traditions of the early church were, in part at least, first formulated.

With these preliminary remarks about the nature of the Aramaic texts which bring to light some data that are pertinent to age-old New Testament problems, we may pass on to the discussion of two of them: (1) the New Testament *kyrios*-title for Jesus; and (2) the acclamation *maranatha*.

I. *The New Testament* Kyrios-*title for Jesus*

As a title for Jesus, (*ho*) *kyrios* is used by various New Testament writers. It is but one of several titles given to him. As in the case of the others, one invariably has to inquire into three aspects of the title for an adequate understanding of it: (1) its origin or background; (2) its meaning and connotations; and (3) its application—was it used of the earthly Jesus, of the exalted or risen Jesus, or of the parousiac Jesus? The answer that is given to the first question (its origin and background) often colors the meaning and connotations which the title carries and eventually even the quest for the stage of Jesus' career to which it was originally applied. The new evidence bears on the question of the origin or background of the *kyrios*-title.

At issue is the absolute usage of (*ho*) *kyrios* for Jesus, i.e., the unmodified title, without any adjectival, possessive, or genitival attributes.[7] In the second part of this paper, we shall be discussing the acclamation *marantha*, which does contain the possessive, "our Lord." But the question is, How did it come about that early Christians came to call Jesus "Lord" or "the Lord" simply? This New Testament Greek absolute usage is not to be confused with the Aramaic absolute state of the noun, for in reality both the absolute (or indeterminate) state of the noun, *mārê*, "Lord," or the emphatic (or determinate) state, *māryā*, "the Lord," could be regarded as the Aramaic substratum of the Greek absolute usage—if there be evidence for it.

Currently, four different views are proposed for the origin or background of the absolute usage in the New Testament. (1) *A Palestinian-Semitic Secular Origin:* (*Ho*) *kyrios* as a religious title for Jesus would have developed from the ordinary vocative or suffixal form for "Sir" or "Milord" (in either Hebrew [*'ādōn*] or Aramaic [*mārê*]). This secular usage would be reflected in the address *kyrie*, "Sir," the vocative, used even of Jesus at times in the New Testament (e.g., Matt 8:2). (2) *A Palestinian-Semitic Religious Origin:* (*Ho*) *kyrios* would have developed as a title for Jesus from the religious title *'ādōn* or *mārê'* used by Palestinian Jews of Yahweh and extended by Jewish Christians of Palestine to Jesus. This view has usually cited the *maranatha* acclamation of 1 Cor 16:22 as evidence, but it has normally encountered the objection that the title preserved in *maranatha* is not absolute, but modified, "our Lord," and hence cannot explain the emergence of the absolute usage. (3) *A Hellenistic-Jewish Religious Origin:* Greek-speaking Jewish Christians of the diaspora, in carrying the Christian message to the Hellenistic world, would have applied to Jesus the title *kyrios* used in the Greek Old Testament as the translation of the tetragrammaton, as, e.g., in the so-called LXX. Indeed, for some New Testament interpreters, this explanation is often joined to the preceding. (4) *A Hellenistic Pagan Origin:* The absolute title (*ho*) *kyrios* was derived by Christian missionaries, carrying the kerygma of the primitive Palestinian church to the Hellenistic world, from the use of *kyrios* for gods and human rulers in the eastern Mediterranean world of the first centuries B.C. and A.D. In this case, *kyrios* was not a kerygmatic title, i.e., it was not part of the original kerygma, but rather the product of Greek-speaking Christian evangelization of the eastern Mediterranean world.[8]

O. Cullmann popularized the combination of the second and third explanations.[9] The fourth explanation has been widely advocated by R. Bultmann and his followers. The Hellenistic pagan origin has been proposed mainly for the three following reasons: (*a*) Paul's allusion to "many 'gods' and many 'lords' "—yet "for us there is one God, the Father, . . . and one Lord, Jesus Christ" (1 Cor 8:5–6)—seems to allude to such an origin; (*b*) *kyrios* as a title for Yahweh or as a translation of the tetragrammaton is said to be found only in Christian copies of the LXX, whereas pre-Christian Greek translations of the Old Testament, made by Jews or for Jews, preserve in the Greek text itself the tetragrammaton written in either the Aramaic "square" characters or paleo-Hebrew writing (thus Papyrus Fuad 266; 8HevXII gr); and (*c*) the conviction that Palestinian Jews simply did not refer to Yahweh as "Lord" or "the Lord" and hence the title for Jesus could not have been an extension of this to him. To quote R. Bultmann, "At the very outset the unmodified expression 'the Lord' is unthinkable in Jewish usage. 'Lord' used of God is always given some modifier; we read: 'the Lord of heaven and earth,' 'our Lord' and similar expressions."[10]

The evidence that comes from Palestinian Aramaic and Hebrew texts that bear on this issue now supports, in my opinion, the second of the views set forth above: that the absolute use of *kyrios* for Jesus was originally of Palestinian-Semitic religious background. I set forth the

arguments in full in an article in the Conzelmann Festschrift.[11] From
the various evidence available today it seems quite likely that there was
an incipient custom among both Semitic- and Greek-speaking Jews of
Palestine to call Yahweh *'ādōn, mārê'*, or *kyrios*. The Hebrew evidence
was cited from Ps 114:7 in the canonical psalter, from Ps 151:4 (in
11QPs[a] 28:7–8), and from deuterocanonical Ben Sira 10:7. Greek
evidence can be found in Josephus, *Ant.* 20.4,2 §90; 13.3,1 §68 (in the
latter case, even in a quotation from Isa 19:19); and also in
Philo (*De mut. nom.* 2 § 12; *Quis rer. div. heres* 6 §22–29; *De somn.* 1.63), if I
may be permitted to add a non-Palestinian source. The Aramaic
evidence was cited from two Qumran texts: (a) 11QtgJob 24:6–7,
which translated Job 34:12, "Of a truth, God will not act wickedly,
and the Almighty will not pervert justice. In Aramaic this becomes,
hk'n ṣd' 'lh' / yšqr wmr' [*y'wt dyn'*], "Now will God really act treacher-
ously, and will the Lord [pervert justice]?"[12] Here the absolute state
mārê', "Lord," stands in parallelism with *'elāhā'*, "God." *Mārê'* here is
not a translation of *Yhwh*, but of *šadday*, because the tetragrammaton
is used in the Book of Job only in the prologue, epilogue, and final
speech of Yahweh, whereas in the dialogues of the book it is practically non-existent.[13] Another instance of the absolute usage of
"Lord" can be found in the *Genesis Apocryphon* from Qumran Cave
1: *bryk 'nth 'l 'lywn mry lkwl 'lmym dy 'nth mrh wšlyṭ 'l kwl'*, "Blessed
are you, O God Most High, my Lord for all ages; for you are (the)
Lord and ruler over all" (1QapGen 20:12–13; cf. also 20:15).[14] In
these instances, which I had already set forth earlier, the title for
God is found not only in the absolute usage, but also in the absolute
state of the noun in Aramaic, *mr'/mrh*. Now, however, in the new
Enoch material from Qumran Cave 4, we have a clear instance of
the absolute usage of the title for God in the emphatic state of the
noun, *māryā'*. It is found in 4QEn[b] 1 iv 5: [*wlgbry'l 'mr m*]*ry' 'z*[*l n' 'l
mmzry' . . .*], "[And to Gabriel] the [L]ord [said]: 'G[o now to the
bastards . . .']".[15] Moreover, what is striking here is that the Greek
translation of Enoch, which is extant for this part of *1 Enoch* (10:9),
reads: *kai tō Gabriēl eipen ho KS*.[16] Although the first letter of *mry'* is
missing in this Aramaic text, it is nevertheless certainly restored on
the basis of the Greek version. We had often suspected that the
emphatic form of the noun would be written with the final radical
yodh, as in later Aramaic and Syriac, but now the form with it is
clearly attested in this Palestinian Aramaic text from Qumran,
which copy Milik dates "in the middle . . . of the second century"
B.C.[17] This text, then, supplies further evidence to that which has
gradually been building up for what was an incipient custom among
Semitic-speaking and Greek-speaking Jews of Palestine in the last

century prior to Christianity of referring to Yahweh as "Lord" or "the Lord." Even though we do not yet have a clear case of *Yahweh*, the tetragrammaton, being translated directly as *mārê'* or *māryā'*, it was scarcely "unthinkable in Jewish usage" to refer to God as "the Lord."

If such evidence be acceptable, then another aspect of the *kyrios*-title for Jesus in the New Testament has to be reconsidered. If, as seems likely, the title *'ādōn*, or *mārê'*, or *kyrios* were, indeed, in use among Palestinian Jews for Yahweh, and the title were borrowed by Palestinian Jewish Christians for Jesus from such a usage, then it would seem that it was used of him as a means of expressing his transcendent and regal status. In this, I find myself thrust back to the explanation of the meaning of the title that O. Cullmann once advocated, even though for reasons quite different from his.[18] The title would suggest a *Gleichsetzung* of Jesus with Yahweh, a setting of him on a par with Yahweh, but not an *Identifizierung*—because he is not *'abbā'*. This would, then, imply perhaps a higher christology for him than the *kyrios*-title derived from a Hellenistic pagan context of the eastern Mediterranean world. It would also imply that the *kerygma* of the Palestinian church actually included a recognition of him as *mārê'* and *kyrios*. It would root in Palestine itself the christological confession of *Kyrios Iēsous* (1 Cor 12:3; Rom 10:9), among the Hebraists as well as the Hellenists. It would, therefore, deny that the title was solely the product of the evangelization of the Greek world, being applied to Jesus by Greek-speaking apostles or disciples alone.

The absolute usage of this title would also make intelligible the acclamation preserved in 1 Cor 16:22, *maranatha*—an acclamation that may be as old and as primitive as the absolute usage itself. Perhaps the acclamation does not explain the emergence of the absolute title, but it does help to provide a context in which the absolute title is intelligible.

II. *The Aramaic Acclamation* Maranatha

The ancient acclamation *maranatha* has been called by J. H. Moulton and G. Milligan "an old Aramaic watchword . . . misunderstood in most of our English versions down to the AV."[19] It is preserved for us, first of all, by Paul and, strangely enough, in that most Greek of his letters, 1 Corinthians (16:22). There it forms part of his final farewell to the Corinthians and of his blessing upon them: "I, Paul, write this greeting with my own hand. If any one has no love for the Lord, let him be accursed. *Maranatha!* The grace of the Lord Jesus be with you." Moreover, it is also preserved in *Didache* 10:6, where it forms part of the final blessing of an ancient eucharistic liturgy: "Let grace come and let this world pass away. Hosanna to the God of David. If any one be holy, let him/her come! If any one be not, let him/her repent. *Maranatha!* Amen." Cf. *Apostolic Constitutions* 7.26,5.

In neither case is this Aramaic phrase preserved in a context of a miracle-story, like *ephphatha* (Mark 7:34) or *talitha koum* (Mark 5:41). Hence its preservation cannot be explained as the use of *onoma thespesion ē rhēsis barbarikē,* "a holy name or a foreign phrase," used in healing stories, as Lucian likes to caricature them.[20] R. Bultmann has compared the use of Aramaic phrases in miracle stories of the Gospel tradition to such extrabiblical descriptions.[21] Though one might have to reckon with this character of the Aramaic phrases used in such miracle stories, this does not seem to be the reason for the preservation of *maranatha.* In Paul's use of it, it seems rather to be the use of a familiar phrase in his farewell to the Corinthians—who are presupposed to understand it. And in the *Didache* it is, in a somewhat similar way, part of a liturgical blessing.

Patristic writers such as John Chrysostom and John of Damascus thought that the expression *maranatha* was Hebrew;[22] but eventually it was correctly identified as Aramaic in the patristic tradition: Theodoret of Cyrrhus speaks of it as written in "the language of the Syrians."[23]

Attempts to explain the meaning of the phrase throughout the centuries have been numerous. It is clear, however, that the first problem to be resolved is the division of the words involved in it, for the meaning depends on how the phrase is to be divided. It is precisely on this point that the new Palestinian Aramaic texts of Enoch shed some light. However, before we consider this new evidence, it may be wise to recall how the problem of the division arose.

In the major Greek majuscle MSS of the New Testament the phrase is normally written as one word. At the end of the last century N. Schmidt studied the reading of the phrase in the main Greek MSS then available.[24] The problem of the division is aggravated in these MSS by the custom of *scriptio continua,* in which there were generally no division of words, no accents, and no breathings. In some cases, however, accents/breathings were later added, and these give a clue to the interpretation of the phrase then in vogue. Schmidt found four different forms of the continuous writing of the phrase as one word:

(a) MAPANAΘA (in codices of the Pauline corpus ℵ, A, B, C);
(b) MAPANNAΘA (in codices F, G);
(c) MAPANAΘÁ (with an acute accent on the ultima, in codex M and in 6 minuscles);
(d) MAPÁNAΘA (with an acute accent on the propenult, in codex E).[25]

He also found suggestions for the division of the phrase in the accents and breathings eventually added to the one-word writing of it:

> (*e*) MAPÀN᾽AΘÁ (with a grave accent on *maràn* and an acute on the final syllable, added by a ninth-century scribe to codex Claromontanus, and also found in codex L);
> (*f*) MAPÂN᾽AΘÂ (with a circumflex accent on *marân* and on the final vowel, added by a ninth/tenth-century scribe to codex Vaticanus).

Both of these readings, therefore, suggest the division *maran atha*.

Since Schmidt's research, only one new Greek MS of 1 Corinthians, containing 16:22, has come to light, P[46], the Chester Beatty Papyrus text of the Pauline letters.[26] It preserves the phrase written as one word, agreeing with the codices listed above under (*a*).

In the Greek text of the *Didache* published by J. Rendel Harris, the phrase is written in ligated minuscule letters and clearly as one word, *maranathá.*[27]

The ancient attempts to divide the phrase in the Greek MSS, by the addition of accents or breathings, date from the end of the first Christian millennium and reflect the division and interpretation of it already present in patristic and early medieval writers. For it is written as one word in the homilies or commentaries of John Chrysostom, Theodoret of Cyrrhus, John of Damascus, Oecumenius, and Theophylact.[28] But here we are hampered by the lack of critical editions of most of these commentaries on 1 Corinthians. In any case, it is significant that all these writers interpret the phrase as meaning *ho Kyrios hēmon ēlthe*, "our Lord has come," and the later writers are undoubtedly merely repeating what their predecessors had written. However, this is the meaning that is also preserved in the Peshitta (*māran ᾽ethā᾽*),[29] and a fifth century Coptic translation of the *Didache* preserves a similar sense: *pjs afi amēn*, "The Lord has come. Amen."[30]

When one consults the various critical editions of the New Testament in modern times, one finds three varieties of readings:

> (*a*) *maranatha* (written as one word): C. Tischendorf (*Novum Testamentum graece et latine*, 1848), K. Lachmann (1850).
> (*b*) *maran atha* (divided after the *ny*): J. J. Griesbach (1818), A. Mai (following the accentuation added to Codex Vaticanus, 1859), C. Tischendorf (in the *edito octava*, 1872), B. F. Westcott and F. J. A. Hort (1890), H. von Soden (*Handausgabe*, 1913), the British and Foreign Bible Society's text (1914), A. Merk (9 editions from 1933–64), H. J. Vogels (1950).
> (*c*) *marana tha* (divided after the third *alpha*): E. Nestle (at least since the 20th ed., 1961), J. M. Bover (since 1953), R. V. G. Tasker (1964), K. Aland et al. (*UBSGNT* 1961), Nestle-Aland, 26th ed. (1979).

Here one notes the weight of tradition: either the phrase was printed as one word (as in the main Greek MSS) or was divided as *maran atha* (according to the accents and breathings added to certain manuscripts or, more likely, according to the patristic and early medieval interpretation of the phrase). For it is only in the more recent modern critical editions that the division *marana tha* is found. The traditional division, however, was defended in modern times by no less a scholar than P. de Lagarde: "muss man *maran atha* schreiben oder auf den Ruhm ein verständiger Mann zu sein verzichten."[31]

The division *marana tha*, however, can be traced back at least to such scholars as J. Wellhausen, T. Nöldeke, and G. Dalman.[32]

The meanings that have been given to the phrase have been numerous; some of them are quite implausible, e.g.:

(1) "Our Lord is the sign," understanding the divided words as *māran ʾāthā* (A. Klostermann, E. Hommel),[33] in which the "sign" would be the liturgical kiss.
(2) "A Lord art thou," understanding the words as *mār ʾantā* (J. C. K. Hofmann, who even changed the Greek text to suit his interpretation).[34]
(3) "Devoted to death," understanding the words as *maharam motha* (M. Luther, giving an explanation that does not correspond to the Greek transcription).[35]
(4) "Our Lord has come," the patristic interpretation, which understood the phrase as *māran ʾāthā* (the perfect tense). (I consider this implausible because there is no way to justify the past tense interpretation in the context of 1 Corinthians or the *Didache*.)[36]
(5) "Our Lord will come," understanding the perfect as a prophetic future (C. L. W. Grimm).[37]

Apart from these implausible interpretations, there are three others which would have to be considered seriously:

(6) "Our Lord is coming," understanding the phrase to stand for *māran ʾathê*, the active participle.[38] But then the problem would be to explain how the Greek *maranatha* would reflect the Aramaic participle *ʾathê*; one would rather expect *maranathē*.
(7) "Our Lord cometh," understanding the phrase as divided *māran ʾāthā*, the perfect tense with a present meaning (J. Buxtorf, E. Kautzsch).[39]
(8) "Our Lord, come!", understanding the phrase to be divided *māranā thā*, with the second element taken either as the apocopated imperative (*thā*) or as an elided form of the imperative (*ʾāthā*), i.e., with the elision of *aleph* and the reduced vowel because of the preceding final long *a* of the pronominal suffix.[40]

In favor of the imperatival interpretation, "Our Lord, come!", commentators have often appealed to Rev 22:20, where in a similar final greeting at the end of that apocalyptic writing the seer makes the testifying heavenly Jesus say, "Surely I am coming soon," and he adds his own response, "Amen, come, Lord Jesus" (*amēn, erchou, kyrie Iēsou*). Here the imperative *erchou* supports the interpretation of the second element of *maranatha* as imperatival. This meaning does no violence to the *Didache* context, with its reference to the close of a eucharistic liturgy, especially when it is thought by some commentators to echo the sentiment of Paul in 1 Cor 11:26, "proclaiming the Lord's death until he comes" (*achri hou elthē*).

In the light of these varied interpretations, we can see that the real problem is still that of the division of the phrase *maranatha*. Should one divide it *maran atha* or *marana tha*? No little part of the problem is the form of the suffixal ending in Aramaic. Is it *-an* or *-ánāʾ*? When the suffix of the first plural is first attested in Old Aramaic texts (from 925–700 B.C.), it is *-an* (e.g., in the Hazael ivory inscription from Arslan Tash, *mrʾn* [*KAI* 232:1]).[41] Similarly, in the period of Imperial or Official Aramaic (from 700–200 B.C.), it is invariably written as *-an* in extrabiblical inscriptions or papyri (thus, *mrʾn* in *AP* 17:1, 5; 27:2, 10, 19, 21, 22; 30:1, 2, 18, 23; 31:17, 22; 33:7, 12, 13; *KAI* 273:9; on other words: *AP* 7:6; 2:3, 9, 13; 3:4; 20:8, 9; etc.).[42] Toward the end of this period one begins to meet the fuller ending *-ánāʾ* (in *AP* 81:110, 115); this is also found in Biblical Aramaic (Ezra 5:12; Dan 3:17). When one looks for evidence from Middle Aramaic texts from Palestine (from the last two centuries B.C. and the first century A.D.), one finds only the fuller form *-ánāʾ* (thus in 1QapGen 12:16; 19:12, 13; 21:5; 11QtgJob 26:5; the Hyrcania inscription, frg. 2, line 3 [*lnpšnʾ*][43]). Moreover, to clinch the matter, we may cite the very form that we have long been looking for, since this suffixal form of *mārēʾ* has now turned up in the Enoch fragments recently published by J. T. Milik.

In 4QEn[b] 1 iii 14 (= *1 Enoch* 9:4) we read about Raphael and Michael, who are described as great Watchers and holy ones, who go in before God's presence and say: [*ʾnth hwʾ*] *mrnʾ rbʾ* [*hwʾ*]ʾ *mrʾ ʿlmʾ* [. . . *wkwrsʾ*]ʾ *yqrk lkl* {*l*}*dr dryʾ dy mn ʿlm*[ʾ], "[You are] our great Lord; (you) are Lord of the world . . . and your glorious [thron]e (is) for every generation of generations which are from eter[nity]."[44] Here we have the missing link, *mrnʾ*, which is to be vocalized as *māránāʾ*. This form now puts to rest the question about how the Aramaic word for "our Lord" would have been pronounced (and written) in first-century Palestine.[45]

However, it still leaves a problem, for, although the verb *ʾătāʾ* is well attested in Qumran texts, there is so far no example of the peal imperative of it. When imperatives of other *Pe Aleph* verbs appear in this literature,

they usually appear with the initial *aleph*, as in 1QapGen 20:23, *'zl*, "go!";
4QEn^b 1 iv 5, *'z*[*l*], quoted above in part I of this paper;[46] 4QEn^c 5 ii 29, *'zl*,
"go!" There is no sign, however, in these texts, which are purely
consonantal, of how the imperatives were pronounced. The presumption
is that the initial *aleph* was still being pronounced.[47] But in a number of
other forms of the verb *'ty*, "come," the *aleph* has disappeared in the
writing, reflecting the quiescence of it in the pronunciation (e.g., *ytwn*,
11QtgJob 16:1, 2 [for *y'twn*]; *lmth*, 4QEnastr^b 7 iii 2 [for *lm'th*]; *lmt'*,
4QEnastr^b 7 iii 5 [for *lm't'*]).

So far, however, there is no evidence for the apocopated imperative
tā' in the Aramaic of Palestine of this period (200 B.C.–A.D. 200), such
as one finds later in Palestinian Jewish Aramaic texts[48] or in Syriac
writings.[49]

In the light of these data, I should prefer to regard the Greek
transcription *maranatha* of 1 Cor 16:22 and *Did.* 10:6 as a representation of an elision of Aramaic *māránā' 'āthā'*, "our Lord, come!" (an
imperative with the elision of the reduced vowel and initial *aleph*
because of the preceding long *a*).[50]

That the phrase is intended to be a liturgical acclamation in a eucharistic
context in *Did.* 10:6 seems clear,[51] but I hesitate to find the ending of 1
Corinthians reflecting a similar eucharistic situation, *pace* J. A. T.
Robinson.[52]

On the other hand, the collocation of *marana tha* in 1 Cor 16:22 with
ētō anathema, immediately preceding it, has suggested to some commentators that *marana tha* might itself have had an imprecatory meaning.[53]
Most of the evidence for this sort of interpretation of *marana tha* comes
from a later period, when the Pauline collocation of the two phrases
was taken up into a context of malediction. It seems that at some point
the original sense of *marana tha* was completely lost, and it was thought
to be a foreign curse (a sort of abacadabra), formulating perhaps the
anathema which immediately precedes. In this way it became what
J. H. Moulton and G. Milligan have called a *symbolon*.[54] And this undoubtedly accounts even for the misspelling of it in a 4th/5th-century
inscription, *maranathan*,[55] where it *is* used as an imprecation. But as far
as I can see, there is not the slightest hint that *marana tha* itself was to be
so understood in the time of Paul. To read it thus in 1 Corinthians
is to be guilty of either eisegesis or anachronism.[56]

The best explanation of *marana tha* remains that of an ancient
acclamation, held over from some primitive Palestinian liturgical
setting,[57] which can no longer be specified more precisely. Paul would
have made use of it at the end of 1 Corinthians as part of his final

blessing on the community to which he writes. The brief, almost disjointed, concluding phrases of that blessing make it difficult to say whether *marana tha* goes with the preceding or the following phrase. To me it makes more sense to relate it to what follows and to regard it as an acclamation referring to Jesus' parousiac coming, understood at least as eschatological and regal, and perhaps also as judicial.[58]

In any case, the Palestinian Aramaic evidence that now bears on the phrase helps to relate the words to a primitive Jewish-Christian context, the same to which I sought earlier to relate the *kyrios*-title for Jesus itself. It thus gives evidence of a veneration of Jesus by early Jewish Christians as the "Lord," as a figure associated with Yahweh of the Old Testament, even as one on the same level with him, without saying explicitly that he is divine.[59]

NOTES

* Submitted for the forthcoming Bo Reicke Festschrift, published here with the permission of the editor.

[1] See R. de Vaux and J. T. Milik, *Qumrân Cave 4: II/I. Archéologie; II. Tefillin, mezuzot et targums (4Q128–4Q157)* (DJD 6; Oxford: Clarendon, 1977) 8.

[2] Twenty-nine of the Cave 4 fragments have been published by J. M. Allegro, *Qumrân Cave 4: I (4Q158–4Q186)* (DJD 5; Oxford: Clarendon, 1968); and thirty more by J. T. Milik in the volume mentioned in n. 1 (pp. 31–91). Fourteen more were published by him in the volume to be mentioned in n. 4 below. For further Cave 4 texts, published in preliminary or partial form, see my book, *The Dead Sea Scrolls: Major Publications and Tools for Study, With an Addendum (January 1977)* (SBLSBS 8; Missoula, MT: Scholars, 1977) 23–34.

[3] For reports on the literature of Cave 4, see P. Benoit et al., "Editing the Manuscript Fragments from Qumran," *BA* 19 (1956) 75–96, esp. pp. 89, 94; "Le travail d'édition des fragments manuscrits de Qumrân," *RB* 63 (1956) 49–67, esp. pp. 60, 66; J. T. Milik, *Ten Years of Discovery in the Wilderness of Judaea* (SBT 26; Naperville, IL: Allenson, 1959) 33–34. For the preliminary Enochic publications, see J. T. Milik, "Hénoch au pays des aromates (ch. xxvii à xxxii): Fragments araméens de la grotte 4 de Qumran," *RB* 65 (1958) 70–77 (= 4QEn^{c,e}); "Problèmes de la littérature hénochique à la lumière des fragments araméens de Qumrân," *HTR* 64 (1971) 333–78 (= 4QEnastr^{a-d}); "Turfan et Qumran: Livre des Géants juif et manichéen," *Tradition und Glaube: Das frühe Christentum in seiner Umwelt: Festgabe für Karl Georg Kuhn zum 65. Geburtstag* (eds. G. Jeremias et al.; Göttingen: Vandenhoeck & Ruprecht, 1971) 117–27.

[4] *The Books of Enoch: Aramaic Fragments of Qumran Cave 4* (Oxford: Clarendon, 1976). Unfortunately, despite the claim that Milik makes that the "main purpose of this edition is to present . . . all the fragments identified among the manuscripts of Qumrân Cave 4 as forming part of different Books of Enoch" (p.

3), he has not yet presented *all* of them. See my remarks in "Implications of the New Enoch Literature from Qumran," *TS* 38 (1977) 332–45.

⁵ For a recent critical edition of this text, see M. A. Knibb (in consultation with E. Ullendorff), *The Ethiopic Book of Enoch: A New Edition in the Light of the Aramaic Dead Sea Fragments* (2 vols; Oxford: Clarendon, 1978). See my review of this edition in a forthcoming issue of *JBL*.

⁶ See my remarks in *TS* 38 (1977) 342–44. Cf. M. A. Knibb (with E. Ullendorff), *BSOAS* 40 (1977) 601–2; "The Date of the Parables of Enoch," *NTS* 25 (1978–79) 345–59; J. C. Greenfield, "Prolegomenon," in H. Odeberg, *3 Enoch or the Hebrew Book of Enoch* (reprinted; New York: Ktav, 1973) xi–xlvii; J. C. Greenfield and M. E. Stone, "The Enochic Pentateuch and the Date of the Similitudes," *HTR* 70 (1977) 51–65; "The Books of Enoch and the Traditions of Enoch," *Numen* 26 (1979) 89–103; C. L. Mearns, "Dating the Similitudes of Enoch," *NTS* 25 (1978–79) 360–69.

⁷ On this crucial distinction, see further my article, "The Semitic Background of the New Testament *Kyrios*-Title," *WA,* 115–42, esp. pp. 117, 133–34; or "Der semitische Hintergrund des neutestamentlichen Kyriostitels," *Jesus Christus in Historie und Theologie: Neutestamentliche Festschrift für Hans Conzelmann zum 60. Geburtstag* (ed. G. Strecker; Tübingen: Mohr [Siebeck], 1975) 267–98, esp. pp. 271–72.

⁸ These four views have been described in greater detail in the articles cited in n. 7: in German, pp. 269–71; in English, *WA,* 115–17.

⁹ *Christology of the New Testament* (London: SCM, 1963) 195–237.

¹⁰ *Theology of the New Testament* (2 vols.; London: SCM, 1956), 1. 51.

¹¹ See n. 7 above; in German, pp. 290–96; in English, *WA,* 123–27.

¹² See J. P. M. van der Ploeg and A. S. van der Woude, *Le targum de Job de la grotte xi de Qumrân* (Koninklijke nederlandse Akademie van Wetenschappen; Leiden: Brill, 1971) 58.

¹³ But see Job 12:9 and the *apparatus criticus.*

¹⁴ See N. Avigad and Y. Yadin, *A Genesis Apocryphon: A Scroll from the Wilderness of Judaea* (Jerusalem: Magnes, 1956), col. XX.

¹⁵ *The Books of Enoch* (n. 4 above), 175–76.

¹⁶ See M. Black, *Apocalypsis Henochi graece* (PVTG 3; Leiden: Brill, 1970) 25. *Ho kyrios* is, however, lacking in the Greek text preserved in George Syncellus.

¹⁷ *The Books of Enoch* (n. 4 above), 5. The form *mry'* also shows that the emphatic form was not *mārā', pace* K. G. Kuhn (*TDNT* 4 [1967] 467).

¹⁸ *The Christology of the New Testament* (n. 9 above), 218.

¹⁹ *The Vocabulary of the Greek Testament Illustrated from the Papyri and Other Non-Literary Sources* (London: Hodder and Stoughton, 1930; reprinted, 1957) 388. Cf. E. J. Goodspeed, *Problems of New Testament Translation* (Chicago: Chicago University, 1945) 166–68.

²⁰ *Philopseudes* 9 (LCL, 3. 334–35).

²¹ *The History of the Synoptic Tradition* (Oxford: Blackwell, 1968) 222.

²² John Chrysostom, *In Ep. I ad Cor. hom.* xliv (PG,61. 377); John of Damascus, *In Ep. ad Cor I,* 123 (PG,95. 705). This identification is also found in an eleventh century Greek MS (Vat. gr. 179): *hebraikē estin hē lexis, ho Kyrios hēkei.*

²³ *Interpr. ep. I ad Cor.,* cap. 16, 21 (PG,82. 373); cf. Oecumenius, *Comment. in ep. I ad Cor.* (PG,118. 904–5); Theophylact, *Expos. in ep. I ad Cor.,* 16.22 (PG,124. 793).

²⁴ "Maranatha, I Cor. xvi. 22," *JBL* 13 (1894) 50–60; cf. *JBL* 15 (1896) 44 n. 14 for a correction.

²⁵ *JBL* 13 (1894) 50. I have been able to check the reading in the major MSS in this list.

²⁶ See F. C. Kenyon, *The Chester Beatty Biblical Papyri: Descriptions and Texts of Twelve Manuscripts on Papyrus of the Greek Bible: Fasciculus III Supplement, Pauline Epistles, Plates* (London: E. Walker, 1937), f. 60 v. (last line). The phrase is actually somewhat unclear here; the *theta* is obscure. But it is almost certainly to be read as one word. The papyrus is dated ca. A.D. 200.

²⁷ *The Teaching of the Apostles* (Didachē tōn apostolōn) *Newly Edited, with Facsimile, Text and a Commentary* (Baltimore: Johns Hopkins University; London: C. J. Clay and Sons, 1887), pl. VII, fol. 79a, line 12 (accented with an acute on the ultima).

²⁸ See nn. 20–21 above. Some of the Latin patristic tradition also echoes this interpretation: Jerome, *Lib. interpr. Hebr. nom.*, ad I Cor. (CC,72. 154): "*Maranatha*, dominus noster venit. Syrum est"; *In ep. I ad Cor.*, 16 (PL, 30. 806): "*Maranatha*. Magis Syrum est, quam Hebraeum; tametsi ex confinio utrarumque linguarum, aliquid Hebraeum sonet. Et interpretatur, *Dominus noster venit.*" Cf. *Ep.* 26.4 (PL, 22. 431). Ambrosiaster, *In ep. ad Cor. I*, 16:22 (CSEL 81.194): "Maranatha enim 'dominus venit' significat. Hoc propter Judaeos qui Jesum non venisse dicebant, hi ergo anathema sunt a Domino, qui venit." Augustine, however, is said to have recorded another interpretation which refers the phrase not to the incarnation, but to the parousia ("Anathema dixit graeco sermone: condemnatus; maranatha definivit: Donec dominus redeat"), but I have been unable to verify this interpretation in Augustine's writings. This interpretation, however, is echoed in a ninth century codex G (Boernerianus): "Anathema sit in adventu domini." Cf. Du Cange, *Glossarium mediae et infimae latinitatis* (Niort: L. Favre, 1885), 5. 258. On this sort of interpretation, see p. 228.

²⁹ *The New Testament in Syriac* (London: British and Foreign Bible Society, 1950) 101.

³⁰ See G. Horner, "A New Papyrus Fragment of the Didache in Coptic," *JTS* 25 (1924) 225–31 (= Brit. Mus. Or. 9271). Cf. C. Schmidt, "Das koptische Didache-Fragment des British Museum," *ZNW* 24 (1925) 81–99; L.-Th. Lefort, *Les Pères apostoliques en copte* (CSCO 135; Louvain: Imprimerie orientaliste L. Durbecq, 1952) 32 (Lefort reads *pj*[š] *afi* ⟨*h*⟩*amēn*, and translates: "Le seigneur est venu, amen" [CSCO 136, 26]). Cf. E. Peterson, "Ueber einige Probleme der Didache-Ueberlieferung," *Rivista di archeologia cristiana* 27 (1951) 37–68, esp. pp. 60 n. 80, 61 n. 86.

³¹ Quoted by N. Schmidt, *JBL* 13 (1894) 51.

³² See T. Nöldeke, Review of E. Kautzsch, *Grammatik des Biblisch-Aramäischen mit einer kritischen Erörterung der aramäischen Wörter im Neuen Testament* (Leipzig: F. C. W. Vogel, 1884), *GGA* 1884/2, 1014–23, esp. p. 1023. Nöldeke there cites the agreement of J. Wellhausen with him in adopting the suggestion of G. Bickell ("Die neuentdeckte 'Lehre der Apostel' und die Liturgie," *ZKT* 8 [1884] 400–12, esp. p. 403 n. 3), who was apparently the first person in modern times to suggest this division and meaning of the phrase. He compared Rev 22:20. See further J. Halévy, "Découvertes épigraphiques en Arabie," *REJ* 9 (1884) 1–20, esp. p. 9; G. Dalman, *Grammatik des jüdisch-palästinischen Aramäisch nach den Idiomen des palästinischen Talmud, des Onkelostargum und Prophetentargum, und der*

jerusalemischen Targume (2d ed.; Leipzig: Hinrichs, 1903; reprinted, Darmstadt: Wissenschaftliche Buchgesellschaft, 1960) 357 n. 1. There is now no longer any reason to appeal to Nabatean forms, as did Dalman and Halévy.

[33] These different meanings have been well discussed by K. G. Kuhn, *"Maranatha," TDNT* 4 (1967) 466–72. Cf. A. Klostermann, *Probleme im Aposteltexte neu erörtert* (Gotha: Perthes, 1883) 200–46; E. Hommel, "Maran atha," *ZNW* 15 (1914) 317–22.

[34] J. C. K. von Hofmann, *Die heilige Schrift neuen Testaments zusammenhängend untersucht: II/2 Der erste Brief Pauli an die Korinther* (Nördlingen: G. H. Beck, 1874) 401–3.

[35] *Sämmtliche Werke: 4. Abt., Vermischte deutsche Schriften 12* (Frankfurt/ Erlangen: Heyder und Zimmer, 1855), 64. 233; *Deutsche Bibel 1522–1546, 7. Das Neue Testament, 2. Hälfte* (Weimar: H. Böhlaus, 1931) 136–37 ("So jemandden HErrn Jhesu Christ nicht lieb hat, der sey Anathema Maharam Motha." His marginal gloss reads: "Bann auf deutsch, Anathem, Griechisch, Maharam auff Ebreisch ist ein ding. Moth aber heisst tod. Wil nu S. Paulus sagen, Wer Christus nicht liebet, der ist verbannet zum tode"). Luther was, however, aware of another interpretation, that of the Fathers and Scholastics before him, for he wrote in his commentary of 1519 on Galatians: "Si quis non amat dominum Iesum Christum, sit anathema maranata (quod Burgensis pessimum maledicendi genus apud Hebreos esse dicit, ubi nostri maranata 'dominus venit' intelligunt, non absque errore, ut puto): nihil mirum sit, si et hic [i.e., in Galatians] maledicat, externi hominis malum detestans, quo bonum spiritus impediri cernebat" (Weimar Ausgabe, 2. 573). "Dominus venit" is, of course, ambiguous, because it could be the perfect or the present tense. The translator of the Commentary on Galatians in *Luther's Works* (ed. J. Pelikan and W. A. Hansen; Saint Louis: Concordia Publishing House, 1964), 27. 345, translated it, "the Lord is coming," but I daresay that that is not what Luther meant, since the tradition before him almost unanimously understood it as the past tense (perfect). The translator has here been influenced apparently by a modern understanding of the phrase, in preferring the present.

The passage to which Luther refers can be found in Nicolaus de Lyra, *Postilla super totam bibliam, cum additionibus Pauli Burgensis* (Unveränderter Nachdruck der Ausgabe Strassburg, 1492; Frankfurt: Minerva, 1971), vol. 4, no pagination: Ad Corinthios I, in 16:22. (I am indebted to Prof. Karlfried Froehlich for this reference.)

The interpretation, *maḥaram motha*, "devoted to death," is ascribed by Cornelius a Lapide (*Commentarii in Sacram Scripturam* [Milan: F. Pagnoni, 1870], 17. 456) to Erasmus, Theodore de Bèze, and Bullinger. His own comment on this interpretation is: "Sed hoc tortum est et longe distat *macharam mota* a *maran ata.*" A similar judgment was made by Melanchthon, "cum adpareat longius accersitam esse" (*Comm. in ep. Pauli ad Cor.*, cap. xvi; C. G. Bretschneider, *Philippi Melanthonis opera quae supersunt omnia* [Corpus reformatorum, 15; Halle/S.: C. A. Schwetschke, 1848] 1190–92).

I have been unable to find the use of this explanation in the works of Erasmus. In his *Novum instrumentum: Annotationes Novi Testamenti* (Basel: Froben, 1516), 2. 483, he gives the usual translation, "Dns noster venit." This is repeated in the printing of 1519, and also in his revision, *In annotationes Novi Testamenti* (Basel: Froben, 1540) 522 (= *Des. Erasmi roter. operum sextus tomus,* 522).

Theodore de Bèze gives the explanation of *maranatha* which relates it to Hebr.

ḥerem; see *Annotationes maiores in Novum Dn. nostri Jesu Christi Testamentum* (2 vols.; [no place or publisher], 1594), 2. 250–51. Cf. J. Calvin, *Commentary on the Epistle of Paul the Apostle to the Corinthians* (Grand Rapids, MI: Eerdmans, 1948), 2. 80–83.

[36] According to this interpretation, the phrase was often said to be a "confession," to distinguish it from other interpretations. See K. G. Kuhn, "*Maranatha,*" *TDNT* 4 (1967) 470–72. The reason why this is still preferred by some commentators is the patristic tradition that is associated with it. It seems rather obvious that the Fathers either did not understand what the phrase meant or related it to the preceding *anathema,* or simply repeated what earlier interpreters had said it meant. The past tense was often used in patristic and early scholastic writings to affirm the incarnation in the face of unorthodox views of Jesus, either Docetic or Jewish. See especially B. Botte, "Maranatha," *Noël-Epiphanie, retour du Christ: Semaine liturgique de l'Institut Saint-Serge* (Paris: Cerf, 1967) 25–42, esp. pp. 37–39. Cf. F. Field, *Notes on the Translation of the New Testament: Being Otium norvicense (pars tertia)* (Cambridge: University Press, 1899) 190; R. Payne Smith, *Thesaurus syriacus* (2 vols.; Oxford: Clarendon, 1901), 2. 2205; also G. Klein, "Maranatha," *RGG* 4 (1960) 732–33, esp. col. 732.

[37] In J. H. Thayer, *A Greek-English Lexicon of the New Testament, Being Grimm's Wilke's Clavis Novi Testamenti Translated, Revised and Enlarged* (New York: Harper, 1892) 389. See K. G. Kuhn, "*Maranatha,*" *TDNT* 4 (1967) 472. Cf. M. Black "The Maranatha Invocation and Jude 14, 15 (1 Enoch 1:9)," *Christ and Spirit in the New Testament: In Honour of Charles Francis Digby Moule* (ed. B. Lindars and S. S. Smalley; Cambridge: University Press, 1973) 189–96, esp. p. 196; "The Christological Use of the Old Testament in the New Testament," *NTS* 18 (1971–72) 1–14, esp. p. 10 n. 4. I remain skeptical, along with G. Dalman and K. G. Kuhn, about the so-called prophetic perfect or *perfectum futurum* in Aramaic, especially in main clauses, as this phrase would be. Cf. H. Bauer and P. Leander, *Grammatik des Biblisch-Aramäischen* (Hall/S.: Niemeyer, 1927) §77a, 79n.

[38] See A. Adam, "Erwägungen zur Herkunft der Didache," *ZKG* 68 (1957) 1–47, esp. p. 6 n. 14. He cites as an authority for this interpretation "ein arabisch, syrisch, englisch sprechender Mönch" of St. Mark's Syrian Orthodox Monastery in Jerusalem, who pronounced it *mōran ōṯe* and translated it, "Der Herr ist im Kommen" (!).

[39] J. Buxtorf, *Lexicon chaldaicum, talmudicum et rabbinicum* (2 vols.; ed. B. Fischer; Leipzig: M. Schaefer, 1875) 633; E. Kautzsch, *Grammatik des Biblisch-Aramäschen,* 12; J. Weiss, *Der erste Korintherbrief* (MeyerK 5; 9th ed.; Göttingen: Vandenhoeck & Ruprecht, 1910) 387.

[40] This explanation is given by E. Kautzsch (*Grammatik des Biblisch-Aramäischen,* 12) as an alternative. The same suggestion was made by J. Hehn, recorded in F. J. Dölger, *Sol salutis: Gebet und Gesang im christlichen Altertum* (Liturgiegeschichtliche Forschungen, 16/17; Münster in W.: Aschendorff, 1925) 201.

[41] True, *-anaʾ* should be regarded as the older form. On the basis of comparative Northwest Semitic grammar, one would postulate a Proto-Semitic from *-ană* (see H. Bauer and P. Leander, *Grammatik des Biblisch-Aramäischen* [n. 37 above], 79 §20t'; C. Brockelmann, *Grundriss der vergleichenden Grammatik der semitischen Sprachen* [2 vols.; Berlin: Reuther & Reichard, 1908; reprinted, Hildesheim: Olms, 1966], 1. 309 [§105d]). But the earliest historically attested Aramaic forms end simply in *-n;* there is no evidence that this was merely a consonantal writing for *-nă.* See F. M. Cross and D. N. Freedman, *Early Hebrew*

Orthography: A Study of the Epigraphic Evidence (AOS 36; New Haven: American Oriental Society, 1952) 21–34; J. A. Fitzmyer, *The Aramaic Inscriptions of Sefire* (BibOr 19; Rome: Biblical Institute, 1967) 139–49; R. Degen, *Altaramäische Grammatik der Inschriften des 10.-8. Jh. v. Chr.* (Abh. f. d. Kunde des Morgenlandes, 38/3; Wiesbaden: Deutsche morgenländische Gesellschaft, 1969) 44 36. S. Segert (*Altaramäische Grammatik mit Bibliographie, Chrestomathie und Glossar* [Leipzig: VEB Verlag Enzyklopädie, 1975] 5.1.3.4.1 [sic!]) considers it a possibility that final -*n* was pronounced -*na,* but he offers not a shred of evidence for the possibility. Cf. L. A. Bange, *A Study of the Use of Vowel-Letters in Alphabetic Consonantal Writing* (Munich: Verlag-UNI-Druck, 1971) 78; he offers no proof for the actual pronunciation of final -*n* beyond the postulated Proto-Semitic ending that everyone acknowledges. When final long *a* was preserved in the pronunciation, it was invariably written with *h* (see *znh* [= *zĕnāh*], "this," Sf I A 36, 40; I B 28, 33; I C 17; *'nh* [= *'ānāh*], "I," Sf II C 8; III 6).

[42] This evidence shows that -*an* was the historically older ending of the first plural suffix in Aramaic, at least as far as what is attested, and that -*ánā'* prevailed at a later date. The latter may, of course, represent a preservation of the more original Proto-Semitic ending -*ană* in certain areas—or at least a return to an older pronunciation. This evidence should at least make one cautious in describing the fuller ending as the "old suffix form *māránā'*" over against what is sometimes called "the more recent popular *māran*" (F. Hahn, *The Titles of Jesus in Christology: Their History in Early Christianity* [London: Lutterworth, 1969] 93).

[43] See J. Naveh, "Ktwbt 'rmyt mhwrqnyh [An Aramaic Inscription from Hyrcania]," *'Atiqot: Hebrew Series* 7 (1974) 56–57 (+ pl. XV/8).

[44] *The Books of Enoch* (n. 4 above), 171. Literally, the text reads, "[You are] our Lord, the Great One."

[45] This evidence is, consequently, significant, because several writers in recent times have insisted on the division *maran atha,* citing evidence for the short ending -*an* from Palestinian pentateuchal targums, Samaritan Aramaic, and Christian Palestinian Aramaic. Thus, e.g., H.-P. Rüger, "Zum Problem der Sprache Jesu," *ZNW* 59 (1968) 113–22, esp. p. 121: "Und in der Tat heisst das Suffix der 1. communis pluralis am konsonantisch auslautenden Nomen im Idiom des palästinischen Pentateuchtargums, im samaritanischen Aramäisch und im Christlich-palästinischen stets -*an,* teils -*ana'.*" Rüger cites F. Schulthess, *Grammatik des christlich-palästinischen Aramäisch,* (Tübingen: Mohr [Siebeck], 1924) 33 §57; G. Dalman, *Grammatik des jüdisch-palästinischen Aramäisch,* 95 and 202-3. The short ending reappears, indeed, in the Late Phase of the language (for the phases in question, see *WA,* 57–84). The question has always been, What form did the first plural suffixal ending take in first-century Palestine? None of the evidence that Rüger cites answers that question; and the same has to be said for most of what is cited by K.-G. Kuhn, *TDNT* 4 (1967) 467–68. See further J. A. Emerton, "Maranatha and Ephphata," *JTS* ns 18 (1967) 427–31, esp. p. 427.

[46] See p. 222 above.

[47] Cf. E. Qimron, "Initial *Alef* as a Vowel in Hebrew and Aramaean Documents from Qumran Compared with Other Hebrew and Aramaean Sources," *Leš* 39 (1975) 133–46.

[48] See G. Dalman, *Grammatik des jüdisch-palästinischen Aramäisch,* 357, 300. Cf. H. Odeberg, *The Aramaic Portions of Bereshit Rabba, with Grammar of Galilaean*

Aramaic (Lunds Universitets Årsskrift, ns 1/36 n. 4; Lund: Gleerup; Leipzig: Harrassowitz, 1939) 77, 160.

[49] See T. Nöldeke, *Compendious Syriac Grammar* (London: Williams and Norgate, 1904) 133 (§183). Cf. the Peshitta of Rev 22:20: *tāʾ māryāʾ Yēšūᶜ*.

[50] As suggested earlier by E. Kautzsch and J. Hehn (see n. 40 above).

[51] There it occurs at the end of a rather lengthy description of an early eucharistic liturgy. See B. Botte, "Maranatha," 33–34.

[52] "The Earliest Christian Liturgical Sequence," *JTS* ns 4 (1953) 38–41; reprinted in *Twelve New Testament Studies* (SBT 34; Naperville: Allenson, 1962) 154–57.

[53] See C. F. D. Moule, "A Reconsideration of the Context of Maranatha," *NTS* 6 (1959–60) 307–10. He takes up a suggestion of E. Peterson, *Heis theos: Epigraphische, formgeschichtliche und religionsgeschichtliche Untersuchungen* (Göttingen: Vandenhoeck & Ruprecht, 1926) 130–31. For the later evidence on which this interpretation is based—apart from the implication of it in patristic writing—see H. Leclercq, "Maranatha," *DACL* 10/2 (1932) 1729–30. Cf. W. Dunphy, "Marantha: Development in Early Christology," *ITQ* 37 (1970) 294–308; M. Black, "The Maranatha Invocation" (see n. 37 above), 189–96. According to B. Botte ("Marantha," 29–34), this linking of *maranatha* with what precedes was the source of the long-standing patristic and medieval understanding of the phrase. My own investigations agree with his on this score.

[54] *The Vocabulary* (see n. 17 above), 33.

[55] See *CIG*, 4. 9303; J. H. Moulton and G. Milligan, *The Vocabulary*, 33. *Pace* C. F. D. Moule (*NTS* 6 [1959–60] 308), the misspelling is precisely the evidence for the misunderstanding of the phrase.

[56] Still further wide of the mark is the interpretation of the text of 1 Cor 16:22 set forth by W. F. Albright and C. S. Mann, "Two Texts in I Corinthians," *NTS* 16 (1969–70) 271–76.

[57] The attempt of W. Heitmüller ("Zum Problem Paulus und Jesus," *ZNW* 13 [1912] 320–37, esp. pp. 333–34) to seek a Hellenistic Christian origin for the title, either in bilingual Antioch or Damascus, has found little support. Cf. W. Bousset, *Kyrios Christos: A History of the Belief in Christ from the Beginnings of Christianity to Irenaeus* (Nashville: Abingdon, 1970) 129. On Bousset's vacillations, see S. Schulz, "Marantha und Kyrios Jesus," *ZNW* 53 (1962) 125–44, esp. p. 125. Cf. V. H. Neufeld, *The Earliest Christian Confessions* (NTTS 5; Leiden: Brill, 1963) 55 n. 4.

[58] See further B. Botte, "Maranatha," 40–42; G. Bornkamm, *Early Christian Experience* (London: SCM, 1969) 169–76, 178–79; P.-E. Langevin, *Jésus Seigneur et l'eschatologie: Exégèse de textes prépauliniens* (Studia, 21; Bruges/Paris: Desclée de Brouwer, 1967) 168–208.

[59] See G. Klein, "Maranatha," *RGG* 4 (1960) 732–33.

Eleven

HABAKKUK 2:3–4
AND THE NEW TESTAMENT*

IT IS WELL KNOWN that in the New Testament, Hab 2:4 is used by Paul in Gal 3:11 and Rom 1:17, and Hab 2:3–4 by the author of the Epistle to the Hebrews (10:37–38). This Old Testament text is also commented on by the author of the *pešer* on Habakkuk from Qumran Cave 1. The different forms of the quotation from Habakkuk have at times been discussed.[1] But it is puzzling why the differing Hebrew and Greek forms of these verses, which must have been behind the New Testament use of this famous quotation, have not been more adequately treated. Moreover, the original verses in the Hebrew form of Habakkuk have concealed problems that would have to be considered in an adequate treatment, since many of the modern translations of the passage have been greatly influenced by—at least—a Greek version of it. The dependence of New Testament writers on the Habakkuk passage is rather obvious, but it is not always clearly stated that the dependence is on a rather narrowly understood Greek version of it. Consequently, it might be well to survey the data now available in a more comprehensive way with the hope that they may shed some light on the problems that one has in the interpretation and use of Hab 2:3–4 in the New Testament.

I. *The Text of Hab 2:3–4 in Pre-New Testament Usage*

The passage that concerns us reads as follows in the Hebrew of the MT (Hab 2:3–4):

3 כי עוד חזון למועד ויפח לקץ ולא יכזב

אם־יתמהמה חכה־לו כי־בא יבא לא יאחר:

4 הנה עפלה לא־ישרה נפשו בו וצדיק באמונתו יחיה:

The Hebrew text of Hab 2:3–4 has usually been translated somewhat as follows:

> [3]For still the vision awaits its time;
>   it hastens to the end—it will not lie.
> If it seem slow, wait for it;
>   it will surely come, it will not delay.
> [4]Behold, he whose soul is not upright in him shall fail,
>   but the righteous shall live by his faith. (*RSV*)

Or:

> [3]For the vision still has its time,
>   presses on to fulfillment, and will not disappoint;
> If it delays, wait for it,
>   it will surely come, it will not be late.
> [4]The rash man has no integrity;
>   but the just man, because of his faith, shall live. (*NAB*)

In the original context of Habakkuk, these verses form part of Yahweh's reply to the prophet's second complaint about the continuing oppression of Judah. Chaldean invaders, who are expected and whose god is their might, are contrasted with Judah, whose deliverance lies in fidelity to Yahweh. Yahweh has just ordered the prophet to record the vision clearly upon tablets so that even a runner can read it. Then follow vv. 3–4, which tell of a vision destined for an appointed time, which will make clear that Judah's deliverance will not depend on its wealth; rather, only fidelity to Yahweh will prove its righteousness and bring life. The Hebrew word *'ĕmûnāh*, "fidelity, steadfastness," expresses the key idea.

The meaning of these verses has been queried in recent times by a number of writers. In particular, v. 3, as translated above, may really express a slightly different idea. The crucial word is *wyph* (vocalized in the MT as *wĕyāpēaḥ*) and is usually translated, "hastens"; related to it is *'wd* (vocalized as *'ôd*), "still." Frequently enough, the word *wyph* has been regarded as a verb, derived from the root *pwh/pyh*, and related to a similar form *yāpîaḥ* in Proverbs (6:19; 12:17; 14:5, 25; 19:5, 9, 26) and Ps 27:12. Recently, however, it has become clear that *yph* must mean "witness" in a good number of these instances, since this root is now abundantly attested in Ugaritic.[2] Baumgartner has admitted this explanation for *yāpēaḥ* in Ps 27:12.[3] W. McKane has made use of this meaning, "witness," for the passages in his commentary on Proverbs.[4]

Because of the parallelism found there between *yāpîaḥ* and *ʿēd*, which has the same meaning, it has been further suggested that possibly in Hab 2:3 one should rather read *ʿwd* as *ʿyd* in the first bicolon, and then take *wyph* in parallelism with it. Recently, D. Pardee essayed such an interpretation:

> For there is yet a vision (or: the vision is a witness) for a set time,
> Even a witness for the end,
> One that will not lie.[5]

If Pardee's suggestion proves correct—though he is still somewhat tied to the older mode of rendering the bicola, given his double translation—then it is clear that Habakkuk's text here carries a nuance slightly different from that to which we have been accustomed.

However, Hab 2:3 is quoted in full in 1QpHab 7:5–10. The second word of v. 3 was read there by M. Burrows as *ʿwd* in the *editio princeps*.[6] However, the word could just as easily be read as *ʿyd*.[7] If so, then possibly the Qumran reading would support this more recent mode of understanding Hab 2:3. The difficulty is that *waw* and *yod* in this Qumran text are not always clearly distinguished; and Burrows almost certainly read *ʿwd* under the influence of the MT. In eliminating the *waw* before *ypyḥ*, the Qumran form removes the possibility of understanding the word as a verb, as is done in various Greek translations (see below).

The text of 1QpHab 7:5–8:3 is presented below so that one can see how it has interpreted Hab 2:3–4 and preserved parts of those verses.

כיא עיד חזון	5
למועד יפיח לקץ ולוא יכזב	6
פשרו אשר יארוך הקץ האחרון ויתר על כול	7
אשר דברו הנביאים כיא רזי אל להפלה	8
אם יתמהמה חכה לו כיא בוא יבוא ולוא	9
יאחר פשרו על אנשי האמת	10
עושי התורה אשר לוא ירפו ידיהם מעבודת	11
האמת בהמשך עליהם הקץ האחרון כיא	12
כול קיצי אל יבואו לתכונם כאשר חקק	13
להם ברזי ערמתו הנה עופל}ה{ לוא יושרה	14
נפשו בו] פשרו אשר יכפלו עליהם	15
חטאתיהם] ול]וא] ירצו במשפטם] [ל] [	16
] וצדיק באמונתו יחיה]	17

פשרו על כול עושי התורה בבית יהודה אשר	1
יצילם אל מבית המשפט בעבור עמלם ואמונתם	2
במורה הצדק	3

[5]*For a vision (is) a witness* [6]*for a set-time, a witness for the end-time, and it will not lie.* [7]The interpretation of it: The final end-time will be long and (will be) an extension beyond all [8]that the prophets have said, because the mysteries of God are amazing. [9]*If it tarries, wait for it, because it will surely come and will not* [10]*delay.* The interpretation of it concerns the men of truth, [11]the observers of the Law, whose hands slacken not in the service of [12]the truth, as the final end-time is prolonged over them, for [13]all God's times will come according to their appointment, as he has determined [14]for them in the mysteries of his providence. *Now (as for the) puffed-up one, [his soul] is not found upright* [15][*within him*]. The interpretation of it: [Their sins] will be doubled upon them, [16][and] they will n[ot] be found acceptable at their judgment [[17]   ; *but (the) righteous one because of his fidelity shall find life*]. [8:1]The interpretation of it concerns the observers of the Law in the house of Judah, whom [2]God shall deliver from the house of judgment because of their struggle and their fidelity to the Teacher of Righteousness.[8]

Unfortunately, the *pēšer* sheds little light on the words *ʿwd/ʿyd* or *ypyḥ*, since the author concentrates only on the extension of the final end-time beyond that which was announced by the prophets. Again, the *pēšer* in lines 9–14 assures the sectarians of the coming of the end-time and recalls to them their need not to slacken their allegiance. The commentary on v. 4a does not present a clear interpretation of the words of Habakkuk, because it is almost as incomprehensible as the original, and the two last words of it (*npšw bw*) may not be correctly restored. Hesitation about this restoration will be more evident when one considers the Greek translation in the LXX where *eudokei* may correspond in some way to the verb *yrṣw* (from *rṣy*), even though the form itself seems to be different. The phrase *hē psychē mou en autō*, which changes the sense of the MT, may be closer to what the author of the *pēšer* originally wrote. In any case, vv. 4a and 4b in the commentary seem to contrast two types of persons, those not upright and those who are righteous. Though the lemma of v. 4b is missing in the fragmentary col. 7, the comment on it makes it clear that it was once there. Because of struggle and loyalty to the Teacher of Righteousness God will deliver them from the house of judgment.

Over against such an understanding of the text of Habakkuk one has to consider the various Greek translations of it that exist today. The oldest is probably that of the so-called Septuagint, which runs as follows:

3 *dioti eti horasis eis kairon kai anatelei eis peras*
    kai ouk eis kenon·
ean hysterēsē, hypomeinon auton, hoti erchomenos
    hēxei kai ou mē chronisē.
4 *ean hyposteilētai, ouk eudokei hē psychē mou en autō·*
    ho de dikaios ek pisteōs mou zēsetai.[9]

Mss ℵ, B, Q, W* read *ek pisteōs mou;* MSS A, C read *dikaios mou ek pisteōs;* and MS W^c omits *mou.* A corrector of ℵ² read *apangelei* instead of *anatelei,* subsequently erased. The LXX may be translated thus:

> ³For (there is) still a vision for the set-time, and it will appear for the end, and not for naught; if it tarries, wait for it, because it will surely come and will not delay. ⁴If one draws back, my soul takes no delight in him; but the righteous one because of my fidelity shall find life (MSS A, C: but my righteous one shall find life).

When one compares this LXX text with the MT, one notes that its Hebrew *Vorlage* clearly read *ʿwd,* here translated as *eti,* "still." Moreover, the Hebr. *wyph* (with the conjunction) was understood as a verbal form, here translated as *anatelei,* "will appear" (lit., will spring up on the horizon). The reading in MS ℵ², introduced by a corrector, *apangelei,* "will announce," shows that the same word was also understood as a verb. Through this could be seen as expressing the function of a witness, the Greek translator scarcely had this in mind. In any case, these words, *eti* and *anatelei* (or *apangelei*), are undoubtedly the reason for the more or less traditional mode of translating v. 3.

In the treatment of v. 4, the LXX has understood Hebr. *ʿuppělāh* as a verb (*hyposteilētai*) and *yāšěrāh* similarly (*eudokei*); the latter seems to be related to *rsh,* found in 1QpHab 7:16. Above, I followed the vocalization of E. Lohse, who took *yršw* as a niphal impf.;[10] if correct, then it seems that both the Qumran commentator and the LXX translator understood the Hebr. *Vorlage* in a somewhat similar way. But the LXX translator obviously read Hebr. *napšô* as *napšî,* "my soul."

It is, however, the last clause in v. 4 that is of more interest. Whereas the MT has *wěṣaddîq beʾěmûnātô yiḥyeh,* "but the righteous one because of his fidelity shall find life," the LXX has either changed it to Yahweh's righteousness (MSS ℵ, B, Q, W*: *ek pisteōs mou,* "because of my fidelity") or introduced a close connection between the righteous one and Yahweh himself (MSS A, C: *ho de dikaios mou ek pisteōs,* "my righteous one because of [his] fidelity will find life").[11] What is at work here again is the confusion of a *waw* and a *yodh* (*bʾmwntw/bʾmwnty*), as in *npšw/npšy* above.

There is, however, another Greek translation of Habakkuk, unfortunately fragmentary, with which that of the LXX can be compared. It is found in the scroll of the Minor Prophets in Greek that comes from the eighth cave of Wadi Ḥabra (Naḥal Ḥever), 8ḤevXIIgr, col. 12. What is preserved of it reads as follows:

3 [k]*airon kai emphanēset*[*ai*   *kai ou di*]*a-*
pseusetai. Ean stran[*geusētai*   *au*]*ton hoti*
erchomenos hē[*xei*   ]

4 *id*[*ou*] *skotia ouk eutheia psychē autou*[   ]
'[*dik*]*aios en pistei autou zēset*[*ai*].[12]

³[se]t-time and it will appea[r and it will not]
lie. If it (*or:* he) tar[ries,   i]t (*or:* h]im), because it (*or:*
he) will surely co[me   .] ⁴No[w] (as for) darkness,
his soul is not upright[; but the ri]ghteous one with his
fidelity will find li[fe].

The hexaplaric *apparatus criticus* of Ziegler's edition of the LXX
Minor Prophets reveals that Aquila read *kai dikaios en pistei autou zēsetai*
(see also Eusebius, *Dem. evang.,* p. 269). But Symmachus had a
significant addition *ho* ⟨*de*⟩ *dikaios tē heautou pistei zēsei.*[13]

What is striking here is that the Greek translation from Wadi
Ḥabra, usually regarded as from Proto-Theodotion,[14] seems to be
independent of the so-called LXX. The few words that it has in
common with LXX are *kairon kai, ean, auton, hoti . erchomenos hēxei,
ouk, psychē, dikaios, zēsetai* (with *pistis* in a different case).

More striking, however, is the use of *emphanēsetai* for *yph* and *skotia*
for *ᶜuppēlāh*. In the LXX the verb *emphainein* is used to translate *ypᶜ*; and
skotia the noun *ᵓōpel*. Is a confusion of *h/ᶜ* and *ᶜ/ᵓ* at the bottom of this?
More noteworthy is the translation of the last clause of v. 4: [*ho de
di*]*kaios en pistei autou zēsetai.* This is a closer rendering of the Hebrew of
the MT and differs from the various preserved LXX forms.

In any case, it is clear that the New Testament passages that make use
of Hab 2:3–4 are more dependent on a Greek translation-tradition that
is related to the LXX than to this Greek text of the Wadi Ḥabra cave, of
Palestinian provenience. It is not easy to say to what extent this New
Testament Greek text might represent a Palestinian *tradition.* In any
case, the New Testament quotations of Hab 2:3–4 stand closer to
what is found in the Egyptian text-tradition.

II. *The Text of Hab 2:3–4 in the New Testament*

In turning to the New Testament passages in which Hab 2:3–4
occurs we can treat the two Pauline passages with more dispatch than
that in Hebrews, since they make use of only the last clause of Hab 2:4.
In Gal 3:11 Paul really only alludes to the passage. It reads:

*hoti de en nomō oudeis dikaioutai para tō theō dēlon,
hoti ho dikaios ek pisteōs zēsetai.*

It is evident that no one is accepted as righteous by God for obeying the
Law, since the righteous one because of faith will find life. (My translation)

And in Rom 1:17 Paul writes, quoting Habakkuk explicitly:

kathōs gegraptai. ho de dikaios ek pisteōs zēsetai

. . . , as it has been written (in Scripture), 'The righteous one because of faith shall find life.' (My translation)

Now Paul, in using *ek pisteōs,* is clearly dependent on the text-tradition which we know from the LXX; he does not translate the Hebrew text of Habakkuk, nor does he use the Proto-Theodotionic version, *en pistei autou.*[15] Strikingly, he omits the personal pronoun entirely, and undoubtedly the reason for this omission is that, although the word *pistis* is the same in his texts as in either the LXX or the Proto-Theodotionic version, he fills that word with his own Christian meaning of "faith." The meaning of *'ĕmûnāh* which we preferred earlier, "fidelity, steadfastness," seems to be demanded by the original context. In 1QpHab 8:2 the word also has to be translated in the same way, again not only because of the context which speaks of "the observers of the Law" (*'ŏśê hattôrāh*), but also because *'mwntm* is set in juxtaposition to *'mlm,* "their struggle," suggesting that the former must have some meaning like "fidelity" or "loyalty" to the Teacher of Righteousness.[16] For Paul, however, the word *pistis* is pregnant with all that he means by that in his view of Christian experience.[17] It would not have been impossible for Paul to use the reading *ek pisteōs mou* (referring to God); but that would have introduced an entirely different notion, since Paul was speaking of something that involved a human self-involving act. In this regard, the reading of MSS A and C (*ho de dikaios mou ek pisteōs zēsetai*) would probably have been more congenial to him. But he avoids both of them, omitting the *mou,* probably because of the sense in which he wanted *pistis* to be understood.[18]

When one turns to Heb 10:37–38, the matter is a little more complicated. The author has finished his main exposé of christology and soteriology, of the way in which he understood Jesus Christ and what he once did for all human beings. He makes use of Hab 2:3–4 as part of an exhortation addressed to his readers, which recalls their struggles and sufferings when they first became Christians and encourages them to endurance, confidence, and faith. After having quoted Hab 2:3–4, he says, "But we are not of those who draw back and are liable to destruction, but of those who have faith and acquire life" (10:39). On the heels of that declaration, he introduces his famous description of faith and his recital of its Old Testament heroes and heroines. Into such a context he introduces the quotation of Habakkuk, which reads as follows:

> [37] *eti gar mikron hoson hoson*
> *ho erchomenos hēxei kai ou chronisei.*
> [38] *ho de dikaios mou ek pisteōs zēsetai*
> *kai ean hyposteilētai, ouk eudokei hē psychē mou en autō.*

[37]For yet a little while (and) the coming one will come and will not delay; [38]my righteous one because of fidelity will find life; and if one draws back, my soul delights not in him. (My translation)

First of all, the author of Hebrews has conflated the verses of Habakkuk with a phrase from Isa 26:20 (LXX: *mikron hoson hoson*), which is added to the adverb *eti*, "still," undoubtedly derived from the LXX of Hab 2:3 (the conjunction *gar* serves as the author's introduction of the quotation from Habakkuk). The phrase is impossible to translate; it merely intensifies "yet."

Second, the author of Hebrews adds the definite article to the participle *erchomenos*, which served in the LXX as the translation of the intensifying infinitive absolute of the Hebr. *b᾽ yb᾽*. In adding the article *ho*, the translator has personalized the participle and made it refer to Jesus himself (in this parousiac appearance). The steadfastness that he demands of the Christians to whom he addresses his hortatory homily is that demanded by the coming of Christ.

Third, the author of Hebrews has inverted the order of phrases in Hab 2:4, and the reason for it is not clear. There does not seem to be at present any justification for this order in the various MSS of the LXX; so it must be the work of the author of Hebrews.

Fourth, the author of Hebrews reads Hab 2:4b as in MSS A and C of the LXX: *ho de dikaios mou ek pisteōs zēsetai*, "my righteous one because of fidelity will find life" (or possibly, "because of faith"). "My righteous one" in this context must mean the person who finds a righteous status in the sight of God. It may be queried whether one should translate *pistis* here in Hebrews as "fidelity" or as "faith." The former certainly suits the general context of the homily, but some other passages in Hebrews may demand a different understanding of the word. Certainly, the word in Heb 4:2 has to be understood as a reaction to a "word of hearing" (*ho logos tēs akoēs*) and the description of *pistis* in chap. 11 would also color the notion. In any case, *pistis* here in Hebrews should not be simply equated with Pauline "faith," even though Christian faith is meant.

Of Hab 2:3–4 used in Heb 10:37–38 G. Howard has said that the use is "unlike either" the Hebrew text of Habakkuk or the LXX, but is under "LXX influence."[19] This is a correct assessment of the textual situation. He has also noted that it is not right "to characterize the quotations in Hebrews as always Septuagintal," since "a great many of them do not correspond exactly to any Septuagint, and some agree with a known Hebrew text, either whole or in part, against the Septuagint."[20] He has also asked whether the New Testament might not have influenced the MSS of the LXX. His query takes on significance in the light of the reading *ho de dikaios mou ek pisteōs zēsetai* in Heb 10:38. Is it possible that this reading in MSS A and C of the LXX has been influenced by the text of Hebrews? After all, those LXX MSS are Christian copies and do not antedate the fourth/fifth century A.D.[21]

NOTES

* Originally published in *De la Loi au Messie: Le développement d'une espérance: Etudes d'historie et de théologie offertes a Henri Cazelles* (ed. J. Doré et al.; Paris: Desclée, 1981).

[1] See P. J. M. Southwell, "A Note on Habakkuk ii. 4," *JTS* 19 (1968) 614–17; A. S. van der Woude, "Der Gerechte wird durch seine Treue leben: Erwägungen zu Habakuk 2:4–5," *Studia biblica et semitica Theodoro Christiano Vriezen . . . dedicata* (Wageningen: Veenman & Zonen, 1966) 367–75.

[2] See D. Pardee, "*Yph* 'Witness' in Hebrew and Ugaritic," *VT* 28 (1978) 204–13 (and the literature cited by him). Cf. J. Obermann, "Survival of an Old Canaanite Participle and Its Impact on Biblical Exegesis," *JBL* 70 (1951) 204–6.

[3] *Hebräisches und aramäisches Lexikon zum Alten Testament* (3d ed.; Leiden: Brill), Lief. 2 (1974) 405. Cf. P. D. Miller, Jr., "*Yāpîaḥ* in Psalm xii 6," *VT* 29 (1979) 495–501.

[4] *Proverbs: A New Approach* (London/Philadelphia: Westminster, 1970) 229, 445.

[5] "*Yph* 'Witness,' " 210. At first sight, it might seem that the Hebrew syntax would be against such an interpretation. What we would have is a predicate + subject + prepositional phrase (dependent on the predicate). This construction, though not the most common, is found in the MT. See Exod 14:3 (*nĕbūkîm hēm bāʾāreṣ*); Num 10:29 (*nōsĕʿîm ʾănaḥnû ʾel hammāqôm . . .*); Deut. 7:17 (*rabbîm haggóyîm haʾēlleh mimmennî*); see further Gen 4:13; 49:12; F. I. Andersen, *The Hebrew Verbless Clause in the Pentateuch* (SBLMS 14; Nashville: Abingdon, 1970) 66–67.

[6] *The Dead Sea Scrolls of St. Mark's Monastery: Volume I, The Isaiah Manuscript and the Habakkuk Commentary* (New Haven: A.S.O.R., 1950) pl. lviii. See also F. M. Cross et al. (eds.), *Scrolls from Qumran Cave I: The Great Isaiah Scroll, The Order of the Community, The Pesher to Habakkuk, from Photographs by John C. Trever* (Jerusalem: Albright Institute of Archaeological Research and the Shrine of the Book, 1972) 156–57.

⁷ Cf. CD 9:23; 10:1.

⁸ Note the following differences in the Qumran text from the MT of Hab 2:3–4 (apart from *scriptio plena* like *bw'* or *ky'*): *'yd* (if correctly read) for *'wd; ypyḥ* (without initial *waw*); *ywšrh* (pual pf. 3d sg. fem.). The form *'wplh*, apart from the *scriptio plena*, is as enigmatic here as in the MT. I follow the suggestion in BHS (1051, *app. crit.*) to read *'uppāl* or *'appāl*. The latter is more difficult for the consonants in 1QpHab, but seems to be a better form; a masc. substantive is needed (without the article) for the parallelism with *ṣaddîq*. In line 16 I have followed the emendation of E. Lohse, *Die Texte aus Qumran hebräisch und deutsch* (Munich: Kösel, 1964) 236.

Another Hebrew text of Habakkuk is found in the scroll of the Minor Prophets from a Murabba'at cave (Mur 88); see P. Benoit, J. T. Milik, and R. de Vaux (eds.), *Les grottes de Murabba'ât* (DJD 2; Oxford: Clarendon, 1961) 199. But only *wyph* is preserved of the verses in which we are interested (col. xviii, line 19 + pl. lxviii).

See further K. Elliger, *Studien zum Habakuk-Kommentar vom Toten Meer* (BHT 15; Tübingen: Mohr [Siebeck], 1953) 191–96. For further use of *'mwnh* in QL, see 1QS 8:3; 1QM 13:3; 1QH 16:17; 17:14; 1QSb 5:26; 11QPsᵃ 19:14.

⁹ See J. Ziegler, *Septuaginta: Vetus Testamentum graecum, XIII: Duodecim Prophetae* (Göttingen: Vandenhoeck & Ruprecht, 1967) 264. See C. Tischendorf, *Bibliorum codex sinaiticus petropolitanus* (4 vols.; Hildesheim: G. Olms, 1969), 1. xvi*.

¹⁰ *Die Texte aus Qumran*, 236.

¹¹ It is scarcely likely that *mou* in MSS A, C is to be understood as a prepositive modifier of *ek pisteōs*. Note too that a corrector of MS W deleted the *mou;* but he may well have been influenced by the Pauline use of the text. It is certainly not demanded by the Hebrew of the MT.

¹² See D. Barthélemy, *Les devanciers d'Aquila: Première publication intégrale du texte des fragments du Dodécaprophéton trouvés dans le Désert de Juda, précédée d'une étude sur les traductions et recensions grecques de la Bible réalisées au premier siècle de notre ère sous l'influence du rabbinat palestinien* (VTSup 10; Leiden: Brill, 1963) 175.

¹³ *Septuaginta, XIII: Duodecim Prophetae*, 264–65. It is this text-tradition (Proto-Theodotion, Aquila, and especially Symmachus) that is related to the Latin Vulgate translation, *iustus autem in fide sua vivet.*

Eusebius (*Dem. evang.* 6.14 §276–77 [GCS 23. 268–69]) shows his dependence on Heb 10:37–38 when he quotes the Greek text of Habakkuk in 6.14,1 with the article *ho* before *erchomenos*. The *erchomenos hēxei* of Hab 2:3 was understood in a personal sense by Eusebius because of Zech 6:12 (*anatolē onoma autou* is used to explain the mysterious verb *anatelei*). He actually quotes Hebrews 10. Actually, he reads the verse in three ways: (a) *ho de dikaios ek pisteōs mou zēsetai* (16.4,3); (b) *ho de dikaios ek pisteōs zēsetai* (16.4,6—influenced by Paul's phrase?); (c) *ho de dikaios mou ek pisteōs zēsetai* (16.4,8).

¹⁴ See F. M. Cross, "The History of the Biblical Text in the Light of Discoveries in the Judaean Desert," *Qumran and the History of the Biblical Text* (ed. F. M. Cross and S. Talmon; Cambridge, MA: Harvard University, 1975) 177–95, esp. p. 178.

¹⁵ The original hand of MS C inserted *mou* after *ho de dikaios* in Rom 1:17, obviously making the passage conform to its own reading of Hab 2:4b.

¹⁶ J. Carmignac ("Interprétation de prophètes et de psaumes," *Les textes de*

Qumran traduits et annotés [ed. J. Carmignac et P. Guilbert; 2 vols.; Paris: Letouzey et Ané, 1961, 1963], 2. 107) remarks: "Le contexte, qui parle de la pratique de la Loi, indique suffisamment qu'il s'agit de la fidelité aux directives du Docteur de Justice sur l'observation de cette Loi. Ce contexte interdit de projeter ici la notion chrétienne de la 'foi' (c'est-à-dire: adhésion de l'intelligence) et de comprendre: 'La foi aux paroles du Docteur de Justice', ou à plus forte raison: 'la foi à la personne du Docteur de Justice'." Carmignac is correct, but I should hesitate to say that for Paul *pistis* can be simply defined as an "adhésion de l'intelligence." J. A. Sanders ("Habakkuk in Qumran, Paul, and the Old Testament," *JR* 39 [1959] 232–44) has noted, however, that the interpretation in 1QpHab shares with Paul a notion of faith that is "centered in a person" and a belief which involves commitment and and [sic] perseverance in the face of adversity and suffering" (p. 233). Does it really?

[17] For an attempt to describe Pauline *pistis,* see my *Pauline Theology: A Brief Sketch* (Englewood Cliffs, NJ: Prentice-Hall, 1967) 67–65; cf. *JBC,* art. 79, §125–27.

[18] See further A. Feuillet, "La citation d'Habacuc ii. 4 et les huit premiers chapitres de l'épître aux Romains," *NTS* 6 (1959–60) 52–80.

[19] "Hebrews and the Old Testament Quotations," *NovT* 10 (1968) 208–16, esp. p. 210.

[20] Ibid., 215.

[21] Note that, when Eusebius quotes Heb 10:37–38 (*Dem. evang.* 6.14, 3 [GCS, 23.268]), he reads *ek pisteōs mou.* See n. 13 above.

See further J. C. McCullough, "The Old Testament Quotations in Hebrews," *NTS* 26 (1979–80) 363–79, esp. pp. 376–77; J. G. Janzen, "Habakkuk 2:2–4 in the Light of Recent Philological Advances," *HTR* 73 (1980) 53–78.

INDEXES

A. Index of Subjects

(The subjects are those of the main text; the reader should check the
Notes referring to the passages indicated by the following page numbers.)

B. Index of Modern Writers

C. *Index of Scripture References*

D. Index of Other Ancient Writings